ROUTLEDGE LIBRARY EDITIONS: VLADIMIR LENIN

Volume 4

LENINISM

LENINISM
Volume One

JOSEPH STALIN

Taylor & Francis Group
LONDON AND NEW YORK

First published in Russian in 1926.
First published in English in 1928 by George Allen & Unwin Ltd
Translated from the Russian by Eden & Cedar Paul

This edition first published in 2017
by Routledge
2 Park Square, Milton Park, Abingdon, Oxon OX14 4RN

and by Routledge
711 Third Avenue, New York, NY 10017

Routledge is an imprint of the Taylor & Francis Group, an informa business

© 1928 English Translation George Allen & Unwin Ltd

All rights reserved. No part of this book may be reprinted or reproduced or utilised in any form or by any electronic, mechanical, or other means, now known or hereafter invented, including photocopying and recording, or in any information storage or retrieval system, without permission in writing from the publishers.

Trademark notice: Product or corporate names may be trademarks or registered trademarks, and are used only for identification and explanation without intent to infringe.

British Library Cataloguing in Publication Data
A catalogue record for this book is available from the British Library

ISBN: 978-0-415-79274-5 (Set)
ISBN: 978-1-315-20438-3 (Set) (ebk)
ISBN: 978-1-138-70027-7 (Volume 4) (hbk)
ISBN: 978-1-138-70046-8 (Volume 4) (pbk)
ISBN: 978-1-315-20474-1 (Volume 4) (ebk)

Publisher's Note
The publisher has gone to great lengths to ensure the quality of this reprint but points out that some imperfections in the original copies may be apparent.

Disclaimer
The publisher has made every effort to trace copyright holders and would welcome correspondence from those they have been unable to trace.

LENINISM

BY
JOSEPH STALIN

Translated from the Russian by
EDEN & CEDAR PAUL

VOLUME ONE

LONDON
GEORGE ALLEN & UNWIN LTD
MUSEUM STREET

The Russian original, Moscow, 1926, is entitled
Вопросы Ленинизма

First published in English in 1928
Second Impression. 1932

(*All rights reserved*)

Printed in Great Britain by
Henderson & Spalding Ltd
London S E 15

TABLE OF CONTENTS

	PAGE
PREFACE	9
PROBLEMS OF LENINISM	11
1. Definition of Leninism	13
2. Core of Leninism	15
3. The Question of " Permanent " Revolution	17
4. The Proletarian Revolution and the Dictatorship of the Proletariat	20
5. The Party and the Working Class within the System of the Dictatorship of the Proletariat	29
6. The Problem of the Victory of Socialism in one Country alone	52
7. The Fight for the Realisation of Socialism	64
FOUNDATIONS OF LENINISM (A Lecture delivered at Sverdloff University in the beginning of April 1924)	77
Introduction	79
1. Historical Roots of Leninism	81
2. Method	87
3. Theory	94
a. The Importance of Theory	94
b. Criticism of the Theory of Spontaneity	95
c. The Theory of the Proletarian Revolution	98
4. The Dictatorship of the Proletariat	110
a. As the Instrument of the Proletarian Revolution	110
b. As the Rule of the Proletariat over the Bourgeoisie	113
c. The Soviet Power as the Form of State embodying the Dictatorship of the Proletariat	118
5. The Peasant Problem	122
a. General Statement of the Problem	122
b. The Peasantry during the Bourgeois-Democratic Revolution	124
c. The Peasantry during the Proletarian Revolution	127
d. The Peasantry after the Consolidation of the Soviet Power	129
6. The National Question	135
a. General Statement of the Question	135
b. The Movement of the Oppressed Peoples to secure Liberation, and the Relationship of that Movement to the Proletarian Revolution	140
7. Strategy and Tactics	145
a. Strategy and Tactics as the Science of the Leadership of the Proletarian Class Struggle	145

	PAGE
b. Strategy and the Phases of the Revolution	146
c. Tactics and the Ebb and Flow of the Movement	148
d. Strategical Leadership	149
e. Tactical Leadership	154
f. Reformism and Revolutionism	157
8. The Party	161
a. The Party as the Vanguard of the Working Class	162
b. The Party as the Organised Detachment of the Working Class	165
c. The Party as the Highest Form of Class Organisation of the Proletariat	167
d. The Party as the Instrument for the Dictatorship of the Proletariat	169
e. The Party is the Expression of a Unity of Will incompatible with the Existence of Fractions	171
f. The Party is strengthened by purging itself of Opportunist Elements	173
9. Style in the Work	175

THE OCTOBER REVOLUTION AND THE TACTICS OF THE RUSSIAN COMMUNISTS (PREFACE TO THE WORK ENTITLED *Towards October*) 179

1. Conditions at Home and Abroad favouring the October Revolution 181
2. Two Peculiarities of the October Revolution, or October and Trotsky's Theory of Permanent Revolution 184
3. Some Characteristics of the Tactics of the Bolsheviks during the Period of Preparation for the October Revolution . . 199
4. The October Revolution as Prelude to the World Revolution . 212

WORK OF THE FOURTEENTH CONFERENCE OF THE COMMUNIST PARTY OF THE SOVIET UNION (REPORT TO THE PARTY OFFICIALS IN MOSCOW ON MAY 9, 1925) . . 217

1. The International Situation 220
2. Immediate Tasks of the Communist Parties in Capitalist Countries 229
3. Immediate Tasks of the Communist Elements in Colonies and Dependencies 233
4. Future of Socialism in the Soviet Union 236
5. Party Policy in the Rural Districts 246
6. The Metallurgical Industry 252

TABLE OF CONTENTS

PAGE

THE NATIONALIST QUESTION IN YUGOSLAVIA (Speech to the Yugoslav Committee of the E.C.C.I. on March 30, 1925) 257

POLITICAL TASKS OF THE UNIVERSITY OF THE PEOPLES OF THE EAST (Speech to the Students of the University on May 18, 1925) 265
  1. Tasks of the University in the Matter of the Soviet Republics of the East 269
  2. Tasks of the University in the Matter of Colonies and Dependencies in the East 276

THE NATIONALIST QUESTION ONCE MORE (Comment on Semich's Article) 283

QUESTIONS AND ANSWERS (Speech at Sverdloff University on June 9, 1925) 293
  First Question 295
  Second Question 301
  Third Question 308
  Fourth Question 315
  Fifth Question 317
  Sixth Question 322
  Seventh Question 324
  Eighth Question 326
  Ninth Question 328
  Tenth Question 337

TASKS OF THE UNION OF YOUNG COMMUNISTS (An Answer to the Questions propounded by the Editorial Board of "Komsomolskaya Pravda", the Organ of the Young Communists) 341
  First Question 343
  Second Question 344
  Third Question 346
  Fourth Question 347
  Fifth Question 349

POLITICAL REPORT OF THE CENTRAL COMMITTEE TO THE FOURTEENTH CONGRESS OF THE COMMUNIST PARTY OF THE SOVIET UNION . . 351

I. The International Situation 354
    1. Stabilisation of Capitalism 355
    2. Imperialism, Colonies, and Half-Colonies . . . 359
    3. Conquerors and Conquered 361
    4. Conflicts between the Victorious Countries . . 366
    5. The Capitalist World and the Soviet Union . . 369
    6. Foreign Situation of the Soviet Union 374
    7. Tasks of the Party 380

II. Internal Situation of the Soviet Union 382
    1. General Economic Position 382
    2. Industry and Agriculture 395
    3. Commercial Problems 397
    4. Classes, their Activities, and their Mutual Relationships . 399
    5. Three of Lenin's Slogans on the Peasant Problem . . 402
    6. Two Dangers and Two Deviations in the Matter of the Peasants 410
    7. Tasks of the Party 414

III. The Party 418

IV. Concluding Words at the Congress 426
    1. Sokolnikoff and the " Dawesation " of our Country . . 426
    2. Kameneff and our Concessions to the Peasants . . 428
    3. Who have miscalculated ? 431
    4. How Sokolnikoff defends the Poor Peasants . . 432
    5. Conflict of Ideas, or Calumny ? 433
    6. Nep 435
    7. State Capitalism 435
    8. Zinovieff and the Peasantry 441
    9. History of our Differences 447
    10. Platform of the Opposition 453
    11. Their " Love of Peace " 455
    12. The Party will maintain its Unity 456

INDEX 458

PREFACE

THE section entitled *Foundations of Leninism* should be regarded as one of the most important parts of the present volume. It was first published, as a separate booklet, in April 1924. [An English translation, entitled *Theory and Practice of Leninism*, has been published by the Communist Party of Great Britain.] During these two years much water has flowed under the bridge. The Party has lived through two discussions; quite a number of pamphlets and manuals on Leninism have appeared; and new practical problems have become urgent in the work of socialist construction. It is obvious that these new problems, and the two recent discussions, could not find a place in the *Foundations of Leninism*. Furthermore, the concrete problems of socialist construction (the New Economic Policy, State capitalism, the problem of the middle peasantry, etc.) could not be adequately considered in a booklet which did not aim at being more than a summary exposition of the foundations of Leninism. Light could only be shed on these and kindred topics in the later sections of the book, such as *The October Revolution and the Tactics of the Russian Communists, The Work of the Fourteenth Congress of the Communist Party of the Soviet Union, Questions and Answers*, etc.

which are organically connected with the main ideas expounded in the section entitled *Foundations of Leninism*. The facts above stated justify the publication of the present collection, which thus forms a unified and complete work upon the problems of Leninism.

The discussions at the Fourteenth Party Congress drew up a balance sheet of the ideological and constructive work of the Party during the period that had elapsed since the Thirteenth Congress. These discussions also made it possible to examine the theses put forward by the new opposition. We are now entitled to ask, What are the results of this examination?

PROBLEMS OF LENINISM

(DEDICATED TO THE LENINGRAD ORGANISATION
OF THE COMMUNIST PARTY OF THE SOVIET UNION)

1. DEFINITION OF LENINISM

My booklet *Foundations of Leninism* contains a definition of Leninism which seems to have made its way in the world. It runs as follows :

> Leninism is the Marxism of the epoch of imperialism and of the proletarian revolution. To be more precise : Leninism is the theory and the tactic of the proletarian revolution in general, and the theory and the tactic of the dictatorship of the proletariat in particular.

Is this definition correct ?

I think so. It is correct, first of all, because it gives an accurate demonstration of the historical roots of Leninism, which is described as Marxism *of the epoch of imperialism*—this being an answer to certain critics of Lenin who falsely suppose that Leninism did not originate until after the imperialist war. It is correct, in the second place, because it accurately indicates the *international* character of Leninism—this being an answer to the social democrats, who consider that Leninism is not applicable anywhere except in Russia. It is correct, in the third place, because it accurately shows the organic connexion between Leninism and the teaching of Marx, describing Leninism as *Marxism* of the epoch of imperialism—this being an answer to certain critics of Lenin who believe that Leninism is not a further development of Marxism, but merely a revival of Marxism and an application of Marxism to Russian conditions.

One would think that all this might pass without further comment.

Nevertheless, there are comrades in our Party who want to define Leninism in a different way. For example, Comrade Zinovieff writes :

> Leninism is Marxism of the epoch of imperialist wars and of the world revolution *which took its direct rise in a country where the peasantry predominates.*[1] (*Bolshevism or Trotskyism?* " Pravda," November 30, 1924.)

What is the meaning of the words underlined by Comrade Zinovieff ? Why, when he is defining Leninism, does he introduce

[1] Italicised by Zinovieff.

into the definition the backwardness of Russia ? Why does he refer to the predominantly peasant character of our country ?

His definition means that Leninism is not to be regarded as an international doctrine, but is to be looked upon as a product of Russian primitiveness.

He thus plays into the hands of Bauer and Kautsky, who deny that Leninism can be of any value in countries where capitalist development is farther advanced.

We are all agreed in thinking that the peasant question is of immense importance in Russia, that our country is a peasant land. But what is the bearing of this fact upon the decision as to the fundamentals of Leninism ? Does it mean that Leninism has grown only upon Russian soil, and for Russia alone ; not upon imperialist soil, and for imperialist countries generally ? Are we to suppose that Lenin's writings, such as *Imperialism, The State and Revolution*, *The Proletarian Revolution and Kautsky the Renegade*, and *Left-Wing Communism, an Infantile Disorder*, have a meaning only for Russia, and are not applicable to imperialist countries throughout the world ? Are we not to regard Leninism as a generalisation of *universal* revolutionary experience? Are not Leninist theory and tactic suitable for, is not their adoption obligatory upon, proletarian parties in *every* land ? Was Lenin wrong when he said : " Bolshevism is a model tactic for *all* " ? (*Works*, Russian edition, vol. xv., p. 503.) Did he make a mistake in speaking of the " *international significance* [1] of the Soviet power and of bolshevist theory and tactic " ? (*Works*, Russian edition, vol. xvii., p. 116.) Was Lenin mistaken when he wrote :

> In Russia, the dictatorship of the proletariat will necessarily exhibit certain features peculiar to that country, dependent upon its backward and petty-bourgeois character as contrasted with lands of more advanced development. But the basic forces and the essential forms of social economy are just the same in Russia as in any other capitalist country, so that *the before-mentioned peculiarities do not affect the fundamentals of the question.* (*Works*, Russian edition, vol. xvi., p. 348.)

If Lenin was right about all these matters, does it not follow that Comrade Zinovieff's definition of Leninism is wrong ?

How can this definition of Leninism, nationally restricted in its scope, be reconciled with internationalism ?

[1] Italicised by Stalin.

2. CORE OF LENINISM

In my booklet *Foundations of Leninism* I say :

> Some think that the essential foundation of Leninism, its starting-point, is the peasant problem, the role of the peasantry, the importance of the peasantry. This is absolutely wrong. The essential foundation of Leninism, its starting-point, is the question of the dictatorship of the proletariat, the question how that dictatorship is to be established and strengthened. The peasant problem, the question how the workers in their struggle for power are to secure the support of the peasants, is a subsidiary one.

Is that contention sound ?

I think so. It is a logical inference from my definition of Leninism. For, if Leninism is the theory and tactic of the proletarian revolution, and if the dictatorship of the proletariat is the essence of the proletarian revolution, it obviously follows that the dictatorship of the proletariat—the working out of this problem, the rendering of it concrete—must form the very core of Leninism.

It is plain, however, that Comrade Zinovieff does not accept this view. In his article *To Lenin's Memory*, he writes :

> As I have already said, the question as to the role of the peasantry is the *fundamental problem* [1] of bolshevism, of Leninism. ("Pravda", February 13, 1924.)

We see at once that Comrade Zinovieff's attitude is the direct outcome of his erroneous definition of Leninism, and that the position he adopts is necessarily as wrong as the definition.

Was Lenin right in contending that " the dictatorship of the proletariat is the tap-root of the revolution " ? (*Works*, Russian edition, vol. xv., p. 447.) Unquestionably he was right. Is it true that Leninism is the theory and the tactic of the proletarian revolution ? I think so. What follows ? We naturally infer that the fundamental question of Leninism, the starting-point, must be the question of the dictatorship of the proletariat.

Consider : imperialism ; its varying rate of development in different countries ; the possibility of a victory for socialism

[1] Italicised by Stalin.

in one country alone; the proletarian State; the Soviet form of the workers' State; the role of the Party in the system of the dictatorship of the proletariat; the methods of socialist construction—were not all these questions analysed by Lenin? Do not these same questions form the kernel of the idea of the dictatorship of the proletariat? Without a preliminary study of these problems would not the study of the peasant question from the outlook of the dictatorship of the proletariat be inconceivable?

No one will deny that Lenin had an expert knowledge of the peasant question. No one will deny that the peasant question, all that concerns these allies of the workers, is of immense importance to the proletariat, and forms an integral part of the fundamental question of the dictatorship of the proletariat. Is it not plain, however, that unless Leninists had to solve the fundamental problem of the dictatorship of the proletariat, they would have no occasion to trouble themselves about a problem which only arises out of the former—the problem of the workers' allies, the peasants? Is it not plain that if Leninists were not faced with the practical problem of the conquest of power by the proletariat, they would have no concern with the question of an alliance between the workers and the peasants?

Lenin was in actual fact the greatest of all proletarian thinkers. But he would not have been this, he would have been nothing more than the simple " peasant philosopher " that literary wiseacres are fond of depicting, had he been content to study the peasant problem, not on the basis of the theory and the tactic of the dictatorship of the proletariat, but independently of this basis and apart from it.

We must make our choice.

Either the peasant problem is the core of Leninism, and in that case Leninism is unsuitable for, is inapplicable to, countries where capitalism is in an advanced state of development, to non-peasant countries.

Or else the dictatorship of the proletariat forms the core of Leninism, and in that case Leninism is the international doctrine of the workers of all lands, is suitable for and essential to all countries, not excepting those where capitalist development is far advanced.

One thing or the other!

3. THE QUESTION OF "PERMANENT" REVOLUTION

In the booklet *Foundations of Leninism*, the "theory of permanent revolution" is described as one which underestimates the importance of the part played by the peasantry. Let me quote (from the first edition):

> Lenin therefore opposed the champions of "permanent revolution", not because they asserted the continuity of the revolution (a theory he himself never ceased to support), but because they underestimated the importance of the part played by the peasantry which forms the great reserve force for the proletariat.

This characterisation of the Russian champions of the theory of permanent revolution has till recently found general acceptance. None the less, though correct as far as it goes, it cannot be regarded as exhaustive. On the one hand the discussions of 1924, and on the other hand a detailed analysis of the works of Lenin, have shown that the mistake of the Russian champions of the theory of permanent revolution consists, not only in their undervaluation of the importance of the part played by the peasantry, but also in their undervaluation of the strength of the proletariat, of the capacity of the workers to induce the peasants to follow their lead—in a lack of faith in the idea of the leadership of the proletariat.

For this reason, in my pamphlet *The October Revolution and the Tactics of the Russian Communists* (December 1924) I expanded the foregoing characterisation. Here is what I then wrote:

> Hitherto it has been usual to draw attention to only one aspect of the theory of "permanent revolution", namely the lack of faith in the revolutionary possibilities of the peasant movement. Now we must supplement this by drawing attention to another aspect, namely the lack of faith in the strength and the capacity of the Russian proletariat.

Of course this does not mean that Lenin and Leninists have been or are opposed to the idea of permanent revolution as formulated by Marx in the forties of the last century. On the contrary, Lenin was the only Marxist who accurately understood the idea of permanent revolution and developed that idea. The difference between Lenin and those whom I will call the "permanentists" was that these latter distorted Marx's idea of permanent revolution, transforming it into something lifeless, something bookish and doctrinaire, whereas Lenin accepted it in its pristine simplicity and made it one of the chief pillars of his own theory of the revolution. We must not forget that the idea of the growth of the bourgeois-democratic revolution into the socialist revolution (an idea propounded by Lenin as long ago as 1905) is one of the modes of realisation of the Marxist theory of permanent revolution. Here is what Lenin wrote about this in 1905 :

> As far as lies within our power, within the power of the class-conscious and organised proletariat, we shall at once begin to move on from the democratic revolution to the socialist revolution. *We are for continuous revolution.*[1] We shall not be content with half measures. . . .
> Without lapsing into adventurism, without being untrue to our scientific conscience, without seeking for cheap popularity, we can say and we do say only one thing : With all our strength we shall help the united peasantry to make a democratic revolution, that it may be easier for us, the party of the proletariat, to pass on as speedily as possible to a new and higher task—to the socialist revolution. (*Works*, Russian edition, vol. vi., pp. 449–450.)

Writing on the same topic sixteen years later, after the conquest of power by the proletariat, Lenin said :

> Kautsky, Hilferding, Martoff, Chernoff, Hillquit, Longuet, MacDonald, Turati, and the other champions of "two-and-a-half" Marxism, have not understood . . . the relationships between the bourgeois-democratic and the proletarian-socialist revolution. *The former grows into the latter.*[1] As it goes along, the latter solves the problems of the former. The latter consolidates the work of the former. Struggle, and nothing but struggle, decides how far the proletarian-socialist revolution can succeed in growing out of the bourgeois-democratic revolution. (*Works*, Russian edition, vol. xviii., part I., pp. 365–366.)

I wish to draw special attention to the first of the two foregoing quotations, which is from an article by Lenin entitled *The Attitude of the Social Democracy towards the Peasant Movement*,

---
[1] Italicised by Stalin.

published on October 1, 1905. I do this for the enlightenment of the comrades who continue to assert that Lenin only conceived the idea of the transformation of the bourgeois-democratic revolution into the socialist revolution, the idea of permanent revolution, after the outbreak of the imperialist war, somewhere about the year 1916. The passage I have quoted shows that these comrades are mistaken.

4. THE PROLETARIAN REVOLUTION AND THE DICTATORSHIP OF THE PROLETARIAT

What are the special features that distinguish the proletarian revolution from the bourgeois revolution?

The differences between the two may be summarised under five main heads.

1. The bourgeois revolution usually begins at a time when the capitalist forms which, prior to the manifest revolution, have made their appearance and begun to ripen within the womb of feudal society, are already more or less developed. The proletarian revolution begins at a time when socialist forms either do not exist at all, or are almost completely lacking.

2. The fundamental task of the bourgeois revolution is to seize power, and to adapt that power to the already existing bourgeois economy. The fundamental task of the proletarian revolution is, on seizing power, to construct a new socialist economy.

3. The bourgeois revolution usually ends with the seizure of power. For the proletarian revolution the seizure of power is only a beginning; power, when seized, is used as a lever for the transformation of the old economy and for the organisation of a new one.

4. The bourgeois revolution, being no more than the replacement of one group of exploiters by another in the seat of power, has no need to destroy the old State machine; but the proletarian revolution means that the groups of exploiters one and all have been excluded from power, and that the leaders of all the workers, the leaders of all the exploited, the leaders of the proletarian class, have come to occupy the seat of power, and they therefore have no option but to destroy the old State machine and to replace it by a new one.

5. The bourgeois revolution cannot for any long period enjoy the support of the working and exploited masses, for the simple reason that the millions, the masses, are workers and are exploited; but the proletarian revolution can and must consolidate all who labour and all the exploited in a lasting alliance with the pro-

THE PROLETARIAN REVOLUTION

letariat, for otherwise it cannot carry out its fundamental task of consolidating the power of the proletariat and upbuilding a new, a socialist economy.

Here are some of Lenin's contentions about this matter:

> One of the basic differences between the bourgeois revolution and the socialist revolution is that in the case of the bourgeois revolution (which is always born out of feudalism) the new economic organisations gradually arise within the womb of the old order, even if it be only in the form of a development of commercial relationships which by degrees modify all the aspects of feudal society. The bourgeois revolution has but one task to perform: to get rid of, to destroy, all the fetters of the old society. As soon as this has been effected, every bourgeois revolution has completed its work, for the upshot is that commodity production can now develop unchecked and the growth of capitalism can proceed apace.
>
> But the socialist revolution is in a very different position. The more backward the country in which, thanks to the zigzag course of history, the socialist revolution has begun, the more difficult will be the change from the old capitalist conditions to socialist conditions. Here, to the tasks of destruction there are superadded new tasks, incredibly difficult—organisational tasks. . . . .
>
> Had not the creative energy of the masses, fortified by the great experiences of the year 1905, been able to set up soviets in February 1917, these soviets could not have seized power in October of the same year, for success depends upon the existence of organisations numbering millions of members. These organisations took the form of soviets, not because in Russia such soviets had already secured striking successes in the political arena, not because our advance had been that of a triumphal campaign, but because the new political form was ready to our hands, so that we had nothing more to do than issue a few decrees, and thus evolve the Soviet power out of the embryonic condition in which it had remained during the opening months of the revolution, into the officially recognised form of the Russian State—the Russian Soviet Republic. . . .
>
> There still remain two gigantic and extremely difficult tasks, neither of which is in any way solved by the fact that our revolution has been a triumphal progress. . . .
>
> First of all comes the task of internal organisation, which every socialist revolution must necessarily undertake. For the difference between the socialist revolution and the bourgeois revolution consists in this, that the bourgeois revolution has ready to its hand the forms of capitalist organisation, whereas the proletarian revolution does not receive these relationships ready-made—if we exclude from consideration the most highly developed forms of capitalism,

which in truth exist only upon the peaks of industry, whereas the broad levels of agricultural production are still practically untouched by them. The organisation of account-keeping, the control of large-scale enterprises, the changing of the whole State economic mechanism into one single great machine, into an economic organism which shall work so perfectly that hundreds of millions of persons shall have their activities guided in accordance with one comprehensive plan—such is the tremendous organisational task we have to perform. From its very nature it is one which cannot be performed by simply shouting loud hurrahs, even though we were able to cope with the difficulties of the civil war in that easy fashion. . . .

The second crucial problem is that of the world revolution. If we found it comparatively easy to get the upper hand of Kerensky and his associates, if we had little difficulty in establishing the Soviet power, if the decree concerning the socialisation of the land and concerning workers' control encountered so little opposition, this was only because for a brief space of time the circumstances were such as to protect us from the onslaughts of international imperialism. But international imperialism, which wields all the forces of united capital and all the acquirements of military technique, is a mighty power, and a very real power. In no circumstances, under no possible conditions, can it live at peace with the Soviet Republic. The objective situation of the capitalist imperialists, the economic interests of the capitalist class (incorporated, as they are, in international imperialism), the various commercial treaties between the capitalist nations, and all their international and financial relationships, combine to make this impossible. A conflict with international imperialism was inevitable. Here is the greatest difficulty of the Russian revolution, its supreme historical problem—the need to solve international problems, the need to promote the world revolution. (*Works*, Russian edition, vol. xv., pp. 124–127.)

Such is the true inwardness, such is the basic significance of the proletarian revolution.

Is an upheaval of the kind, is a radical transformation of the old bourgeois system of society, possible without a forcible revolution; is it possible without establishing the dictatorship of the proletariat?

Obviously not. To think that such a revolution can be carried out peacefully within the framework of bourgeois democracy, within the framework of the system that is adapted to maintain bourgeois rule, means one of two things. Either it means madness, an inability to understand the normal signifi-

THE PROLETARIAN REVOLUTION 23

cance of words; or else it means a cynical repudiation of the proletarian revolution.

It is necessary to insist on this all the more strongly, all the more categorically, seeing that we have to do with a proletarian revolution which as yet has triumphed in one land only, in a land surrounded by hostile capitalist countries, in a land whose bourgeoisie international capital cannot fail to support.

That is why Lenin writes:

> The deliverance of the oppressed class is impossible without a forcible revolution, and also without the destruction of the State machine which has been created by the ruling class. (*Works*, Russian edition, vol. xiv., part II., p. 302.)

Elsewhere he writes:

> Here is the view of the petty-bourgeois democrats, who call themselves "socialists" but are really the henchmen of the bourgeoisie. They say: "Not until the majority of the population has declared itself on the side of the party of the proletariat"—this while private property is still maintained, while capital is still enthroned, while the people is still under its yoke!—" can power be assumed by that majority"....
>
> But we say: "Let the revolutionary proletariat overthrow the bourgeoisie, break the yoke of capital, destroy the bourgeois State apparatus. Then the victorious proletariat will speedily gain the sympathy and win the support of the majority of the working (though non-proletarian) masses, whose wants will then be satisfied at the cost of the exploiters." (*Works*, Russian edition, vol. xvi., pp. 456–457.)
>
> If the proletariat is to win over the majority of the population, it must first of all overthrow the bourgeoisie and seize the powers of the State. Next, it must establish the Soviet authority, breaking up the old State apparatus, and thus at one blow counteracting the influence which the bourgeoisie and the petty-bourgeois apostles of class collaboration exercise over the working (though non-proletarian) masses. In the third place, the proletariat must *completely and finally destroy* the influence which the bourgeoisie and the petty-bourgeois compromisers exercise over the majority of the working (though non-proletarian) masses; it must do so by the *revolutionary satisfaction of the economic needs of these masses at the cost of the exploiters.* (*Works*, Russian edition, vol. xvi., p. 450.)

Such are the characteristics of the proletarian revolution.

Now, if it be agreed that the dictatorship of the proletariat forms the very essence of the proletarian revolution, what are the fundamental characteristics of the dictatorship of the proletariat ?

Here is Lenin's most generalised definition of the dictatorship of the proletariat :

> The dictatorship of the proletariat is not the end of the class struggle ; it is the continuation of that struggle under new forms. The dictatorship of the proletariat is the class struggle of the proletariat (after it has been victorious, after it has seized political power) against the bourgeoisie, which has been defeated but not annihilated, which still exists, which is still able to resist and is able to consolidate its forces of resistance. (*Works*, Russian edition, vol. xvi., pp. 240-241.)

As against those who confuse the dictatorship of the proletariat with a " popular " authority, " elected by universal suffrage ", and " standing above class ", Lenin writes :

> The class which has seized political power has done so knowing that it has seized power *for itself alone*. This is implicit in the idea of the dictatorship of the proletariat. When we speak of the " dictatorship " of a class, we do not mean anything at all unless we mean that this class consciously takes all political power into its own hands, and does not fool either itself or others by any verbiage about " a national authority, elected by universal suffrage, and consecrated by the will of the whole people." (*Works*, Russian edition, vol. xviii., part I., p. 175.)

This must not be taken to mean that the power of this one class, the class of the proletarians (who do not and cannot share this power with any other class), can get along without an alliance with the labouring and exploited masses of other classes. On the contrary, the proletarians need such an alliance for the realisation of their aims. This power, the power of a single class, cannot be firmly established, cannot be realised to the full, without a special kind of alliance between the proletariat and the working masses of the petty-bourgeois classes—in especial, the working masses of the peasantry.

What is this special kind of alliance ? In what does it consist ? Does not the idea of an alliance with the working masses of other classes, of non-proletarian classes, conflict with the idea of the dictatorship of the proletariat ?

No, for the alliance is such, that, within it, the proletariat takes the lead. The essence of the matter is that we have to do with an alliance in which the leader of the State, the leader within the system of the dictatorship of the proletariat, is one party alone, the party of the proletariat, the party of the communists, which does not and cannot share that leadership with other parties.

We see that the contradiction is apparent merely. I quote Lenin once more:

> The dictatorship of the proletariat is *a peculiar form of class alliance* [1] between the proletariat (the vanguard of all those who labour) and the various strata of the non-proletarian labouring masses (the petty bourgeoisie, independent artisans, peasants, members of the intelligentsia, etc.), or with the majority of these; it is an alliance against capital; an alliance aiming at the complete overthrow of capital, at the crushing of bourgeois resistance and the frustrating of any attempt at a bourgeois restoration; an alliance designed for the establishment and the definitive consolidation of socialism. This peculiar form of alliance is entered into under special circumstances, at a time when civil war is raging; it is an alliance between the convinced supporters of socialism and its wavering allies. (Some of the allies may be " neutrals ", and then an agreement to fight may be replaced by an agreement to maintain neutrality.) *It is an alliance between classes which differ economically, politically, socially, and ideologically.*[1] (*Works*, Russian edition, vol. xvi., p. 241.)

In one of his instructive reports, Comrade Kameneff, taking up the cudgels against such a conception of the dictatorship of the proletariat, writes:

> The dictatorship of the proletariat is not an alliance between one class and another (" Pravda ", Jan. 14, 1925).

I believe that Comrade Kameneff was mainly thinking of the passage in my pamphlet *The October Revolution and the Tactics of the Russian Communists*, where I write:

> The dictatorship of the proletariat is not simply an administrative clique at the head of affairs, " cleverly selected by experienced strategists ", and " sagely relying on the support " of this, that, or the other section of the populace. The dictatorship of the proletariat is a class alliance of the proletariat with the labouring masses of the peasantry; an alliance entered into for the overthrow of capitalism, for bringing about the final victory of socialism; an alliance formed upon the understanding that, within it, the leadership belongs to the proletariat. (See below, p. 185.)

---

[1] Italicised by Stalin.

I stand by this formulation of the dictatorship of the proletariat, for I think that it is in perfect conformity with Lenin's formulation, as above quoted.

I maintain that Comrade Kameneff's categorical declaration that "the dictatorship of the proletariat is not an alliance between one class and another" conflicts hopelessly with the Leninist theory of the dictatorship of the proletariat.

I maintain that Comrade Kameneff's view of the matter is possible only to persons who have never grasped the idea of the smychka,[1] the idea of the alliance between the workers and the peasants, the idea of the leadership of the workers within that alliance.

Such a view can be held only by persons who have failed to grasp what Lenin meant when he wrote :

> *Nothing but an understanding with the peasants*[2] can save the socialist revolution in Russia until the revolution takes place in other lands. (*Works*, Russian edition, vol. xviii., part I., p. 138.)

Such a view can be held only by persons who cannot fathom Lenin's meaning when he says :

> The first principle of the dictatorship is the safeguarding of the alliance between the proletariat and the peasantry, in order that the proletariat may continue to play the leading part and to wield State authority. (*Works*, Russian edition, vol. xviii., part I., p. 331.)

With reference to the crushing of the exploiters, as one of the chief aims of the dictatorship, Lenin writes :

> Scientifically defined, a dictatorship is an authority based directly on force, an authority which is absolutely unrestricted by any laws or regulations. . . . The dictatorship means (let the cadets[3] grasp the fact once for all !) power, unlimited power, based on force and not on law. When civil war is raging, the authority of the victors cannot be anything but a dictatorship. (*Works*, Russian edition, vol. xvii., pp. 355 and 361.)

Of course, the dictatorship of the proletariat does not mean

---

[1] *Smychok*, diminutive *smychka*, a leash. Metaphorically applied to the alliance of the workers and the peasants, conceived of as hounds leashed together and hunting in a couple.—E. and C. P.

[2] Italicised by Stalin.   [3] The constitutional democrats.—E. and C. P.

force and nothing else, although a dictatorship cannot be maintained except by force. To quote Lenin :

> The dictatorship does not mean force alone, though it is impossible without force. It likewise betokens a higher organisation of labour than has previously existed. (*Works*, Russian edition, vol. xvi., p. 222.)
>
> The dictatorship of the proletariat . . . is not merely the exercise of force against the exploiters, and indeed does not chiefly consist in the use of force. The economic basis of this revolutionary force, the guarantee of its vitality and success, is that the proletariat represents and realises a type of social organisation of labour higher than that represented and realised by the capitalist system. That is the main point. Herein lies the source of the strength of communism; herein we find assurance of its inevitable victory. (*Works*, Russian edition, vol. xvi., pp. 247–248.)
>
> The essence of the dictatorship is to be found in the organisation and discipline of the workers' vanguard, of their only leader, the proletariat. The purpose of the dictatorship is to establish socialism, to put an end to the division of society into classes, to make all the members of society workers, to make the exploitation of one human being by another for ever impossible. This end cannot be achieved at one stride. There will have to be a transitional period, a fairly long one, between capitalism and socialism. The reorganisation of production is a difficult matter. Time is requisite for the radical transformation of all departments of life. Furthermore, the power of custom is immense; people are habituated to a petty-bourgeois and bourgeois economy, and will only be induced to change their ways by a protracted and arduous struggle. That was why Marx, too, spoke of a transitional period between capitalism and socialism, a whole epoch of the dictatorship of the proletariat. (*Works*, Russian edition, vol. xvi., pp. 226–227.)

Such are the characteristics of the dictatorship of the proletariat.

We see, then, that it has three fundamental aspects :

1. The use of the power of the proletariat in order to crush the exploiters, in order to defend the country, in order to strengthen the ties with proletarians in other lands, and in order to favour the revolution everywhere.

2. The use of the power of the proletariat in order to detach the labouring and exploited masses once for all from the bourgeoisie, in order to strengthen the alliance of the proletariat with these masses, in order to enlist these masses in the work

of socialist construction, and in order to ensure that in the State the proletariat shall function as leader of these masses.

3. The use of the power of the proletariat in order to organise socialism abolish classes, and found a society without classes and without a State.

The dictatorship of the proletariat is a combination of all three. It is wrong to put any one of the three aspects to the front, or to regard it as of unique significance. On the other hand, should any one of the three characteristics be lacking, the result will be, in a capitalist environment, that the dictatorship of the proletariat will cease to be a dictatorship. Therefore not one of the three can be omitted without running the risk of distorting the conception of the dictatorship. The idea of the dictatorship of the proletariat is not complete, is not fully rounded off, unless all three of the before-mentioned characteristics are present in combination.

The dictatorship of the proletariat has its periods, its special forms, its diversified methods of work. While civil war is raging, the coercive aspect of the dictatorship is peculiarly prominent. But we must not infer from this that no constructive work can be carried on during the phase of civil war. The civil war itself cannot be waged without constructive work. During the period of socialist construction, on the other hand, the organisational and cultural work of the dictatorship is especially conspicuous, together with revolutionary legislation, etc. Here, again, we must be careful to avoid coming to the conclusion that during the period of socialist construction the dictatorship dispenses or can dispense with the use of force. The army and other organs of repression are no less necessary in this phase than they are in the phase of civil war. Without the force provided by these institutions there can be no guarantee for the safeguarding of the constructive work of the dictatorship. We must not forget that hitherto the revolution has taken place in one country only. We must not forget that so long as we live in a capitalist environment we are exposed to the danger of intervention, with all its disastrous consequences.

5. THE PARTY AND THE WORKING CLASS WITHIN THE SYSTEM OF THE DICTATORSHIP OF THE PROLETARIAT

HITHERTO I have been writing about the dictatorship of the proletariat from the standpoint of its historical necessity; from the standpoint of its nature as a class manifestation; from the standpoint of its political characteristics; and, lastly, from the standpoint of its destructive and creative tasks, which persist throughout an entire historical epoch known as the period of transition from capitalism to socialism.

Now we have to consider the dictatorship of the proletariat from the standpoint of its structure; its "mechanism"; the function and the importance of the "belts", the "levers", and the "guiding force", which comprise in their totality "the system of the dictatorship of the proletariat" (Lenin), and with the aid of which the daily work of the dictatorship of the proletariat is carried on.

What are these "belts" or "levers" in the system of the dictatorship of the proletariat? What is the "guiding force"? Why are they needed?

The levers and the belts are the mass organisations of the proletariat, without whose aid the dictatorship cannot be realised in practice.

The guiding force is that of the advanced section of the proletariat, the workers' vanguard, which constitutes the veritable leader of the dictatorship of the proletariat.

The proletariat needs these belts, these levers, and this guiding force, because without them it would, in its struggle for victory, be like a weaponless army in face of organised and armed capital. It needs these organisations, because without them it would inevitably be defeated in the fight for the overthrow of the bourgeoisie, for the consolidation of its own power, for the upbuilding of socialism. The systematic help of these organisations and of the guiding force of the workers' vanguard is indispensable, because otherwise the dictatorship of the proletariat could not be durable or steadfast.

What are these organisations ?

First of all there are the *trade unions*, with their national and local ramifications in the form of productive, educational, cultural, and other organisations. In these, the workers of all trades and industries are united. They are not Party organisations. Our trade unions can be regarded as the general organisation of the working class now holding power in Soviet Russia. They constitute a school of communism. From them are drawn the persons best fitted to occupy the leading positions in all branches of administration. They form the link between the more advanced and the comparatively backward sections of the working class, for in them the masses of the workers are united with the vanguard.

Secondly we have the *soviets* with their manifold national and local ramifications, taking the form of administrative, industrial, military, cultural, and other State organisations, together with a multitude of spontaneous mass groupings of the workers in the bodies which surround these organisations and link them up with the general population. The soviets are the mass organisations of all those who labour in town and country. They are not Party organisations, but are the direct expression of the dictatorship of the proletariat. All kinds of measures for the strengthening of the dictatorship and for the upbuilding of socialism are carried out by means of the soviets. Through them, the political guidance of the peasantry by the proletariat is effected. The soviets unite the labouring masses with the proletarian vanguard.

Thirdly we have *cooperatives* of all kinds, with their multiple ramifications. These, too, are non-Party organisations, being mass organisations in which the workers are united, primarily as consumers, but also, at a later stage, as producers (agricultural cooperatives). The cooperatives play a specially important part after the consolidation of the dictatorship of the proletariat, during the period of widespread construction. They form a link between the proletarian vanguard and the peasant masses, and provide a means whereby the latter can be induced to share in the work of socialist construction.

Fourthly there is the *League of Youth*. This is a mass organisation of the young workers and peasants, not a Party organisation, but in close touch with the Party. Its work is to help the Party in training the younger generation in a socialist spirit. It provides young reserves for all the other mass organisations of the proletariat in every branch of administration. The League of Youth acquires peculiar importance after the consolidation of the dictatorship of the proletariat, during the period when widespread cultural and educational work is incumbent upon the proletariat.

Lastly we come to the *Party* of the proletariat, the proletarian vanguard. Its strength lies in the fact that it attracts to its ranks the best elements of all the mass organisations of the proletariat. Its function is to *unify* the work of all the mass organisations of the proletariat, without exception, and to *guide* their activities towards a single end, that of the liberation of the proletariat. Unification and guidance are absolutely essential. There must be unity in the proletarian struggle; the proletarian masses must be guided in their fight for power and for the upbuilding of socialism; and only the proletarian vanguard, only the Party of the proletariat, is competent to unify and guide the work of the mass organisations of the proletariat. Nothing but the Party of the proletariat, nothing but the Communist Party, is able to act as universal leader in the system of the dictatorship of the proletariat.

Why is this? Let me quote from my pamphlet *Foundations of Leninism*:

> First of all, because the Party is the rallying-point for the best elements of the working class, of those who are in touch with the non-Party proletarian organisations, and are often leaders in these. In the second place, because the Party, as rallying-point for the best elements of the working class, forms the best training school for leaders competent to guide every kind of working-class organisation. Thirdly, because the Party, as the best training school for working-class leaders, is the only organisation competent, in virtue of its experience and authority, to centralise the leadership of the proletarian struggle, and thus to transform all non-Party working-class organisations into accessory organs and connecting belts linking up the Party with the working class as a whole.

The Party is the fundamental guiding force within the system of the dictatorship. As Lenin puts it, the Party is the supreme form of class organisation of the proletariat.

To sum up: the *trade unions*, as mass organisations of the proletariat, linking the Party with the working class as a whole, especially in the industrial field ; the *soviets*, as mass organisations of all who labour, linking the Party with these latter, especially in the political field ; the *cooperatives* as mass organisations, chiefly of the peasants, linking the Party with the peasant masses, especially in the economic field and as concerns peasant participation in the work of socialist construction ; the *League of Youth*, as a mass organisation of the young workers and peasants, whose function it is to help the proletarian vanguard in the socialist education of the rising generation and in the formation of young reserves ; finally, the *Party*, as the essential guiding force within the system of the dictatorship of the proletariat, and called upon to lead all the before-mentioned mass organisations—here we have, in broad outline, a picture of the " mechanism " of the dictatorship, a picture of the " system of the dictatorship of the proletariat ".

Without the Party as the essential guiding force, there cannot be a lasting and firmly consolidated dictatorship of the proletariat.

To quote Lenin :

> We thus have a supple, broadly based, and extremely powerful proletarian apparatus. In point of form, considered as a whole, it is not communist ; but by means of it the Party is closely linked to the *class* and to the *masses ;* and, thanks to it, under the leadership of the Party, a *class dictatorship* is realised. (*Works*, Russian edition, vol. xvii., p. 139.)

Of course this does not mean that the Party can or should become a substitute for the trade unions, the soviets, and the other mass organisations. The Party effectively realises the dictatorship of the proletariat. It does this, however, not directly, but with the help of the trade unions, and through the instrumentality of the soviets and their ramifications. Without these " belts ", a stable dictatorship would be impossible.

Lenin writes :

> The dictatorship cannot be effectively realised without " belts " to transmit power from the vanguard to the mass of the advanced class, and from this to the mass of those who labour. . . . The Party comprises the proletarian vanguard, and this vanguard realises the dictatorship of the proletariat. In the absence of such a basis to work upon as the trade unions constitute, the dictatorship could not become effective, the functions of the State could not be fulfilled. They have to be fulfilled *through the instrumentality*

of [1] a series of special institutions which are likewise of a new type, *through the instrumentality of* [1] the soviet apparatus. (*Works*, Russian edition, vol. xviii., part I., pp. 8-9.)

Here is a fact which may be considered the supreme expression of the guiding function of our Party. In the Soviet Union, in the land where the dictatorship of the proletariat is in force, no important political or organisational problem is ever decided by our soviets and other mass organisations without directives from the Party. *In this sense* we may say that the dictatorship of the proletariat is, *substantially*, the " dictatorship " of its vanguard, the " dictatorship " of its Party, as the force which guides the proletariat. Consider what Lenin said in reference to this matter at the Second Congress of the Communist International:

> Tanner tells us that he is in favour of the dictatorship of the proletariat, but he does not understand the term in precisely the same sense as we do. He says that by the dictatorship of the proletariat we mean, *substantially*,[1] the dictatorship of its organised and class-conscious minority. In actual fact, under capitalism, when the working masses are subject to unceasing exploitation and cannot develop their human faculties, one of the main characteristics of working-class political parties is that such parties can only enrol a minority of the working class. The reason is that, under capitalism, effectively class-conscious workers form a minority of the workers as a whole. We have, therefore, to admit that the broad masses of the workers must be led and guided by the class-conscious minority. When Comrade Tanner says that he is opposed to the Party, and in the same breath declares that a minority of the best organised and most revolutionary workers must show the way to the proletariat as a whole, I answer that really there is no difference between our views. (*Works*, Russian edition, vol. xvii., p. 270.)

Does this mean that the dictatorship of the proletariat and the guiding function of the Party (the " dictatorship " of the Party) are *one and the same thing*, that the latter can be *substituted* for the former without producing any change? Of course it means nothing of the kind. Comrade Sorin declares that " the dictatorship of the proletariat is the dictatorship of our Party " (*What Lenin teaches about the Party*, p. 95). Obviously, to say that is to identify the " dictatorship of the Party " with the dictatorship of the proletariat. Can this be admitted while

[1] Italicised by Stalin.

remaining within the confines of Leninism ? No, for the following reasons :

1. In his speech to the Second Congress of the Communist International, Lenin does not identify the guiding role of the Party with the dictatorship of the proletariat. He says that the broad masses of the workers must be led and guided by the class-conscious minority—by the Party. He says that, *in this sense*, by the dictatorship of the proletariat we mean, *substantially*, the dictatorship of its organised and class-conscious minority. When he uses the word "substantially", he implies that he does not mean "wholly". We often say that the national problem is, substantially, a peasant problem. This is perfectly true. But when we say it we do not mean that the national question covers exactly the same ground as the peasant question ; that the peasant question is of precisely the same scope as the national question, that the peasant question and the national question are one and the same thing. There is no need to prove that the scope of the national question is much wider than that of the peasant question, that the content of the former is much richer than that of the latter. There is an analogous relationship between the concept of the dictatorship of the proletariat and the concept of the guiding function of the Party. Even though the Party carries out the dictatorship of the proletariat, so that, in this sense, the dictatorship of the proletariat is *substantially* a "dictatorship" of the Party of the proletariat, that does not signify that "the dictatorship of the Party" (the guiding function of the Party) is *identical* with the dictatorship of the proletariat, that the former is *coextensive* with the latter. There is no need to prove that the scope of the dictatorship of the proletariat is much wider than that of the guiding function of the Party, that the content of the former concept is much richer than that of the latter. The Party carries out the dictatorship of the proletariat ; but what it carries out is the dictatorship of the *proletariat*, and not the dictatorship of something else. Any one who identifies the guiding function of the Party with the dictatorship of the proletariat, is substituting the "dictatorship" of the Party for the dictatorship of the proletariat.

2. No important decision is ever arrived at by the mass organisations of the proletariat without directives from the Party. This is perfectly true. But does it mean that the

dictatorship of the proletariat is the guiding function of the Party *and nothing more* ? Does it mean that the issuing of directives by the Party is one and the same thing as the dictatorship of the proletariat ? Of course it does not mean this. The dictatorship of the proletariat is the issuing of directives by the Party, plus the carrying of these directives into effect on the part of the mass organisations of the proletariat, plus their being made actual by the population at large. Obviously, we are faced here with a whole series of transitions and graduations which comprise important elements of the dictatorship of the proletariat. Between the directives of the Party and their being made actual, come the will and the activities of those who carry out these directives, the will and the activities of the class, its willingness (or unwillingness) to act in accordance with the directives, its capacity (or incapacity) for acting upon them, its capacity (or incapacity) for realising them as circumstances may demand. It is hardly necessary to prove that the Party, when it has shouldered the burden of leadership, has to take into account the wills, the states of mind, the degrees of class consciousness, of those who are being led—of the members of the class as a whole. Consequently, any one who identifies the guiding function of the Party with the dictatorship of the proletariat, is substituting the directives of the Party for the will and the activities of the class.

3. " The dictatorship of the proletariat ", says Lenin, " is the class struggle of the proletariat after its victorious seizure of political power ". (*Works*, Russian edition, vol. xvi., p. 240.) How can this *class* struggle find expression ? It may take the form of a series of armed activities on the part of the proletariat designed to resist the onslaughts of the bourgeoisie which has been overthrown, or to resist the intervention of a foreign bourgeoisie. If the power of the proletariat is not yet fully established, it may take the form of civil war. After that power has been consolidated, it may take the form of widespread organisational and constructive work on the part of the proletariat, with the enlistment of the masses in these activities. In all cases alike, the " personality " at work is the proletariat *as a class*. Never has the Party, simply as a Party, been able to undertake all these activities solely in virtue of its own strength, and without the support of the class. Ordinarily the Party does no more than lead them, and it can lead them only in so

far as it has the support of the class. For the Party is not the same thing as the class, and cannot replace the class. The Party, however important it may be, however indispensable its guiding function, is still nothing more than a *part* of the class. Consequently, any one who identifies the guiding function of the Party with the dictatorship of the proletariat, is substituting the Party for the class.

4. The Party effectively realises the dictatorship of the proletariat. Lenin writes : " The Party is the directly managing vanguard of the proletariat ; it is the leader ". This is the sense in which the Party wields power, in which the Party governs the country. But that does not mean that the Party realises the dictatorship of the proletariat outside the limits of the State authority ; that the Party governs the country independently of the soviets, for it governs through the soviets. But this, again, does not mean that the Party can be identified with the soviets, or that it can be identified with the State authority. The Party is the substantial wielder of authority, but it cannot be identified with the State authority. Lenin writes : " Since we are the ruling Party, we cannot but amalgamate the chiefs of the soviets with the chiefs of the Party ; in Soviet Russia they are thus amalgamated, and will remain so ". (*Works*, Russian edition, vol. xviii., part I., p. 112). This is perfectly correct. But Lenin does not mean that our Soviet institutions as a whole (such as the army, the transport service, the economic institutions, etc.) are Party institutions ; he does not mean that the Party can take the place of the soviets and their ramifications, or that the Party can be identified with the State authority. Lenin says again and again that " the Soviet system is the dictatorship of the proletariat " and that the Soviet power is the dictatorship of the proletariat. (*Works*, Russian edition, vol. xvi., pp. 44-46.) Nowhere does he say that the Party is the State authority, or that the soviets and the Party are one and the same. The Party, with its membership of a few hundred thousand, guides the soviets both nationally and locally, the soviets and their ramifications, comprising several million persons, some of whom are Party members but the majority of whom are not ; it neither can nor ought to take the place of the soviets. That is why Lenin writes : " The dictatorship is realised by the proletariat organised in the soviets, and the proletariat itself is guided by

THE PARTY AND THE WORKING CLASS 37

the Communist Party of the bolsheviks"; why he tells us that "all the work of the Party is carried out *through* [1] the soviets, which unite the labouring masses without distinction of occupation" (*Works*, Russian edition, vol. xvii., pp. 138-140); and why he declares that the dictatorship " must be realised . . . *through* [1] the Soviet apparatus". (*Works*, Russian edition, vol. xviii., part I., p. 8.) Consequently, any one who identifies the guiding function of the Party with the dictatorship of the proletariat, is substituting the soviets, the State authority, for the Party.

5. The concept of the dictatorship of the proletariat is a political concept, a State concept. The dictatorship of the proletariat necessarily involves the idea of force. Without force there can be no dictatorship in the strict sense of the term. Lenin defines the dictatorship of the proletariat as " power based directly on force ". (*Works*, Russian edition, vol. xvii., p. 124.) Any one, therefore, who talks as if the dictatorship of the Party *were exercised over the proletarian class*, and identifies *this* dictatorship with the dictatorship of the proletariat, is in effect saying that in relation to its own class the Party must be, not only guide and teacher, but also in some sort a State authority which rules that class by force. Consequently, any one who identifies the " dictatorship of the Party " with the dictatorship of the proletariat is tacitly assuming that the authority of the Party can be grounded on force—which is absurd, and utterly incompatible with Leninism. The authority of the Party is maintained by the confidence of the working class. The confidence of the working class is not to be won by force; for the use of force would kill confidence. It can only be won if Party theory is sound, if Party policy is correct, if the Party is devoted to the cause of the working class, if the Party is closely linked with the masses of the working class, and if the Party is ready and able to *convince* the masses that its slogans are the right ones.

What follows from all these considerations?

Here we have the deductions:

1. When Lenin speaks of a dictatorship of the Party, he does not use the word dictatorship in its literal meaning of " power based directly on force ", but uses it figuratively, to mean leadership.

2. Any one who identifies leadership by the Party with the

[1] Italicised by Stalin.

dictatorship of the proletariat distorts Lenin's meaning, wrongly attributing to the Party the use of force in relation to the working class as a whole.

3. Any one who attributes to the Party a non-existent use of force in relation to the working class, violates the elementary principles of the proper mutual relationships between the workers' vanguard and the working class as a whole, between the Party and the proletariat.

This brings us to the question of the relationships between the Party and the working class, between those in the working class who are and those who are not members of the Party.

Lenin defines these relationships as " mutual confidence between the workers' vanguard and the working masses " (*Works*, Russian edition, vol. xviii., part I., p. 135.)

What does this mean ?

First of all, that the Party must have a good ear for the voice of the masses, must pay close attention to their revolutionary instinct, must study the actualities of their struggle, must carefully enquire whether their policy is sound—and must, therefore, be ready, not only to teach the masses, but also to learn from them.

This means, in the second place, that the Party must from day to day win the confidence of the proletarian masses ; that, by its policy and its activities, it must secure the support of the masses ; that it must not order but persuade, helping the masses to become aware by their own experience that the Party policy is right ; that it must, therefore, be the guide, the leader, the teacher of the proletariat.

To violate these conditions is to violate the proper mutual relationships between the vanguard and the class as a whole, to undermine the " mutual confidence ", to imperil discipline both within the class and within the Party.

Lenin writes :

> Beyond question, almost every one knows by this time that the bolsheviks would not have been able to hold power for two and a half years, nor even for two and a half months, had there not been the strictest possible discipline, a truly iron discipline, within the Party ; nor would they have been able to hold power *without the whole-hearted support of the entire mass of the working class,*[1] or at any rate the full support of all the members of the working class

---

[1] Italicised by Stalin.

who are class-conscious, sincere, devoted, influential, and competent to lead those who are comparatively backward or attract them into the forward movement. (*Works*, Russian edition, vol. xvii., p. 117.)

The dictatorship of the proletariat is a hard-fought fight against the forces and traditions of the old society; a fight that is both bloody and unbloody, both violent and passive, both military and economic, both educational and administrative. The power of habit, ingrained in millions and tens of millions, is a terrible power. Without the Party, a party of iron which has been tempered in the struggle, a party *that enjoys the confidence of all the straightforward members of the working class*,[1] a party able to understand and to influence the psychology of the masses, success in such a struggle would be impossible. (*Works*, Russian edition, vol. xvii., p. 136.)

But how is the Party to win the confidence and gain the support of the class? The iron discipline necessary for the dictatorship of the proletariat—how is it fashioned, upon what soil does it grow?

Here is what Lenin has to say about the matter:

How is discipline maintained within the revolutionary Party of the proletariat? What controls this discipline, and what strengthens it? First of all, there is the class consciousness of the proletarian vanguard, its devotion to the revolution, its self-control, its self-sacrifice, its heroism. Secondly, there is the capacity of the proletarian vanguard for linking itself with, for keeping in close touch with, for to some extent *amalgamating with, the broad masses of those who labour*,[1] primarily with the proletarian masses, *but also with the non-proletarianised masses of those who labour*.[1] Thirdly, we have the soundness of the vanguard's political leadership, the soundness of its political strategy and tactic—with the proviso that the broad masses must become convinced *by their own experience*[1] that the leadership, the strategy, and the tactic are sound. Unless these conditions are fulfilled, there is no possibility of achieving the discipline which is indispensable for a revolutionary party that shall be able to become the Party of the most advanced class, the Party whose task it is to overthrow the bourgeoisie and to transform the whole of society. Unless these conditions are fulfilled, the attempts to establish such a discipline will never get beyond empty talk and unmeaning gestures—hot air. On the other hand, these conditions cannot be fulfilled betwixt night and morning. Much labour and pains, hard-won experience, will be required. Their fulfilment must be guided by accurate revolutionary theory, which, however, must

---

[1] Italicised by Stalin.

never harden into dogma, but must always be formulated in close touch with the practical activity of the masses and the daily work of the revolutionary movement. (*Works*, Russian edition, vol. xvii., pp. 118–119.)

Again:

> In order to win the victory over capitalism there must be a proper relationship between the leading party, the Communist Party, the revolutionary class, the proletariat, on the one hand, and the mass, the totality of those who labour and are exploited, on the other. The Communist Party, as the vanguard of the revolutionary class, enrolling as members all the best elements of that class, consisting of fully class-conscious and devoted communists who have been enlightened and steeled by their experience in the stubborn revolutionary struggle, inseparably connected with the whole life of the working class and through this class linked up with the wider mass of the exploited, enjoying the *full confidence*[1] of one and all of these—only the Communist Party, if it fulfils all the before-mentioned conditions, is competent to lead the proletariat in the last, the ruthless, the decisive campaign against the united forces of capitalism. On the other hand, only under the leadership of such a party is the proletariat able to develop the full power of its revolutionary onslaught, to render harmless the inevitable apathy (and sometimes the active hostility) of the small minority of the workers, of the working-class aristocracy which has been corrupted by capitalism, of the old leaders in the trade unions and the cooperatives, etc. Only under the leadership of such a party can the proletariat develop all its strength, which, in virtue of the economic structure of capitalist society, is incomparably greater than its numerical ratio to the rest of the population. (*Works*, Russian edition, vol. xvii., p. 232.)

From the foregoing considerations it follows that:

1. The authority of the Party, and the iron discipline of the working class indispensable to the dictatorship of the proletariat, are based, not upon fear nor upon the concession of " unrestricted " rights to the Party, but upon the confidence of the working class in the Party and upon the support of the Party by the working class.

2. The Party does not win the confidence of the working class in the twinkling of an eye, or by the use of force against the working class. Trust is gradually inspired by the prolonged work of the Party among the masses; thanks to the soundness of Party policy; because the Party is able to convince the masses

---
[1] Italicised by Stalin.

THE PARTY AND THE WORKING CLASS

by their own experience that its policy is sound, thus ensuring the support of the working class and inducing the broad masses of the workers to follow its lead.

3. The Party does not and cannot effectively lead unless its policy is sound, and strengthened by experience in the working-class struggle ; it does not and cannot effectively lead unless it has the full confidence of the working class.

4. If the Party enjoys the confidence of the working class and if its leadership is effective, the Party and its leadership cannot be contraposed to the dictatorship of the proletariat, for a firmly established dictatorship of the proletariat is impossible unless the Party leads the working class (the " dictatorship " of the Party) and enjoys the confidence of the working class.

Unless these conditions are fulfilled, " the authority of the Party " and " the iron discipline of the working class " are but empty phrases, are but an idle boast.

There is no justification for contraposing the dictatorship of the proletariat to the leadership (the " dictatorship ") of the Party. The contraposition is inadmissible for the reason that the Party leadership is the most important element in the dictatorship of the proletariat—if we are thinking of a firmly established and effective dictatorship, and not of such a dictatorship as that of the Commune of Paris, which was neither firmly established nor effective. The contraposition is inadmissible because the dictatorship of the proletariat and the Party leadership are, as it were, complementary parts of one piece of work, and act together along the same line.

Lenin writes :

> Any one who states the question in this way, speaking of the dictatorship of the Party *or* the dictatorship of the class, speaking of dictatorship of the leaders and dictatorship of the masses as *alternatives*, shows by this very formulation that his mind is incredibly and hopelessly confused. . . . Every one knows that the masses are split up into classes ; . . . that (in modern civilised countries, at least) classes are usually led by political parties ; that these parties are, as a rule, managed by more or less stable groupings of the most authoritative, influential, and experienced persons among their members, elected to responsible posts and spoken of as leaders. . . . To imply that there is, in general, a contraposition between the dictatorship of the masses and the dictatorship of the leaders is utterly absurd. (*Works*, Russian edition, vol. xvii., pp. 133-134.)

The statement is perfectly correct, but it presupposes the existence of sound relationships between the vanguard and the working masses, between the Party and the class. It assumes that the relationship between the vanguard and the class are, so to say, normal; that they are inspired by mutual confidence. But what will happen if the relationship between the vanguard and the class is disturbed, if the mutual confidence which ought to subsist is shaken or destroyed? Suppose that in one way or another the Party begins to set itself up against the class, thus undermining the foundations of proper relationships between the two, the foundations of mutual confidence! Can such a thing happen? Certainly it can happen, if the Party begins to base its authority among the masses, not upon its work, not upon the trust it inspires, but upon its " unrestricted " rights; if the Party is manifestly wrong in its policy, and yet will not admit and rectify its errors; or if the policy of the Party, though sound in the main, is one which the masses are not yet ready to adopt, and the Party will not or cannot wait until the masses have had a chance of learning by their own experience that the Party policy is right. The history of our Party presents a number of instances of the kind. Various groupings and fractions of the Party have failed and have broken up because they infringed one of the three conditions just mentioned—or sometimes infringed them all.

No one, therefore, is entitled to speak of the " dictatorship " (the leadership) of the Party as equivalent to the dictatorship of the proletariat unless he has in mind one of the three following cases :

1. The case in which, when we speak of the dictatorship which the Party exercises over the working class, we mean what Lenin meant when he used the phrase, not a dictatorship in the strict sense of the term (" power based directly on force "), but the guiding function of the party exercised without the use of force directed against the class as a whole — against its majority.

2. The case in which the Party is really qualified to act as leader of the class, the implication being that the Party policy is sound, and in conformity with the interests of the class.

3. The case in which the class, the majority of the class, accepts the Party policy, makes that policy its own, and, being

THE PARTY AND THE WORKING CLASS

convinced by the daily work of the Party that the policy is sound, has confidence in the Party and supports it.

Failure to satisfy these conditions will inevitably lead to a conflict between the Party and the class.

Can the Party impose its leadership on the class by force? No, it cannot. Or, if such a thing were done, the leadership would not last long. If the Party is to remain the Party of the proletariat, it must know that, above all, it is the *guide*, the *leader*, the *teacher* of the working class. We must not forget what Lenin said about this matter in *The State and Revolution*:

> By educating the workers' party, Marxism educates the vanguard of the proletariat, thus fitting it to seize power and to lead the whole people towards socialism, to carry on and to organise the new order, to become the *teacher*, the *guide*, the *leader* [1] of all who labour and are exploited—their teacher, guide, and leader in the work of organising their social life without the bourgeoisie and against the bourgeoisie. (*Works*, Russian edition, vol. xiv., part II., p. 317.)

But can we look upon the Party as the effective leader of the working class if the Party policy is wrong, if its policy conflicts with working-class interests? Of course not! In such circumstances, the Party, if it is to remain the leader, must reconsider its policy, must rectify its policy, must acknowledge its mistakes and amend them. Consider, for instance, the compulsory levies of grain. At a certain period in the history of our Party it became obvious that the masses of workers and peasants disapproved of these levies. Thereupon the Party openly and honestly revised its policy, and the levies were abolished. At the Tenth Party Congress, Lenin discussed this question of the abolition of the forced levies, and that of the introduction of the New Economic Policy. Here is an extract from his speech:

> We must not try to hush up anything. We must frankly admit that the peasants are discontented with the system we have established, and that they will not put up with it any longer. This is indisputable. They have expressed their wishes very plainly indeed. We are confronted with the wishes of the great mass of the labouring population. Their wishes have to be taken into account, and, as politicians, we are realists enough to say: "*Let us reconsider the question.*" [1] (*Works*, Russian edition, vol. xviii., part I., p. 138.

---

[1] Italicised by Stalin.

Now let us contemplate another possibility. Let us suppose that, owing to the political backwardness of the working class, the Party policy (though right in the main) does not inspire general confidence or command general support; let us suppose that the Party has not yet been able to convince the working class that its policy is sound, the reason being that (as the phrase runs) the time is not yet ripe. In such a case, is the Party to take a decided initiative? Should the Party try to give a strong trend to the actions of the masses? No, certainly not! In such cases the Party, if it is to lead effectively, must know how to wait until it has convinced the masses that its policy is sound, must help the masses to learn this by their own experience.

Lenin writes:

> If the revolutionary Party is not supported by a majority in the advanced sections of the revolutionary classes and throughout the country, then there can be no question of a rising. (*Works*, Russian edition, vol. xiv., part II., p. 255.)

Again:

> No revolution is possible without a change of views in the majority of the working class. Such a change of views is brought about, in the masses, by political experience. (*Works*, Russian edition, vol. xvii., p. 172.)

Once more:

> The proletarian vanguard has been won over to our ideas. That is the main thing. Until so much has been achieved, we cannot take even the first step towards victory. But from this first step it is still a long way to the victory. The vanguard cannot conquer unaided. It would be worse than a blunder, it would be a crime, to send the vanguard into the fighting line before the class as a whole (the broad mass) is ready to support it, or at least ready to show benevolent neutrality and fully determined not to go over to the enemy. But propaganda and agitation alone will not suffice to ensure that the class as a whole, the broad masses of those who labour and are exploited by capitalism, are to be depended on. For this the masses must have learned by their own political experience. (*Works*, Russian edition, vol. xvii., p. 179.)

We know that the Party worked along this line from the days when Lenin wrote his April theses down to the time of the October revolution. The armed rising of October (November)

THE PARTY AND THE WORKING CLASS

1917 was successful for the very reason that Lenin's teaching had gone home.

Such are the fundamental characteristics of a proper mutual relationship between the vanguard and the class as a whole.

What does *leadership* mean when the Party policy is sound and when the relationships between the vanguard and the class as a whole are all that can be wished?

In such circumstances, leadership means: ability to convince the masses that the Party policy is right; ability to issue and to act upon slogans that will bring the masses nearer to the Party standpoint, and will make it easier for them (as the outcome of their own experience) to realise the soundness of the Party policy; ability to raise the masses to the Party level, and thus to ensure their cooperation at the decisive hour.

Thus the method of persuasion must be the chief method employed by the Party in its leadership of the class.

Lenin writes:

> If in Russia to-day, after two and a half years of unexampled success in the fight against the Russian bourgeoisie and the Entente capitalists, we were to make the " recognition of the dictatorship " a condition of membership of the trade unions, we should commit a gross blunder, should forfeit our influence over the masses, should play into the hands of the mensheviks. For the essential task of the communists is to *convince* the backward members of their class, to work *among* them, and *not to set themselves apart* by artificial and childishly "left-wing" slogans. (*Works*, Russian edition, vol. xvii., p. 144.)

Of course this does not mean that the Party must convince all the workers without exception, and must not till then take any action. It means nothing of the sort. What it means is that before entering upon decisive political activities the Party must, by prolonged revolutionary work, make sure of the support of the great majority of the working masses, or at least of their benevolent neutrality. Otherwise there would be absolutely no meaning in Lenin's contention that a victorious revolution is impossible unless the Party has first won over the majority of the working class.

What is to be done if the minority refuses to submit to the will of the majority? When the Party enjoys the confidence of the majority, may it and must it force the minority to comply?

Yes, it may and it must. The fundamental way in which the Party acts upon the masses is by persuasion; it is by *persuading* the majority that the leadership is safeguarded. This however does not exclude compulsion. On the contrary, it presupposes the use of compulsion when compulsion is supported by the confidence of the majority of the working class, and when the Party does not apply it to the minority until the majority has been won over. In this connexion let us recall the discussions that went on in our Party during the time when the trade-union problem was under consideration. What was the error of the opposition, of the Central Committee of the Transport Workers' Union? Did that error consist simply and solely in this, that the use of force was contemplated? Not at all! The mistake was that the opposition contemplated the use of force in spite of the fact that it was unable to convince the majority that its views were sound, in spite of the fact that it had forfeited the confidence of the majority; the mistake was that in these circumstances the opposition wanted " to make a clean sweep " of persons who enjoyed the confidence of the majority.

Here is what Lenin said at the Tenth Congress of the Party, in his speech on the trade-union question:

> To restore mutual confidence between the workers' vanguard and the working masses, it was necessary that the Central Committee of the Transport Workers' Union, made having a blunder, . . . should correct its error. When people who have made a mistake try to defend it, the political situation grows dangerous. Unless the utmost possible had been done in the democratic direction in order to carry into effect the views expressed here by Kutuzoff, there would have been a political explosion. *We must convince first, and keep force in reserve. At any cost, we must convince first, and not use force till afterwards.*[1] In this case we did not succeed in convincing the broad masses, and we therefore impaired the relationships between the vanguard and the masses. (*Works*, Russian edition, vol. xviii., part I., p. 135.)

Lenin writes to the same effect in his pamphlet *Concerning the Trade Unions*:

> We have applied force rightly and successfully in those cases in which we have paved the way for it by persuasion. (*Works*, Russian edition, vol. xviii., part I., p. 19.)

This is perfectly correct, for on no other supposition is

---
[1] Italicised by Stalin.

THE PARTY AND THE WORKING CLASS

leadership possible. In no other way can the unity of the Party or the unity of the working class as a whole (as the case may be) be safeguarded. Otherwise there will be disunion, disarray, in the ranks of the workers.

Such are the fundamental characteristics of correct Party leadership.

Any other conception of leadership may be syndicalism, anarchism, bureaucracy, or what you will; it is certainly not bolshevism, certainly not Leninism.

If there are sound relationships between the Party and the working class, between the vanguard and the working masses, then there can be no ground for contraposing the leadership (the " dictatorship ") of the Party to the dictatorship of the proletariat. It follows from this that there is no warrant for identifying the Party with the working class, or the leadership (" dictatorship ") of the Party with the dictatorship of the working class. From the circumstance that the " dictatorship " of the Party must not be contraposed to the dictatorship of the proletariat, Comrade Sorin draws the erroneous conclusion that " the dictatorship of the proletariat is the dictatorship of our Party ". But Lenin does not merely tell us that to contrapose the " dictatorship " of the Party to the dictatorship of the proletariat is inadmissible; in the same connexion he declares that we must not contrapose the " dictatorship of the masses " to the " dictatorship of the leaders ". Are we, for this reason, to identify the dictatorship of the leaders with the dictatorship of the proletariat? If we took that road, we might declare that the dictatorship of the proletariat is the dictatorship of our leaders. Such is the absurdity to which we are led if we set out from an identification of the " dictatorship " of the Party with the dictatorship of the proletariat.

What are Comrade Zinovieff's views on this subject?

In reality, Comrade Zinovieff holds that the " dictatorship " of the Party and the dictatorship of the proletariat are one and the same thing. The only difference between him and Comrade Sorin is that Comrade Sorin says plainly what he means, whereas Comrade Zinovieff " wriggles ". Read, for instance, what Comrade Zinovieff writes in his *Leninism* :

> What is the prevailing system in the U.S.S.R. when considered from the class standpoint? It is the dictatorship of the prole-

tariat. What is the mainspring of power in the U.S.S.R.? Who incorporates the power of the working class? The Communist Party! In this sense, *the dictatorship of the Party prevails*.[1] What is the legalised form of power in the U.S.S.R.? What is the new type of State system brought into being by the October revolution? The Soviet system.. There is no contradiction between one and the other. (*Leninism*, pp. 370–371.)

Certainly there is no contradiction between the one and the other—provided always that when we speak of a dictatorship exercised by the Party over the working class we mean the leadership of the Party. But how is it possible, for that reason, to identify the dictatorship of the proletariat with the " dictatorship " of the Party, or to identify the Soviet system with the " dictatorship " of the Party? Lenin identified the Soviet system with the dictatorship of the proletariat, and he was right to do so, for the soviets, *our* soviets, are organisations in which the masses of those who labour are united round the proletariat under the leadership of the Party. But when, where, and in which of his writings, has Lenin identified the " dictatorship " of the Party with the dictatorship of the proletariat, or the " dictatorship " of the Party with the Soviet system, in such a way as that in which Comrade Zinovieff is now identifying them? There is no contradiction between the leadership (" dictatorship ") of the Party and the dictatorship of the proletariat, or between the guiding function (" dictatorship ") of the leaders and the dictatorship of the proletariat. But should we, for that reason, declare that our country is the country of the dictatorship of the proletariat, *that is to say* the country of the dictatorship of the Party, *that is to say* the country of the dictatorship of the leaders? This is the absurdity to which we are led by the " principle " of the identity of the " dictatorship " of the Party with the dictatorship of the proletariat, the " principle " surreptitiously and timidly maintained by Comrade Zinovieff.

In Lenin's numerous works there are, to the best of my knowledge and belief, only five passages in which he touches (and lightly) upon the question of the dictatorship of the Party.

The first of these is one directed against the social revolutionaries and the mensheviks. Here he writes:

[1] Italicised by Stalin.

THE PARTY AND THE WORKING CLASS 49

> When they complain that we have established a dictatorship of one party, and, as you have heard, propose a united socialist front, we reply: "Yes, the dictatorship of one party! We stand by this, and have no intention of giving it up, for it is the Party which, in the course of decades, has fought for and won the position of vanguard to all the factory and industrial proletariat. (*Works*, Russian edition, vol. xvi., p. 296.)

The second allusion is in the *Letter to the Workers and Peasants about the Defeat of Kolchak*. He writes:

> Some people (especially the mensheviks and the social revolutionaries—even those among them who claim to belong to the left wing) try to frighten the peasants with the bogey of the "dictatorship of one party", the Party of Communist Bolsheviks. The Kolchak affair has taught the peasants not to be terrified by this spectre. Either the dictatorship of the ground landlords and the capitalists (the Iron Heel), or else the dictatorship of the working class. (*Works*, Russian edition, vol. xvi., p. 306.)

The third passage is in the answer to Tanner at the Second Congress of the Communist International. I quoted it on p. 33.

The fourth reference comprises several allusions made in *Left-Wing Communism, an Infantile Disorder*. The passage in question was quoted by me on p. 41. See also the quotations from the same booklet on pp. 38-40.

The fifth and last occasion on which Lenin refers to this matter is in his draft scheme of the dictatorship of the proletariat, where "Dictatorship of One Party" is used as a sub-title. (*Choice Works of Lenin*, Russian edition, vol. iii., p. 497.)

The reader should note that in two of these passages, the second and the fifth, Lenin has the words "dictatorship of one party" in quotation marks, thus emphasising his view that the phrase lacks precision and is used metaphorically.

I must also point out that in *every one* of these instances when Lenin speaks of the "dictatorship of the Party" *as exercised over the working class*, he obviously does not mean dictatorship in the strict sense of the term ("power based directly on force"); he means nothing more than Party leadership.

Noteworthy is the fact that in *none* of the works, major or minor, where Lenin discusses or merely alludes to the dictatorship of the proletariat and speaks of the function of the Party in the system of the dictatorship of the proletariat, does he imply in any way whatever that (as Sorin puts it) "the dictatorship of the proletariat is the dictatorship of our Party". On the contrary, every page, every line, of these works is a strong protest against any such formulation. (See *The State and Revolution, The Proletarian Revolution and Kautsky the Renegade, Left-Wing Communism, an Infantile Disorder*, etc.)

Even more noteworthy is the fact that in the theses of the Second Congress of the Communist International concerning the function of a political party (theses worked out under Lenin's supervision, often quoted in his speeches, and regarded by him as a masterly formulation of the tasks of our Party) there is not a word, literally not one word, about Party dictatorship.

What does all this mean?

It means that:

1. Lenin did not regard the formula "the dictatorship of the Party" as unobjectionable; he did not look upon it as accurate. That was why he rarely used the phrase, and sometimes put it in quotation marks.

2. On the few occasions when Lenin found it necessary, for controversial reasons, to speak of the dictatorship of the Party, he usually explained that when he referred to the dictatorship of the Party as exercised over the working class he was to be understood as meaning Party leadership.

3. Whenever Lenin thought it necessary to give a scientific definition of the function of the Party in the system of the dictatorship of the proletariat, he spoke of Party leadership and nothing else (innumerable instances!).

4. That was why, at the Second Congress of the Communist International, when a resolution of fundamental importance concerning the function of the Party was adopted, Lenin never dreamed of including in it the formula of "the dictatorship of the Party".

5. Those who identify or try to identify the "dictatorship" of the Party or the "dictatorship of the leaders" with the dictatorship of the proletariat, are out of touch with Leninism, and are politically blind, for these comrades infringe the right relationships between the vanguard and the class.

It is hardly necessary to say that the phrase "dictatorship of the Party", when used without the before-mentioned qualifications, may involve us in serious dangers and give rise to a number of mistakes in our practical political work. When employed without qualification, the expression implies that we are saying :

1. *To the non-Party masses :* " Don't dare to contradict, or to discuss matters ; the party is supreme ; the dictatorship of the Party has been established ".

2. *To the members of the Party :* " Act more resolutely ; tighten up the screw ; pay no heed to what the non-Party masses say ; the dictatorship of the Party is in force ".

3. *To the Party leaders :* " You can enjoy the luxury of self-satisfaction ; you can have a touch of swelled head if you like ; a Party dictatorship has been set up, and of course that really means the dictatorship of the leaders ".

The present moment is one at which it is more than ever incumbent on us to keep these dangers well in mind, at a time when the political activity of the masses is increasing. Now, in especial, the Party must be ready to pay close attention to the voice of the masses ; must have a fine ear for their demands ; must display extreme caution and show peculiar elasticity in its policy. Now, more than ever, will the Party leadership of the masses be imperilled if communists should suffer from swelled head.

Let us never forget Lenin's golden words at the Eleventh Party Congress :—

> Among the masses of the people, we communists are but drops in the ocean, and we cannot rule unless we give accurate expression to the folk consciousness. Otherwise the Communist Party will not be able to lead the proletariat, the proletariat will not be able to lead the masses, and the whole machine will fall to pieces. (*Works*, Russian edition, vol. xviii., part II., p. 55.)

Give accurate expression to the folk consciousness ! Only on condition that it does this, can the Party have the honour of being the essential guiding force in the system of the dictatorship of the proletariat.

6. THE PROBLEM OF THE VICTORY OF SOCIALISM IN ONE COUNTRY ALONE

My pamphlet *Foundations of Leninism*, which dates from April 1924, contains two formulations of the problem of the victory of socialism in one country alone. The first of these runs as follows:

> It used to be supposed that the victory of the revolution in one country alone would be impossible, the assumption being that the conquest of the bourgeoisie could only be achieved by the united action of the proletarians of all advanced countries, or at any rate those in the majority of these. This contention no longer fits the facts. We must now set out by assuming the possibility of such a victory: for the varying speed of social evolution in different capitalist countries (proceeding in some, under imperialist conditions, by leaps and bounds); the development of catastrophic conflicts as the outcome of imperialist rivalries, inevitably culminating in wars; the growth of the revolutionary movement in all countries throughout the world—these factors, working together, make proletarian victories in separate countries not merely possible but necessary. (*Foundations of Leninism*, Section Three.)

This argument is perfectly sound, and needs no comment. It is directed against the theory of the social democrats, who regard as utopian the belief that the proletariat can seize power in one country alone, and without the simultaneous victory of the revolution in other lands.

But my pamphlet contains a second formulation. Here it is (I quote from the first edition):

> But the overthrow of the power of the bourgeoisie and the establishment of the power of the proletariat in one country alone does not, per se, mean the complete victory of socialism. The chief task, the organisation of socialist production, still lies ahead. Can this task be performed, can the final victory of socialism be gained, in one country alone, and without the joint efforts of the proletarians in several of the most advanced countries? No, this is out of the question. The history of the Russian revolution shows that the proletarian strength of one country alone can overthrow the bourgeoisie of that country. But for the final victory of socialism, for the organisation of socialist production, the strength

of one country (especially a peasant country, such as Russia) does not suffice. For this, the united strength of the proletarians in several of the most advanced countries is needed. (*Foundations of Leninism*, Section Three.)

This second formulation was directed against some of the critics of Leninism, against the Trotskyists who declared that the dictatorship of the proletariat " could not be maintained against conservative Europe " in one country alone, and in the absence of a proletarian victory in other lands.

In view of its purpose (and only in view of this), that formulation was adequate in April 1924, and doubtless had its uses.

Subsequently, when that particular criticism of Leninism from the quarter named had been refuted within the Party, and when a new question had come to the fore (the question as to the possibility of establishing a fully socialised society by our unaided strength, and without any help from abroad), the second formulation became obviously inadequate, and therefore inaccurate.

In what does the inadequacy consist?

That two different questions are here confounded in one. First of all there is the question: Can socialism *possibly* be established in one country alone by that country's unaided strength? This question must be answered in the affirmative. Then there is the question: Can a country where the dictatorship of the proletariat has been established, regard itself as *fully safeguarded* against foreign intervention, and the consequent restoration of the old regime, unless the revolution has been victorious in a number of other countries? This question must be answered in the negative. What is wrong with the second formulation is that it may be interpreted as implying that the organisation of a socialist society by the unaided forces of one country is impossible—a manifest error.

In my pamphlet *The October Revolution and the Tactics of the Russian Communists* (December 1924) I therefore rectified the formulation by splitting up the question into two, and discussing under separate heads: 1. the question of *full safeguards against a restoration of the bourgeois regime* ; and 2. the question of *the possibility of establishing a fully socialised society in one country alone*. This was effected: first of all, by treating the " complete victory of socialism " as an " absolute guarantee against the restoration of the old regime ", this being attainable only through "the joint efforts of the proletarians in several countries"; and, secondly, by proclaiming (on the basis of Lenin's pamphlet *Cooperation*) the indisputable truth, that we [here in Soviet Russia] have all the requisites for the establishment of a fully socialised society. (See below, *The October Revolution and the Tactics of the Russian Communists*, p. 212.)

This new way of formulating the question underlay the resolution "Concerning the tasks of the Comintern and the Communist Party of Russia" adopted in April 1925 at the Fourteenth Party Conference. The resolution dealt with the problem of the victory of socialism in one country alone in connexion with the stabilisation of capitalism. It declared that that establishment of socialism in Soviet Russia was possible and necessary by the unaided forces of that country.

The new formulation also formed the basis of my report in May 1925 on the *Work of the Fourteenth Congress of the Communist Party of the Soviet Union*. (See below, pp. 217 et seq.)

In that report, when discussing the problem of the victory of socialism in one country alone, I wrote:

> Our country exhibits two groups of contradictions. One of these is the group of contradictions (or cross-purposes) in our homeland, as between the proletariat and the peasantry—these cross-purposes affecting the question of the establishment of socialism in one country alone. The other is the group of contradictions (or cross-purposes) as between our country, a socialist country, and foreign countries, capitalist countries—these cross-purposes affecting the question of the final victory of socialism. . . .
> To confound the first group of contradictions, which the unaided forces of one country are fully competent to solve, with the second group of contradictions, which can only be solved by the united efforts of the proletarians of several countries—is to commit a grave fault against the principles of Leninism, and one who commits it must either be muddle-headed or else a hopeless opportunist.

As regards the problem of the victory of socialism in our country, I wrote:

> We can establish socialism, and we shall be able to do so with the help of the peasantry and under the leadership of the working class; . . . for, under the dictatorship of the proletariat, . . . we have all the requisites for establishing a fully socialised society, inasmuch as we can overcome all the domestic difficulties—for these we must and can overcome by our unaided forces.

SOCIALISM IN ONE COUNTRY ALONE

As regards the problem of the final victory of socialism, I wrote:

> The final victory of socialism will provide full guarantees against attempts at intervention, and therefore against the restoration of the old regime; for no serious attempt at such a restoration can be made without extensive foreign support, without the support of international capital. Consequently the support of our revolution by the workers of all lands, and (even more than this) the victory of the workers in a few countries at least, are indispensable preliminary conditions without which there can be no adequate guarantees against intervention in the first land where the workers have been victorious and against a restoration of the old regime there, and without which the final triumph of socialism cannot be assured.

Those statements seem to me perfectly clear.

The matter in question was treated on similar lines in my pamphlet *Questions and Answers* (Speech at Sverdloff University on June 9, 1925), which is included in the present work; and in the *Political Report of the Central Committee to the Fourteenth Congress of the Communist Party of the Soviet Union* (December 1925), which is also reprinted below (pp. 351 et seq.).

Such are the facts.

They are known to every one, not excepting Comrade Zinovieff. If now (after the lapse of nearly two years, after the ideological struggle which has been going on within the Party and after the passing of a resolution on the subject at the Fourteenth Party Conference held in April 1925) Comrade Zinovieff finds it possible in his concluding words to the Fourteenth Party Congress (December 1925) to dig up the old and quite inadequate formulation contained in my pamphlet of April 1924, and to make it the basis for a settlement of the already settled problem as to the victory of socialism in one country alone—this characteristic action on his part serves only to show the utter confusion that prevails in his mind on the topic. He wants to drag the Party back when it has taken a step forward; he wants to ignore the resolution of the Fourteenth Party Conference after it has been confirmed by the Plenum of the Central Committee. Thus he involves himself in hopeless contradictions, shows his lack of faith in constructive socialism, wanders away from the road of Leninism, and acknowledges his defeat.

What do we mean when we say that the victory of socialism in one country alone is *possible*?

We mean that it is possible, with the unaided forces of our own land, to find a way of putting an end to the existence of cross-purposes as between the workers and the peasants. We mean that the proletariat, having seized power in Soviet Russia, can use that power for the establishment of a fully socialised society there. For this to be possible, the Russian workers need the sympathy and the support of the workers in other lands; but it is not essential that there should have been a victorious proletarian revolution in these other lands.

In the absence of such a possibility there can be no outlook for socialist construction, no faith in the upbuilding of socialism. We cannot upbuild socialism without a belief in the possibility of what we are trying to do; we cannot establish socialism unless we are convinced that the backwardness of our country in technical matters *does not impose insuperable difficulties* in the way of the establishment of a fully socialised society. To deny the possibility of this is a lack of faith in constructive socialism, is a deviation from Leninism.

What do we mean when we say that the final victory of socialism is *impossible* in one country alone, and without the victory of the revolution in other lands?

We mean that unless the revolution has been victorious, if not everywhere, at least in several countries, there can be no full safeguards against intervention, or against a restoration of the bourgeois regime. To deny this indisputable fact is to deviate from internationalism, to deviate from Leninism.

Lenin writes:

> We are living, not merely in one State, but in a system of States; and it is inconceivable that the Soviet Republic should continue to exist interminably side by side with imperialist States. Ultimately, one or other must conquer. Pending this development, a number of terrible clashes between the Soviet Republic and the bourgeois States must inevitably occur. This means that the proletariat, as ruling class, if it wants to rule and to make its rule effective, must manifest its power to rule through a military organisation as well as in other ways. (*Works*, Russian edition, vol. xvi., p. 102.)

Again:

> A balance has been attained, a highly unstable one, but certainly a balance. Will it last long? I don't know; nor do I think

that any one can tell. We must, therefore, show the greatest possible wariness. The first principle of our policy (a principle which is the logical deduction from our governmental activities during the past twelvemonth, and one which all the workers and peasants must accept as their own) will have to be that we must be always on guard ; must never forget that we are surrounded by persons, by classes, by governments, which openly express their intense hatred for us. We must never forget that nothing but a hair's breadth separates us from intervention at any moment. (*Works*, Russian edition, vol. xviii., part I., p. 425.)

That seems perfectly clear.

But what are Comrade Zinovieff's views concerning the problem of the victory of socialism in one country alone ?

Here they are :

When we talk of the final victory of socialism we must mean this much, at least : 1. the abolition of classes ; and, 2. the abolition of the dictatorship of a class, which means (in the case we are now considering) the abolition of the dictatorship of the proletariat. . . . If we are to get a clearer grasp of the way in which the question presents itself to us here in the U.S.S.R. and in the year 1925, we must distinguish between two things : 1. an assured *possibility* of upbuilding socialism (and the upbuilding of socialism, of course, is perfectly *conceivable* within the limits of one country alone) ; and, 2. the final establishment and the final consolidation of socialism, by which I mean the realisation of the socialist system, of socialist society. (*Leninism*, Russian edition, pp. 291 and 293.)

What does all this mean ?

It means that when Comrade Zinovieff thinks of the final victory of socialism in one country alone, he is not thinking of safeguards against intervention and restoration, but of the possibility of establishing a socialist society. What he has in mind is the sort of socialist construction which cannot possibly lead to the establishment of socialism. Comrade Zinovieff is thinking of chance construction, of construction without foresight, of construction (I repeat) which cannot possibly lead to the establishment of socialism.

Let us upbuild socialism where there is *no possibility* of establishing it, let us upbuild it where *we know that we cannot establish it*—such are the inconsistencies in which Comrade Zinovieff has involved himself.

This is to trifle with the problem, not to solve it !

Now I will quote another of Comrade Zinovieff's utterances

on this topic, from his concluding speech at the Fourteenth Party Congress :

> Consider, for instance, the conclusion reached by Comrade Yakovleff at the last Kursk Provincial Party Conference. He said : " Is it possible for us, surrounded as we are by capitalist enemies, to establish socialism in such conditions and in one country alone ? " He answered his own question as follows : " On the ground of all that has been said, we are entitled to declare, not only that we are upbuilding socialism, but also that—in spite of the fact that we are the one and only Soviet country, the one and only Soviet State, in the world—we shall establish this socialism " (" Kursk Pravda ", December 8, 1925). *Is that a Leninist way of stating the question? Does it not seem tinged with a narrow nationalism?* [1]

Thus, according to Comrade Zinovieff, one who recognises the possibility of establishing socialism in one country alone, entertains views tinged with a narrow nationalism ; and one who denies this possibility is a sound internationalist.

If so, is it worth while to fight for victory over the capitalist elements in our own economic life ? Is it not a natural sequence of Comrade Zinovieff's views, to contend that such a victory is impossible ?

Surrender to the capitalist elements of our economic life—such is the logical outcome of Comrade Zinovieff's arguments.

This absurdity, which has absolutely nothing in common with Leninism, is presented to us by Comrade Zinovieff as " internationalism ", as " hundred-per-cent. Leninism " !

I maintain that here, as regards the most important problem of socialist construction, Comrade Zinovieff deviates from Leninism, and lapses to the menshevist standpoint of Suhanoff.

Let us turn to Lenin. In August 1915, more than two years before the October revolution, he said :

> Irregularity in economic and political development is an invariable law of capitalism. It is, therefore, possible for socialism to triumph at the outset in a small number of capitalist countries, nay even in one alone. The victorious proletariat in such a land, *having expropriated the capitalists and having organised socialist production*,[1] would rise against the remainder of the capitalist world, winning over to its cause the oppressed classes in other lands, inciting them to revolt against the capitalists, and even, when

---
[1] Italicised by Stalin.

needs must, having recourse to armed intervention against the exploiting classes and their States. (*Works*, Russian edition, vol. xiii., p. 133.)

What does Lenin mean by the phrase " having organised socialist production " ? He means that the victorious proletariat *can* and *must* organise socialist production ; and by " organising socialist production " he means " establishing a socialist society ". Lenin's phrasing is so clear, that further comment is hardly needed. If he meant anything else than this, his appeals to the proletariat to seize power in October 1917 would be incomprehensible.

You see that Lenin's thesis is perfectly lucid, and is utterly different from Comrade Zinovieff's muddle-headed and anti-Leninist contention that within the limits of one country the upbuilding of socialism is possible while at the same time the establishment of socialism is impossible.

Lenin's utterance quoted above dates from 1915, before the proletariat had seized power. Perhaps he modified his views after that event, after 1917 ? Let us turn to his pamphlet *Cooperation*, penned in 1913. Here he writes :

> In actual fact, all the means of large-scale production are in the hands of the State, and the powers of State are in the hands of the proletariat ; there is the alliance of this same proletariat with the many millions of middle and poor peasants ; there is the assured leadership of these peasants by the proletariat ; and so on, and so forth. Have we not already, here and now, all the means for making out of the cooperatives (which, in the past, we treated as trading concerns and which, even to-day, we have a certain justification for treating similarly under the new economic policy), out of the cooperatives alone—have we not *all the means requisite for the establishment of a fully socialised society ?* [1] Of course we have not yet established a socialist society, but we have *all the means requisite for its establishment*.[1] (*Works*, Russian edition, vol. xviii., part II., p. 140.)

In other words, we can and must establish a fully socialised society, for we have at our disposal all the means requisite for its establishment.

I do not think that anything could be stated in plainer terms.

Compare Lenin's classical thesis with Comrade Zinovieff's anti-Leninist rejoinder to Comrade Yakovleff, and you will

---

[1] Italicised by Stalin.

realise that Comrade Yakovleff was only repeating Lenin's words about the possibility of establishing socialism in one country alone, whereas Comrade Zinovieff, who is campaigning against this thesis and is castigating Comrade Yakovleff, has turned away from Lenin to adopt the standpoint of Suhanoff, the menshevik, who contends that the technical backwardness of our country makes it impossible for us to establish socialism here.

The only puzzle is, why we seized power in October (November) 1917, unless we intended to establish socialism !

We ought not to have seized power in October 1917—such is the conclusion to which Comrade Zinovieff's train of argument leads us.

I declare, further, that, as regards the fundamental problem of the victory of socialism, Comrade Zinovieff has taken a line which is opposed to the plain decisions of the Party, as expressed in the resolution " Concerning the Tasks of the Communist International and the Communist Party of Russia in conjunction with the Enlarged Executive Committee (the Plenum) of the Communist International "—a resolution adopted at the Fourteenth Party Conference.

Here is the wording of the clauses in which the resolution refers to the victory of socialism in one country alone :

> The existence of two directly opposed forms of social system gives rise to a perpetual menace of a capitalist blockade, of other forms of economic pressure, of armed intervention, of a restoration. Consequently, nothing but a victorious socialist revolution in several countries can furnish guarantees for the final victory of socialism, that is to say *guarantees against a restoration.*[1] . . . It is a Leninist principle that the final victory of socialism, in the sense of *a full safeguard against the restoration of bourgeois conditions,*[1] is only possible on the international scale. . . . But *there is absolutely no justification for deducing from this principle the inference that it is impossible to establish a fully socialised society in a backward country like Russia without " State aid " (Trotsky) from countries in a more advanced condition of technical and economic development.*

You see that the resolution is based on the contention that the significance of the final victory of socialism is that it is a guarantee against intervention and against a bourgeois restoration —an outlook which is in sharp conflict with the views expressed by Comrade Zinovieff in his *Leninism*.

[1] Italicised by Stalin.

You see that the resolution recognises the possibility of establishing a fully socialised society in one country alone—Russia, for instance—without " State aid " from countries in a more advanced condition of technical and economic development. Once more, this is in sharp conflict with the views expressed by Comrade Zinovieff in his concluding speech (the rejoinder to Comrade Yakovleff) at the Fourteenth Party Congress.

Am I not right in saying that Comrade Zinovieff is up in arms against the resolution of the Fourteenth Party Conference ?

Of course, the resolutions of the Party are not always faultless. We may admit the possibility that the resolution of the Fourteenth Party Conference errs here and there. Perhaps Comrade Zinovieff thinks that the resolution in question is mistaken. If so, he should say as much frankly and in plain terms, like a good bolshevik. Comrade Zinovieff does nothing of the kind. He prefers to attack the resolution in the rear ; to attack it without speaking of it, and without a frank criticism of its terms. Comrade Zinovieff obviously thinks that this will be the best way of achieving his purpose. But what is his purpose ? He wants to " improve " the resolution, and to rectify Lenin " just a little ". I need not trouble to prove that he is somewhat out in his calculations.

What is the source of Comrade Zinovieff's mistake ? What are its roots ?

I think the main source of this error lies in Comrade Zinovieff's conviction that the backwardness of our country in the matter of technical development imposes an *insuperable* obstacle in the way of the establishment of a fully socialised society in Russia ; in his belief that, owing to the aforesaid backwardness, the Russian proletariat cannot establish socialism. At one of the sittings of the Central Committee of the Party shortly before the April Party Conference, both Comrade Zinovieff and Comrade Kameneff brought forward this argument. It was effectively answered ; they had to beat a retreat ; and, to outward seeming, they accepted the views of the majority of the Central Committee. But, in spite of this formal compliance, Comrade Zinovieff went on with the campaign on behalf of his original contention, as is witnessed by his book *Leninism* and his concluding speech at the Fourteenth Party Congress. This is what the Moscow Committee of our Party has to say (in answer to a letter issued by the Leningrad Provincial Party Conference) about the "incident" in the Central Committee of the Party:

> In the Politbureau, not long ago, Comrades Kameneff and Zinovieff declared that we should not be able to cope with the difficulties arising out of the backwardness of our technical and economic development unless an international revolution were to come to our rescue. But we hold (and the majority of the members of the Central Committee are of the same opinion) that we can upbuild socialism, and that we shall be able to establish it, notwithstanding the backward condition of our technical development. We believe, of course, that the upbuilding of socialism will go on far more slowly than it would if our cause had been victorious throughout the world; but it will go on none the less. Furthermore we consider that the outlook of Comrade Kameneff and Comrade Zinovieff is an indication of their lack of faith in the internal forces of our working class and of the peasant masses that follow its lead. We consider that these comrades' view is a deviation from Leninism.

This document was published in the press during the first sittings of the Fourteenth Party Congress, and Comrade Zinovieff, therefore, had ample opportunity of taking the floor at the congress against the opinions therein expressed. But it is characteristic of Comrade Zinovieff and Comrade Kameneff that they should have not thought fit to answer at the congress the grave charges made against them by the Moscow Committee. Was it by chance that they failed to do so? I trow not! The accusation was well founded. They were silent because they had no trump card to play.

The new opposition is mortified because Comrade Zinovieff is accused of a lack of faith in the possibility of establishing socialism in our country. But the question of the victory of socialism in one country alone has been eagerly discussed for a whole year; Comrade Zinovieff's view was condemned by the Politbureau of the Central Committee in April 1925; this happened after the Party as a whole had expressed a definite opinion on the matter in the resolution adopted at the Fourteenth Party Conference (April 1925). If, none the less, Comrade Zinovieff thinks fit to return to the charge, and to express his dissent from the Party point of view—doing so both in *Leninism* (September 1925) and subsequently at the Fourteenth Party Congress—how can we explain this stubborn determination, this persistent defence of an error, except on the supposition that he is incredulous, hopelessly incredulous, as to the possibility of upbuilding socialism in Russia?

Of course it is open to Comrade Zinovieff to dignify his lack of faith by calling it internationalism. But since when has any one else in Soviet Russia been willing to describe as "internationalism" a deviation from Leninism upon a matter of cardinal importance?

Surely it would be more accurate to say that Comrade Zinovieff, and not the Party, is sinning against internationalism and the world revolution? For what else is our country, "the country that is building up socialism", but the base of the world revolution? And how can it effectively function as the base of the world revolution unless it is competent to establish a socialist society? At present, beyond question, Soviet Russia is a great centre of attraction for the workers of all lands. But can Soviet Russia continue to be this unless it prove able to gain the victory over the capitalist elements in its own economy, unless it prove equal to the task of establishing socialism? I do not think so. But does it not follow from this that a lack of faith in the possibility of upbuilding socialism in Russia, and the propaganda of that lack of faith, will undermine the position of our country as the base of the world revolution, with the result that the world-revolutionary movement will be seriously weakened? How have the social democrats tried to scare the workers away from us? By their incessant propaganda to the effect that: "the Russians will get nowhere". How do we now refute the social democrats, with the result that one workers' delegation after another comes to visit our country, and by this the position of communism is strengthened throughout the world? By our successes in upbuilding socialism. Is it not obvious, then, that any one who disseminates a lack of faith in our success as builders of socialism, thereby indirectly helps the social democrats, weakens the impetus of the international revolutionary movement, inevitably deviates from internationalism?

We see that, in the matter of the upbuilding of socialism in one country alone, Comrade Zinovieff is in no better case with his "internationalism" than with his "hundred-per-cent. Leninism".

That is why the Fourteenth Party Congress did well to define the views of the new opposition as "lack of faith in the upbuilding of socialism", and as a "perversion of Leninism".

7. THE FIGHT FOR THE REALISATION OF SOCIALISM

In my opinion, a lack of faith in the upbuilding of socialism is the basic error of the new opposition. I call it a " basic error " because all the other mistakes of the new opposition are grounded upon it. The mistakes of the new opposition in the matter of the new economic policy, State capitalism, the nature of our socialist industry, the function of cooperation under the dictatorship of the proletariat, the best way of fighting the kulaks, the role and the importance of the middle peasants—all these mistakes are the outcome of the one primary blunder, they all depend upon a lack of faith in the establishment of a socialised society by the forces of our own country.

What are the implications of this lack of faith in the upbuilding of socialism in our own land ?

It implies, first of all, a failure to believe that (thanks to the special developmental conditions of our country) the great majority of the peasants *can be induced* to participate in the upbuilding of socialism.

It implies, secondly, a failure to believe that the proletariat of our country, which holds the strategic positions of the national economy, is *competent to induce* the great majority of the peasants to participate in the upbuilding of socialism.

Tacitly—perhaps consciously, perhaps unconsciously—it is from those two failures to believe that the opposition sets out when it is formulating its views concerning the course of Russian development.

Can the great majority of the peasants be induced to participate in the upbuilding of socialism ?

In my pamphlet *Foundations of Leninism* I put forward two fundamental propositions bearing upon this matter, as follows :

> 1. The peasantry of the Soviet Union cannot be compared with the peasantry of western Europe. A peasantry which has been schooled by three revolutions ; which, shoulder to shoulder with the proletariat and under the leadership of the proletariat, fought the tsar and the bourgeoisie ; which, thanks to the

FIGHT FOR THE REALISATION OF SOCIALISM 65

proletarian revolution, had its land-hunger satisfied and its longing for peace fulfilled; and which, in this way, has become a reserve force for the proletariat—such a peasantry is radically different from a peasantry which fought under the leadership of the liberal bourgeoisie in the days of the bourgeois revolution; which received the land from the hands of the bourgeoisie; and which, in this way, has become a reserve force for the bourgeoisie. It is evident that the peasants of the U.S.S.R., who have learned to value their political friendship with the proletariat, and have realised the importance of *political* collaboration with the workers, will not be slow to realise that it is equally important for them to collaborate in the *economic* field. . . .

2. The Russian rural economy cannot be compared with the rural economy of western Europe. The latter has developed along the familiar capitalist lines, so that there is a broad distinction between the well-to-do agriculturists with large estates and big farms, on the one hand, and smallholders and the impoverished wage-slaves of agriculture, on the other. There is a profound cleavage between these two sections of the rural population. Things are very different in Russia. In that country, thanks to the existence of the Soviet authority and thanks to the nationalisation of the principal means of production, evolution is necessarily taking a different path. In Russia, rural economy progresses by the formation of cooperatives among the millions upon millions of poor peasants and middle peasants, by the formation of agricultural cooperatives which are assisted by the provision of State credit upon favourable terms. In his articles on cooperation, Lenin has rightly pointed out that our rural economy must enter upon a new form of development, by involving the majority of the peasants in the work of upbuilding socialism by means of cooperatives; and by gradually permeating agriculture with the principles of collectivism—at first for the sale of agricultural produce, and in due course for agricultural production. . . . It is evident that the immense majority of the peasants will gladly enter upon this new path of development, in order to avoid the road leading to the formation of large capitalistic private farms; the road leading to wage slavery, poverty, and ruin.

Are these propositions correct?

I think they are correct; and that throughout the period of construction under the new economic policy, our development will necessarily take the course above indicated.

These propositions are nothing but the expression of Lenin's famous theses concerning the smychka,[1] the alliance between the workers and the peasants; concerning the inclusion of

[1] See translators' note on p. 26.

peasant economy within the system of the socialist development of our country; concerning how essential it is that the proletariat, in its advance towards socialism, should march shoulder to shoulder with the overwhelming majority of the peasants; concerning the need for involving the millionfold masses of the peasants in cooperative undertakings, as the chief way of upbuilding socialism in the rural districts; and concerning the growth of our socialist industry, as to which he says that " for us the simple growth of cooperation is identical with the growth of socialism " (*Works*, Russian edition, vol. xviii., part II., p. 144.)

In actual fact, what is the possible and necessary course of development in the case of peasant economy in Russia?

Peasant economy is not capitalist economy. As far as the overwhelming majority of the peasants is concerned, peasant economy is a system of small-scale production for the market. What does this mean? It means that peasant economy stands at the parting of the ways leading to capitalism and to socialism. It means that the peasant economy can take either road. It may develop towards capitalism, as it is now developing in capitalist countries; and it may develop towards socialism, as it is developing in contemporary Russia under the dictatorship of the proletariat.

Why is the peasant economy thus unstable? What is the explanation of its lack of independence?

The explanation is to be found in the disaggregated character of peasant farms; in their lack of organisation; in their dependence on the town, upon manufacturing industry, upon the credit system, and upon the nature of the ruling power in the country; and, lastly, upon the social fact that both in material and in cultural matters the village follows and necessarily must follow the town.

If peasant agriculture takes the capitalist road, this leads to a tremendous differentiation among the peasantry, to the formation of huge estates in the hands of rich farmers, on the one hand, and to the impoverishment of the great mass of the peasants on the other. Such a development is inevitable in capitalist countries, because the villages are dependent (because peasant agriculture is dependent) upon the town, upon manufacturing industry, upon the concentrated credit of the town, upon the

FIGHT FOR THE REALISATION OF SOCIALISM 67

circumstances of power—and because in the town the bourgeoisie holds sway, capitalist industry is dominant, the capitalist credit system prevails, and the capitalist State is in power.

Is it inevitable that peasant agriculture should take this course in Soviet Russia, where the town has a very different aspect, where manufacturing industry, the means of transport, the credit system, etc., are in the hands of the proletariat; where the nationalisation of the land has been universally established by law? Of course it is not inevitable. The inevitability is the other way about. For the very reason that the town leads the village, and because in Soviet Russia the proletariat holds sway and occupies all the strongholds of economic life—for that very reason, peasant agriculture in Russia must take a different road, the road of socialist construction.

What is that road?

It leads by way of the mass cooperation of millions upon millions of peasant farmers, joining up to form cooperatives of all kinds; by way of the union of the scattered and disintegrated peasant farms around socialist manufacturing industry; by way of the implantation of collectivist principles among the peasantry. First of all, these cooperative developments will concern the *marketing* of agricultural produce, and the *supply* of the peasants with the products of urban industry; and subsequently they will become concerned with the actual work of agricultural *production*.

Under the dictatorship of the proletariat, such developments will become more and ever more inevitable, for only by the cooperative organisation of the sale of rural produce, by the cooperative organisation of the supply of rural needs, and, at length, by the cooperative organisation of rural credit and rural industry (by the formation of agricultural productive cooperatives), can the wellbeing of the villages be secured. Thus only can the masses of the peasants be saved from poverty and ruin.

We are told that the Russian peasantry is not socialistically inclined, and therefore cannot develop towards socialism. It is true that the Russian peasantry is not socialistically inclined. But that is no argument against the view that peasant agriculture will take the socialist road—provided it can be shown that the village follows the town, and that socialist industry is dominant in the town. At the time of the October revolution, likewise, the peasants were not socialistically inclined; and they had no desire to establish socialism in Russia. Their main desires then were: to make an end of the rule of the great landowners; and to have done with the war—they wanted peace. None the less, they followed the lead of the socialist proletariat. Why did they do this? Because there was no other way of ending the imperialist war, no other way of bringing peace to Russia, than by overthrowing the bourgeoisie, and by establishing the dictatorship of the proletariat. Because our Party succeeded in linking up the specific interests of the peasantry (the destruction of landlordism and the making of peace) with the general interests of the country (the dictatorship of the proletariat) in a way which the peasants regarded as advantageous to themselves and were therefore willing to accept. That was why the peasants, though not socialistically inclined, followed the lead of the socialist proletariat.

Like considerations apply to the work of upbuilding socialism in Russia, and to the problem of inducing the peasants to participate in that work. The peasantry is not socialistically inclined. But the peasants will inevitably march along the road leading to socialism, for in no other way can they be saved from poverty and ruin than by an alliance with the proletariat, by making common cause with socialist manufacturing industry, by involving peasant agriculture in the general current of socialist development thanks to the widespread cooperative organisation of the peasant masses.

But why through the widespread cooperative organisation of the peasant masses?

Because the widespread cooperative organisation of the peasant masses will provide (as Lenin said) " the precise amount of coordination of private interest, private trading interest, with State supervision and control, the precise degree of subordination of private interest to the general interest " which will be advantageous to the peasants and which the peasants will therefore be willing to accept—and which, for that reason, will enable the proletariat to enlist the great majority of the peasants for the work of socialist construction. The peasants will organise themselves cooperatively on the grand scale for the simple reason that it will be to their advantage to organise the cooperative marketing of their produce and to organise the cooperative purchase of the machinery they need.

What will be the significance of the widespread cooperative organisation of the peasant masses under a system in which socialist industry rules?

It means that petty-peasant farming will be *withdrawn* from the old capitalist road (along which the peasant masses march towards ruin), and will be *transferred* to a new path of development, to the road leading towards socialist construction.

That is why the campaign on behalf of this new directive for peasant agriculture, and the struggle to enlist the peasant masses in the work of socialist construction, are among the most pressing tasks of our Party.

The resolution passed at the Fourteenth Congress of the Communist Party of the Soviet Union is therefore right in declaring: " The chief method of upbuilding socialism in this country must be that, thanks to the growing economic leadership exercised by socialist State industry, State credit institutions, and other economic strongholds occupied by the proletariat, the broad masses of the peasantry will become enrolled in cooperative organisations, and these organisations will be given a socialist trend, any capitalist elements they may contain being utilised, vanquished, or expelled ".

The fundamental error of the new opposition is its lack of faith in this new trend of peasant development, its failure to see or to understand how inevitable it is that events will follow this road under the dictatorship of the proletariat. The new opposition's failure to understand is the outcome of its lack of faith in the building of socialism in our country, its lack of faith in the competence of our proletariat to lead the peasantry towards socialism.

That is why the new opposition fails to understand the twofold character of Nep (the new economic policy), its exaggeration of the negative aspect of Nep, and its view that Nep is a retreat and nothing more.

That is why the new opposition exaggerates the part played by capitalist elements in our economic life, and underestimates the part played by the motive forces of our socialist development (socialist industry, the credit system, cooperation, the rule of the proletariat, etc.).

That is why the new opposition fails to understand the socialist character of our State industry, and doubts the soundness of Lenin's cooperative plan.

That is why the new opposition overstates the case as regards the differentiation which has taken place among the peasants, why it is so much alarmed about the kulaks (the rich peasants), minimises the role of the middle peasants, tries to counteract the endeavours of the Party to enter into a firm alliance with the middle peasants—and, speaking generally, wobbles as regards the Party policy in the rural districts.

That is why the new opposition fails to understand the immense amount of work our Party is doing in the way of attracting the millionfold masses of the workers and peasants to the upbuilding of industry and agriculture ; to the task of livening up the cooperatives and the soviets ; to the administration of the country ; to the struggle against bureaucracy ; to the campaign for the betterment and the transformation of our State apparatus, which is entering upon a new developmental phase, and without which socialist construction is unthinkable.

That is why the members of the new opposition are hopelessly at a loss when they have to face the difficulties of socialist construction ; that is why they doubt whether it will be possible to industrialise our country ; that accounts for their pessimistic chatter about the degeneration of the Party.

" In the other camp, among the bourgeois, all is going on fairly well. In our camp, among the proletarians, things are in a bad way ; and unless the revolution occurs in the West pretty soon, our cause is lost." Such is the general tone of the new opposition, and I cannot but regard it as a defeatist tone, although those who use it dignify it (surely they must be jesting ?) with the name of " internationalism ".

" Nep is capitalism," declares the opposition. " Nep is a retreat and nothing more," says Comrade Zinovieff. Of course, both these assertions are false. The actual fact is that Nep is a Party policy based on the recognition that there is a struggle between socialist and capitalist elements, and upon the belief that the socialist elements will conquer. In reality, it is only at the outset that Nep can be looked upon as a retreat. It is so designed that in the course of this initial retreat we may be able to regroup our forces and then resume the offensive. In very truth, we resumed the offensive several years ago, and successfully, for we are developing our industries, are promoting Soviet commerce, and are pressing privately owned capital hard.

What underlies the assertions that Nep is capitalism, that Nep is a retreat and nothing more ? Whence do they arise ?

Out of the erroneous hypothesis that in Soviet Russia a simple reestablishment of capitalism, a simple " return to capitalism ", is now taking place ! Only because they entertain this hypothesis, do the members of the new opposition doubt the socialist character of our industry. Only for that reason are they in such a panic about the kulaks. Only for that reason have they been in such a hurry to accept the inaccurate statistics regarding differentiation among the peasants. Only for that reason have they been so ready to forget that in Russia the middle peasants form the core of the rural population. Only for that reason do they underestimate the importance of the middle peasants and adopt a sceptical attitude towards Lenin's scheme for promoting cooperation among peasant farmers. Nothing but the fact that they start from this erroneous hypothesis can account for their lack of faith in the new developments that are taking place in the villages, their scepticism as regards the possibility of enlisting the villages in the work of socialist construction.

What is really going on in contemporary Russia is, not a one-sided process leading to the reestablishment of capitalism, but a twofold process leading to the simultaneous development of capitalism and socialism, a contradictory process characterised by a struggle between the socialist and the capitalist elements therein, a process in which the socialist elements are getting the better of the capitalist elements. This is plain in the towns, where State industry forms the basis of socialist evolution ; it is equally plain in the rural districts, where a mass development of cooperation, linked up with socialist industry, will be the main factor of socialist development.

The simple reestablishment of capitalism is impossible in Soviet Russia, were it only for the reason that power there is in the hands of the proletariat, that large-scale industry is controlled by the proletariat, that the transport system and the credit system belong to the proletarian State.

Differentiation among the peasants cannot regain its old

proportions. The middle peasants nowadays form the great mass of Russian agriculturists. The kulaks, the rich peasants, cannot get back to their old position of power, now that the land has been nationalised and has ceased to be an article of commerce ; now that, in Russia, trade, credit, fiscal, and cooperative policy are all guided by the aim of limiting the rich peasants' capacity to exploit their poorer neighbours, and by the aim of promoting the welfare of the generality of peasants and abolishing the chasm that used to separate " rich " and " poor ". Besides, whilst the old way of fighting the kulaks was to organise the poor peasants against them, we have found a new and better way. Nowadays we strengthen the alliance of the proletariat with both the middle peasants and the poor peasants, and direct the forces of this alliance against the kulaks. The opposition fails to grasp the significance, overlooks the importance, of this new way of fighting the rich peasants. The fact gives further proof (if further proof were needed) that the members of the new opposition are still in the old rut, that they are still thinking of village life in the terms of its capitalistic development, when the rich peasants and the poor peasants formed the outstanding elements of the rural population, and the middle peasants were " a wash-out " !

" Cooperation is a variety of State capitalism," says the new opposition, appealing, in confirmation of this assertion, to Lenin's *Taxation in Kind*. For this reason they consider it impossible to use cooperation as a fundamental link in socialist evolution. But here, likewise, the opposition commits a gross blunder. Such a view of cooperation was adequate in 1921, when *Taxation in Kind* was written, when our socialist industry was still comparatively undeveloped, when Lenin thought that State capitalism might perhaps become the basic form of our economic life, and when he thought of cooperation as linked up with State capitalism. This view has now become inadequate ; history has marched over it. Times have changed. Our socialist industry has developed ; State capitalism has not struck root so firmly and extensively as could be wished ; but cooperation, enrolling more than ten million members, is closely interconnected with socialist industry.

In 1923, two years after *Taxation in Kind* was written, Lenin began to look at cooperation in a different light, and declared that " under the conditions that obtain in Russia, cooperation

FIGHT FOR THE REALISATION OF SOCIALISM

is perfectly identical with socialism ". (*Works*, Russian edition, vol. xviii., part II., p. 144.)

How can this change of view be explained except by the fact that during these two years socialist industry had grown a good deal, whereas State capitalism had failed to become established to the desired extent; and that, consequently, Lenin had begun to regard cooperation as linked up, not with State capitalism, but with socialist industry?

Now that the conditions under which cooperation is developing have changed, there must be a change in the approach to the problem of cooperation.

The following remarkable passage from Lenin's pamphlet on *Cooperation* (1923) throws light on this matter:

> *Under State capitalism,*[1] cooperative enterprises differ from State-capitalist enterprises in two ways: first, because they are private enterprises; and, secondly, because they are collective enterprises. *Under our extant system,*[1] cooperative enterprises differ from private capitalist enterprises inasmuch as they are collective enterprises; but they *do not differ*[1] from socialist enterprises if they are established upon land, and work with means of production, belonging to the State, that is to say the working class. (*Works*, Russian edition, vol. xviii., part II., pp. 143–144.)

In the foregoing passage, short though it is, two great problems are solved. First of all, Lenin makes it plain that " our extant system " is not State capitalism. Secondly he declares that, in connexion with " our extant system ", cooperative enterprises " do not differ " from socialist enterprises.

I think it would be difficult to put the matter more clearly.

Here is another quotation from the same pamphlet:

> With the " trifling " exception mentioned above, for us the simple growth of cooperation is identical with the growth of socialism, and in this connexion it is incumbent on us to make a radical change in our outlook upon socialism. (*Works*, Russian edition, vol. xviii., part II., p. 144.)

Obviously in the pamphlet *Cooperation* we have a revaluation of cooperation, although the new opposition cannot recognise this or tries to hush it up—in defiance of the facts, in defiance of the plain truth, in defiance of Leninism.

[1] Italicised by Stalin.

Cooperation linked up with State capitalism is one thing, and cooperation linked up with socialist industry is another.

But this does not justify the inference that between Lenin's *Taxation in Kind* and his *Cooperation* there is a great gulf fixed. Such an inference would be false. To show that, as regards the valuation of cooperation, there is a close tie between the two booklets, it will suffice to quote the following passage from *Taxation in Kind*:

> Between concessions and socialism, the transition is from one form of large-scale industry to another. Between cooperation among petty proprietors and socialism, the transition is from small-scale production to large-scale. This latter transition is a much more complicated affair; but if it be successfully accomplished it will influence far more extensive masses of the population; and its result will be to tear up the deep and tenacious roots of *pre-socialist* [1] and even pre-capitalist relationships—relationships which are most obstinately resistant to innovation. (*Works*, Russian edition, vol. xviii., part I., p. 220.)

The foregoing quotation shows clearly that Lenin, at the time when he wrote *Taxation in Kind*, and before we had a well-developed socialist industry in Russia, was already of opinion that cooperation, *if successful*, might become a weapon in the fight against " pre-socialist ", and therefore *against capitalist conditions*. I fancy that this idea was the starting-point for his pamphlet *Cooperation*.

What follows from all this?

My inference is that the members of the new opposition approach the problem of cooperation, not as Marxists, but as metaphysicians. They do not look upon cooperation as a historical phenomenon, as something which has to be considered in its interconnexions with other historical phenomena —with State capitalism if we are dealing with the year 1921, and with socialist industry if we are dealing with the year 1923. They look upon cooperation as something fixed and unchangeable, as a " thing-by-itself ".

That accounts for their errors as regards the problem of cooperation; for their lack of faith in the possibility of the villages progressing towards socialism through the growth of the

---

[1] Italicised by Stalin.

FIGHT FOR THE REALISATION OF SOCIALISM

cooperative movement; for their backsliding on to the old road, the road of capitalist development for the peasantry.

Stated in general terms, such is the position of the new opposition as concerns the practical problems of socialist construction.

Only one conclusion can be drawn. The line of the new opposition (so far as the new opposition has a line!)—its vacillations and wanderings, its lack of faith and its confusion of mind in face of the difficulties to be encountered—leads to a surrender to the capitalist elements of our economic life. If Nep is a retreat and nothing more, if the socialist character of State industry is questionable, if the rich peasants are wellnigh all-powerful, if there is little hope in cooperation, if the importance of the middle peasants is steadily declining, if it is dubious whether a new type of evolution can occur in the rural districts, if the Party is almost degenerate, and if there is no near prospect of a revolution in the West—what remains in the arsenal of the new opposition, what weapons can they use in the struggle against the capitalist elements of our economic life? An army cannot go into battle with no better resource than " the philosophy of the epoch ".

The arsenal of the new opposition, if it can be dignified by the name of arsenal, is not an enviable one. It is not the sort of arsenal with which people win victories.

Obviously, if the Party were to enter the fray with no better arsenal than this, it would be defeated in the twinkling of an eye, and would simply have to surrender to the capitalist elements in our economic life.

That is why the Fourteenth Congress of the Party was right in its decision that " the fight for the victory of socialist construction in the U.S.S.R. is the immediate task of our Party "; that one of the most indispensable requisites for the performance of this task is " to campaign against a lack of faith in the upbuilding of socialism in our country, and against attempts to represent as State-capitalist enterprises those of our enterprises which Lenin described as belonging to the ' consistently socialist type ' "; that " such ideological trends, which make it impossible for the masses to adopt a class-conscious attitude towards the upbuilding of socialism in general and socialist industry in particular, can have no other effect than that of hindering the growth of the socialist elements of our economic life and of helping private capital in its fight against these elements "; that " the congress therefore regards it as essential to inaugurate a widespread educational campaign to refute these distortions of Leninism ".

The historical significance of the Fourteenth Congress of the Communist Party of the Soviet Union lies in this, that it was able to disclose the roots of the errors of the new opposition, to make short work of the new opposition's unfaith and whimperings, and to give a clear lead in the fight for the establishment of socialism. The Fourteenth Congress opened for the Party a perspective of victory, and thereby at the same time equipped the proletariat with an inextinguishable faith in the success of socialist construction.

January 25, 1926

FOUNDATIONS OF LENINISM

A LECTURE DELIVERED AT SVERDLOFF UNIVERSITY
IN THE BEGINNING OF APRIL 1924.

*In this, the second, edition there are some changes
in the third section.*

(DEDICATED TO THE LENIN RECRUITS)

INTRODUCTION

THE foundations of Leninism: it is a big subject. To expound it thoroughly, a whole volume, or several, would be needed. Obviously, then, the present exposition cannot possibly be exhaustive. At best, it can be nothing more than an outline of the foundations of Leninism. Nevertheless, it may be of considerable use.

An exposition of the foundations of Leninism is a different thing from an exposition of the foundations of Lenin's philosophy. Lenin is a Marxist, so of course his philosophy is based upon Marxism. But this does not mean that an account of Leninism ought to begin with an account of the foundations of Marxism. To expound Leninism means to expound what is distinctive in the work of Lenin, what new thing Lenin brought to Marxism, what is particularly connected with Lenin's name. Only in this sense shall I speak here of the foundations of Leninism.

What, then, is Leninism?

According to some, it is the application of Marxism to the peculiar conditions of Russia. This definition contains only part of the truth, not the whole. It is true that Lenin applied Marxism to the Russian situation, and that his application was masterly. But if Leninism were nothing more than the application of Marxism to the peculiar conditions of Russia, it would have a purely Russian and exclusively national character. Nevertheless, as we know, Leninism is an international phenomenon. It is rooted in internationalism, and is not solely Russian. That is why the foregoing definition is too narrow.

Others declare that Leninism is a revival of the Marxism of the late forties, as contrasted with the Marxism of subsequent years, which (they contend) became " moderate ", and lost its revolutionary fire. Although it is stupid to split up Marx's teaching in this way into " revolutionary Marxism " and " moderate Marxism ", we have to admit that the second definition of Leninism, for all its inadequacy, likewise embodies part of the truth. It is a fact that Lenin brought to light once more the revolutionary content of Marxism, which had been glossed over by the opportunists of the Second International. But that is only a fragment of the truth. The whole truth is that Leninism is not merely a revival of Marxism, but is a step forward. Leninism is a development of Marxism adapting it to the new conditions of capitalism and to the class struggle of the proletariat.

What, then, is Leninism?

Leninism is the Marxism of the epoch of imperialism and of the proletarian revolution. To be more precise: Leninism is the theory and the tactic of the proletarian revolution in general, and the theory and the tactic of the dictatorship of the proletariat in particular. Marx and Engels lived in a prerevolutionary period,[1] when imperialism was still in an embryonic condition, when the workers were only preparing for the revolution, when the proletarian revolution had not yet become an immediate and practical necessity. Lenin, the disciple of Marx and Engels, lived in a period of fully developed imperialism; in a period when the proletarian revolution was already under way; in a period when the proletarian revolution had already triumphed in one country, had made an end of bourgeois democracy, and had begun the era of proletarian democracy, the era of soviets.

That is why I describe Leninism as a development of Marxism.

It is usual to point out that Leninism is preeminently combative and revolutionary. There are two reasons why Leninism has these peculiar characteristics. First of all, Leninism issued from the proletarian revolution, and therefore necessarily bears the imprint of that revolution. Secondly, Leninism originated and grew strong in conflict with the opportunism of the Second International—a conflict essential to success in the struggle against capitalism. We must never forget that between the epoch of Marx and Engels and the epoch of Lenin came the epoch when the opportunism of the Second International held unrestricted sway; and that a ruthless fight with this opportunism was one of Lenin's chief tasks.

---

[1] When I use the word "prerevolutionary", I am thinking only of the *proletarian* revolution.

1. HISTORICAL ROOTS OF LENINISM

LENINISM has grown and become established in the age of imperialism, when the conflicts within capitalism have reached a climax, when the proletarian revolution has become a question of practical politics, when the period of working-class preparation for the revolution is passing into that in which the capitalist fortress is being stormed.

Lenin spoke of imperialism as " capitalism on its death-bed ". Why ? Because imperialism carries the conflicts inherent in capitalism to their farthest limits, beyond which the revolution begins. Among the most important contradictions of the capitalist system, special mention may be made of the three following :

First Contradiction. The conflict between labour and capital. Imperialism means the omnipotence of monopolist trusts and syndicates, of banks and the financial oligarchy, in industrial countries. The usual methods of the working-class struggle (trade unions, cooperatives, parliamentary parties, and the fight in parliament) are unable to cope with this omnipotence. The workers are now faced by two alternatives : either they must surrender to capitalism, vegetating and degenerating more and more ; or else they must arm themselves with new weapons. Thus imperialism ripens the working class for the revolution.

Second Contradiction. The conflict between the various financial groups and the different imperialist powers in their competition for control of the sources of raw material, for foreign territory. Imperialism is the export of capital to the sources of raw material ; a pitiless struggle for monopolist ownership of these sources ; a fight for the redistribution of the spoils in a world which has already been shared out ; a fight which is waged with especial savagery by new financial groups and powers seeking " a place in the sun," against old-established groups and powers retaining a firm grip on their acquisitions. Imperialist wars, wars for the seizure of foreign territory, are the inevitable outcome of these capitalist rivalries. Such wars, in their turn, result in the weakening of the imperialists by one another, and lead to the general weakening of the capitalist position; they hasten the coming of the proletarian revolution, and make it practically inevitable.

Third Contradiction. The conflict between the small group of dominant " civilised " nations, on the one hand, and the hundreds of millions of persons who make up the colonial and dependent peoples of the world, on the other. Imperialism means the most shameless exploitation and the most inhuman oppression of the hundreds of millions who comprise the populations of the colonies and dependencies. Gain, the drawing of large profits—that is the object of the exploitation and oppression. But, in order to exploit these countries effectively, the imperialists have to construct railways in them, to build factories, to establish industrial and commercial centres. This policy inevitably leads to the formation of a proletariat, to the appearance of a class of native intellectuals, to the awakening of national consciousness, to the strengthening of the movement for national independence. In evidence of these changes, there occurs a strengthening of the revolutionary movement in all colonies and dependencies. Such changes are of the utmost importance to the proletariat, for they undermine the position of capitalism. The colonies and dependencies, which have hitherto been imperialist reserves, become proletarian reserves—reserve forces of the proletarian revolution.

Such are the chief among the contradictions inherent in imperialism; and it is due to them that capitalism, once flourishing, is now moribund.

The historical significance of the great war, the imperialist war, was (among other things) that it concentrated these conflicts, and brought them simultaneously into play, thus facilitating and accelerating the revolutionary battles of the proletariat.

In other words, the growth of imperialism has not only made the revolution a practical necessity; it has also created conditions favourable to an immediate onslaught on the strongholds of capitalism.

It was in this international situation that Leninism took its rise.

" That is all very fine," we are told. " But where does Russia come in—Russia, which is not and cannot be one of the countries where imperialism has assumed a typical form ? What has Lenin got to do with it, seeing that Lenin worked primarily in Russia and for Russia ? Why has Russia been the birthplace of Leninism, the birthplace of the theory and the practice of the proletarian revolution ? "

The reason is that Russia has been the focus of the three great contradictions of imperialism.

The reason is that Russia was ripe for the revolution, more ripe than any other country in the world. Russia was the only land ready to solve the three contradictions by means of revolution.

First of all, every kind of oppression—capitalist, colonial, and military—was rife in tsarist Russia; and in tsarist Russia these kinds of oppression took on peculiarly inhuman and barbarous forms. Every one knows that in Russia capitalist omnipotence walked hand in hand with tsarist despotism; aggressive nationalism, with the most ferocious oppression of non-Russian peoples; the exploitation of whole regions of Turkey, Persia, and China, with the military conquest of these regions by the forces of the tsar. Lenin was right when he declared that tsarism was "feudal-militarist imperialism". Tsarism was the quintessence of the negative aspects of imperialism.

Secondly, tsarist Russia was a huge reserve force for western imperialism, and this in more ways than one. Not only did it welcome the entry of foreign capital, which controlled such important branches of Russian economic life as the engineering industry and the supply of fuel. In addition, Russia could provide millions of soldiers to fight the battles of the western imperialists. You will remember that a Russian army numbering twelve millions fought and bled on the imperialist front in order to safeguard the limitless profits of the Anglo-French capitalists.

Thirdly, tsarism was not only the watchdog of imperialism in eastern Europe; it was also the agency through which the western imperialists collected from the Russian population the huge sums of interest that were payable upon loans floated in Paris, London, Berlin, and Brussels.

Finally, tsarism was the faithful ally of the western imperialists in the partitioning of Turkey, Persia, China, etc. Every one knows that the imperialist war was carried on by tsarist Russia in alliance with the imperialists of the Entente, and that Russia was an essential element in the war.

That is why the interests of tsarism and of western imperialism became so closely intertwined, so that, in the last resort, the two came to constitute a single coterie of imperialist interests. Could the western imperialists be expected to accept the loss of so powerful a support in the East, so rich a reserve of men and money, as the old, tsarist, bourgeois Russia, without rallying all their forces for a ruthless struggle against the Russian revolution, in the hope of maintaining and protecting tsarism? Of course not!

The logical deduction is that any one who wanted to strike a blow at tsarism must perforce strike a blow at imperialism, that any one who rose in revolt against tsarism must also rise in revolt against imperialism; for he who wished to overthrow tsarism must overthrow imperialism as well—if he wished to get rid of the roots of tsarism, and not merely to cut down the surface growth. That was why an anti-tsarist revolution could not fail to develop into an anti-imperialist revolution, into a proletarian revolution.

Well now, in Russia there occurred the greatest popular uprising in history, headed by the most revolutionary proletariat in the world. The Russian proletariat was supported by an exceedingly formidable ally, the revolutionary peasantry of Russia. Is it necessary to prove that such a revolution could not possibly stop half way; that if the revolutionists were successful in overthrowing tsarism they would have to go further, would have no choice but to raise the standard of revolt against imperialism?

Now we understand why Russia could not fail to become the focus of the contradictions of imperialism. This was inevitable, not only because these contradictions were most conspicuous in Russia owing to the peculiarly hideous and intolerable forms they assumed in that country; not only because Russia was the mainstay of western imperialism, an essential link between financial capital in the West and the colonies in the East: but also because only in Russia did there exist the concrete force able to solve the contradictions of imperialism by the method of revolution.

That was why the revolution in Russia could not fail to become a proletarian revolution, could not fail to assume an international character in its very earliest days, could not fail to sap the foundations of international imperialism.

In such circumstances, was it possible for the Russian

communists to confine their activities within the narrow framework of a purely Russian revolution? Of course not! On the contrary, the environing conditions, both at home (the far-reaching revolutionary crisis) and abroad (the war), forced them to transcend such limitations. They had to carry the struggle into the international arena; to lay bare the plague-spots of imperialism; to demonstrate the inevitability of the downfall of capitalism; to make an end of the jingoism and the pacifism that wore a socialist mask; to overthrow capitalism in their own country; and, finally, to formulate the theory and elucidate the practice of the proletarian revolution, thus forging new weapons for the workers of the world to use in the fight against capitalism. The Russian communists had to do these things, for in no other way was there any hope of bringing about the changes in the international situation that would safeguard Russia against a restoration of the bourgeois regime.

That is why Russia was the birthplace of Leninism. That is why a leader of the Russian communists became the founder of Leninism.

The situation in Russia a few years ago, and the position of Lenin in relation to Russia, resembled the situation in Germany eighty years back, and the position of Marx and Engels in relation to Germany at that time. In the late forties of the nineteenth century Germany was pregnant with the bourgeois revolution, just as Russia was at the beginning of the twentieth century. In the *Communist Manifesto* (penned towards the close of 1847 and published early in 1848) we read:

> Communists pay special attention to Germany. There are two reasons for this. First of all, Germany is upon the eve of a bourgeois revolution. Secondly, this revolution will take place under comparatively advanced conditions as far as the general civilisation of Europe is concerned, and when the German proletariat is much more highly developed than was the English proletariat in the seventeenth century or the French proletariat in the eighteenth. Consequently, in nineteenth-century Germany, the bourgeois revolution can only be the immediate precursor of a proletarian revolution.

In other words, the centre of the revolutionary movement had been transferred to Germany.

We can hardly doubt that this explains why Germany, rather

than any other country, was the birthplace of scientific socialism ; and why Marx and Engels, leaders of the German proletariat, were the founders of the new doctrine.

Similar considerations apply, even more powerfully, to twentieth-century Russia. At the beginning of the twentieth century, Russia was upon the eve of the bourgeois revolution. But in Russia the bourgeois revolution was to take place when the general European situation had made great advances since 1848, and when the Russian proletariat was in a much more developed condition than the German proletariat had been in 1848 (to say nothing of the embryonic condition of the proletariat in England and France at the respective times when the bourgeois revolution occurred in those countries). The general indications were, then, such as to encourage the belief that the Russian bourgeois revolution would act like a ferment, and would be the prologue to a proletarian revolution. It was not a chance happening that in the year 1902, when the first rumblings of the coming Russian revolution were heard, Lenin wrote prophetically in his booklet *What is to be done ?* :

> History imposes upon the Russian Marxists an immediate task which is more revolutionary than any of those immediately incumbent upon the proletariat in other lands. Its accomplishment, namely the destruction of the most powerful bulwarks of European and Asiatic reaction, would make the Russian proletariat the vanguard of the international revolutionary proletariat. (*Works*, Russian edition, vol. v., p. 138.)

In other words, the centre of the revolutionary movement was about to be transferred to Russia.

We know that the course of the Russian revolution has fully confirmed Lenin's forecast.

Is there any reason to be surprised that the country which has undergone such a revolution, and has such a proletariat, should have been the birthplace of the theory and the practice of the proletarian revolution ?

Is there any reason to be surprised that the leader of the Russian proletariat, Lenin, should have been the founder of this theory and practice, and should have become the leader of the international proletariat ?

2. METHOD

I SAID above (at the close of the introduction) that between the epoch of Marx and Engels and the epoch of Lenin came the epoch when the opportunism of the Second International held unrestricted sway. It is desirable to explain that, whilst opportunism was in actual fact dominant, the dominance was veiled. Formally, the Second International was led by such " orthodox " Marxists as Kautsky. In reality, the substance of its work was opportunist. The opportunists, being adaptable in virtue of their petty-bourgeois temperament, adapted themselves to the bourgeoisie. The " orthodox " Marxists, in their turn, adapted themselves to the opportunists, doing this " for the sake of unity ", " for the sake of peace within the Party ". Thus the policy of the " orthodox " Marxists was towed along in the wake of bourgeois policy. Opportunism ruled the roast.

This was during what may be called a pre-war phase, during a period when the development of capitalism was comparatively peaceful. The disastrous contradictions of imperialism had not yet become fully manifest ; the industrial struggle, and trade-union development, were taking a more or less " normal " course ; at the polls and in parliament, socialist and labour parties were winning " all along the line " ; paeans were being sung in honour of constitutional methods of struggle, which (it was asserted) would amply suffice to effect the overthrow of capitalism. In short, the parties enrolled in the Second International were putting on fat, were becoming stodgy. Their leaders had ceased to think seriously about revolution, about the dictatorship of the proletariat, about the revolutionary education of the masses.

Unified revolutionary theory had given place to a bundle of contradictory propositions and fragments of theory unrelated to the actual revolutionary struggle of the masses ; had given place to superannuated dogma. To outward seeming, the leaders (in continental countries) conformed to Marxist doctrine, but they deprived Marxism of its revolutionary core.

There was no longer a revolutionary policy. The

"moderates" were in control, "safe and sane" labour leaders, diplomatic parliamentarians, champions of "statesmanlike" coalitions. For window dressing, "revolutionary" resolutions would be passed at congresses, and "revolutionary" slogans would be voiced from time to time—to be shelved with commendable promptitude.

The parties made no attempt to educate themselves, to work out a sound revolutionary tactic from the study of their own mistakes. Thorny problems were carefully avoided, as far as any serious attempt to solve them was concerned. Here, again, for window dressing, they would occasionally be brought up for discussion, but were always, in the end, evaded by means of some elastic resolution.

Such was the aspect of the Second International; such was its method of work; such was its armoury.

But a new epoch began, an epoch of imperialist wars, of revolutionary proletarian struggles. The old weapons were powerless in face of the omnipotence of financial capital.

All the activities of the Second International had to be reconsidered; its methods revised. An end had to be made of its triviality, its narrowness, its compromises, its renegade spirit, its alternations of jingoism and pacifism under a socialist mask. There was urgent need for an overhaul of the armoury of the Second International, rejecting all the weapons that were rusty and out-of-date, and forging new ones. Without this preliminary work, it would have been futile to enter upon a war against capitalism, for the proletariat would have been likely, in the coming revolutionary struggles, to find itself inadequately equipped or even quite weaponless.

To Leninism was assigned the task of undertaking this general inspection, this cleaning of the Augean stables of the Second International.

It was in such a situation that the method of Leninism was born and bred.

What are the demands made by this method?

First of all, there must be a *testing of the dogmas* of the Second International in the fire of the revolutionary mass struggle, in the fire of living practice. This means that the unity between theory and practice must be restored, that the breach between theory and practice must be bridged over, for thus only can there be created a genuine proletarian party, equipped with a revolutionary theory.

Secondly, there must be a *testing of the policy* of the parties affiliated to the Second International—not by their slogans and resolutions (which must not be accepted at face value), but by their deeds, for only by deeds can the confidence of the proletarian masses be won.

Thirdly, there must be a *reorganisation of all the activities* of proletarian parties. Their activities must be given the new revolutionary trend. The masses must be educated and prepared for the coming revolutionary struggle, for the proletarian revolution.

Fourthly, the proletarian parties must undertake *self-criticism*. They must learn by the experience of their own mistakes. Thus only can trustworthy troops and leaders be formed.

Such are the foundations, such is the essence, of the Leninist method.

How has this method been applied ?

The opportunists of the Second International have a number of theoretical dogmas which they have learned by rote, which they repeat mechanically like a parrot. Let us consider some of them.

Dogma number one relates to the conditions under which the proletariat can seize power. The opportunists declare that the proletariat cannot seize power, and must not try to do so, unless it comprises a majority of the inhabitants of the country. They offer no proof of this assertion, which is in fact an absurd one, devoid of either theoretical or practical justification. " Let us admit it for the sake of argument," says Lenin (substantially) to the gentlemen of the Second International. " But let us suppose that a situation arises—that there is a war, for instance, or an agrarian crisis—in the course of which the proletariat, though a minority of the population, is able to group round itself the immense majority of the toiling masses. Why, in that case, should not the proletariat seize power ? Why should it not take advantage of the favourable internal and international situation to break the capitalist front and hasten the general settlement of accounts ? Did not Marx say in the fifties of the nineteenth century that the proletarian revolution in Germany would be in a ' splendid ' position if it could but be supported by a sort of 'second edition of the Peasants' War'? But at that period the proportion of proletarians in Germany was considerably smaller than the proportion of proletarians in Russia at the time of the 1917 revolution." Has not the practical experience of the Russian proletarian revolution taught us that this dogma, so dear to the heroes of the Second International, has no vital significance for the proletariat? Is it not obvious that the realities of the revolutionary mass struggle are daily refuting this outworn dogma?

Dogma number two runs as follows: The proletariat will not be able to keep power in its hands unless it has at its disposal a large number of intellectuals and technicians, sufficient to carry on the public services. A supply of these must first be assured under capitalist conditions, and only then should power be seized. "Suppose that the first part of what you say is true," answers Lenin. "But why can't we arrange matters in this way? Let's seize power first, thus establishing conditions favourable to the development of the proletariat. Then we'll put on our seven-league boots to stride forward in the work of raising the cultural level of the masses and training from among them the intellectuals and technicians we need." Has not Russian experience taught us that the development of leaders from among the ranks of the workers goes on a hundred times quicker under the rule of the proletariat than under the rule of the capitalists? Does not the practical work of the revolutionary mass struggle dispose of the second opportunist dogma quite as effectually as the first?

Dogma number three: The general strike on behalf of political ends is inadmissible as part of proletarian tactic. From the theoretical standpoint, it is open to serious objections (see Engels' criticism). In practice, it is dangerous, for it is likely to disturb the normal course of the economic life of the country and to empty the coffers of the trade unions. The general strike cannot take the place of the parliamentary struggle, which is the most important form of proletarian class struggle. "Well and good," answer the Leninists. "But we have to remind you that Engels' criticism related, not to the general strike per se, but to the purely industrial or economic strike advocated by the anarchists, who looked upon it as a substitute for the political struggle of the proletariat. This criticism has no bearing upon the general strike for political ends. Furthermore, who has proved, and where, that the parliamentary struggle is the most important form of proletarian class struggle ? Does not the history of the revolutionary movement show beyond dispute that the parliamentary struggle can be nothing more than a school for, and an accessory means to, the extra-parliamentary struggle of the proletariat ; that under capitalism the basic problems of the working-class movement are decided by force, by the direct action of the proletarian masses—by a general strike or by an insurrection ? In the third place, why introduce talk about substituting the method of the general strike for political ends, for the method of the parliamentary struggle ? Where and when did the advocates of the general strike for political purposes propose any such substitution ? Fourthly, has not the history of the Russian revolution shown that the general strike for political purposes is an admirable training school for the proletarian revolution, and an invaluable means for mobilising and organising the proletarian masses on the eve of the attempt to storm the capitalist fortress ? Why, then, in this connexion, introduce petty-bourgeois plaints concerning the disorganisation of economic life and the depletion of trade-union funds ? Is it not plain that the practical experience of the revolutionary struggle refutes this opportunist dogma as well as the others ? "

That is why Lenin said that " the revolutionary theory is not a dogma ", and that " it acquires its definitive formulation only in direct contact with the practical activity of the masses and with an actual revolutionary movement " (*Left-Wing Communism, an Infantile Disorder*) ; for theory must serve practice, " theory must answer the questions that arise out of practice " (*The Friends of the People*), and it must be confirmed by the data of practice.

As regards the political slogans and the political decisions of the parties affiliated to the Second International, it will suffice to recall the history of the slogan " War against War ". That will serve to remind you how double-faced these parties were, how base their policy, how skilful they were in veiling their antirevolutionary trend behind revolutionary watchwords and resolutions. Every one will remember the formidable demonstration made by the Second International at the Basle Congress when the imperialists were threatened with all the terrors of an armed rising in the event of war. It was at Basle that the dread slogan " War against War " was issued. But who has forgotten what happened shortly afterwards ? Immediately the war really began, the Basle resolution was shelved, and the workers were given a new watchword—were told to exterminate one another for the greater glory of their respective capitalist countries. Is it not plain that revolutionary slogans and resolutions are not worth a brass farthing unless translated into action ? Enough to compare the Leninist policy of transforming the imperialist war into a civil war, with the treacherous policy of the Second International when the imperialist war began ; this shows us how base a thing is opportunism, how great is Leninism. I cannot refrain from quoting here a passage from Lenin's book *The Proletarian Revolution and Kautsky the Renegade*, in which he scourges Kautsky for judging parties not by their deeds but by their words :

> Kautsky adopts a typical petty-bourgeois attitude when he expresses the opinion that the mere utterance of a slogan makes a difference. The history of bourgeois democracy pricks this bubble. Bourgeois democrats have voiced, and continue to voice, all possible slogans, this being one of the ways in which they humbug the people. The vital matter is that we should test the sincerity of those who utter slogans, should compare their deeds with their words, that we should not be content with idealist and cheapjack phraseology, but should find how much actual class content lies behind the words. (*Works*, Russian edition, vol. xv., p. 493.)

I shall allude only in passing to some of the other characteristics of the parties affiliated to the Second International : their dread of self-criticism ; their way of trying to hide their blunders, and to gloss over thorny problems ; their fondness for window dressing as a pretence that everything in the interior is in the best possible order, thus stifling healthy thought and hindering the revolutionary education of their members. Lenin pilloried this incapacity for self-criticism in his *Left-Wing Communism, an Infantile Disorder*, writing with mordant sarcasm :

> The attitude of a political party towards its own mistakes is one of the surest tests of its seriousness, and of its ability to fulfil its duties towards its class and towards the labouring masses. Frank admission of an error, discovery of its causes, analysis of

the situation in which it occurred, careful study of the ways by which the mistake can be remedied—these are the signs whereby a serious party can be recognised. That is fulfilment of duty. That is the education of the class and of the masses. (*Works*, Russian edition, vol. xvii., p. 147.)

Many people declare that self-criticism is dangerous to a party, that by a frank admission of its errors a proletarian party will put weapons into the hands of the enemies of the proletariat. In Lenin's view, no weight can be attached to this objection. Here is what he said about the matter in *One Step Forward*. The words were penned in 1904, when our Party was still weak and insignificant.

> Our adversaries, the enemies of the Marxists, are overjoyed at our dissensions. They will naturally make the most of certain passages in my pamphlet where I refer to the mistakes and shortcomings of our Party, and will try to exploit these admissions for their own purposes. The Russian Marxists have been in the firing line so long that they will disregard such pinpricks. They will, in spite of them, go on with the work of self-criticism. They will continue, unsparingly, to expose their own weaknesses, which will inevitably disappear as the working-class movement gathers strength. (*Works*, Russian edition, vol. v., p. 307.)

Such are the general characteristics of Leninist method.

Substantially, the elements of Lenin's method are to be found already in Marxist doctrine, which is (to quote Marx's own words) " in essence, critical and revolutionary ". This critical and revolutionary spirit permeates Lenin's method from start to finish. But it would be a mistake to suppose that Lenin's method is nothing more than a revival of that of Marx. It is not a mere revival ; it is a practical application and an extension of Marx's critical and revolutionary method, of Marx's materialist dialectics.

3. THEORY

UNDER this head, three matters come up for consideration: *a.* the importance of theory to the proletarian movement; *b.* criticism of the theory of spontaneity; *c.* the theory of the proletarian revolution.

a. THE IMPORTANCE OF THEORY

Some think that Leninism signifies the supremacy of practice over theory, in this sense, that the chief thing in Leninism is the translation of Marxist principles into the realm of fact, the " fulfilment " of these principles. Leninism of this sort pays little heed to theory. We know that Plehanoff again and again made fun of Lenin for his indifference to theory, and especially to philosophy. We know, too, that many of those who are engaged in the practical application of Leninism care little for theory, their attitude being due, above all, to the extent to which their time is engrossed in practical work. My business here is to show that this peculiar view of Lenin and Leninism is utterly wrong-headed. It is quite out of touch with the world of reality. The endeavour of " practical " persons to have no truck with " theories " runs counter to the whole spirit of Leninism and is a great danger to our cause.

Revolutionary theory is a synthesis of the experience of the working-class movement throughout all lands—the generalised experience. Of course theory out of touch with revolutionary practice is like a mill that runs without any grist, just as practice gropes in the dark unless revolutionary theory throws a light on the path. But theory becomes the greatest force in the working-class movement when it is inseparably linked with **revolutionary practice**: for it, and it alone, can give the movement confidence, guidance, an understanding of the inner links between events; it alone can enable those engaged in the practical struggle to understand the whence and the whither of the working-class movement. Again and again, Lenin said:

> Without a revolutionary theory, there cannot be **a revolutionary movement** (*Works*, Russian edition, vol. v., p. 135.)

Lenin knew better than any one else the immense importance of theory, especially for such a party as ours, one called to form the vanguard of the international proletariat; and above all in view of the complicated situation, both at home and abroad, with which the Party is confronted. As far back as 1902, foreseeing the special role of our Party, he thought it necessary to point out that:

> Only a party guided by an advanced theory can act as vanguard in the fight. (*Works*, Russian edition, vol. v., p. 136.)

To-day, when Lenin's forecast of the role of our Party has been fulfilled, it would be superfluous to labour the point that what he had to say about the matter is of fundamental importance.

The immense importance attached by Lenin to theory is perhaps best shown by this, that he himself undertook the great task of generalising, on behalf of materialistic philosophy, the main achievements of science since the days of Engels, and of comprehensively criticising the anti-materialistic trends of certain Marxists. Engels said that "materialism should take on a new aspect with each new discovery". For his own epoch, Lenin performed this task in his remarkable work *Materialism and Empirio-Criticism*. Plehanoff, on the other hand, though he had been so ready to condemn Lenin for "indifference to philosophy", did not himself make a serious attempt to perform the necessary task.

b. Criticism of the Theory of Spontaneity, or the Part played by the Vanguard in the Movement

The theory of spontaneity is the theory of opportunism; the theory that we must bow before the spontaneity of the working-class movement; the theory which in practice amounts to a denial that the vanguard of the working class, the Party of the working class, can act as leader for the class as a whole.

This theory that we must bow before the spontaneity of the working-class movement is the theory of those who deny the revolutionary character of the working-class movement, the theory of those who oppose any endeavour to lead the working-class battalions into an attack upon the foundations of capitalism.

It is the theory of those who consider that the movement should be content to formulate demands that are " reasonable ", demands that will be " acceptable " by the capitalists ; it is the theory of those who are glad to follow " the line of least resistance ". The theory of spontaneity is the ideology of trade unionism.

The theory that we must bow our heads before the spontaneity of the working-class movement is the theory of those who are decisively opposed to an attempt to give the spontaneous movement a deliberate and purposive character ; it is the theory of those who do not want our Party to march in front of the working class, stimulating the masses till they reach the level of conscious action, leading the movement. It is the theory of those who consider that the thinking elements should let the movement go its own way, that the Party should listen for the voice of the spontaneous movement and be content to trot along in the rear, to hold on to the tail, to follow where the movement leads. It is the theory of those who underestimate the importance of the thinking elements, the theory of those whose ideology is that of " hvostism " or " tailism " [1]—the logical foundation of every kind of opportunism.

In practice this theory, which was current in Russia before the revolution of 1905, led those who were guided by it (they were known as the " economists ") to deny the need for an independent working-class party in Russia. The " economists " were opposed to the development of a revolutionary working-class struggle for the overthrow of tsarism ; they advocated a trade-unionist policy within the movement ; they wished the working-class movement to remain under the thumb of the liberal bourgeoisie.[2]

The campaign of the old " Iskra ", and Lenin's brilliant criticism of " tailism " in *What is to be done ?*, not only smote the " economists " hip and thigh, but also provided a theoretical

---

[1] The ideology of those who cling to the tail (Russian, *hvost*) of the movement instead of trying to lead it ; the ideology of those who await the progress of events, and are therefore " opportunists ".—E. and C. P.

[2] The name " economists " was coined because in Russia it is usual to contrast the *political* struggle with the *economic* struggle, whereas we in Britain usually speak of the contrast between the struggle in the *political* and that in the *industrial* fields. Thus the " economists " wanted the working-class struggle to be confined to the industrial plane, and to the formation of trade unions in which there would be " no politics ". In politics, the workers were to follow the liberal lead.—E. and C. P.

foundation for a truly revolutionary Russian working-class movement.

Had it not been for this preliminary work in the theoretical field, it would have been impossible to create an independent party of class-conscious workers in Russia, and impossible for that party to take the lead in the revolution.

But the theory that we must bow before the spontaneity of the movement is not an exclusively Russian phenomenon. This theory (varying a little in form) is voiced in all the parties affiliated to the Second International. I am thinking now of the theory of "the forces of production". On this theory, as distorted by the leaders of the Second International, everything can be justified and every one can be conciliated; facts obvious to all the world are established and proved; and the mere observing and recording of the facts becomes an end in itself. Marx said that materialist theory must not be content with explaining the world, but must change it. Kautsky and Co., however, are satisfied with explaining, and leave the change to take care of itself. Here is an instance (among many which might be given) of the way in which this precious theory is applied. Just now I reminded you (see above, p. 92) how, at the Basle Congress, the parties affiliated to the Second International threatened to declare "War against War" if the imperialists began a war. But, you will remember, directly the imperialist war began, the "War against War" business was scrapped, and the workers were told to fight "all out" in defence of their several imperialist fatherlands. As a result of this change of front, millions of workers were butchered. But it would be a great mistake to suppose that any one is to blame for this, that any one betrayed the working class. Nothing of the sort! Everything happened as it had to happen. For, first of all, the International is an "instrument of peace", not a "weapon of war". Secondly, in view of "the level of the forces of production" at the time of the outbreak of the war, there was no option. The fault lies with "the forces of production". Mr. Kautsky's "theory of the forces of production" explains this quite clearly, and those who challenge the soundness of the theory are not Marxists.

"The Party?" you venture to ask at this stage. "Has the Party no function?"

"What are you talking about?" comes the ready answer. "Can the Party do anything to affect the working of so decisive a factor as ' the level of the forces of production ' ? "

A host of such instances of the falsification of Marxism could be marshalled. Their aim is to raise a smoke-screen thick enough to hide the opportunism of those who utter them, and it is self-evident that they are nothing more than the western European variety of the " tailism " which Lenin was combating in Russia as long ago as the days before the revolution of 1905.

Surely, too, the abandonment of this radically false outlook is an essential preliminary to the formation of genuinely revolutionary parties in western Europe.

c. The Theory of the Proletarian Revolution

The Leninist theory of the proletarian revolution is based on three fundamental theses.

First Thesis. The dominion of financial capital in countries of advanced capitalist development; the issue of stocks and bonds, as the chief activity of financial capital; the export of capital to the sources of raw material, this being one of the main foundations of imperialism; omnipotence of the financial oligarchy, as a result of the rule of financial capital—all these circumstances disclose the intensely parasitic character of monopolist capital, make the yoke of the capitalist trusts and syndicates a hundred times more intolerable, intensify the workers' indignation, and spur the masses on towards the proletarian revolution, as their only means of deliverance. (See Lenin's *Imperialism*.)

As a result, the revolutionary crisis in capitalist countries becomes more acute; there is a heaping up of combustible material on the internal front, on the proletarian front, in the " mother countries ".

Second Thesis. Increasing export of capital to colonies and dependencies; a widening of " spheres of influence " and colonisation until all the land in the world has been grabbed; the transformation of capitalism to become a worldwide system thanks to which a handful of " advanced " countries is able to hold the vast majority of the population of our planet in a state of financial bondage and colonial oppression—all these changes have, first of all, transformed the separate economies of national areas into parts of a unified system known as the "world economy"; and have, secondly, divided the population of the world into two camps. One of these camps contains the small number of "advanced" capitalist countries, which exploit and oppress the rest of the world, the colonial and dependent lands (far more numerous), so that these latter are now compelled to struggle in the hope of freeing themselves from the imperialist yoke. (See Lenin's *Imperialism*.)

As a result, the revolutionary crisis in colonies and dependencies becomes more acute; and the spirit of revolt against imperialism becomes intensified all along the external front, the colonial front.

Third Thesis. Monopolist rule over "spheres of influence" and colonies; differences in the degree of capitalist development attained by various countries, with the result that there is a fierce struggle between the countries that have secured and those that would like to secure a large "share of the spoils"; imperialist wars as the only means of "readjusting the balance", of securing the redistribution desired by the countries that are excluded from "a place in the sun"—all these influences co-operate in leading to the accumulation of tensions on the third front, the intercapitalist front, thus weakening the imperialist forces and promoting a union between the proletarian and the colonial fronts for the fight against imperialism. (See Lenin's *Imperialism*.)

As a result, under imperialism, wars become inevitable; and, under imperialism, there must necessarily ensue a coalition between the proletarian revolution in Europe and the colonial revolution in the East, this leading to the formation of a united world-front of the revolution against the world-front of imperialism.

All the foregoing inferences are unified and generalized by Lenin in the conclusion that "*imperialism is the immediate forerunner of the socialist revolution*". (*Works*, Russian edition, vol. xiii., p. 243.)

As a result, our attitude towards the problem of the proletarian revolution has undergone a change. We have new lights upon its character, its scope, its general scheme.

Study of the antecedents of the proletarian revolution used, in general, to be undertaken from an outlook upon the economic conditions peculiar to the country under consideration. This formulation of the problem has to-day become inadequate. We have, nowadays, to approach the matter from a more general outlook, from that upon all or most of the countries in the world, from that upon the world economy. Individual countries and individual national economies have ceased to be independent entities. They have become parts of a united whole, which is spoken of as the world economy. The old " civilising " capitalism has developed into imperialism, which is a worldwide system of financial bondage, a system whereby the inhabitants of colonies and dependencies (forming the great majority of the population of the globe) are oppressed by a small number of " advanced " countries.

In former days the question which came up for discussion was whether the objective conditions requisite for the proletarian revolution were or were not present in this or that highly developed country. This formulation of the problem, likewise, has to-day become inadequate. Our business, nowadays, is to discuss whether the objective conditions requisite for the proletarian revolution do or do not exist in the world economy, in the worldwide imperialist system regarded as a unified whole. Within that system there are certain countries where industrial development is backward, but this is not an insurmountable obstacle to the revolution *if* the system as a whole (it would be more accurate to say, *inasmuch as* the system as a whole) is already ripe for the revolution.

In former days, again, it was usual to think of the proletarian revolution, in this country or that, as an independent magnitude, confronted by another independent magnitude, the capitalist forces of the same country; these two independent magnitudes faced one another upon an independent national front. To-day this formulation is obsolete. Nowadays we have to think in terms of the worldwide proletarian revolution, for the various national capitalist fronts, isolated of yore, have coalesced into a unified whole, the worldwide imperialist front, against which must be arrayed the unified front of the revolutionary movement in all lands.

In former days, finally, it was customary to regard the proletarian revolution as an outcome of conditions that were purely local to the country under consideration. Once more, this formulation is obsolete. Nowadays we have to regard the proletarian revolution, first and foremost, as the outcome of the growth of antagonisms within the worldwide system of imperialism, as the outcome of an effort which (in this country or in that) breaks the chains of worldwide imperialism.

Where will the revolution begin? In what country can the capitalist front be first broken?

The usual answer was that this would happen where industrial development was most advanced, where the proletariat formed the majority of the population, where the level of civilisation was high, where democracy was thoroughly established.

But, according to Leninist theory, this reasoning is unsound. There are no grounds for the belief that the capitalist front will first be broken where industrial development is most advanced, and so on, and so on. The capitalist front will be broken where the chain of imperialism is weakest, and it is there that the proletarian revolution (which follows upon the defeat of imperialism) must begin. It is likely enough, therefore, that the country where the revolution begins, the country where the capitalist front is broken, will be one where capitalist development is comparatively backward; and that, while the revolutionary movement is being successful in such a country, others, where industrial development is much farther advanced, will remain within the framework of capitalism.

In 1917, the weakest part of the imperialist world-front was in Russia. There the front was broken, so that the way was opened for the advance of the proletarian revolution. Why did this happen? Because, in Russia, there occurred a great uprising of the people, led by the revolutionary proletariat, which has as its formidable ally the peasantry, the millions upon millions of those who had been oppressed and exploited by the landowners. Because, in Russia, the forces of imperialism, the forces that faced the revolution, were incorporated in the execrable figure of tsarism, which was devoid of moral authority and was universally detested. Russia was the weakest part of the imperialist world-front, although in Russia capitalism was so much less developed than in France, Germany, Great Britain, or the United States of America.

Where is the front likely to be broken next? Again at the weakest point, obviously. Perhaps that will be in British India, where there is a young and combative revolutionary proletariat, allied to the champions of the movement for national liberation—a movement which is certainly very powerful. In India, moreover, the antirevolutionary forces are incorporated in a foreign imperialism, which has completely forfeited moral credit and has incurred the general hatred of the oppressed and exploited masses.

Another possibility is that the next breach in the imperialist world-front will occur in Germany. The factors at work in India are beginning to operate in Germany as well. But, naturally, the immense difference in evolutionary level between British India and Germany must not be forgotten. The course and the upshot of the revolution in Germany will necessarily have their own peculiar stamp.

That was why Lenin wrote:

> The capitalist countries of western Europe will accomplish their evolution towards socialism, . . . not by the methodical maturing of socialism in these lands, but through the exploitation of some of the States by others (the exploitation of the first State that is defeated during the imperialist war), and through the exploitation of the whole of the East. Thanks to the first imperialist war, the East has definitively been drawn into the revolutionary movement, has definitively been swept into the vortex of the world-wide revolutionary movement. (*Works*, Russian edition, vol. xviii., part II., p. 136.)

To put the matter more concisely, the imperialist front will usually be broken where it is weakest. This weak spot will not necessarily be where capitalism is most highly developed, where industrial workers are numerous and peasants scarce, and so on.

That is why statistical data concerning the proportion of proletarians among the population of this country or that, have less bearing on the problem of the proletarian revolution than the statisticians of the Second International (who do not understand imperialism, and are as much afraid of the revolution as of the plague) like to think.

Furthermore, the heroes of the Second International have asserted, and continue to assert, that between the bourgeois-democratic revolution and the proletarian revolution there is a great gulf fixed, or at any rate a sort of Chinese wall. But the gulf or the wall is temporal, not spatial. We are told that there must be a long interval between the bourgeois revolution and the proletarian revolution, an interval of many decades at least, during which the bourgeoisie (having risen to power) is developing the resources of capitalism, while the proletariat is slowly consolidating its forces and preparing for the "decisive struggle" against capitalism. Is it not self-evident that this theory is devoid of scientific foundation under imperialist conditions, and is nothing more than a mask for the concealment of the counter-revolutionary appetites of the bourgeoisie? Surely it is self-evident that, under imperialist conditions, when clashes and wars are germinating; on the eve of the socialist revolution, when "thriving" capitalism is on the way to become "dying" capitalism, and when the revolutionary movement is on the up grade all over the world; at a time when imperialism is allied with the forces of reaction, including autocracy and serfdom, thus making it even more essential that there should be a consolidation of the revolutionary forces from the proletarian movement in the West to the movement on behalf of national liberation in the East; at an hour when the uprooting of the vestiges of the feudal regime has become impossible without a revolutionary struggle against imperialism—surely at such a time and in such circumstances it is self-evident that the bourgeois-democratic revolution will tend to develop into the proletarian revolution! The history of the Russian revolution has abundantly and irrefutably confirmed this view. With good reason did Lenin, as long ago as 1905, on the eve of the first Russian revolution, describe (in his pamphlet *Two Tactics*) the bourgeois-democratic revolution and the socialist revolution as two links of one chain, as two natural stages of the Russian revolution:

> The proletariat must push the democratic revolution through to an end, inducing the mass of the peasantry to join forces with the workers, in order to break the power of the autocracy and to overcome the vacillations of the bourgeoisie. The proletariat must push the socialist revolution through to an end, inducing the mass of the semi-proletarian elements to join forces with the proletariat, in order to break the power of the bourgeoisie and to overcome the vacillations of the peasantry and the petty bourgeoisie. Such are the tasks of the proletariat, of which the adherents of the new "Iskra" show so narrow a conception in their arguments and resolutions concerning the scope of the revolution. (*Works*, Russian edition, vol. vi., p. 371.)

Here I shall make no more than a passing allusion to Lenin's later works, in which the idea of the metamorphosis of the bourgeois revolution into the proletarian revolution is brought into much greater relief than in *Two Tactics*, so that it forms one of the corner stones of the Leninist theory of the revolution.

Certain comrades appear to believe that Lenin did not happen upon this idea until 1916. They think that before that year he supposed that in Russia the revolution would only be a bourgeois revolution; that power would pass to the bourgeoisie and not to the proletariat. It is said that this erroneous belief regarding Lenin's views has even been championed in our communist press. Let me assure you that there is no warrant for any such belief.

Let me remind you, for instance, of Lenin's famous speech at the Third Party Congress (1905), when he described the dictatorship of the proletariat and peasantry, that is to say the victory of the democratic revolution, as being, " not the organisation of order, but the organisation of war ". (*Works*, Russian edition, vol. vi., p. 171.)

Again, I may refer to Lenin's well-known articles *The Provisional Government* (1905), in which, describing the prospects of the Russian revolution, he writes:

> The Party ought to act in such a way as will ensure that the Russian revolution shall not be an affair of a few months, but an affair of many years; that it shall not lead merely to trifling concessions on the part of the authorities, but to the complete overthrow of the powers that be. . . . If we succeed, then the revolutionary conflagration will spread to the rest of Europe. The workers of western Europe, weary of the misdeeds of the bourgeois reaction, will rise in their turn and give us an ' object lesson ' in revolution. Thereupon the revolutionary impetus of western Europe will react upon Russia, and will transform an epoch of a few revolutionary years into an epoch of several revolutionary decades. (*Works*, Russian edition, vol. vi., p. 129.)

Once more, there is the article published by Lenin in November 1915, in which he says:

> The proletariat fights and will continue to fight with all its strength for the conquest of power, for the establishment of a republic, for the confiscation of the land, . . . and to induce the " non-proletarian masses of the people " to participate in the liberation of bourgeois Russia from the militarist-feudal imperialism which passes by the name of tsarism. This freeing of bourgeois

Russia from tsarism, from the territorial dominion of the landowners, will *immediately* [1] be turned to account by the proletariat —not in order to help the well-to-do peasants to get the better of the poorer peasants, the agricultural labourers ; but in order, having joined forces with the proletarians of western Europe, to complete the socialist revolution. (*Works*, Russian edition, vol. xiii., p. 214.)

Finally I may mention the passage in *The Proletarian Revolution and Kautsky the Renegade*, where Lenin, having referred to the passage just quoted from *Two Tactics* (the one on p. 201 in which he speaks about the scope of the Russian revolution), draws the following inference :

> Things have turned out as we said they would. The course of the revolution has confirmed the accuracy of our view. First of all the proletariat marched with the peasantry as a whole : against the monarchy, against the landlords, against the vestiges of medievalism (and up to this point the revolution was still bourgeois, was still bourgeois-democratic). Then the proletariat marched with the poorer peasants, with the semiproletarians, with the exploited : against capitalism, and against its embodiments in the countryside, against the kulaks, the speculators (so that now the revolution became a socialist revolution). The attempt to build a Chinese wall between the two phases, the contention that they are separated one from the other by anything more than differences in the degree of preparedness of the proletariat and in the intimacy of the union between the workers and the poorer peasants, is a gross distortion of Marxism, a debasement of Marxism, a confounding of Marxism with liberalism. (*Works*, Russian edition, vol. xv., pp. 508–509.)

Why, then, say the objectors, did Lenin oppose the idea of " permanent revolution " ?

Because he wanted to make the fullest possible use of the revolutionary capacities and energies of the peasantry for the complete liquidation of tsarism and for the transition to the proletarian revolution, whereas the champions of " permanent revolution " did not understand how important a part the peasantry had and has to play in the Russian revolution. They underestimated the revolutionary energy of the peasantry. At the same time they underestimated the strength of the Russian proletariat, and its power of rallying the peasants to the revolutionary cause. Thus they tended to hinder the emancipation of the peasants from bourgeois influences, and to check the

[1] Italicised by Stalin.

inclination of the peasants to join forces with the revolutionary workers.

Lenin's aim was to *crown* the revolution by the rise of the proletariat to power. On the other hand, the champions of " permanent revolution " wanted to *begin* by establishing the power of the proletariat right away, not realising that when they made this their aim they were closing their eyes to such little matters as survivals of serfdom, were neglecting so puny a force as the Russian peasantry ! Thus they were hindering the peasants from rallying to the proletariat.

Lenin therefore opposed the champions of " permanent revolution ", not because they asserted the continuity of the revolution (a theory he himself never ceased to support), but because they underestimated the importance of the part played by the peasantry, which forms the great reserve force for the proletariat—and because they did not really understand the nature of proletarian supremacy.

The idea of " permanent revolution " is not new. It dates from 1850, when Marx expounded it in the circular from the central committee to the members of the Communist League. The Russian champions of " permanent revolution " lifted it from that document, but in the process they botched it in such a way as to unfit it for practical use. The skilful hand of Lenin was needed to rectify this error, to restore Marx's idea of permanent revolution to its pristine form, and to make it one of the corner stones of our theory of revolution.

In the 1850 circular, Marx, after enumerating the revolutionary demands which the communists ought to put forward, went on as follows :

> Whereas the petty-bourgeois democrats want the revolution to be brought to a close as speedily as possible (as soon as their scanty demands are satisfied), it is incumbent upon the workers to make the revolution permanent until the more or less possessing classes have been excluded from power, until the proletariat has achieved the conquest of State authority, and until—not in one country alone, but in all the advanced countries of the world—the association of the proletarians has developed so far that competition among the proletarians of these lands has ceased to exist and the key industries at least are in proletarian hands.

In other words :

1. Whatever our champions of "permanent revolution" may say, Marx did not, in 1850, propose that the revolution in Germany should *begin* by a proletarian conquest of State authority.

2. Marx's idea was that the conquest of State authority by the proletariat would *crown* the work of the revolution. The workers, having successively overthrown one fraction of the bourgeoisie after another, and having attained power, would then kindle the torch of revolution in all the countries of the world.

This is perfectly consistent with what Lenin taught. It is perfectly consistent with what Lenin did in the course of our revolution, guided by his theory of the proletarian revolution as it takes place under imperialist conditions.

Thus the Russian champions of "permanent revolution" have not been content with underestimating the importance of the part played by the peasantry in the Russian revolution, and have not only misunderstood the significance of the idea of the leadership of the proletariat ; but they have also degraded Marx's idea of "permanent" revolution, so as to deprive it of practical value.

That is why Lenin ridiculed their theory, and declared that they had closed their eyes to avoid having to see the way in which, for decades, life had been refuting so "original" and "charming" a notion. This was in articles written in 1915, ten years after the formulation of the Russian version of the theory of "permanent revolution". (*Works*, Russian edition, vol. xiii., p. 213.)

That is why Lenin considered the theory tainted with menshevism. He wrote :

> While it borrows from the bolsheviks the call to the proletariat to engage in a decisive revolutionary struggle and to achieve the conquest of political power, it borrows from the mensheviks the denial that the peasants have an important part to play. (See *The Two Lines of Revolution*, in *Against the Stream*, reference as above.)

Such were Lenin's ideas concerning the way in which the bourgeois-democratic revolution would develop into the proletarian revolution, concerning the way in which the bourgeois-democratic revolution could be turned to account in order to bring about a prompt transition to the proletarian revolution.

It used to be supposed that the victory of the revolution in one country alone would be impossible, the assumption being that the conquest of the bourgeoisie could only be achieved by the united action of the proletarians of all advanced countries, or at any rate those in the majority of these. This contention no longer fits the facts. We must now set out by assuming the possibility of such a victory : for the varying speed of social evolution in different capitalist countries (proceeding in some, under imperialist conditions, by leaps and bounds) ; the development of catastrophic conflicts as the outcome of imperialist rivalries, inevitably culminating in wars ; the growth of the revolutionary movement in all countries throughout the world—these factors, working together, make proletarian victories in separate countries not merely possible but necessary. The history of the Russian revolution is striking evidence of this. We have, nevertheless, to remember that certain preliminary conditions must be fulfilled before the bourgeoisie can be overthrown, and that unless these conditions have been fulfilled it is futile for the proletariat to think of seizing power.

Here is what Lenin wrote about these indispensable preliminaries in his *Left-Wing Communism, an Infantile Disorder* :

> The fundamental law of revolution, confirmed by every revolution, and especially by the three Russian revolutions of the twentieth century, runs as follows. For the revolution, it is not enough that the exploited and oppressed masses should have become aware that they cannot go on living in the old way, and that they should demand changes ; in addition, the exploiters must find it impossible to live and rule in the old way. *Not until the " lower classes " cannot put up with the old conditions any longer, and the " upper classes " cannot carry on under the old conditions, can the revolution triumph.*[1] To express this truth in other words : *revolution is impossible unless there is a national crisis affecting both exploited and exploiters.*[1] This means that there are two essentials for the revolution. First of all, the majority of the workers (or at any rate the majority of the class-conscious, the thoughtful, the politically active workers) must be fully aware that a revolution is necessary and must be ready to go to their deaths for its sake. Secondly, the ruling classes must be in the throes of a governmental crisis which draws even the most backward masses into the political arena, and enfeebles the government to such an extent that the revolutionists can speedily overthrow it. (*Works*, Russian edition, vol. xvii., p. 172.)

---

[1] Italicised by Stalin.

But the overthrow of the power of the bourgeoisie and the establishment of the power of the proletariat in one country alone does not, per se, mean the complete victory of socialism. Having consolidated its power and having secured the support of the peasantry, the victorious proletariat can and must proceed to upbuild a socialist society. Does this mean that thereby the victorious proletariat will achieve the final victory of socialism? Does this mean that the workers in one country alone, unaided, can definitively instal socialism, guaranteed against intervention, guaranteed against a restoration of the old regime? No, certainly not. For that, the victory of the revolution, if not everywhere, at least in several countries, will be requisite. That is why the fostering of revolution, the support of revolution, in other countries, is incumbent upon the country where the revolution has triumphed. That is why a country in which the revolution has triumphed must not look upon itself as an independent magnitude, but as an auxiliary, as a means for hastening the victory of the proletariat in other lands.

Lenin expressed this idea pithily as follows:

> In any country, the victorious revolution must do its utmost to develop, support, and awaken the revolution in all other countries. (*Works*, Russian edition, vol. xv., p. 502.)

Such, in broad outline, are the characteristics of Lenin's theory of the proletarian revolution.

4. THE DICTATORSHIP OF THE PROLETARIAT

THIS question must be considered under three main heads: *a.* The dictatorship of the proletariat as the instrument of the proletarian revolution; *b.* the dictatorship of the proletariat as the rule of the proletariat over the bourgeoisie; *c.* the Soviet power as the form of State embodying the dictatorship of the proletariat.

a. THE DICTATORSHIP OF THE PROLETARIAT AS THE INSTRUMENT OF THE PROLETARIAN REVOLUTION

The question of the dictatorship of the proletariat is, above all, the question of the fundamental meaning of the proletarian revolution. The proletarian revolution, with its movement, its impetus, and its achievements, only becomes a reality through the dictatorship of the proletariat. This dictatorship is the chief fulcrum of the proletarian revolution, its main instrument. The first aim of the dictatorship is to break the resistance of the defeated exploiters. Next, it must lead the revolution onward to the final victory, to the complete triumph of socialism. The revolution can achieve the first conquest of the bourgeoisie, the overthrow of bourgeois dominion, without the dictatorship of the proletariat. But if the resistance of the bourgeoisie is to be crushed, if the conquests of the revolution are to be maintained, if the final victory is to be won by the establishment of socialism, this special revolutionary organ, the dictatorship of the proletariat, must be created in the appropriate phase of the revolution.

Lenin says: " The fundamental question of the revolution is the question of power ". Does this mean that the revolution is the seizure of power and nothing more? It does not, for the seizure of power is only the first step. When deprived of power in any one country, the bourgeoisie still remains (for various reasons) stronger than the proletariat which has overthrown it. Power has not merely to be seized; it has to be held, to be consolidated, to be made invincible. To fulfil these aims, it is necessary, on the morrow of the first overthrow of the bourgeoisie, to work along three main lines:

1. We must break the resistance of the landowners and capitalists who have been deprived of power and expropriated by the revolution, and must frustrate their efforts to restore the dominion of capital.

2. We must organise the process of socialist reconstruction by rallying all the toilers to the support of the proletariat, and by preparing for the gradual disappearance of classes.

3. We must arm the revolution, must organise the army of the revolution for the fight against the enemies outside our borders, for the fight against imperialism.

The dictatorship of the proletariat is essential to the performance of these three tasks. Lenin writes:

> The transition from capitalism to socialism occupies an entire historical epoch. While the transition is still going on, the exploiters will continue to cherish hopes of a capitalist restoration, and these hopes will find practical expression in attempts to bring about such a restoration. After their first serious defeat, the exploiters (who never expected anything of the kind, and can hardly believe in it now that it has taken place) throw themselves with redoubled energy, with furious passion, with implacable hatred, into the battle for the recovery of their lost paradise, into the fight to restore their family fortunes, to regain " comfortable " positions for those whom the " rabble " would now condemn to poverty and ruin (or to the simple necessity of work !). . . . The lead of these capitalist exploiters will be followed by the broad masses of the petty bourgeoisie. Experience in all countries has shown that the members of this stratum of the population have no steadfastness; that to-day they will march with the proletariat; but to-morrow, alarmed by the difficulties of the revolution, panic-stricken at the first check to the workers' advance, they grow nervous, do not know where to turn, and rush whining from one camp to another. (*Works*, Russian edition, vol. xv., p. 467.)

For a long time after its overthrow, the bourgeoisie remains stronger than the victorious proletariat, and has therefore good grounds for attempting to re-establish its position. Lenin writes:

> If the exploiters have been defeated in one country only (and this is what usually happens, for simultaneous revolutions in many countries are exceptional), they remain very much stronger than the exploited. (*Works*, Russian edition, vol. xv., pp. 466-467.)

How can we account for the strength of the bourgeoisie after it has been overthrown? There are three reasons:

1. There is the power of international capital, the strength and the intimacy of the international ties that unite the bourgeoisie. (*Works*, Russian edition, vol. xvii., pp. 117-118.)

2. There is the fact that for a long time after the revolution the exploiters necessarily retain a number of enormous advantages. They have money (which cannot be immediately done away with); they have portable property; often valuables to a considerable amount; they have personal ties, together with organisational and administrative experience and a knowledge of all the " secrets " of government (habits, methods, means, possibilities); they are better educated; they have close connexions with the leading technicians (who are all bourgeois in their modes of life and ways of thought); they are profoundly versed in the art of war (this is very important); and so on, and so on. (*Works*, Russian edition, vol. xv., p. 466.)

3. There is the force of habit, together with the power of small-scale production. Unfortunately, small-scale production is still widespread, continually (day by day and hour by hour), with elemental energy, and in vast proportions, generating capitalism and the bourgeoisie. . . . If we want to make an end of classes, we must do something more than drive out landowners and capitalists (we have done that without much difficulty); we must make an end of small-scale production. Now, it is impossible to drive out the petty producers, it is impossible to suppress them offhand; we have, for the time being, to live with them as best we may, while we are transforming them. This transformation is indispensable. We can achieve it; we can re-educate them, but a lengthy, tedious, and carefully considered organisational task lies before us. (*Works*, Russian edition, vol. xvii., p. 118 and pp. 135-136.)

That is why Lenin says :

The dictatorship of the proletariat is a fight, fierce and ruthless, of the new class against an enemy of preponderant strength, against the bourgeoisie, whose determination to resist has been increased tenfold by its overthrow. (*Works*, Russian edition, vol. xvii., p. 117.)

He also writes in this connexion :

The dictatorship of the proletariat is a hard-fought fight against the forces and traditions of the old society; a fight that is both bloody and unbloody, both violent and passive, both military and economic, both educational and administrative. (*Works*, Russian edition, vol. xvii., p. 136.)

Obviously, these tasks cannot be hurried; we shall not be able to finish them within the space of a few years. The dictatorship of the proletariat, the transition from capitalism to

DICTATORSHIP OF THE PROLETARIAT

socialism, must not be contemplated as a fleeting period whose whole content is a number of doughty revolutionary deeds and impressive decrees. It will be an entire historical epoch, an era of civil wars and international conflicts, of steadfast organisational work and economic reconstruction, of advances and withdrawals, of victories and defeats. This lengthy historical epoch is essential, not only to create the economic and cultural prerequisites for the complete victory of socialism, but also to provide an opportunity for the proletariat, first of all to educate itself and to consolidate its forces so that it may become capable of carrying on the administration of the country, and secondly to re-educate and transform the petty-bourgeois sections of the community so as to ensure the organisation of socialist production.

This is how Marx looked at the matter (he was apostrophising the workers, at the close of the year 1851):

> You will have to go through fifteen, twenty, fifty years of civil wars and international wars, not only in order to change external conditions, but also in order to change yourselves and in order to fit yourselves for the exercise of political power. (*Enthüllungen über den Kommunistenprozess zu Köln*, § 1—p. 52 of the fourth reprint, Berlin, 1914.)

Developing Marx's thought, Lenin wrote:

> During the dictatorship of the proletariat, it will be necessary to re-educate millions of peasants and petty proprietors, hundreds of thousands of employees, officials, and bourgeois intellectuals; to subject them all to the proletarian State and to proletarian guidance; to rid them of bourgeois habits and traditions. . . . In like manner, it will be necessary, in the course of a long struggle and under the aegis of the dictatorship of the proletariat, to re-educate the proletarians themselves—for even proletarians do not shake off their petty-bourgeois prejudices in the twinkling of an eye, as if by miracle, through the grace of the Virgin Mary, thanks to watchwords, resolutions, or decrees; but only as the outcome of a tedious and difficult mass struggle against massed petty-bourgeois influences. (*Works*, Russian edition, vol. xvii., pp. 197 and 198.)

b. The Dictatorship of the Proletariat as the Rule of the Proletariat over the Bourgeoisie

Enough has been said to show that the dictatorship of the proletariat does not mean a mere change of the personnel of the government, a change of cabinet as it were, while the old economic and political order persists unaltered. Mensheviks and opportunists in all lands, dreading the dictatorship as they dread the plague, and (in their alarm) substituting the notion of the "conquest of power" for the notion of the dictatorship of the proletariat, usually water down the idea still farther by thinking of the conquest of power as nothing more than a change of cabinet—as the installation of a new ministry composed of such men as Scheidemann and Noske, MacDonald and Henderson. There is no need to waste words in proving that such a cabinet change has nothing in common with the dictatorship of the proletariat, with the conquest of real power by the real proletariat. So long as bourgeois order remains in being, to put the Scheidemanns and the MacDonalds in power, to let them form what is called a "government", can mean nothing more than to put a new tool into the hands of the bourgeoisie, nothing more than to plaster the sores of imperialism, nothing more than to give the bourgeoisie weapons for use against the revolutionary movement of the oppressed and exploited masses. Such a government serves as a screen at times when the capitalists find it inconvenient, disadvantageous, or difficult, to oppress and exploit the masses openly. It is true that the formation of such a government is symptomatic, is an indication that a certain uneasiness, a certain disorder, prevails in the capitalist camp. None the less, behind the screen of the "labour" cabinet, capitalism continues to govern. From the government of a MacDonald or a Scheidemann to the real conquest of power by the proletariat, it is as far as from earth to heaven. The dictatorship of the proletariat is not a change of ministry, but a new State, with new central and local administrative organs; it is a proletarian State which rises like the phoenix out of the ashes of the old bourgeois State.

The dictatorship of the proletariat is not established upon the foundation of the bourgeois system of things; it is established in the course of the destruction of that system, after the overthrow of the bourgeoisie, when the landowners and the capitalists are being expropriated, when the most important means of production are being socialised, and when the proletarian revolution is making its way by force. The dictatorship of the proletariat is a revolutionary authority forcibly imposed upon the bourgeoisie.

The State is an instrument in the hands of the dominant class, used to break the resistance of the adversaries of that class. In this respect, the dictatorship of the proletariat does not differ fundamentally from the dictatorship of any other class, seeing that the proletarian State is an instrument used to break the resistance of the bourgeoisie. But in another respect there is a fundamental difference. Hitherto, the class State has always been the dictatorship of an exploiting minority over the exploited majority, whereas the dictatorship of the proletariat is the dictatorship of the exploited majority over the exploiting minority.

To put it briefly, *the dictatorship of the proletariat is the rule of the proletariat over the bourgeoisie, a rule unrestricted by law, based upon force, enjoying the sympathy and the support of the labouring and exploited masses.* (Cf. *The State and Revolution.*)

From this two important inferences may be drawn.

First inference. The dictatorship of the proletariat cannot possibly be "complete democracy"; cannot be democracy for all, for the rich as well as the poor. Lenin writes:

> The dictatorship of the proletariat must be a State that embodies a new kind of democracy, *for* [1] the proletarians and the dispossessed; and a new kind of dictatorship, *against* [1] the bourgeoisie. (*Works*, Russian edition, vol. xiv., part II., p. 324.)

The sermons of Kautsky and Co. on "universal" equality, "pure" democracy, "complete" democracy, and the like, are but bourgeois verbiage to mask the indisputable fact that there can be no equality between exploited and exploiters. The theory of "pure" democracy is the theory of a favoured labour caste which has been tamed by the imperialist robbers and has learned to feed out of their hands. It was formulated in order to plaster the sores of capitalism, to camouflage imperialism, and to give the exploiters moral strength in their fight against the exploited masses.

Under capitalism, there can be no real "freedom" for the exploited, were it only for the reason that the buildings, the printing presses, and the paper supplies necessary for the utilisation of this freedom are in privileged hands, in the hands of the exploiters. Under capitalism, the exploited masses cannot effectively participate in the government of the country, were it

[1] Italicised by Stalin.

only because in the countries where bourgeois democracy is most fully developed, governments are set up, not in reality by the people, but by such financiers and industrialists as Rothschild, Stinnes, Rockefeller, and Morgan. Under capitalism, democracy is *capitalist* democracy, the democracy of the exploiting minority, based upon a restriction of the rights of the exploited majority and directed against that majority. Only under the dictatorship of the proletariat can there be real freedom for the exploited masses, and only under the dictatorship of the proletariat can the workers and the peasants effectively participate in the government of the country. Under the dictatorship of the proletariat, democracy is *proletarian* democracy, the democracy of the exploited majority, based upon a restriction of the rights of the exploiting minority and directed against that minority.

Second inference. The dictatorship of the proletariat cannot arise as the outcome of the peaceful development of bourgeois society and bourgeois democracy. It can only arise as the outcome of the destruction of the bourgeois State machine, the bourgeois army, the bourgeois bureaucracy, and the bourgeois police force.

Marx and Engels, guided by the experience of the Paris Commune, wrote:

> The working class cannot simply lay hold of the ready-made State machinery and wield it for its own purposes. (*The Civil War in France*, Truelove, London, 1871, p. 15.)

Again, writing to Kugelmann in 1871, Marx said:

> The aim of the proletarian revolution is no longer (as used to be thought) to transfer the bureaucratic and military machine from one set of hands to another, but to *smash* that machine. This is the indispensable prerequisite for any genuine folk-revolution on the Continent.

Marx's reservation " on the Continent " has given the opportunists and mensheviks of all lands the chance of shouting in chorus that at any rate as regards certain countries that were not on the continent of Europe (Britain and the United States) he conceded the possibility of the peaceful development of bourgeois democracy into proletarian democracy. Marx did, in actual fact, admit this possibility, and he had good reason for doing so in regard to the Britain and the United States of the early seventies, before the days of monopolist capitalism and imperialism, and at a time when in those countries (owing to the peculiar conditions of their development) militarism and bureaucracy were but little in evidence. That was at an epoch when imperialism was in its infancy. But several decades later, when the position in the English-speaking lands had radically changed, when imperialism had grown to its full stature and was dominant in all capitalist countries without exception, when militarism and bureaucracy had become established in Britain and the United States as well as on the continent of Europe, and when the exceptional conditions favourable to a peaceful development in the English-speaking world had passed away—then Marx's reservation " on the Continent " had become obsolete, and what he said of continental Europe applied with equal force to Britain and the United States.

In 1917, Lenin wrote :

> Nowadays, in the epoch of the first great imperialist war, Marx's reservation lapses. Britain and the United States, which have been up till now (thanks to their exemption from militarism and bureaucracy) the last and greatest embodiments of Anglo-Saxon " freedom ", have at length come, like the other nations, to wallow in the foul and bloody mire of bureaucratic and militarist institutions, which establish a universal tyranny. To-day in Britain and the United States, no less than elsewhere, the *smashing*, the *destruction* of " the ready-made State machinery " (which in those lands has during the years 1914–1917 achieved the same imperialist perfection as on the continent of Europe) " is the indispensable prerequisite of any genuine folk-revolution ". (*Works*, Russian edition, vol. xiv., part II., p. 327.)

In other words, as far as the imperialist countries are concerned, we must regard it as a universally applicable law of the revolutionary movement that the proletarian revolution will be effected by force, that the bourgeois State machine will have to be smashed, as an indispensable preliminary to the revolution.

No doubt in the distant future, if the proletariat has triumphed in the chief countries that are now capitalist, and if the present capitalist encirclement has given place to a socialist encirclement, it will be possible for a " peaceful " transition to be effected in certain capitalist countries where the capitalists, in view of the " unfavourable " international situation, will deem it advisable " of their own accord " to make extensive concessions to the proletariat. But this is to look far ahead, and to contemplate extremely hypothetical possibilities. As concerns the near future, there is no warrant for any such expectations.

That is why Lenin is perfectly right when he says:

> The proletarian revolution cannot take place without the forcible destruction of the bourgeois State machine and its replacement by a new machine. (*Works*, Russian edition, vol. xv., p. 453.)

c. The Soviet Power as the Form of State embodying the Dictatorship of the Proletariat

The triumph of the dictatorship of the proletariat means the crushing of the bourgeoisie, the break-up of the bourgeois State machine, and the replacement of bourgeois democracy by proletarian democracy. That is plain enough. But what are the organisations through whose instrumentality these colossal undertakings can be carried out? It can hardly be supposed that the old forms of proletarian organisation, which are rooted in the soil of bourgeois parliamentarism, will prove equal to the task. The question is, what new types of organisation will be able, not only to smash the bourgeois State machinery and clear the fragments away, not only to substitute proletarian democracy for bourgeois democracy, but also to constitute the foundations of the proletarian State authority.

The soviets are this new type of proletarian organisation.

What is the secret of the strength of the soviets, as compared with organisations of the familiar kind?

1. Soviets are the most comprehensive mass organisations of the proletariat, being the only organisations to which all the workers, without exception, belong.

2. Soviets are the only mass organisations which enrol all the oppressed and exploited, workers and peasants, soldiers and sailors, so that, through the instrumentality of the soviets, the political leadership of the mass struggle by the proletarian vanguard can be effectively realised.

3. Soviets are the most powerful instruments of the revolutionary struggle of the masses, of the political activity of the masses, of the revolt of the masses; they are instruments

competent to break the power of financial capital and its political satellites.

4. Soviets are the direct organisations of the masses, consequently the most democratic, and therefore the most influential, mass organisations; thus they are able to have a maximal effect in the way of inducing the masses to participate in the upbuilding of the new State, facilitating its administration, and, to the greatest possible extent, developing the revolutionary energy, the initiative, and the creative faculty of the masses in the struggle for the destruction of the old order and the upbuilding of the new proletarian order.

The Soviet power is the unification and transformation of the local soviets to constitute a general State organisation, the State organisation of the proletariat as the vanguard of the oppressed and exploited masses and as the ruling class. This unified State organisation is the Soviet Republic.

The essential nature of the Soviet power is this, that the most revolutionary and most comprehensive organisations of those very classes which have been oppressed by the capitalists and the landowners, have now become " the permanent and exclusive foundation of the whole State power, of the whole State apparatus "; that the masses—which even in the most democratic republics (where by law all men are equal) " are as an actual fact by manifold devices excluded from participation in political life and from the enjoyment of democratic rights and liberties "—have now been enabled to share effectively and permanently in the democratic administration of the State. (Cf. Lenin, *Works*, Russian edition, vol. xvi., p. 44.)

That is why the Soviet power is a new form of State organisation, essentially different from the old bourgeois-democratic and parliamentary form; a new type of State, adapted, not for the exploitation and oppression of the labouring masses, but for their full and final liberation from every kind of oppression and exploitation—adapted for the work of the dictatorship of the proletariat.

Lenin was right when he said that the establishment of the Soviet power " marks the end of the era of bourgeois-democratic parliamentarism, and the opening of a new chapter in universal history, the epoch of proletarian dictatorship ".

What are the main characteristics of the Soviet power?

1. The Soviet power is, of all State organisations possible while classes continue to exist, the most comprehensive and the most democratic. In actual fact, seeing that the Soviet power is the expression of the smychka,[1] the expression of the collaboration of the workers and the exploited peasants in the struggle against the exploiters, and is dependent upon the smychka in all its activities, it is, consequently, the power exercised by the majority of the population over the minority, is the State of that majority, is the embodiment of a majoritarian dictatorship.

2. The Soviet power is the most international of all the State organisations that are possible in a class society, for, by making an end of all national oppression and by being based upon the collaboration of the labouring masses of various nationalities, it facilitates the coalescence of these masses to form a federation of States.

3. The Soviet power, in virtue of its structure, facilitates the guidance of the oppressed and exploited masses by their vanguard, the proletariat, which forms the stalwart and pre-eminently class-conscious core of the soviets. " The experience of all movements of oppressed classes, the experience of the worldwide socialist movement, teaches us that the proletariat alone is competent to bring together the scattered and comparatively backward sections of the labouring and exploited population, and to lead them onward." (Lenin, *Works*, Russian edition, vol. xvi., p. 45.) The structure of the Soviet power favours the application of the knowledge gained by such experience.

4. The Soviet power, uniting legislative and executive authority into a single organ, and replacing territorial electoral areas by electoral units based on production (factories and workshops), establishes direct ties between the workers and the labouring masses, on the one hand, and the administrative apparatus on the other, and teaches the former how to use the latter.

5. The Soviet power (and only the Soviet power) is able to withdraw the army from bourgeois command, and to change it from an instrument for the oppression of the people (which is what it is under the bourgeois system) into an instrument for

[1] See note to p. 26.

DICTATORSHIP OF THE PROLETARIAT

freeing the people from the yoke of the bourgeoisie at home and abroad.

6. " The Soviet power (and only the Soviet power) can destroy, once and for all, the old bourgeois bureaucratic and judicial apparatus." (Lenin, loc. cit.)

7. The Soviet form of State (and no other form of State), admitting the mass organisations of the workers, and the exploited generally, to direct and unconditional participation in the management of public affairs, is able to pave the way for the gradual dying out of the State, which is an essential phase of the progress towards the stateless communist society of the future.

Thus the Republic of Soviets is the long sought and at length discovered political form within whose framework the economic emancipation of the proletariat, the complete triumph of socialism, will ultimately be realised.

The Commune of Paris was the germ of this political form. The Soviet power is its culmination.

That is why Lenin says:

> The Republic of Soviets of Workers', Soldiers', and Peasants' Delegates is not only a higher type of democratic institution; it is, furthermore, the only form capable of ensuring an almost painless transition to socialism. (*Works*, Russian edition, vol. xv., p. 50.)

5. THE PEASANT PROBLEM

THIS problem will be considered under four sub-heads: *a.* general statement of the problem; *b.* the peasantry at the time of the bourgeois-democratic revolution; *c.* the peasantry at the time of the proletarian revolution; *d.* the peasantry after the establishment of the Soviet power.

a. GENERAL STATEMENT OF THE PROBLEM

Some think that the essential foundation of Leninism, its starting-point, is the peasant problem, the role of the peasantry, the importance of the peasantry. This is absolutely wrong. The essential foundation of Leninism, its starting-point, is the question of the dictatorship of the proletariat, the question how that dictatorship is to be established and strengthened. The peasant problem, the question how the workers in their struggle for power are to secure the support of the peasantry, is a subsidiary one.

Even so, though subsidiary, the peasant problem is of vital importance to the proletarian revolution. It was on the eve of the revolution of 1905 that Russian Marxists began to pay serious heed to the peasant problem. At this time, the Party was faced with the immense tasks of the overthrow of tsarism and the establishment of proletarian supremacy, and the question of finding an ally in the imminent bourgeois revolution became a pressing one for the proletariat. Later, in 1917, the peasant problem in Russia became a matter of still more urgent importance, for in the days of the proletarian revolution the question of the dictatorship of the proletariat—how it was to be established and maintained, what allies the proletariat could find—had become actual. Obviously, those who are getting ready to seize and hold power, cannot afford to be indifferent about the possibility of finding powerful allies.

In this sense, the peasant problem is part of the general question of the dictatorship of the proletariat, and as such it constitutes one of the most vital elements of Leninism.

The parties affiliated to the Second International have, as a rule, been indifferent to the peasant problem, and have even been antagonistic to its discussion. This attitude has deeper reasons than the peculiarities of agrarian conditions in western Europe. The main reason is that these parties do not believe in the dictatorship of the proletariat. They are afraid of revolution, and have no wish to lead the proletariat to the conquest of power. Now, one who dreads revolution, one who does not wish to lead the proletariat to the conquest of power, is not likely to be interested in finding allies for the proletarians. To such persons, the question of revolutionary allies will seem to be subsidiary, to be up in the air. The sarcastic attitude displayed towards the peasant question by the leaders of the Second International is regarded by them as a praiseworthy one, as a sign of the genuineness of their Marxism. Really, there is no trace of Marxism in such an attitude, for, on the eve of the proletarian revolution, indifference to so important a problem as the peasant problem is tantamount to the repudiation of the dictatorship of the proletariat, and is an open betrayal of Marxism.

In virtue of the special conditions of its existence, the peasantry has certain revolutionary possibilities. Are these already exhausted? If not, is there any justification for the hope that they can be turned to account on behalf of the proletarian revolution? Is there any hope of transforming the peasantry, or, rather, its exploited majority, from a reserve of forces for the bourgeoisie (which the rural masses were in the days of the bourgeois revolutions in the West, and still are in that part of the world) into a reserve of forces for the proletariat? Can the rural masses become the allies of the urban workers?

The Leninist answer to this question is in the affirmative. The Leninist answer is that as regards the exploited majority of the peasants there exist revolutionary possibilities which can be turned to account in support of the dictatorship of the proletariat. The history of the three Russian revolutions confirms this deduction abundantly.

From these considerations we draw the practical conclusion that the labouring masses of the peasantry must be unhesitatingly supported in their fight against servitude and exploitation, against oppression and impoverishment. Of course this does not mean that the proletariat should support every peasant movement without exception. But they should support those peasant movements, those peasant struggles, which tend directly or indirectly to promote the emancipation of the proletariat, to supply motive power to the proletarian mill, to make the peasants a proletarian reserve, to transform them into allies of the urban workers.

b. The Peasantry during the Bourgeois-Democratic Revolution

For Russia, the period of the bourgeois-democratic revolution extends from the time of the first revolution (1905) up to the time of the second revolution (the February revolution—March 1917, new style). During this period the peasants were freed from the influence of the liberal bourgeoisie, were detached from the cadets (constitutional democrats), and were moving towards the proletariat, towards the bolsheviks. The history of this period is the history of a struggle to secure the allegiance of the peasantry, a struggle between the cadets, the liberal bourgeoisie, on the one hand, and the bolsheviks, the proletariat, on the other. The parliamentary period decided the upshot of this struggle. The four dumas were an object lesson for the peasants, who learned from this experience that it was no use looking to the cadets for the gifts of land and liberty. They came to realise that the tsar sided unconditionally with the great landowners, that the cadets supported the tsar, and that there was only one force upon whose aid they could count—that of the urban workers, the proletariat. The imperialist war merely confirmed the lesson of the parliamentary period, completing the severance of the peasantry from the bourgeoisie, completing the isolation of the liberal bourgeoisie. As the war went on, it became plain that it was futile to expect the tsar and his bourgeois allies to make peace. The rule of the proletariat could not have been established but for the object lesson of the parliamentary period.

Thus the alliance between the workers and the peasants was formed during the bourgeois-democratic revolution; and the rule, or rather the leadership, of the proletariat was established in the common struggle of the workers and peasants for the overthrow of tsarism, a leadership which resulted in the February revolution.

THE PEASANT PROBLEM

As every one knows, the bourgeois revolutions of the West, those of Britain, France, Germany, and Austria, followed a different course. When the bourgeois revolutions occurred in the West, the proletariat was too weak to constitute an independent political factor, and leadership in the revolution devolved upon the liberal bourgeoisie. Deliverance from serfdom came to the peasants from the bourgeoisie, and not from the proletariat, for the proletarians were then few in number and imperfectly organised. When the peasants marched to the attack on the old regime, they marched shoulder to shoulder with the bourgeoisie. The peasantry was a reserve force for the bourgeoisie. Consequently, the revolution greatly enhanced the political importance of the bourgeoisie.

In Russia, however, the effects of the bourgeois revolution were the precise opposite. Here the revolution did not strengthen the bourgeoisie as a political force, but weakened it; the revolution did not amplify the political reserves of the bourgeoisie, but deprived it of its main reserve, the peasantry. In Russia the bourgeois revolution brought to the front not the liberal bourgeoisie but the revolutionary proletariat, rallying the millions upon millions of the peasants to the support of the latter.

That is one of the reasons why the bourgeois revolution in Russia was so speedily followed by the proletarian revolution. The leadership of the proletariat blossomed into the dictatorship of the proletariat.

How are we to account for the peculiar course of the Russian revolution, which has no precedent in the history of the West?

The answer to this question is that when the bourgeois revolution occurred in Russia, the class struggle there was in a much more advanced phase of development than it was in the various western countries when the bourgeois revolution took place in these. The Russian proletariat had already become an independent political force. On the other hand the liberal bourgeoisie, greatly alarmed by the revolutionary trend of the proletariat, had itself lost all its revolutionary fire (especially after the lessons of the year 1905), and had joined forces with the tsar and the great landowners, against the revolution, against the workers and the peasants.

If we wish to understand the peculiarities of the Russian

I

bourgeois revolution, we must take the following circumstances into account :

1. On the eve of the revolution, Russian industry was concentrated to an unprecedented extent. For instance, in Russia fifty-four per cent. of all the industrial workers were employed in enterprises where the number of workers engaged was five hundred and upwards, whereas even in so highly developed a country as the United States the proportion of workers employed in such large-scale enterprises was only thirty-three per cent. It is hardly necessary to say that this fact, in conjunction with the existence of so revolutionary a party as that of the bolsheviks, sufficed to make the Russian working class the dominant political factor in the country.

2. Industrial exploitation in Russia took peculiarly horrible forms, and the tsarist police system was of an intolerably odious character. Hence every considerable strike became a political act of far-reaching importance, tending to steel the working class and to direct its activities into revolutionary channels.

3. After the revolution of 1905, the Russian bourgeoisie was in a state of decay, politically speaking. Scared by the revolutionary trend of the proletariat, and dependent upon the government in business matters (for the government was one of its chief customers), it had become a servile tool of tsarism and a directly counter-revolutionary force.

4. The vestiges of serfdom in the rural districts, where the territorial magnates were all-powerful, stimulated the revolutionary sentiments of the peasants.

5. Under the tsarist regime, all stirrings of activity among the people were crushed and the oppression of the capitalists and the landowners was intensified. This promoted the coalescence of the struggle of the workers and the struggle of the peasants into a single torrent of revolution.

6. The imperialist war gave a unified direction to these conflicting trends in Russian political life, and supplied a tremendous impetus to the revolution.

Whither, under such conditions, was the peasantry to turn? Where could they seek help against the omnipotence of the landed proprietors, against the despotism of the tsar, against the devastating war? From the bourgeois liberals? The experience of the four dumas had convinced the peasants that the bourgeois liberals were their enemies. From the essers (the social revolutionaries) ? The essers were, indeed, somewhat better than the cadets (the constitutional democrats), and their program was acceptable to the peasants—was almost a peasant program. But what could be hoped from the essers, since they themselves relied almost exclusively on the peasants for support; and were weak in the towns, the very places where the strength of the enemy was concentrated ? Where was the new force which would fear no adversaries, whether in the countryside or in the towns; which would courageously man the front ranks for the struggle against the tsar and the great landowners; which would help the peasants to break their chains, to satisfy their land hunger, to rid themselves of the war ? Was there any such force in Russia ? Yes, there was the Russian proletariat, which in 1905 had already shown its strength, its willingness to fight to the bitter end, its undaunted courage, its revolutionary impetus.

That was why the peasants, who, after turning away from the cadets, had clung to the essers for a while, at length became convinced that they must follow the virile leadership of the Russian proletariat.

Such were the factors which determined the special characteristics of the Russian bourgeois revolution.

c. THE PEASANTRY DURING THE PROLETARIAN REVOLUTION

This period extended from the February revolution (March 8, 1917, new style) to the October revolution (November 7, 1917, new style). It was thus comparatively short, but in the matter of the political enlightenment and the revolutionary education of the masses the eight months it comprises outweighed whole decades of ordinary constitutional development, for they were eight months of revolution. The main characteristic of this period was that the peasants became more and more revolutionary. They lost confidence in the essers, drew away from these, and were increasingly disposed to enter into an alliance with the proletariat, which seemed to them the one and only steadfastly revolutionary force, the only force able to bring peace to the country. The history of this period is the history of the struggle between the essers (the petty-bourgeois democracy) and the bolsheviks (the proletarian democracy) to gain a dominating influence among the peasantry. The upshot of the struggle was determined by the events of the coalition period, by the events of the Kerensky regime : the refusal of the essers and the mensheviks to confiscate the estates of the great landed proprietors ; the attempt of the same groups to continue the war ; the June offensive ; the re-establishment of capital punishment in the army ; the Korniloff rising.

Before March 1917, the fundamental question of the revolution had been the overthrow of tsarism and the breaking of the power of the great landowners. After the February revolution, when the tsar had been dethroned, and when the interminable war was ruining the economic life of the country and leading to the hopeless impoverishment of the peasants, the fundamental question of the revolution was a new one—how to end the war. The centre of gravity had shifted. " Stop the war ! " This was the universal cry throughout the exhausted country, and was voiced with especial vehemence by the rural masses.

But it was impossible to stop the war without overthrowing the provisional government ; without breaking the power of the bourgeoisie ; without defeating the essers and the mensheviks, for it was they, and they only, who wanted to " fight to a finish ". Coming down to bed rock, there was no other way of stopping the war than by getting the bourgeoisie out of the saddle.

This meant another revolution, a proletarian revolution this time. It meant a revolution that would sweep from power the extreme left wing of the imperialist bourgeoisie, would deprive the essers and the mensheviks of their authority, and would set up a new power, a proletarian power, the power of the soviets. This revolution must establish the authority of the party of the revolutionary proletariat, the party of the bolsheviks, the party pledged to resist the continuance of the imperialist war and to make a democratic peace. The majority of the peasants supported the workers' struggle for peace, and rallied to the workers' slogan " All power to the soviets ! "

There was not and could not be any other way out for the peasantry.

Thus the Kerensky regime was an admirable object lesson for the labouring masses of the peasantry, giving as it did a plain demonstration that under the rule of the essers and the mensheviks the war would continue indefinitely, and the peasants longing for land and liberty would remain unsatisfied; that the essers and the mensheviks only differed from the cadets in that the former were readier with fine speeches and delusive promises, while in reality they pursued the same imperialist policy as the cadets; that the soviets were the only power able to guide the country along the right path. The continuance of the war confirmed these deductions, hastened the coming of the proletarian revolution, led the millions upon millions of soldiers and peasants to line up behind the workers. The essers and the mensheviks were now hopelessly isolated. But for the lessons of the coalition period, it would not have been possible to set up the dictatorship of the proletariat.

Such were the factors which facilitated the transformation of the bourgeois revolution into a proletarian revolution.

That was how the proletarian dictatorship was established in Russia.

d. THE PEASANTRY AFTER THE CONSOLIDATION OF THE SOVIET POWER

During the first phase of the revolution, the main problem was the overthrow of tsarism; during the second phase, after the February revolution, the main problem was the overthrow of the bourgeoisie in order to stop the imperialist war; during the third phase, when the civil war had been brought to a successful conclusion, and when the Soviet power had been firmly established, the main problem was economic reconstruction. To foster the growth of the nationalised industries and to increase their output; to establish close ties between industry and agriculture by means of State-regulated commerce; to substitute taxation in kind for compulsory levies, with subsequent gradual reduction of taxation in kind, in order to replace it by a system of the exchange of industrial products for agricultural; to liven up commerce and encourage cooperation, inducing the peasants to participate in the latter—such were the measures of economic reorganisation recommended by Lenin as urgently necessary for the laying of the foundations of a socialist economy.

We are told that a peasant country like Russia is unequal to these tasks. Some sceptics go as far as to declare that such schemes are utopian. The peasants, they say, are nothing but peasants. A peasant is only a small-scale producer, and petty producers cannot be used as bricks wherewith to build the foundations of a socialist system of production.

These sceptics are wrong. They have failed to take certain vital factors into account. Let us consider some of these factors.

1. The peasantry of the Soviet Union cannot be compared with the peasantry of western Europe. A peasantry which has been schooled by three revolutions; which, shoulder to shoulder with the proletariat and under the leadership of the proletariat, fought the tsar and the bourgeoisie; which, thanks to the proletarian revolution, had its land-hunger satisfied and its longing for peace fulfilled; and which, in this way, has become a reserve force for the proletariat—such a peasantry is radically different from a peasantry which fought under the leadership of the liberal bourgeoisie in the days of the bourgeois revolution; which received the land from the hands of the bourgeoisie; and which, in this way, has become a reserve force for the bourgeoisie. It is evident that the peasants of the U.S.S.R., who have learned to value their political friendship with the proletariat, and have realised the importance of *political* collaboration with the workers, will not be slow to realise that it is equally important for them to collaborate in the *economic* field.

Writing about the peasantry of the West in the nineties of the last century, Engels said :

> The conquest of power by the Socialist Party is imminent. In order to achieve the conquest of power, this Party will have to extend its activities from the town into the countryside, will have to become a power in the rural districts. (*Die Bauernfrage in Frankreich und Deutschland.*)

The Russian communists have, during three revolutions, done an immense amount of work in this direction, and have thereby secured such an influence in rural life as our western comrades can hardly dream of. How can this fail to make very much easier the economic collaboration between the Russian peasants and the Russian workers?

The before-mentioned sceptics insist that rural petty proprietorship is incompatible with the establishment of a socialist economy. Well, hear what Engels has to say about the petty peasants of the West :

We are very definitely on the side of the petty peasant. We shall do everything we can to make his lot more tolerable, and to make it easier for him to join with his fellows in cooperative farming, should he so desire. If he is not yet ripe for such a decision, then we shall do our utmost to secure for him plenty of time for thinking the matter over on his little plot of land. We shall do this, not only because we regard the smallholder who farms his own land as substantially one of ourselves, but also in the direct interest of our Party. The more numerous the peasants whom we can save from slipping down into the proletariat, whom we can win over to our cause while they are still peasants, the quicker and easier will be the social transformation. It will not be to our advantage that we should have to wait for this social transformation until capitalist production has worked itself out to its fullest and final consequences; until the last independent artizan and the last smallholder have become the prey of large-scale capitalism. From the outlook of capitalist economics, the material sacrifices which must be made from the common funds of society to promote the interests of the peasants in this direction may seem to be so much money thrown away. Really, such expenditure is an excellent investment, for it will save our having to spend perhaps ten times as much, as part of the general cost of social reorganisation. In this sense, therefore, we can afford to be very generous to the peasants. (*Die Bauernfrage in Frankreich und Deutschland.*)

Now, where can Engels' theories regarding the peasantry be realised more easily or more thoroughly than in the country where the dictatorship of the proletariat has been established? It is surely obvious that only in Soviet Russia to-day are we fully entitled to " regard the smallholder who farms his own land as substantially one of ourselves ". Only there is it possible unhesitatingly to make the necessary " material sacrifices . . . from the common funds of society ", and " to be very generous to the peasants ". In Soviet Russia, these and similar measures for the benefit of the peasantry have, indeed, already been carried out. Surely no one will venture to deny that all this will react by facilitating and advancing the economic reorganisation of our country?

2. The Russian rural economy cannot be compared with the rural economy of western Europe. The latter has developed along the familiar capitalist lines, so that there is a broad distinction between the well-to-do agriculturists with large estates and big farms, on the one hand, and smallholders and the

impoverished wage-slaves of agriculture, on the other. There is a profound cleavage between these two sections of the rural population. Things are very different in Russia. In that country, thanks to the existence of the Soviet authority and thanks to the nationalisation of the principal means of production, evolution is necessarily taking a different path. In Russia, rural economy progresses by the formation of cooperatives among the millions upon millions of the poor peasants and the middle peasants, by the formation of agricultural cooperatives which are assisted by the provision of State credit upon favourable terms. In his articles on cooperation, Lenin has rightly pointed out that our rural economy must enter upon a new form of development, by involving the majority of the peasants in the work of upbuilding socialism by means of cooperatives; and by gradually permeating agriculture with the principles of collectivism—at first for the sale of agricultural produce, and in due course for agricultural production.

There have, in this connexion, been some extraordinarily interesting developments in the Russian countryside, as the outcome of the activities of the agricultural cooperatives. Under the aegis of the Selskosoyus (the central cooperative for agriculture), extensive new organisations have been formed for carrying on various branches of agriculture and dairy farming, such as the production of flax, potatoes, butter, etc. The future of these organisations is full of promise. Take, for instance, the " Flax Centre " (L'no-tsentr). This is an amalgamation of a large number of local productive cooperatives formed by peasant flax growers. The Flax Centre supplies the flax growers with seed and farming implements, buys from them all their crop, sells it wholesale in the market, guarantees to the peasants a share in the profits, and thus (through the Selskosoyus) links up peasant farming with State industry. What is the proper name for such an organisation of production? In my opinion we must speak of it as a domestic system of State-socialist production in the domain of agriculture. I use the term by analogy with the domestic system of capitalist production (home industry) in the domain of textile production, for instance, where the home workers get their raw materials and their tools from the capitalist, to whom they hand over all their product, thus becoming in actual fact semi-wage-workers (on piece-work), in their own houses. The achievements of the Selskosoyus are but some among many indications of the direction in which rural economy will develop in Russia, but the example I have given will suffice.

It is evident that the immense majority of the peasants will gladly enter upon this new path of development, in order to avoid the road leading to the formation of large capitalistic private farms; the road leading to wage slavery, poverty, and ruin.

Here are Lenin's views regarding the course of our agricultural development:

> All the means of large-scale production are in the hands of the State, and the powers of State are in the hands of the proletariat; there is the alliance of this same proletariat with the many millions of middle and poor peasants; there is the assured leadership of these peasants by the proletariat; and so on, and so forth. Have we not already, here and now, all the means for making out of the cooperatives (which, in the past, we treated as trading concerns, and which, even to-day, we have a certain justification for treating similarly under the new economic policy), out of the cooperatives alone—have we not all the means requisite for the establishment of a fully socialised society? Of course we have not yet established a socialist society, but we have all the means requisite for its establishment. (*Works*, Russian edition, vol. xviii., part II., p. 140.)

Speaking farther on about the need for giving financial and other support to cooperation, as "the new principle in the organisation of the population", and as a "new social system" under the dictatorship of the proletariat, Lenin writes:

> Every social system comes into being only in consequence of the financial support of a particular class. What need is there to speak of the hundreds upon hundreds of millions of roubles that were spent upon the inauguration of "free" capitalism? Our business now is to realise that the social system it especially behoves us to support is the cooperative system. But here I mean that we must support cooperation in the true sense of the term. It is not enough to support this or that enterprise simply because it calls itself cooperative. We have to support the cooperative enterprises in which the mass of the people effectively participate. (*Works*, Russian edition, vol. xviii., part II., p. 141.)

What do all these facts show?
They show that the sceptics are wrong.

They show that Leninists are right in regarding the labouring masses of the peasantry as a reserve force for the proletariat.

They show that the proletariat, having secured power, can and should make use of this reserve force in order to link up industry with agriculture, to hasten socialist reconstruction, and to provide the dictatorship of the proletariat with the foundation upon which alone a Socialist economic order can be built up.

6. THE NATIONAL QUESTION

The national question must be considered under two main departments: *a.* general statement of the question; *b.* the movement of the oppressed peoples to secure liberation, and the relationship of that movement to the proletarian revolution.

a. General Statement of the Question

During the last twenty years, the national question has undergone important modifications. Alike in its scope and in its character, it is very different now from what it was in the palmy days of the Second International.

At that time, when people spoke of the problem of nationality they were thinking, wholly or mainly, of a circumscribed series of questions concerning the "civilised" nations of the western world. The Irish, the Hungarians, the Poles, the Finns, the Serbs—these and a few other European peoples which did not enjoy a full right of self-determination, were of interest to the Second International. The Asiatics and the Africans who, to the number of tens or even hundreds of millions, were subject to the most outrageous forms of oppression, were for the most part beyond the horizon of vision. Whites and blacks, "civilised" and "uncivilised", belonged to different categories. The activities of the Second International in this field were limited to occasional insipid resolutions wherein the fundamentals of the position of colonial and dependent peoples were carefully glossed over. To-day, however, duplicity and half-heartedness as concerns the national question have become obsolete. Leninism has disclosed the glaring inconsistency of the old outlook. Making no distinction between whites and blacks, between Europeans and Asiatics, between the "civilised" and the "uncivilised" slaves of imperialism, Leninists link up the national question with the colonial question. Thereby the national question has been broadened out, so that it is no longer the private concern of any one nation, but is a general and international concern. It is now seen to be the worldwide problem of the deliverance of the inhabitants of colonial and dependent countries from the yoke of imperialism.

In former days, the right of self-determination was usually narrowed down to the right of " home rule ". Some of the leaders of the Second International were actually content to restrict the right of self-determination to what was called the right to have " cultural autonomy ", this meaning that an oppressed nation was to be entitled to have its own cultural institutions, but in political matters was to be subject to the dominion of the oppressing nation. Thus interpreted, the notion of self-determination, instead of being a weapon for use in the struggle against annexation, became a justification for annexation ! This confusion of terms has now been dispelled. According to Leninism, self-determination must be understood in a much wider sense, as meaning that the inhabitants of colonies and dependencies have the right of complete severance, the right to independent national existence. The Leninist interpretation makes it impossible to justify annexations on the ground that self-determination means nothing more than " home rule ". Thereupon " the right of self-determination " ceases to be a mere formula for humbugging the masses (as it undoubtedly was in the hands of the jingo socialists during the imperialist war) ; it becomes a touchstone for the detection of imperialist leanings and chauvinist machinations, and a means for the political enlightenment of the masses in the spirit of internationalism.

In former days, the question of oppressed nationalities was usually looked upon as legal and nothing more. A solemn proclamation of the " equality of national rights ", countless assertions as to the " equality of the nations ", served the turn of the parties affiliated to the Second International, and helped to veil the fact that under imperialist conditions (in which a minority of nations lives by exploiting the majority) the term " equality of the nations " is a mockery of the oppressed peoples. This bourgeois-legalist conception of the national question is now discredited. Leninism has brought the question down from the altitudes of high-flown declarations to mother earth ; has shown that talk about the " equality of the nations " is false and empty declamation unless it is backed up by deeds, unless the proletarian parties give direct support to the oppressed nationalities in their struggle for freedom. Thus the problem of the oppressed nationalities has become the problem of how much genuine and effective help can be given them in their struggle against imperialism, their fight for real national independence, for existence as separate political entities.

Reformists regarded the national question as a problem standing by itself, unrelated to the general problem of the power of capital, that of the oppression exercised by imperialism, that of the proletarian revolution. They tacitly assumed that the European proletariat could win the victory without forming direct ties with the movement for national liberation in the colonies, that the national-colonial question would " solve itself ", apart from the proletarian revolution, apart from the fight against imperialism. This antirevolutionary outlook is now discredited. The imperialist war and the Russian revolution have confirmed the Leninist view that the national problem can only be solved in the arena of the proletarian revolution, and when it is linked up with that revolution ; that for the revolution in the western world the path to victory lies by way of a revolutionary alliance with the struggle of the colonial and dependent nationalities to throw off the yoke of imperialism. The national question is part of the general question of the proletarian revolution, part of the question of the dictatorship of the proletariat.

The problem must be stated thus : Are the revolutionary possibilities of the revolutionary movement for the liberation of oppressed countries already exhausted ; if they are not exhausted, is there any chance of turning these possibilities to account on behalf of the proletarian revolution, is there any chance of transforming the colonial and dependent lands from reserves of force for the bourgeoisie into reserves of force for the proletariat ; can the colonial and dependent nationalities become the allies of the revolutionary proletariat ?

The Leninist answer to these questions is that the nationalist movements for the freeing of oppressed countries from the imperialist yoke certainly contain unexhausted revolutionary possibilities ; that these possibilities can be utilised for the overthrow of our common enemy, for the destruction of imperialism. The mechanism of imperialist development, that of the imperialist war, and that of the Russian revolution, have fully confirmed the conclusions of Leninism in this respect.

From these considerations it follows that the proletariat must decisively and actively support the nationalist movements for the liberation of the oppressed and dependent peoples.

Of course this does not mean that the proletariat ought to support any and every nationalist movement, at all times and in all places, no matter what the concrete conditions may be. The proletariat should support nationalist movements which tend to weaken and subvert imperialism, not those which tend to strengthen and maintain it. In certain oppressed countries, nationalist movements may run counter to the general interests of the proletarian movement. Obviously, there can be no question of our helping such movements as these. The problem of national rights does not stand alone; it is part of the general problem of the proletarian revolution, is subordinate thereto, and can only be considered by the proletariat from that angle. In the forties of the last century, Marx supported the Polish nationalist movement and the Hungarian nationalist movement, while he opposed the Czech nationalist movement and the Yugoslav nationalist movement. Why this difference? The reason was that in those days the Czechs and the Southern Slavs were " reactionary peoples ", were " outposts of Russian absolutism ", whereas the Poles and the Hungarians were " revolutionary peoples ", fighting against absolutism. At that epoch, to support the Czech nationalist movement and the Yugoslav nationalist movement would have been to give indirect support to tsarism, which was then the most dangerous enemy of the revolutionary movement in Europe.

Lenin writes :

> The various demands of democracy, and among others the right of self-determination, have no absolute value, but are parts of the worldwide democratic (nowadays, socialist) movement. In concrete instances, the interests of the part may conflict with the interests of the whole. If that is so, we must repudiate the part. (*Works*, Russian edition, vol. xix., pp. 199-200.)

These words apply to the various nationalist movements. Contemplated, not from the outlook of formal, abstract right, but realistically, and with an eye to the interests of the revolutionary movement as a whole, a nationalist movement may be reactionary.

In like manner, though most of the nationalist movements undoubtedly have a revolutionary character, this is no less relative and specific than is the reactionary character of certain others. Under the imperialist yoke, a nationalist movement may have a revolutionary trend even though it does not embody any proletarian elements, even though its program is neither revolutionary nor republican, and even though the movement lacks a democratic foundation. Objectively considered, the struggle of the amir of Afghanistan to secure the independence of his country is a revolutionary struggle, despite the fact that the amir and his adherents are monarchists and not republicans; for the movement on behalf of the independence of Afghanistan tends to weaken, disintegrate, and undermine imperialism. On the other hand, during the imperialist war, the activities of such doughty democrats, " socialists ", " revolutionaries ", and republicans as Kerensky and Tseretelli, Renaudel and Scheidemann, Chernoff and Dan, Henderson and Clynes, were reactionary in trend, for the upshot of their doings was to mask the workings of imperialism, to promote an imperialist victory. By parity of reasoning, we see that the fight of Egyptian business men and bourgeois intellectuals on behalf of the independence of Egypt is, objectively considered, revolutionary, although the leaders of the Egyptian nationalist movement are bourgeois by birth and occupation, and although they are antisocialists. On the other hand, the determination of the British labour government to maintain the dependence of Egypt is a reactionary determination, although the members of this government are proletarian by birth and calling, and although they declare themselves socialists. I need merely allude in passing to the nationalist movement in much larger colonial and dependent countries, such as Hindostan and China, whose every step towards national liberation is revolutionary, even if it infringes the canons of formal democracy—for every such step on the part of one of these countries inflicts a smashing blow on imperialism.

Lenin was right when he said that the nationalist movements of oppressed countries must be considered, not from the outlook of formal democracy, but from the outlook upon their actual results in the general struggle against imperialism; when he said that they must be regarded, " not in isolation, but as parts of the world process ".

b. THE MOVEMENT OF THE OPPRESSED PEOPLES TO SECURE LIBERATION, AND THE RELATIONSHIP OF THAT MOVEMENT TO THE PROLETARIAN REVOLUTION

In order to solve the national problem, Leninism sets out from the following propositions :

1. The world is divided into two camps : the camp of the civilised nations, which comprise no more than a small minority, though they control financial capital and exploit the overwhelming majority of the inhabitants of the globe ; and the camp of the oppressed and exploited peoples in colonial and dependent lands, far more numerous than their exploiters.

2. Colonial and dependent countries, oppressed and exploited by financial capital, form the main field from which imperialism draws its reserve forces.

3. Only by means of a revolutionary struggle against imperialism can the peoples of dependent and colonial lands hope to free themselves from oppression and exploitation.

4. The chief colonial and dependent countries have already entered into the movement for national liberation, and this cannot fail to bring about a crisis in world capitalism.

5. The proletarian movement in advanced countries and the nationalist movement for the liberation of the peoples of colonial and dependent lands being both revolutionary movements, or two different aspects of the same great revolutionary movement, it will be to their interest to unite, to form a united front against the common enemy—imperialism.

6. The victory of the working class in advanced countries and the liberation of oppressed nationalities from the imperialist yoke can only be effected by the formation and consolidation of a united revolutionary front.

7. The formation of this united revolutionary front is impossible unless the proletariat of the oppressor nations gives direct and effective support to the endeavours of the oppressed nations to free themselves from the yoke of imperialism ; and the proletariat of an oppressor nation must do this regardless of the fact that the imperialism of " its own country " functions as oppressor, remembering that (as Marx said) " a people which oppresses another people cannot itself be free ".

THE NATIONAL QUESTION

8. This support involves the defence, the effective realisation, of the principle that the oppressed nationalities are entitled to break away from the oppressor nationalities, and to form themselves into independent political entities.

9. Only through the effective realisation of this principle will it be possible for the nations to combine and to collaborate in a unified worldwide economic system, which is essential as the material foundation for the victory of socialism.

10. This union must be voluntary, must be based on mutual confidence and on brotherly relationships among the peoples.

There are, therefore, two distinct trends in the nationalist movements. First of all, there is the trend towards political emancipation from imperialist fetters and towards the formation of independent national States, a trend determined by the reaction against imperialist oppression and colonial exploitation. Secondly, there is the trend towards the economic union of the nations, a trend determined by the formation of a world market and the organisation of a worldwide economy.

Compare this statement with what Lenin wrote:

> In the course of the development of capitalism, two historical trends are manifest in the national question. First of all, we see an awakening of national life and of nationalist movements, a struggle against all forms of national oppression, the creation of national States. Secondly, we see the formation and the strengthening of all sorts of ties between the nations; the breaking down of the barriers that separate them; the establishment of international unity in capitalism, in economic and political life, in the field of science, etc. Both these trends are universal laws of capitalism. The former is dominant in the early days of capitalism. The latter is characteristic of capitalist maturity, of the days when the transition of capitalist society into socialist society is at hand. (*Works*, Russian edition, vol. xix., p. 46.)

For imperialism, these two trends represent irreconcilable contradictions. Imperialism cannot exist without the exploitation of the colonies, without combining them by force into a " unified whole ". It can only bring the nations together by annexations, by a policy of grab. Otherwise, imperialism is unthinkable.

For communism, on the other hand, the trends are but two aspects of one great movement, or two phases of a single process

—the emancipation of the peoples which are under the imperialist yoke. Communists are well aware that the drawing together of the nations into a worldwide economic system can only be achieved upon a foundation of mutual confidence and voluntary agreement; and they know that the path along which the peoples will enter into a voluntary union must lead in the first instance by way of the severance of the colonies from the " unified whole " into which they have been forcibly aggregated by the imperialists— by way of the interim transformation of the colonies into independent political entities.

Hence the need for a stubborn, incessant, effective struggle against the jingoism of the so-called socialists in the ruling nations (Britain, France, the United States, Italy, Japan, etc.), who, in each country, are unwilling to put up a genuine fight against " their own " imperialist government, or to support attempts of the exploited and oppressed in " their own " colonies to throw off the imperialist yoke and to establish independent States.

Without such a struggle, it is impossible to educate the working class of the ruling nations in the spirit of true internationalism, to bring the workers of the oppressor nations into close touch with the labouring masses of the colonies and dependencies, to diffuse the mentality of the proletarian revolution. The Russian revolution would not have been victorious, Kolchak and Denikin would not have been defeated, unless the Russian proletariat had had the sympathy and support of the oppressed peoples throughout the area which was formerly the Russian empire. But to secure their sympathy and support, the Russian proletariat had, first of all, to break the chains that had been imposed on these peoples by Russian imperialism, to free them from the tsarist yoke. Otherwise it would have been impossible to consolidate the Soviet power, to inculcate true internationalism, to create that remarkable organisation for the collaboration of the peoples which is known as the Union of Socialist Soviet Republics and is the forerunner of the coming union of the nations to form a worldwide economy.

Hence the need for a struggle against the narrowness, the particularism, of those socialists in oppressed lands who cannot see beyond the boundaries of the parish in which they were born, and therefore fail to perceive the intimate connexion between

THE NATIONAL QUESTION

the movement for the liberation of their own country and the proletarian movement in the country by which it is ruled.

Without such a struggle, the proletariat of the oppressed nationality cannot pursue an independent policy, cannot be solidarised with the proletariat of the ruling country for the struggle against the common enemy, for the overthrow of imperialism; without such a struggle, internationalism is impossible.

Only by such a struggle can we educate the labouring masses both of the dominant and of the oppressed nations in the spirit of revolutionary internationalism.

Let us read what Lenin has to say about the twofold task awaiting the communists, who must diffuse among the workers this spirit of internationalism—an educational task:

> Can this education be one and the same in the great nations which oppress, and in the small nations which are oppressed; in the nations which annex, and in the nations which are annexed?
>
> Obviously not! They are marching towards the same goal; towards equal rights, a close approximation of all the nations, ultimate fusion. But they must reach that goal by different roads, just as when we draw a line from the side of a page towards the middle we must move the point of the pencil towards the right from the left-hand margin and towards the left from the right-hand margin. If a socialist who belongs to a great, oppressing, annexing nation, an advocate of the fusion of the peoples, forgets (were it but for a moment) that " his " Nicholas II., " his " William II., " his " George V., or " his " Poincaré, is likewise a fusionist (by way of annexation)—Nicholas II. in favour of " fusion " with Galicia; William II. in favour of " fusion " with Belgium; and so on—then this socialist will be an absurd doctrinaire in the field of theory, and an understrapper to imperialism in the field of practice.
>
> The centre of gravity of the internationalist education of the workers in oppressing countries must take the form of insisting upon the right of oppressed countries to secede and set up for themselves. Short of this, there is no internationalism. We can and should regard as an imperialist and a scoundrel every socialist in an oppressing country who fails to carry on propaganda of this kind. The right to secede is axiomatic, even though, before the coming of socialism, there may not be more than one case in a thousand where the right can be enforced.
>
> On the other hand, the socialist of a small and oppressed nation must mainly stress the second part of our general formula—the " voluntary union " of the nations. Without doing violence

to his obligations as an internationalist, he may (according to circumstances) either advocate the political independence of his nation, or favour its inclusion in some neighbouring State. In all cases, however, he should fight particularism, exclusiveness, a narrow conception of nationalism ; should insist upon the importance of wider issues ; should favour the subordination of special interests to general interests.

Persons who have not troubled to fathom these questions are apt to think it " contradictory " that the socialists of oppressing nations should make the " right of secession " their watchword, whereas the socialists of oppressed nations raise the slogan of the " right of fusion ". Brief reflection will, however, show that there is no other road towards internationalism and the coalescence of the nations than the one pointed out in our thesis. (*Works*, Russian edition, vol. xix., pp. 203-205.)

7. STRATEGY AND TACTICS

THIS topic will be considered under six heads : *a.* strategy and tactics as the science of the leadership of the proletarian class struggle ; *b.* strategy and the phases of the revolution ; *c.* tactics and the ebb and flow of the movement ; *d.* strategical leadership ; *e.* tactical leadership ; *f.* reformism and revolutionism.

a. STRATEGY AND TACTICS AS THE SCIENCE OF THE LEADERSHIP OF THE PROLETARIAN CLASS STRUGGLE

The period during which the Second International was dominant was, mainly, one when the proletarian forces were being marshalled and instructed in a comparatively tranquil time. The class struggle was being carried on, for the most part, within the walls of parliament. Great clashes between the contending classes, the preparation of the proletariat for revolutionary campaigns, methods of establishing the dictatorship of the proletariat—were not topics of discussion. The task of leadership was limited to the utilisation of all the available constitutional and lawful methods for marshalling and training the proletarian army, within the confines of a system where the proletariat was (and was presumably destined to remain) nothing more than the electoral foundation of a parliamentary opposition. Obviously, during this period, and while such a conception of the mission of the proletariat was dominant, there could be no question of systematising proletarian strategy or elaborating proletarian tactics ; there could be nothing more than detached thoughts about these matters, nothing more than isolated fragments of strategy and tactics.

The fatal error of the Second International was, not that for a time it concentrated its energies upon the development of the parliamentary form of the class struggle, but that it overestimated the importance of parliamentarism, and regarded parliamentarism as a practically exclusive and all-sufficient method—with the result that, when the period of open revolutionary conflicts began, and when the question of extraparliamentary forms of struggle became urgent, the parties affiliated to the Second International jibbed, refused the leap, would not face the new tasks.

Not until the next phase, the phase of direct action, of proletarian revolution, when the overthrow of the bourgeoisie had become a question of practical politics, did the problem of finding reserves for the proletarian army (strategy) become actual, and the problem of the organisation of that army whether on the parliamentary or on the extraparliamentary field (tactics) clearly demand a solution. Not until this phase had begun, could proletarian strategy be systematised and proletarian tactics be elaborated.

It was now that Lenin disinterred Marx's and Engels' masterly ideas on strategy and tactics, ideas which the opportunists of the Second International had buried out of sight. Lenin was not content with a mere reiteration of his predecessors' words. He developed what they had said, added fresh thoughts of his own, and unified the whole into a system of rules and precepts for the conduct of the proletarian class war. Thus Lenin's booklets, *What is to be done?*, *Two Tactics*, *Imperialism*, *The State and Revolution*, *The Proletarian Revolution and Kautsky the Renegade*, and *Left-Wing Communism, an Infantile Disorder*, are invaluable contributions to the Marxist revolutionary arsenal. Leninist strategy and tactics are the science of the leadership of the revolutionary proletarian struggle.

b. STRATEGY AND THE PHASES OF THE REVOLUTION

Strategy is the determination of the direction of the main proletarian onslaught in this or that phase of the revolution; the elaboration of the best plan for the distribution of the revolutionary forces (the main reserves and the secondary reserves), and the endeavour to carry out this plan during the whole period of this or that phase of the revolution.

The Russian revolution passed through its first phase from 1903 to the beginning of March 1917 (new style); its second phase between March 1917 and the beginning of November 1917; to enter upon its third phase with the October (November) revolution of that year. Each of these three phases had its appropriate strategy.

STRATEGY AND TACTICS

First Phase, from 1903 to the February (March) revolution in 1917.

Aim : the overthrow of tsarism, and the abolition of the last vestiges of feudalism.

Essential force of the revolution : the proletariat.

First reserve : the peasantry.

Chief line of attack : isolation of the bourgeois liberals (monarchists), who were trying to secure the support of the peasantry and to arrest the progress of the revolution by coming to terms with tsarism.

Plan for the distribution of the revolutionary forces : an alliance between the workers and the peasants.

Consider, in this connexion, Lenin's words :

> The proletariat must push the democratic revolution through to an end, inducing the mass of the peasantry to join forces with the workers, in order to break the power of the autocracy and to overcome the vacillations of the bourgeoisie. (*Works*, Russian edition, vol. vi., p. 371.)

Second Phase, 1917, from the February (March) revolution to the October (November) revolution.

Aim : the overthrow of imperialism in Russia and the withdrawal from participation in the imperialist war.

Essential force of the revolution : the proletariat.

First reserve : the poorer peasants.

Contingent reserve : the proletariat of neighbouring countries.

Favouring circumstances : the protraction of the war and the crisis of imperialism.

Chief line of attack : isolation of the petty-bourgeois democrats (the mensheviks and the essers), who were trying to win over the labouring masses of the peasants and to stop the revolution by coming to terms with imperialism.

Plan for the distribution of the revolutionary forces : an alliance between the proletariat and the poorest peasants.

Consider, in this connexion, Lenin's words :

> The proletariat must push the socialist revolution through to an end, inducing the mass of the semi-proletarian elements to join forces with the proletariat, in order to break the power of the bourgeoisie and to overcome the vacillations of the peasantry and the petty bourgeoisie. (*Works*, Russian edition, vol. vi., p. 371.)

Third Phase, after the October (November) revolution.

Aim : the consolidation of the dictatorship of the proletariat in one country, where it could be used as a fulcrum for the overthrow of imperialism in all countries. This revolution transcends the limits of one country, and begins the epoch of the world revolution.

Essential force of the revolution : the dictatorship of the proletariat in one country, and the revolutionary movement of the proletariat in all countries.

Chief reserves : the semi-proletarian and petty-bourgeois masses in the highly developed countries, the nationalist (liberationist) movements in colonial and dependent lands.

Chief line of attack : isolation of the petty-bourgeois democracy ; isolation of the parties affiliated to the Second International, whose policy it is to come to terms with imperialism.

Plan for the distribution of the revolutionary forces : an alliance between the proletarian revolution and the nationalist (liberationist) movements in colonial and dependent lands.

Strategy is concerned with the essential forces of the revolution and with its reserves. It changes as the revolution moves on from one phase to the next, but remains unchanged in its principles throughout any one phase.

c. Tactics and the Ebb and Flow of the Movement

Tactic is the determination of the line to be taken by the proletariat during a comparatively short period of the ebb or flow of the movement, of advance or retreat of the revolution ; the maintenance of this line by the substitution of new forms of struggle and organisation for those that have become out of date, or by the discovery of new watchwords, or by a combination of new methods with old, etc. Whereas strategy is concerned with such wide purposes as the winning of the war against tsarism or the bourgeoisie, tactic has a narrower aim. Tactic is concerned, not with the war as a whole, but with the fighting of this or that campaign, with the gaining of this or that victory which may be essential during a particular period of the general revolutionary advance or withdrawal. Tactics are thus parts of strategy, and subordinate thereto.

Tactics vary according as the movement is flowing or ebbing.

During the first phase of the Russian revolution, for instance, between 1903 and the revolution of February (March) 1917, there was no change in general strategical plan, though there were several changes in tactics.

From 1903 to 1905, a period of general advance, the Party tactic took the form of an offensive. There were local strikes, directed towards political ends; political demonstrations; a political general strike; boycott of the duma; risings; revolutionary war-cries—such were the changing forms of struggle, which demanded correspondingly different forms of organisation. Factory and workshop committees, committees of revolutionary peasants, strike committees, soviets of workers' deputies, a workers' party carrying on more or less open agitation—such were the forms of organisation during this period.

From 1907 to 1912, the Party tactic had to be one of withdrawal, for the revolutionary movement was in a declining phase, a phase of ebb. The forms of organisation, too, had to be appropriately modified: participation in the duma, instead of boycott of the duma; parliamentary action, instead of direct action; local and partial strikes for purely industrial ends, instead of the general strike for political ends; absolute inaction, even, at times. Of course during this period the Party had to work underground; revolutionary mass organisations had to be replaced by educational and cultural societies, cooperatives, friendly societies, and other " legal and constitutional " bodies.

In like manner during the second phase of the revolution, and yet again during the third phase, there were frequent changes in tactics, whilst—throughout each phase—there was no change in strategy.

Tactics are concerned with the methods of proletarian struggle and the forms of proletarian organisation, and with the modifications and combinations of these. That is why, in a given phase of the revolution, tactics can change repeatedly, according as the revolutionary tide is ebbing or flowing, according as the revolutionary movement is advancing or receding.

d. Strategical Leadership

The reserve forces of the revolution are of two kinds, direct and indirect.

Direct Reserves :
1. The peasantry and the intermediate strata of the population of one's own country.
2. The proletariat of neighbouring countries.
3. The revolutionary movement in colonial and dependent countries.
4. The conquests and achievements of the dictatorship of the proletariat. The proletariat may temporarily renounce one of these conquests or achievements, in order to buy off a powerful adversary or secure a respite.

Indirect Reserves :
1. Antagonisms and conflicts between non-proletarian classes of one's own country, which the proletariat can turn to account in order to weaken an adversary or strengthen its own reserves.
2. Antagonisms, conflicts, and wars (imperialist war, for instance) between capitalist States hostile to the proletarian State, disputes which the proletariat can turn to account for its own purposes—maybe an offensive, maybe manoeuvres to cover an enforced retreat.

The importance of the direct reserves is self-evident. The importance of the indirect reserves may be less obvious, though they are sometimes of very great moment to the cause of the revolution. Incontestable, for example, is the great importance of the quarrel which took place, during and after the first revolution, between the petty-bourgeois democrats (the essers) and the monarchist bourgeois liberals (the cadets). Unquestionably, this dispute helped to free the peasants from bourgeois influences. Even more obvious is the enormous importance of the war to the death among the chief groups of imperialists at the time of the October revolution. Their quarrels made it impossible for them to concentrate their forces against the young Soviet power, which was thus enabled to organise its strength, consolidate its position, and prepare to crush Kolchak and Denikin. To-day, when the antagonisms between the imperialist groups are becoming intensified to a degree which will make a new war inevitable, these indirect reserves grow ever more important to the proletariat.

The function of strategy consists in the right application and utilisation of the various reserves in such a way as to ensure that, during a particular phase of the revolution, there shall be an effective advance towards the goal of the revolution in that phase.

By what methods can this be achieved ?

1. The main forces of the revolution must, at the decisive moment, be concentrated for an attack on the enemy's most vulnerable spot, at a moment when conditions are ripe for revolution, when a general offensive can go ahead with full steam, when armed insurrection is imminent, and when the calling of all the reserves into the fighting line is an indispensable preliminary to success. Consider, for example, the strategy from April to October (old style) 1917. Unquestionably, throughout this period the enemy's most vulnerable point was the war. The matter was fundamental, and it was one which made it possible for the Party to gather the whole population round the proletarian vanguard. At this time, therefore, the Party strategy was, having schooled the vanguard at street-corner meetings and in manifestations and demonstrations, to bring the reserves into action through the instrumentality of the Soviets at the rear and the soldiers' committees on the imperialist fighting front. The course of the revolution showed that this strategy was sound.

Lenin, paraphrasing the well-known utterances of Marx and Engels concerning insurrection, writes as follows about this strategical utilisation of the forces of the revolution :

> Never play with insurrection ; but, having begun one, make up your mind to go through with it to the end. At the right place, and when the time is ripe, assemble forces greatly outnumbering those of the enemy—for otherwise the latter, better prepared and better organised, will annihilate the insurgents. Once the rising has begun, it is essential to act with the utmost resoluteness, and, without fail and unconditionally, to assume the offensive. " A defensive attitude is fatal to an armed rising." We must try to take the enemy by surprise, to seize the moment when his forces are dispersed. We must endeavour to gain some success, however small, day by day (hour by hour, even, if we are operating in a town), so that at all costs we may maintain a superior " morale ". (*Works*, Russian edition, vol. xiv., part II., p. 270.)

2. The moment for the decisive blow, for raising the standard of revolt, must be carefully chosen. This must be when matters have reached a climax, when the vanguard is ready to fight to the bitter end, when the reserves will not hesitate to rally to the support of the vanguard, and when disorder is paramount in the ranks of the enemy. In this connexion, Lenin writes :

> We may consider that the time is ripe for the decisive struggle : when all the class forces arrayed against us are in a state of confusion, are sufficiently embroiled one with another, have been sufficiently weakened in combats for which their strength is inadequate ; when all the vacillating, unsteady, unstable intermediate elements (the petty bourgeoisie, the petty-bourgeois democracy, in contradistinction to the bourgeoisie) have exposed themselves enough before the people, have made a sufficient parade of their utter bankruptcy; when there has arisen and spread widely among the proletariat a strong feeling in favour of decisive and unhesitatingly bold revolutionary action against the bourgeoisie. Then the time is ripe for revolution. Then, if we have kept good account of the before-mentioned conditions, and have chosen our moment well, our victory is assured. (*Works*, Russian edition, vol. xvii., pp. 180–181.)

The conduct of the October revolution may be regarded as a model for such strategy.

A failure to study the conditions carefully may lead to either of two serious blunders. The Party may lag behind the movement ; or it may run on far in advance of the movement, thus risking a setback. As an example of the injudicious choice of the moment may be mentioned the desire of some of the comrades to begin a rising in August 1917 by breaking up the Democratic Conference—at a time when the soviets were still in a vacillating mood, when the soldiers at the front had not yet made up their minds, and before the reserve forces were ready and willing to support the vanguard.

3. Once a line of action has been adopted, it must be followed unerringly to the goal, regardless of hindrances and complications. This is necessary to ensure that the vanguard shall not lose sight of the essential aim of the struggle, and that the masses shall not stray into devious paths, but shall march straight forward towards the goal and consolidate their forces in support of the vanguard. Unless this condition is fulfilled, there will be serious danger that the movement may get (as sailors say of

a ship) off its course. As an example I may mention the mistake made immediately after the Democratic Conference, when our Party decided to participate in the Constituent Assembly. The Party apparently forgot for the moment that the Constituent Assembly embodied an attempt by the bourgeoisie to switch the country off the road of the soviets and on to the road of bourgeois parliamentarism. It forgot that participation in the Constituent Assembly could not fail to confuse the issues, to mislead the workers and peasants who were carrying on a revolutionary campaign under the watchword " All power to the Soviets ". This mistake was rectified when the bolsheviks decided to withdraw from the Constituent Assembly.

4. The reserves must be handled in such a way as to safeguard an orderly retreat should the enemy be very powerful, should a withdrawal be inevitable, should it be obviously undesirable to accept the enemy's offer of battle, should retreat be the only way whereby (in the circumstances) the vanguard can escape destruction and keep the reserves at its disposal. In this connexion, Lenin writes :

> Revolutionary parties must go on learning. They have learned how to attack. Now it is time for them to realise that this knowledge must be supplemented by acquiring a knowledge of how best to retreat. We have got to understand (and a revolutionary class learns this by bitter experience) that victory can only be won by those who have learned the proper method both of advance and of retreat. (*Works*, Russian edition, vol. xvii., p. 121.)

The object of such strategy is to gain time, to scatter the forces of the enemy while consolidating our own for a future advance.

The peace of Brest-Litovsk is a model instance of such strategy. This peace enabled the Party to gain time, to take advantage of the dissensions in the imperialist camp, to disintegrate the enemy forces, to retain the support of the peasants, and to gather strength for an attack on Kolchak and Denikin. In the days of Brest-Litovsk, Lenin wrote :

> By concluding a separate peace, we free ourselves as far as is possible at the present moment from both the contending imperialist groups, turning their mutual hostilities to our own account, taking advantage of the state of warfare between them which prevents their joining forces against us, thus freeing ourselves for a time so that we can further and consolidate the socialist revolution. (*Works*, Russian edition, vol. xv., pp. 68-69.)

Three years after the peace of Brest-Litovsk, Lenin wrote :

> Even the dullest have now come to see that the peace of Brest-Litovsk was a concession which strengthend us while it disintegrated the forces of international imperialism. (*Works*, Russian edition, vol. xviii., part I., p. 355.)

e. TACTICAL LEADERSHIP

Tactical leadership is a part of strategical leadership, subordinated to the tasks and needs of the latter. Its aim is to ensure the control of all the forms of proletarian struggle and organisation, and their right utilisation in such a way that in the given situation the best possible results shall be obtained for the promotion of the strategical victory.

The main conditions requisite for the satisfactory utilisation of all the forms of proletarian organisation and struggle are as follows :

1. We must bring to the front those forms of struggle and organisation which are best suited to the condition of the movement at the time, to its ebb or its flow as the case may be ; those which are best fitted to mobilise the masses and to distribute them conveniently along the revolutionary front.

It does not suffice that the vanguard should realise the impossibility of maintaining the old order and the need for its overthrow. The masses, likewise, the millionfold masses, must come to understand this need, and must show themselves ready and willing to rally to the support of the vanguard. But such a thoughtful insight can only be acquired by the masses in the school of personal experience. Our task is to see that the masses shall be provided with opportunities for the acquirement of such an understanding, that they shall be brought to realise the inevitability of the overthrow of the old order, that we shall put forward methods of struggle and forms of organisation which shall permit the masses to learn from experience the truth and correctness of our revolutionary watchwords.

The vanguard would have become severed from the working class, and the latter would have lost touch with the masses, had not the bolsheviks decided to take part in the duma, to carry on the agitation within its walls, to concentrate their forces on parliamentary action in order to show the masses the utter futility of the duma, the falseness of the cadets' promises, the impossibility of a compromise with tsardom, and the need for an alliance between the peasantry and the working class. Had the masses lacked this experience during the period when the duma functioned, it would have been impossible to unmask the cadets, and to secure the leadership in the hands of the proletariat.

The tactics of the otzovists ("abstentionists"), who demanded the withdrawal of the social-democratic fraction from the duma, thereby repudiating parliamentary action, gave rise to the danger of detaching the vanguard from its countless reserves.

Again, the vanguard would have alienated itself from the working class, and the latter would have forfeited its influence on the peasants and the soldiers, if the Party had followed the lead of the left-wing communists who advocated a rising in April 1917, before the mensheviks and the social revolutionaries had discredited themselves in the eyes of the workers by showing themselves to be partisans of the war and of imperialism, before the masses had learned to their sorrow how lying were the utterances of menshevik and social revolutionary alike concerning peace, land, and liberty. Had the masses been deprived of the experience of the Kerensky regime, the mensheviks and the essers would not have become isolated from the masses, and the establishment of the proletarian dictatorship would have been impossible. The only correct tactic in the circumstances was to lay bare the errors of the petty-bourgeois parties and to carry on an open struggle within the soviets.

The tactics of the left-wing communists threatened to deprive the Party of its position as leader of the proletarian revolution, and to make it a mere handful of futile conspirators having no foothold in reality.

Lenin writes in his *Left-Wing Communism, an Infantile Disorder* :

> A vanguard alone will not lead to victory. To hurl the vanguard into the fray before the masses are ready to support it, or, at least, are willing to remain neutral, would not only be the height of folly but a crime. Agitation and propaganda do not suffice to bring the masses to a suitable frame of mind. They need also to be schooled by political experience. This is the law which lies at the root of all far-reaching revolutions, a law which has been confirmed in a striking manner both in Russia and in Germany.

The Russian masses, uneducated, often illiterate, and the German masses, whose education and culture are at such an incomparably higher level, had each in turn to learn by bitter experience all the powerlessness, the listlessness, the helplessness, the servility of the governments carried on by the leaders of the Second International —henchmen of the bourgeoisie. The masses had to learn by experience that either of two dictatorships was inevitable : the dictatorship of the ultra-reactionaries (such as Korniloff in Russia and Kapp and Co. in Germany), or the dictatorship of the proletariat as a definite step on the road to communism. (*Works*, Russian edition, vol. xvii., p. 173.)

2. We must find just that one particular link in the chain of events, the possession of which at a given moment will render us masters of the whole chain, and will place us in a position to prepare for a strategical victory.

From among all the tasks confronting the Party we have to choose the one which is of the most immediate importance, the one whose accomplishment constitutes the nodal point of our endeavours, the one whose execution will lead to the carrying out of all the other tasks.

Let us consider this statement in the light of two examples, the first taken from the history of the more remote past (the period when we were building up the Party), and the second culled from the history of very recent times (the period of the New Economic Policy).

During the period when we were upbuilding the Party; when there were innumerable circles, clubs, and organisations having no bonds one with the other; when the Party was split from top to bottom by the circle system of organisation, and by the fact that every comrade did what was right in his own eyes; when confused thinking was the order of the day—during this period, the most important link to grasp, the most important item in the chain of many links and many tasks, was to launch a clandestine newspaper which would circulate throughout the whole of Russia. Why was this such an urgent need? Because a solid kernel of Party organisation could not be created in any other way. Only by issuing such a paper could the innumerable circles and other organisations be united to form a compact whole, could the way be prepared for theoretical and tactical unity; and thus only could the foundations be laid whereon an effective Party could be built up.

In the period of transition from war to economic reconstruction, when industry was stagnant on account of the general disorganisation, when agriculture was suffering from the dearth of industrial commodities, and when the welding together of the State industries with the peasant economy was an essential condition for the successful upbuilding of socialism—in this period the most important link in the chain of events, the most important task, is the development of commerce. Why? Because, under the conditions created by Nep, the only thing which can form an intimate bond between industry and agriculture is commerce; because every commodity that does not find a market is, under the system of Nep, a weapon threatening industry with extinction; because industry cannot grow unless the products of industry find a market; because it is only when we have secured a strong foothold in the domain of commerce, when we have made ourselves masters in the realm of commerce, when we have got a permanent hold on this link of the chain, that we shall be able to create the bond between industry and agriculture, be able to carry out other tasks successfully, and be able to lay the foundations of a socialist economic order.

Lenin, in his essay on *The Significance of Gold*, tells us:

> To be a revolutionist, to be a socialist or communist sympathiser, is not enough. It behoves us to find, at any given moment, that particular link in the chain to which we can cling in order to keep the whole chain together, and subsequently to pass on to the next link. . . . For the nonce, the particular link is the stimulation of commerce on the home market, and its effective control and guidance by the State. Commerce is a "link" in the chain of historical events, in the transitional forms of our socialist construction; and we must cling to this link for dear life. (*Works*, Russian edition, vol. xviii., part I., p. 412.)

f. Reformism and Revolutionism

In what way do revolutionary tactics differ from reformist tactics?

There are some who imagine that Leninism is against all reform, compromise, and agreements of any kind with the enemy. This is utterly wrongheaded. The bolsheviks know just as well as any one else that "the smallest contributions will be thankfully received"! They realise that, in certain circumstances, both reforms in general and compromises and agreements in particular are necessary and useful. Here we have Lenin's testimony on the subject :

> To wage war for the overthrow of the international bourgeoisie, a war which is a hundred times more difficult, more prolonged, more complicated, than the most bloodthirsty of wars between States, while renouncing beforehand the use of manœuvring, of playing off (though for a time only) the interests of one foe against the other, of entering upon agreements and effecting compromises (even though these may be of an unstable and temporary character)—would not such renunciation be the height of folly ? We might as well, when climbing a dangerous and hitherto unexplored mountain, refuse in advance to make the ascent in zigzags, or to turn back for a while, to give up the chosen direction in order to test another which may prove to be easier to negotiate. (*Works*, Russian edition, vol. xvii., p. 158.)

What we are concerned with are not the reforms, compromises, and agreements, qua reforms, compromises, and agreements, but with the use they can be put to and the advantages to be gained.

Reform is the first and the last letter of the reformist's alphabet. He looks upon revolutionary work as a matter of no importance. If a reformist speaks of the social revolution, it is for him only a rhetorical flourish, used to throw dust in people's eyes. This is why, under a bourgeois regime, reformist tactics achieve reforms which serve merely to bolster up that regime and to scatter the revolutionary forces.

For the revolutionist, however, the revolution is everything, and reform a means to an end, a by-product of the revolution. For this reason, reform brought about by means of a revolutionary tactic carried on under a bourgeois government inevitably tends to weaken that government and to reinvigorate the forces of revolution, it serves as a base for the further development of the revolutionary movement.

A revolutionist may sponsor a reform because he sees in it a means for linking up constitutional action with unconstitutional action, because he feels he can make use of it as a screen behind which he can strengthen his clandestine work, whose aim is to educate and prepare the masses for the revolutionary overthrow of the bourgeoisie.

This is what we mean by the revolutionary use of reforms and of agreements under the imperialistic regime.

A reformist, on the other hand, stands for reform, rejects every unconstitutional action which might spread enlightenment among the masses and prepare them for revolution, and basks in the sunshine of the reforms he has succeeded in putting through.

There you have the reformist tactic, and such is the inevitable significance of reformism under imperialism.

But under the dictatorship of the proletariat, after the overthrow of imperialism, matters assume a different aspect. In certain cases and under certain conditions, the proletarian power may be compelled for a time to forsake the revolutionary path of completely changing the extant social order, and to enter the path of gradual transformation. In his essay on *The Significance of Gold*, Lenin calls this " the path of reforms ", the path of " circular movements ". Reforms are granted, concessions are made to non-proletarian classes, whereby these classes are weakened. While pursuing this road, the revolutionists gain a breathing space, during which they can assemble their forces and prepare for a new attack. No one will deny that, in a certain sense, this is a reformist tactic. But we need to remember that such reforms have one peculiarity which other reforms do not possess : they emanate from a proletarian State. They serve to strengthen that State; to give the proletariat a breathing space, and they are useful weapons for the disintegration of the non-proletarian classes.

If such a policy is compatible with proletarian rule, it is only because the advance of the revolution in the preceding period has been so great as to allow of sufficient room for retreat when a withdrawal becomes necessary. Then the offensive gives way to a tactic of retreat, of flanking movements, and the like.

Thus we see that, whilst under the dominion of the bourgeoisie reforms are no more than by-products of the revolution, under the dictatorship of the proletariat they arise out of the revolutionary achievements of the proletariat. Lenin writes in this connexion :

> The relation of reform to revolution can be correctly and precisely determined by Marxist theory alone, though Marx himself could only contemplate this relation from one point of view, namely from the point of view of his own period, before

the proletariat had achieved a more or less solid and stable victory even in one single country. In such circumstances, the foundation for a correct relationship between reform and revolution was the formula : Reforms are by-products of the revolutionary class struggle of the proletariat. . . . After the victory of the proletariat, even if that victory has taken place in one country alone, a new element enters into the relationship of reform to revolution. As far as principle is concerned, nothing has been altered. But a change has come over the form, a change which Marx could not possibly foresee. And yet the change can be understood only in the light of Marxist philosophy and Marxist politics. . . . After the victory, reforms (though still no more than by-products in the international arena) become, in the land where the workers have been victorious, a necessary and legitimate breathing space when, despite the most intrepid endeavour, the revolutionary forces are obviously not strong enough to pass on from this or that phase of development to a higher phase. Victory gives such a " reserve of strength " that, even when a retreat becomes unavoidable, the revolutionary forces can hold out both materially and morally. *(Works*, vol. xviii., part I., pp. 414–415.)

8. THE PARTY

DURING the prerevolutionary epoch, the epoch of comparatively peaceful development, when the parties affiliated to the Second International dominated the labour movement and the parliamentary forms of struggle were looked upon as the chief forms—during that epoch our Party had not, nay it could not have, such a profound and decisive significance as it came to have later during the revolutionary struggles. Kautsky, in his defence of the Second International against various attacks, has declared that the parties composing the Second International were instruments of peace and not of war, and that they were, therefore, not in a position, while the great war lasted, to embark on any serious activity during the period of the revolutionary struggle of the proletariat. This is quite true. But what does it imply? It implies that the parties affiliated to the Second International are not adapted to the revolutionary struggle of the proletariat, that they are not fighting organisations capable of leading the proletariat to the seizure of power; they are merely an electoral apparatus, good for parliamentary election campaigns, and appropriate for the parliamentary struggle. This is why, under the aegis of the Second International, the most important political organisation representing the political aspirations of the proletariat was not a party, but a parliamentary fraction. The party, in those days, was no more than an appendage, a servant, of the parliamentary fraction. It can readily be understood that, in such circumstances, and under such a leadership, a party of the kind just described is incapable of preparing the proletariat for the revolution.

But with the advent of a new period, the situation is entirely changed. The new period is one of open class war, a period of revolutionary action on the part of the proletariat, a period of proletarian revolution, a period during which definite preparations are made for the overthrow of imperialism and for the seizure of power by the proletariat. This period sets the proletariat new tasks. One of the first of these is to reorganise the Party work, renewing it and revolutionising it in every way; to educate the workers in the revolutionary struggle for power; to rally the reserves and prepare them for the fight ; to seek alliances with the proletariat of neighbouring lands ; to create firm ties between the proletariat and the movements for independence in colonial and vassal countries ; and so on, and so forth. To rely, for the accomplishment of these tasks, upon the old social-democratic parties, is to doom oneself to despair and defeat. In view of these tasks, to remain under the leadership of such parties is to consent to march forward unarmed into the coming battle.

Hence the need for the creation of a new party, a revolutionary fighting party, bold enough to lead the proletariat forward into the struggle for the seizure of power, experienced enough to find a solution for all the complications arising out of the revolutionary situation, and flexible enough to be able to steer the revolutionary barque safely through the shoals.

Without such a party it is useless to dream of overthrowing imperialism and installing the dictatorship of the proletariat.

This new party is the Party of Leninism.

What are the characteristics of this new Party ?

a. THE PARTY AS THE VANGUARD OF THE WORKING CLASS

First of all the Party should be the vanguard of the working class. Its membership should comprise the pick of the working class. It should embody the experience of the finest stalwarts, their revolutionary spirit, their unbounded devotion to the cause of the proletariat. But in order to be an effective vanguard, the Party must be armed with a revolutionary theory, with a knowledge of the laws of the movement, of the laws of revolution. Lacking this, the Party is not fit to rally the proletariat for the fight, or to take over the functions of leadership. The Party is no true Party if it limits its activities to a mere registration of the sufferings and thoughts of the proletarian masses, if it is content to be dragged along in the wake of the " spontaneous movement " of the masses, if it cannot overcome the inertia and the political indifference of the masses, if it cannot rise superior to the transient interests of the proletariat, if it is incapable of inspiring the masses with a proletarian class consciousness. The Party should march at the head of the working class, it should see farther than the latter, it should lead the proletariat, and not lag in the rear. The parties affiliated to the Second International, the advocates of " hvostism " or " tailism " [see above, p. 96], are the fuglemen of bourgeois policy. Their leadership condemns the proletariat to becoming a tool in the hands of the bourgeoisie. Only a party which is conscious of its function as vanguard of the proletariat, which feels itself able to inspire the masses with a proletarian class consciousness, only such a party can lead the workers out of the narrow path of trade unionism and consolidate them into an independent political force. Such a party is the political leader of the working class.

I outlined above some of the difficulties of the proletarian class struggle, and some of the complications arising therefrom; I spoke of strategy and tactics, of reserves and of manœuvring, of offensive warfare and of retreat. The circumstances arising from the proletarian class struggle are just as complicated, if not more so, than were those arising out of the great war. Who can find a way out of the labyrinth of these complexities? Who is competent to guide the millionfold masses of the proletariat? No army can venture forth to battle without an experienced general staff to direct its actions. If it tries to dispense with a general staff it is foredoomed to defeat. To a greater extent, if possible, does this apply in the case of the proletariat. It, too, must possess a general staff if it is to avoid being handed over to the tender mercies of its enemies. Where shall we find such a general staff? In the revolutionary party of the proletariat. The working class without a revolutionary party is an army without a general staff. Our Party is the war staff of the proletarian army.

But the Party must not content itself with being the vanguard. It must also be a division of the class army, an intimate part of the working class, striking deep roots into the very life of that class. The distinction between the vanguard and the mass of the working class, the distinction between Party members and the non-Party masses, will not disappear so long as classes still continue to exist, so long as elements from other classes come to swell the ranks of the proletariat, and so long as the working class as a whole is not in a position to raise itself to the level attained by the vanguard. On the other hand, the Party would forfeit its position as a Party if this distinction were to lead to its severance from the masses, if the Party were to shut itself up in an ivory tower and thereby effectively cut itself loose from the non-Party masses. The Party cannot be the leader of the working class unless it keeps the closest contact with the non-Party masses, unless there is an alliance between the Party and the non-Party masses, unless the masses accept the Party leadership, unless the Party possesses both moral and political authority among the masses. Our Party has recently added two hundred thousand new working-class members to its ranks. The remarkable thing about these new members is that they have not for the most part entered the Party on their own initiative, but have been sent by their non-Party fellow-workers, who took an active hand in proposing the new members, and without whose approval no new members would have been admitted. This points to the fact that the broad masses of non-Party workers look upon the Party as their Party, a Party which is near and dear to them, a Party in whose development and strengthening they are personally interested, a Party to whose leadership they cheerfully confide their destiny. It is hardly necessary to point out that were it not for these invisible moral threads binding the masses to the Party, the latter could not have become the mainspring of the working-class movement. The Party is an inalienable portion of the working class. Lenin, in his *One Step Forward, Two Steps Backward*, writes :

> We are the Party of the working class. Consequently, nearly the whole of that class (in times of war and of civil war, the whole of that class) should work under the guidance of our Party, should create the closest contacts with our Party. But we should be guilty of " hvostism " and " Maniloffskyism "[1] were we to believe that, under capitalism, all or nearly all the workers will become class-conscious and will be prepared to share the activities of the vanguard, the socialist party. No reasonable socialist has ever believed that, under capitalism, even the trade unions (more primitive organisations and therefore more accessible to the backward strata of the working class) can succeed in enrolling all or nearly all the members of the working class. We should be deceiving ourselves and closing our eyes to the immensity of our task were we to belittle the difficulties ahead of us, were we to overlook the distinction between the vanguard and the masses which are attracted towards it, were we to forget that the perennial duty of the vanguard is to raise ever wider strata of the proletariat to its own level. (*Works*, Russian edition, vol. v., pp. 350–351.)

---

[1] Maniloffsky is one of the characters in Gogol's famous novel *Dead Souls*. He is always dreaming of splendid projects which he never tries to realise in action. " Maniloffskyism " has become an epithet in Russia to describe " all talk and no do ".—E. and C. P.

b. The Party as the Organised Detachment of the Working Class

The Party is not only the vanguard of the working class. If the Party is to function as the genuine leader in the class struggle it must likewise be the organised detachment of the working class. Under the bourgeois regime, the tasks confronting the Party are manifold and of the utmost importance. The Party has to guide the proletariat in its struggle, and has to do so, everywhere, under extraordinarily difficult conditions; it has to lead the proletariat to assume the offensive when events warrant an attack, and it has to withdraw the proletariat from the onslaught upon the foe when retreat is indicated; it has to instil into the minds of the masses of unorganised workers a sense of discipline, of method in the fight, to inspire them with the spirit of organisation and steadfastness. But the Party will not acquit itself of these tasks unless it is itself an embodiment of discipline and organisation, unless it is in very truth the organised detachment of the working class. Lacking this, the Party is in no condition to act as the leader of the millionfold proletarian masses. The Party is the organised detachment of the working class.

The concept of the Party as being an organised whole was formulated by Lenin in the first paragraph of our Party constitution. Here the Party is described as "the sum of all the organisations", and the Party members as "members of one of the Party organisations". The mensheviks, who opposed this formula as early as 1903, proposed a "system" of "individual membership" of the Party. Any university professor or undergraduate, any "sympathiser", any striker, who was willing to give the Party support, was to be entitled to become a member of the Party, even though he did not belong, and did not wish to belong, to any local group of the Party. It is obvious that had this system been adopted, the Party would have become full of professors, students, and the like, would have become sloppy, formless, disorganised, would have been swamped in a sea of "sympathisers", while the line of demarcation between Party and class would have become blurred and the task of raising the unorganised masses to the level of the vanguard would have been whistled down the wind. Under such an "opportunist" system, our Party could not have fulfilled its mission as organiser of the working class during the period of our revolution. Quoting once more from Lenin's *One Step Forward, Two Steps Backward* :

> If we accept Martoff's outlook, the Party frontiers are to be left undefined, so that "every striker" may "declare himself to be a member of the Party". What is to be gained by this vagueness of outline ? It will merely lead to a widespread assumption of the name "Party member". Where it is mischievous, is that it tends to blur the fundamental distinction between Party and class. (*Works*, Russian edition, vol. v., p. 356.)

The Party is, however, not only the sum of all the Party organisations. It is likewise the centre of unity for all these organisations, the formal concentration point for the united whole, possessing higher and lower organs of leadership, having power to subordinate the minority to the majority, to pass resolutions and make practical decisions whose carrying out is binding upon all members. In the absence of such conditions, the Party could not function as an organised whole capable of methodical and organised guidance of the proletariat in the class struggle. To quote once more from Lenin's *One Step Forward, Two Steps Backward* :

> In days gone by, our Party was not a formally organised whole, but the sum of individual groups. Consequently, these groups could exercise no more than an ideological influence one upon the other. To-day we have become an organised Party : and organisation signifies the establishment of power, signifies the transformation of the authority of ideas into the authority of power, signifies the subordination of the lower constituents of the Party to the higher. (*Works*, Russian edition, vol. v., p. 442.)

The principle of subordinating the minority to the majority, the centralisation of the Party leadership, has often been attacked by unstable elements as the embodiment of bureaucracy, of formalism, and the like. We need hardly point out that the methodical work of the Party as a whole and the guidance of the class struggle would be impracticable on any other terms. Leninism is, from the organisational point of view, the putting of this principle into practice. Lenin nicknamed the opposition to this principle " Russian nihilism " and " aristocratic anarchism ",

THE PARTY

and he declared that these should be laughed out of court. Here is what he has to say about the matter in his *One Step Forward* :

> This aristocratic anarchism is peculiar to the Russian nihilist. In his eyes, the Party organisation appears as a monstrous " factory." The subjection of the part to the whole, of the minority to the majority, seems to him a " slavery " ; . . . the apportionment of Party work from and through the Party centre drags from him tragi-comic wails about the transformation of men into " machines " ; . . . the very mention of Party rules elicits a grimace, and the remark that we can quite well do without rules. . . . It is abundantly clear that behind these complaints concerning bureaucracy there lurks a spirit of discontent with the composition of the central organism, a complaint that it is, as it were, a fig leaf. . . . You are a bureaucrat because you have been elected to this or that post by the congress and against my will ; you are a formalist because you act in accordance with congress decisions and against my consent ; you act mechanically because you follow the decisions of the majority and reck little of my approval or my desire to be coopted ; you are an autocrat because you will not hand over power and authority into the hands of our dear and trusted comrades.[1] . . . (*Works*, Russian edition, vol. v., pp. 462 and 438.)

c. THE PARTY AS THE HIGHEST FORM OF CLASS ORGANISATION OF THE PROLETARIAT

The Party, as we have seen, is the organised detachment of the working class. But it is not the only organisation of the working class. The proletariat has fashioned a number of other organisations without which it could not wage war upon capitalism : trade unions, cooperatives, workshop committees, parliamentary labour parties, women's associations, a labour press, educational leagues, Youth societies, revolutionary fighting units (when the struggle assumes an active form), delegate councils or soviets (as soon as the proletariat has seized power), and so on. As often as not, these are non-party organisations, and only a certain proportion of them are linked up with the Party or constitute a ramification of the Party. Under special conditions, every one of these organisations is necessary; for, lacking them, it would be impossible to consolidate the class positions of the proletariat in the various spheres of the struggle,

[1] The reference is to Axelrod, Martoff, Potresoff, and others, who would not submit to the Party decisions agreed upon by the Second Congress, and who accused Lenin of " bureaucratism ".

and to make of the proletariat a force capable of replacing the capitalist order by a socialist order. But how can unity of command be achieved in the presence of such a diversity of organisations ? How are we to guarantee that their multiplicity will not lead to confusion and disagreement in the guidance of the struggle ? Some may contend that these organisations function only within a special sphere of activity, and that therefore they cannot hinder one another. Maybe so. But they must all direct their activities towards the same goal, for each of them serves the same class, the proletariat. It may well be asked, who decides upon the direction, the general direction all these organisations shall take ? Where is the central unit of organisation which, because of its past experience, is not only capable of determining the line of activities these manifold organisations should take, but likewise wields sufficient authority to induce these organisations to keep within the prescribed lines in order to achieve unity of command and to avoid any possibility of confusion ?

This central unit of organisation is the Party.

The Party possesses all the necessary qualifications. It is the rallying point for the best elements of the working class, elements which are intimately connected with the non-Party organisations of the proletariat and are very often the leading spirit in these organisations. As rallying point for these elements of the working class, it is the best school for the training of leaders who shall be capable of guiding all the forms of organisation thrown up in the course of the working-class struggle. Further, the Party, as the best school for the training of leaders, and the most experienced and authoritative of working-class organisations, is specially fitted for the work of centralising the leadership of the proletarian struggle and for converting each and every non-Party organisation of the working class into an auxiliary corps and into a means for linking up the working class as a whole with the Party. The Party is the highest form of the class organisation of the proletariat.

But this does not mean that the non-Party organisations should be formally subject to the Party. All that is requisite is that the Party members who belong to these organisations should use their influence and all their arts of persuasion to bring these non-Party organisations into the closest proximity to the Party, and to lead them to place themselves of their own free will under the political guidance of the Party.

It is from this point of view that Lenin describes the Party as "the highest form of class organisation of the workers", whose political leadership should be exercised over all the other forms of proletarian organisation. (*Works*, Russian edition, vol. xvii., p. 141.)

The opportunists' theory of "independence" and of "neutrality" in respect of the non-Party organisations, the theory which gives rise to "independent" members of parliament, to "unattached" journalists, to "strait-laced" trade unionists, and to "embourgeoised" cooperators, is, in the light of all these considerations, seen to be quite incompatible with the theory and practice of Leninism.

d. The Party as the Instrument for the Dictatorship of the Proletariat

The Party is the highest form of proletarian organisation. The Party is the nucleus of leadership within the working class and among the organisations created by the workers. But the Party must not be looked upon as an end in itself, as a self-sufficing force. The Party is not only the highest form of proletarian class unity, it is also an instrument in the hands of the proletariat for the establishment of the dictatorship, and for consolidating and elaborating that dictatorship after the seizure of power. The Party could not attain so notable a position, it could not soar above all the other organisations of the working class, were it not that the proletariat is faced with the problem of the conquest of power, were it not for the existence of imperialism, for the inevitability of wars, for the advent of crises. All these circumstances make it imperative for the proletariat to concentrate its forces, to unite the threads of the revolutionary movement at one central point in order to overthrow the bourgeoisie and instal the dictatorship of the proletariat. The proletariat has need of the Party as its general staff if the struggle for power is to be crowned with victory. It is plain that without a Party capable of mustering around it the mass organisations of the proletariat and of centralising the management of the movement during the course of the struggle, the Russian proletariat could not have established its revolutionary dictatorship.

Moreover, the Party is not only indispensable to the proletariat for the establishment of the dictatorship. It becomes even more necessary after the seizure of power in order to maintain the dictatorship of the proletariat, to consolidate and to enlarge it with a view to inaugurating a completely socialised order. In his book on *Left-Wing Communism* Lenin observes :

> Beyond question, almost every one knows by this time that the bolsheviks would not have been able to hold power for two-and-a-half years, nor even for two-and-a-half months, had there not been the strictest possible discipline, a truly iron discipline, within the Party ; nor would they have been able to hold power without the whole-hearted support of the entire mass of the working class, or at any rate the full support of all the members of the working class who are class-conscious, sincere, devoted, influential, and competent to lead those who are comparatively backward or attract them into the forward movement. (*Works*, Russian edition, vol. xvii., p. 117.)

What do " consolidate " and " enlarge " signify in relation to the dictatorship of the proletariat ? They mean that the proletarian masses must be imbued with the spirit of discipline and organisation ; that the proletarian masses must be inoculated against the harmful influence of the petty bourgeoisie, must be prevented from acquiring petty-bourgeois habits and customs ; that the organisational activities of the proletariat must be utilised in order to educate and transform the mentality of the petty bourgeoisie ; that the proletarian masses must be taught to help themselves, to cultivate their own strength, so that, in the course of time, class may be abolished and the conditions be prepared for the inauguration of socialist production. None of this is possible, however, unless there exists a Party which has been rendered strong by its solidarity and its discipline. To quote again from Lenin's *Left-Wing Communism* :

> The dictatorship of the proletariat is a hard-fought fight against the forces and traditions of the old society ; a fight that is both bloody and unbloody, both violent and passive, both military and economic, both educational and administrative. The power of habit, ingrained in millions and tens of millions, is a terrible power. Without the Party, a party of iron which has been tempered in the struggle, a party that enjoys the confidence of all the straightforward members of the working class, a party able to understand and to influence the psychology of the masses, success

in such a struggle would be impossible. (*Works*, Russian edition, vol. xvii., p. 136.)

The proletariat needs the Party for the establishment and for the maintenance of the dictatorship of the proletariat. The Party is an instrument for the dictatorship of the proletariat.

It follows from this that as soon as class has been abolished, as soon as the dictatorship of the proletariat has been done away with, the Party likewise will have fulfilled its function and can be allowed to disappear.

e. THE PARTY IS THE EXPRESSION OF A UNITY OF WILL INCOMPATIBLE WITH THE EXISTENCE OF FRACTIONS

The establishment and the maintenance of the dictatorship of the proletariat is impossible without a Party which has been steeled in the school of solidarity and discipline. But an iron discipline is unthinkable without unity of will, without wholehearted and unconditional unity of action on the part of the members. Of course this does not exclude the possibility of a conflict of opinion arising within the ranks of the Party. Quite otherwise. An iron discipline, far from excluding criticism and conflict of opinion, presupposes that such struggles will arise. Neither should we suppose that the discipline is " blind ". On the contrary. Discipline does not exclude, but, rather, presupposes, the existence of conscious and voluntary submission ; for only a conscious discipline can ever become a discipline of iron. But when a difference of opinion has been thoroughly thrashed out, when criticism has had its say, and when a decision has been made, then unity of will and of action on the part of all our members is the indispensable condition without which unity and discipline are impossible. In Lenin's *The Conditions of Admission into the Communist International*, we read :

> During the present epoch of intense civil warfare, the Communist Party can accomplish its task only on condition that it is highly centralised, that it is dominated by an iron discipline which is quasi-military in its severity, that it is guided by a group of comrades at the centre, enjoying the confidence of the rank and file members, endowed with authority, and possessing wide executive powers.

This is what Party discipline should be like during the struggle for the establishment of the dictatorship of the proletariat.

Even more appropriate are the above-quoted words when we consider the condition of affairs after the inauguration of the dictatorship. We read in Lenin's *Left-Wing Communism* :

> He who weakens, no matter how little, the iron discipline of the Party of the proletariat (especially during the period of dictatorship), effectually helps the bourgeoisie against the proletariat. (*Works*, Russian edition, vol. xvii., p. 136.)

It follows from this that the existence of fractions within the Party is directly inimical to unity and discipline. Obviously such fractions can only lead to the setting up of several centres of direction. The existence of several centres means a lack of one general controlling body; it means division of purpose, divided will; it means a weakening and an undermining of discipline, a weakening and an undermining of the dictatorship. The Parties affiliated to the Second International can allow themselves the luxury of fractions; they are actively antagonistic to the dictatorship of the proletariat, they do not want to lead the workers to the conquest of power, and they can follow the custom of the liberals in the matter of fraction-building. For them an iron discipline is not necessary. But the parties affiliated to the Communist International cannot afford themselves any such luxury, for they organise their activities with a view to the establishment and to the consolidation of the dictatorship of the proletariat. They have no time to waste on such " liberal " devices. The Party constitutes a unity of wills which is incompatible with any setting up of fractions and any division of power.

Hence Lenin's explanation of the " danger of setting up fractions within the Party. It is dangerous from the outlook of Party unity and from the outlook of the unity of will among the vanguard of the proletariat. Unity is an essential prerequisite for the successful maintenance of the dictatorship of the proletariat." A special resolution concerning Party unity confirmed and strengthened this idea.

That is why Lenin demanded " the complete abolition of all fractions " within the Party. He further demanded the " immediate disbanding of all groups without exception and irrespective of the platform on which they have come together ", on pain of " instant and unconditional expulsion from the Party ".

(See the resolution " On the Unity of the Party ", passed by the Tenth Party Congress.)

f. THE PARTY IS STRENGTHENED BY PURGING ITSELF OF OPPORTUNIST ELEMENTS

The origin of all fraction-building within the Party is opportunism. The proletariat is not a sharply circumscribed class. A constant stream of recruits from the peasantry, from the petty bourgeoisie, from the intelligentsia, flows into its ranks. In the course of the development of capitalism, these people have become proletarianised. Simultaneously with this influx, a change is taking place in the upper strata of the proletariat, among trade-union leaders, members of parliament and the like, who have been corrupted by the bourgeoisie, bribed with a share of the high profits made by colonial exploitation. In the preface to his book on *Imperialism*, Lenin expresses himself as follows :

> These bourgeois-minded workers, this " labour aristocracy ", petty-bourgeois in its manner of life, in its income, and in its ideology, are the main strength of the Second International, and, here and now, are the most dependable social (not military) supporters of the bourgeoisie. These persons are veritable agents of the bourgeoisie, active for the bourgeoisie in the ranks of the workers, the touts of the capitalist class, the modern protagonists of jingoism and reform. (*Works*, Russian edition, vol. xvii., pp. 248–249.)

These petty-bourgeois groups crowd into the Party by one means or another, and bring with them a spirit of vacillation and opportunism, of disintegration and mistrust. They are mainly responsible for the creation of fractions within the Party, for the falling away of members, for disorganisation in our ranks, and for the endeavour to break up the Party from within. To do battle against imperialism with such " allies " as these is to lay oneself open to attack from two sides at once. If we are to wage successful warfare against imperialism we needs must clear all such persons out of the Party and must conduct a ruthless fight against them.

The assumption that such persons can be won over by moral suasion within the Party, within the framework of one and the same Party, is an unsound and dangerous theory. It is a theory which dooms the Party to paralysis and chronic illness, threatens to hand it over bag and baggage to a policy of opportunism, which would rob the proletariat of its revolutionary Party and deprive it of its best weapon in the fight against imperialism. Our Party could not have led the workers to power and to the inauguration of the dictatorship of the proletariat, it would not have emerged from the civil war as the conqueror, if it had kept all the Martoffs, Dans, Potresoffs, and Axelrods among its members. If our Party has succeeded in creating unity within its ranks, and has welded its membership into a coherent whole, it is because it has shaken itself free from opportunism, has purged itself of the mensheviks and of all those who would fain relinquish the gains of the revolution. The proletarian parties must expel the opportunist and reformist elements, all the socialists who have an imperialist and jingoist bias, all the socialists who are infected with patriotism and pacificism, they must expel all such if they hope to develop and strengthen in the course of the struggle. The more drastic the purge, the more likelihood is there of a strong and influential Party arising. Lenin tells us in his *Lying Speeches about Freedom* :

> With reformists and mensheviks in our ranks, we cannot hope to lead the revolutionary proletariat to victory, or to preserve the gains of victory. This is fundamental. Moreover it has been confirmed by recent experiences in Russia and in Hungary. . . . In Russia we have many times pulled through a difficult situation which, had there been mensheviks, reformists, or petty-bourgeois democrats in our ranks, would have meant the overthrow of the Soviet regime. . . . The opinion is current that the Italian proletariat will soon enter upon a definitive struggle with the Italian bourgeoisie as to which is to become the governing power in Italy. In such circumstances it is essential that the mensheviks, the reformists, and the followers of Turati should be cleared out of the Party. Nay more, even communists should be removed from positions of responsibility if these comrades show any inclination to vacillate or to make common cause with the reformists. . . . On the eve of a revolution, and during the bitterest hours of the battle, the slightest hesitation within the ranks of the Party may ruin everything, may scotch the revolution, may pluck power from the hands of the workers before the spoils of victory are fully secured and while the proletariat is still subject to furious attack If hesitant leaders withdraw at such a time, their action tends to strengthen rather than to weaken the Party. In fact the whole of the workers' movement and the revolution gain thereby. (*Works*, Russian edition, vol. xvii., pp. 372-373.)

9. STYLE IN THE WORK

WE are not concerned here with literary style. What we are about to discuss is the style of work, that which is peculiar and characteristic in the practice of Leninism, that which brings to the fore a special type of Leninist worker. Leninism is a school where the study of the theory and practice of Leninism produces a special type of Party and State official, a special kind of style in public work. What are the characteristics of this style? what its peculiarities?

There are two: *a.* revolutionary zeal, inspired by the Russian spirit; and *b.* businesslike practicality, inspired by the American spirit. The combination of these two in Party and State work constitute what we call " style " in our activities.

Revolutionary zeal is the antidote to laziness, routinism, conservatism, apathy of thought, slavish adherence to tradition and to the beliefs of our forefathers. Revolutionary zeal is a life-giving force which stimulates thought, spurs on to action, throws the outworn into the limbo of forgotten things, and opens the portals of the future. Without such zeal, there can be no advance. But it has a drawback, seeing that in practice it tends to vent itself in revolutionary talk unless it is intimately combined with level-headedness and businesslike action imbued with the American spirit. There is no lack of examples of the kind of degeneration referred to above. Who has not had experience of the fatal disease of " revolutionary " planning, of " revolutionary " projects which are concocted in the blind belief that a decree can change everything, can bring order out of chaos? Erenburg, in his tale *Uskomchel* (The Fully-Fledged Communist), gives us an admirable portrait of a bolshevik overtaken by this kind of sickness. The hero has set himself to produce the ideal man. He is absorbed in his work. Unfortunately the creature is a complete failure. The story is, of course, an extravaganza; nevertheless it is a very shrewd take-off. But no one has ridiculed this unwholesome faith in paper decrees and plans more effectively than Lenin. He stigmatises it as " communist vanity ". At the Second All-Russian Congress of the sections for political education, held in 1921, Lenin said:

> The man who is still a member of the Communist Party (because he has not yet been expelled from the Party !) and who imagines he can succeed in any task he puts his hand to simply by drawing up communist decrees, is suffering from communist vanity. (*Works*, Russian edition, vol. xviii., part I., pp. 384-385.)

Lenin was in the habit of countering revolutionary phrase-mongering by imposing common, everyday tasks, thereby emphasising the fact that revolutionary fantasy is opposed to the whole spirit and practice of Leninism. We read in *The Great Initiative* :

> Fewer high-falutin phrases, and more simple, everyday deeds. . . . Less political chatter, and more attention to the plain but living facts of communist construction. (*Works*, Russian edition, vol. xvi., pp. 256 and 247.)

The best antidote to revolutionary fantasy is practical work imbued with the American spirit. Such businesslike, practical endeavour is an unquenchable force, one which recognises no obstacles, one which, by sheer commonsense, thrusts aside everything which might impede progress, one which invariably carries a thing once embarked upon to completion (even though the affair may seem a puny one), one without which any genuine work of construction is impossible. But the practical, business-like American spirit is liable to degenerate into narrow-minded, unprincipled commercialism, if it be not allied with revolutionary zeal. Who does not know of cases where narrow-minded and unprincipled commercialism has led a so-called bolshevik into devious ways inimical to the revolutionary cause ? Pilnyak describes such types in his story *The Needy Year*. Here we make acquaintance with bolsheviks who are full of good will and practical endeavour, who " function energetically ", but who have no vision, who have no notion of what is seemly to the occasion, who cannot foresee whither their actions will lead, and who, consequently, stray from the revolutionary path. No one has ridiculed this disease of commercialism more bitingly than has Lenin. He stigmatises it as " narrow practicalism ", as " brainless commercialism ". He was wont to contrast it with living, revolutionary work ; he would emphasise the need for revolutionary vision in all the domains of our everyday work ; and would lay especial stress upon the point that commercialism is as opposed to the true spirit of Leninism as is revolutionary fantasy.

A combination of revolutionary zeal with the practical spirit constitutes the essence of Leninism as manifested in Party and in public work.

Such a union of qualities is the only one capable of giving us the perfect type of Leninist worker, and capable of setting the standard for the Leninist style in our work.

THE OCTOBER REVOLUTION AND THE TACTICS OF THE RUSSIAN COMMUNISTS

(PREFACE TO THE WORK ENTITLED *Towards October*)

1. CONDITIONS AT HOME AND ABROAD FAVOURING THE OCTOBER REVOLUTION

THREE events abroad were responsible for making the working-class revolution in Russia comparatively easy to accomplish, for helping the Russian proletariat to break the chains of imperialism and thus to overthrow the power of the bourgeoisie.

In the first place, the October (November) revolution began while the desperate fight between the two main imperialist groups was still raging, while the war between the Anglo-French powers, on the one hand, and the Austro-German powers, on the other, was absorbing so much thought and energy that neither group had time or inclination to give serious attention to a contest with the October revolutionists. This circumstance was of vital importance, for it permitted the Russian workers to reap full benefit from the fierce internal struggle of the warring imperialisms, and to concentrate and organise their own forces.

Secondly, the October revolution took place at a time when the labouring masses, weary of the war and yearning for peace, had been led by the logic of events to look upon the proletarian revolution as the only issue from the imperialist struggle. This state of mind was of the utmost importance to the October revolutionists; for the mighty weapon of peace was thereby placed in their hands, the possibility of linking up the revolution with the termination of the war was thus provided, whereby the sympathy of the masses was aroused in the East no less than in the West.

Thirdly, at that time there existed a powerful working-class movement throughout Europe, and it might be expected that in the West and in the East the revolutionary situation would be brought to a head should the imperialist war be prolonged. This circumstance was of the utmost importance to the revolution in Russia, for it secured faithful allies abroad, allies that were ready to fight alongside the Russian workers against world imperialism.

But, in addition to these conditions abroad, the October

revolution was further aided to its victorious issue by certain circumstances at home.

In the first place, the October revolution could count upon the support of the most active majority of the workers throughout Russia.

Secondly, it could count on the support of the poorer peasants and that of the war-weary and land-hungry soldiers.

Thirdly, it was led by an experienced Party, the Party of the bolsheviks, whose strength lay, not only in its past experience and its discipline forged during long years of training, but also in its intimate ties with the labouring masses.

Fourthly, the October revolution was faced by enemies who were comparatively easy to overthrow. These foes were, the more or less feeble Russian bourgeoisie, the landowners who were now completely demoralised by the peasant revolt, and the compromise parties (such as the mensheviks and essers) which had been ideologically bankrupted by the war.

Fifthly, the vast extent of territory permitted the revolutionists to manœuvre freely, to retreat when necessary, to advance, to gather up their forces, and so on.

Sixthly, during the struggle with the counter-revolution, an adequate supply of food, fuel, and other prime necessaries could be counted upon.

These were the circumstances which, at home and abroad, were responsible for facilitating the victory of the October revolution.

Of course this does not mean that there were not likewise unfavourable circumstances at home and abroad. We need but recall the comparative isolation of the revolution, which had no soviet neighbouring lands on which to rely. There can be no doubt that a similar revolution taking place in Germany at the present day would be in a vastly more advantageous situation in this respect, for it would be backed by a strong Soviet State, its immediate neighbour, the Soviet Union. The lack of a proletarian majority within the confines of Russia constituted another drawback.

Nevertheless, such disadvantages serve merely to emphasise the importance of the special situation at home and abroad at the outbreak of the October revolution.

Nor must we forget these special circumstances. It is above

all seemly to remember them when we are analysing the events of the autumn of 1923 in Germany. In particular, it behoves Comrade Trotsky to recollect these things, he who regards the October revolution in Russia and the revolution in Germany as completely analogous, he who castigates the Communist Party of Germany for its real or imaginary mistakes. Lenin writes :

> The concrete and exceptionally original situation of affairs in 1917 made it easy for Russia to *start* the revolution ; but to *continue* and complete the revolution will be a far harder task for Russia than for any other European country. I had occasion to point this out in the early days of 1918 ; the experience of the last two years has fully confirmed the correctness of my estimate. There were four special circumstances which went to create the highly original situation in Russia during 1917 : (1) The possibility of linking up the Soviet revolution with the ending of the imperialist war, which was causing intense suffering among proletarians and peasants alike ; (2) the possibility of turning to account for a while the life-and-death struggle between two mighty groups of rapacious imperialists, who were too busy cutting one another's throats to turn their attention to the Soviet foe ; (3) the possibility of prolonging the civil war, as much on account of the huge extent of territory involved as on account of the disrepair of the means of communication ; (4) the existence, among the peasant masses, of a bourgeois-democratic movement so deeply rooted that the Party of the proletariat could champion the revolutionary demands of the party of the peasants (the party of the social-revolutionaries, the majority of whose members were violently opposed to the bolsheviks), and could grant all demands as soon as the workers had seized political power. These special conditions do not at present exist in western Europe, and it is far from easy to reproduce the same or analogous conditions a second time. For this reason, among many others, the actual starting of the revolution in western Europe will be much more difficult than it was in Russia. (*Works*, Russian edition, vol. xvii., p. 153.)

Lenin's words must not be forgotten !

2. TWO PECULIARITIES OF THE OCTOBER REVOLUTION, OR OCTOBER AND TROTSKY'S THEORY OF PERMANENT REVOLUTION

THERE are two peculiarities of the October revolution which it behoves us to recognise if we are to understand its true inner meaning and its historical significance.

What are these peculiarities?

First of all there is the fact that the dictatorship of the proletariat arose out of an alliance between the industrial workers and the peasant masses, the latter being guided by the proletariat. In the second place, the dictatorship of the proletariat became established through the victory of socialism in a land of backward capitalistic development while capitalism of a more developed kind persisted in the other countries. By mentioning these two peculiarities I do not suggest that there were no others to influence the October revolution. These two are, however, of moment to us just now; not only because they clearly express the nature of the said revolution, but likewise because they throw a strong light upon the opportunist character of the theory of " permanent revolution ".

Let us briefly examine these peculiarities.

The most important problem of the proletarian revolution is the question as to how the urban and rural masses of the labouring petty bourgeoisie are to be won over to the cause of the proletariat. In the struggle for power, which side are the masses of the town and rural workers going to espouse? Are they going to rally to the bourgeoisie or to the proletariat? For which side are they going to act as a reserve? The fate of the revolution and the security of the dictatorship of the proletariat hang upon this choice. The revolutions of 1848 and 1871 in France were crushed mainly because the peasant reserves rallied to the side of the bourgeoisie. The October revolution was victorious because it was able to rob the bourgeoisie of its peasant reserves and to attract them to the proletarian camp; because in this revolution the proletariat proved to be the only guiding force for the millions of workers in town and countryside alike.

He who has not understood this, will never understand the nature of the October revolution, the significance of the proletarian dictatorship, or the characteristics of the inner policy of our working-class power.

The dictatorship of the proletariat is not simply an administrative clique at the head of affairs, " cleverly selected " by " experienced strategists " and sagely relying on the support of this, that, or the other section of the populace. The dictatorship of the proletariat is a class alliance of the proletariat with the labouring masses of the peasantry ; an alliance entered into for the overthrow of capitalism, for bringing about the final victory of socialism : an alliance formed upon the understanding that, within it, the leadership belongs to the proletariat.

We see, therefore, that there is no question here of underestimating " just a little " or of overestimating " just a little " the revolutionary possibilities of the peasant movement—as certain diplomatic champions of " permanent revolution " are fond of maintaining. We are here concerned with the nature of the new proletarian State which has arisen out of the October revolution. We are concerned with the nature of the proletarian power, with the foundations of the dictatorship of the proletariat. Lenin writes :

> The dictatorship of the proletariat is a special sort of class alliance between the proletariat (the vanguard of the workers) and the numerous non-proletarian strata of those who labour (petty bourgeoisie, small employers, peasants, intelligentsia, and so forth) or the majority of these ; it is an alliance whose objects are the complete overthrow of capitalism, the crushing once for all of the resistance of the bourgeoisie in its attempts at the restoration of the old order, and the definitive inauguration and consolidation of socialism. (*Works*, Russian edition, vol. xvi., p. 241.)
>
> The words " dictatorship of the proletariat " translated from the Latin scientific historical and philosophical setting into our own simpler tongue mean that a certain class—that of the urban workers, and in general the industrial workers—is competent to guide the masses of those who labour and are exploited in order to throw off the yoke of capitalism, to consolidate and uphold the victory, to create a new social order, and to put an end for ever to the division of mankind into classes. (*Works*, Russian edition, vol. xvi., p. 248.)

Such, according to Lenin, is the theory of the dictatorship of the proletariat.

One of the peculiarities of the October revolution was that it was a typical application of Lenin's theory of the dictatorship of the proletariat.

There are some comrades among us who are of opinion that this theory is a purely " Russian " one having no relation to any other circumstances than to those prevalent in Russia. This is an erroneous belief. When Lenin speaks of the non-proletarian labouring masses led by the proletariat, he has in mind, not only the Russian peasants, but also the labouring elements living on the outskirts of the Soviet Union, living in those territories which, until recently, were nothing more than Russian colonies. Lenin was never weary of repeating that the Russian proletariat would not be victorious unless it secured these masses of other nationalities as allies. In his articles upon the nationalist question and in his speeches at the congresses of the Communist International, Lenin more than once maintained that the victory of the world revolution was impossible without the union, without the revolutionary coalition, of the proletariat of the advanced countries with the oppressed people of the enslaved colonies. Now, what are such colonies but the dwelling place of these same labouring masses and, in especial, of the labouring masses of the peasantry ? Who does not know that the question of the liberation of the colonies is, in essence, none other than the question of the liberation of the toiling masses of non-proletarians from the oppression and exploitation of financial capital ?

Hence we may conclude that Lenin's theory of the dictatorship of the proletariat is not a purely " Russian " theory, but that, on the contrary, it is a theory which may be applied to all lands. Bolshevism is not merely a Russian phenomenon. " Bolshevism," said Lenin, " is a model tactic for all ". (*Works*, Russian edition, vol. xv., p. 503.)

Such are the characteristics of the first peculiarity of the October revolution.

What is the value of Comrade Trotsky's theory of permanent revolution in view of this peculiarity of the October happenings ?

We need not dwell upon Comrade Trotsky's attitude during 1905, when he " merely " forgot to count the peasantry as a revolutionary power, and coined the slogan : " No more tsars ! A workers' government ! " This watchword implied a revolution without the backing of the peasants. Even Radek, the diplomatic champion of "permanent revolution", has now to admit that, in 1905, to talk of "permanent revolution" was "cutting capers", a leap which took us away from actualities. (Cf. "Pravda", December 14, 1924.) To-day there is almost unanimous agreement that this "caper" can be ignored.

Neither shall we enlarge upon Trotsky's attitude during the war, when, in 1915, discussing the fact that "we are living during an epoch of imperialism", that imperialism "sets up as opponents, not the bourgeois nation against the old order, but the proletariat against the bourgeois nation", he concludes his article *The Struggle for Power* by maintaining that the revolutionary role of the peasantry was fated to wane and that the slogan concerning the seizure of the land had no longer the same importance as of yore. (See Trotsky's *1905*, pp. 289-292.) Lenin, as we know, in his criticism of Comrade Trotsky's article, accused him of "denying the role of the peasantry". This is what Lenin wrote :

> In actual fact, Trotsky is playing into the hands of the liberal-labour politicians who, seeing that he "denies" the role of the peasantry, imagine that we do not want to muster the peasants for the revolution. (*Works*, Russian edition, vol xiii., p. 214.)

We will pass to more recent works upon this subject, to writings penned by Comrade Trotsky during the period when the dictatorship of the proletariat had already consolidated itself, when Comrade Trotsky had had the possibility of putting his theory of "permanent revolution" to the test, and thereby the chance of rectifying his mistakes. Let us consider his preface to a work entitled *1905*, a book which he wrote in 1922. Here is what Comrade Trotsky says concerning "permanent revolution" :

> It was during the interval between January 9th and the October strike of 1905 that I came to consider the revolutionary development of Russia under the aspect of what ultimately came to be known as the "permanent revolution". This rather abstruse designation was intended to convey the idea that the Russian revolution, though in the immediate future forced to realise certain bourgeois aims, could not stop at that. The revolution could not accomplish its immediate bourgeois tasks unless the proletariat had risen to power. Once the proletariat had seized power, it could not confine its activities within the framework of the bourgeois revolution. On the contrary ; if the proletarian van-

guard was to reap the harvest of its victory, it must at the very outset make the most decisive inroads into the domains both of feudal and of capitalist property. Such action would have led to *hostile collisions*,[1] not only with all the bourgeois groups which had helped the revolution in its early stages, but likewise with the peasant masses whose cooperation had raised the proletariat to power. The contradictions inherent in the position of a workers' government functioning in a backward country where the large majority of the population is composed of peasants, can only be liquidated on an international scale, in the arena of a worldwide proletarian revolution.

So far Comrade Trotsky on the subject of the "permanent revolution".

We need but compare this quotation with those extracts from Lenin's works concerning the dictatorship of the proletariat which we quoted above, in order to understand the depth of the abyss which separates Lenin's theory of the dictatorship of the proletariat from Trotsky's theory of permanent revolution.

Lenin speaks of an *alliance* between the proletariat and the labouring masses of the peasantry; this alliance is the basis of the dictatorship. Trotsky, on the other hand, foresees *hostile collisions* between the proletarian vanguard and the broad masses of the peasantry.

Lenin speaks of the proletariat as the *leader* of the toiling and exploited masses. Trotsky deduces *contradictions* " inherent in the position of a workers' government functioning in a backward country where the large majority of the population is composed of peasants ".

Lenin maintains that the revolution draws all its forces from among the workers and peasants of Russia itself. But Trotsky contends that the indispensable forces are to be found " in the arena of a worldwide proletarian revolution ".

What is to be done if the world revolution is postponed? What, then, are the prospects for our revolution? Trotsky leaves us with no prospects at all! He sees " the contradictions . . . in the position of a workers' government ", contradictions which " can *only* be liquidated . . . in the arena of a worldwide proletarian revolution ". Our prospects? According to this plan, our revolution is to stew in its own contradictions, and to rot as it stews, while awaiting the advent of the world revolution.

[1] Italicised by Stalin.

What, according to Lenin, is the dictatorship of the proletariat?

It is the power which has its roots in the alliance between the proletariat and the labouring masses of the peasantry for " the complete overthrow of capitalism " and for " the definitive inauguration and consolidation of socialism ".

What, according to Trotsky, is the dictatorship of the proletariat?

It is a power coming into " hostile collisions " with the " peasant masses ", and seeking a solution for its inherent " contradictions " *only* " in the arena of a worldwide proletarian revolution ".

In what way does this " theory of permanent revolution " differ from the well-known theory of the mensheviks concerning the negation of the idea of the dictatorship of the proletariat?

In no way at all!

There is no loophole for a doubt. The theory of " permanent revolution " is not simply an underestimate of the revolutionary possibilities of the peasant movement. It is far more than this, for it is so gross an underestimate of the peasant movement that it leads to the *negation* of the Leninist theory of the dictatorship of the proletariat.

Trotsky's " permanent revolution " is a variety of menshevism.

Such is its relationship to the first peculiarity of the October revolution.

What are the characteristics of the second peculiarity of the October revolution?

During his study of imperialism, especially in the course of the war, Lenin was led to formulate the law of the irregular and spasmodic economic and political development of capitalistic countries. According to this law, the growth of enterprises, of trusts, of branches of industry in various lands does not proceed regularly, in a preconceived order, so that one country with its trusts and branches of industry is always in the van, and all the other countries with their branches of industry, trusts, etc., bring up the rear, all keeping to their foreordained places in the procession. On the contrary, this growth is achieved by leaps and bounds, followed by interruptions in certain countries, while other countries spring forward along their lines of development, and so on. Further, the " perfectly legitimate " aspiration of backward countries to hold on to the position they have achieved, and the no less "legitimate" aspiration of the more advanced countries to go forward to fresh conquests, makes armed collisions between the imperialistic States inevitable. Such was the case with Germany fifty years or so ago, in comparison with the more advanced development of England and France. The same may be said of Japan, when we compare its development with that of Russia. Nevertheless, at the beginning of the twentieth century Germany made so mighty a stride forward that German goods had soon ousted French goods and were beginning to oust English goods from the world market. Similarly with Japan. This country's goods were replacing Russian goods in the world market. These clashes of interests gave rise, as we all know, to the recent imperialist war.

The following five facts are responsible for the law formulated by Lenin :

(1) "Capitalism has become a world-wide system of colonial oppression and financial strangulation of most of the globe by a handful of 'advanced' countries." (Lenin, *Works*, Russian edition, vol. xvii., p. 246.)

(2) "Three world powers, the United States of America, Great Britain, and Japan, armed to the teeth, divide the 'spoils' and drag the world into the wars which their squabbles over the booty entail." (Lenin, ibid.)

(3) The contradictions developing within the worldwide system of financial oppression, and the impossibility of avoiding a clash of arms, render international imperialism more vulnerable to the onslaught of the revolution and more liable to being broken up in certain lands.

(4) Such a break-up of the imperialist front is more likely to take place in countries where imperialism is less strongly entrenched, less stabilised, and where, consequently, the revolution can develop more easily.

(5) In view of all this, the victory of socialism in one country alone is possible and probable, even though that country is in a backward state of development in regard to capitalism, and even though capitalism may continue to exist in more advanced countries.

Here we have the fundamental postulates of Lenin's theory of the proletarian revolution.

What, then, is the second peculiarity of the October revolution?

It is that the October revolution is a model of the practical application of Lenin's theory of the proletarian revolution.

He who has not grasped this peculiarity of the October revolution will never understand either the international character of this revolution, or its tremendous international potentiality, or its specific foreign policy. In his book, *Against the Stream*, Lenin writes :

> Irregularity in economic and political development is an invariable law of capitalism. It is, therefore, possible for socialism to triumph at the outset in a small number of capitalist countries, nay even in one alone. The victorious proletariat in such a land, having expropriated the capitalists and having organised socialist production, would rise against the remainder of the capitalist world, winning over to its cause the oppressed classes in other lands, inciting them to revolt against the capitalists, and even, when needs must, having recourse to armed intervention against the exploiting classes and their States. . . . For a free union of nations under socialism cannot be achieved without a more or less prolonged and fierce struggle on the part of the socialist republics against the backward States. (*Works*, Russian edition, vol. xiii., p. 133.)

The opportunists in every land maintain that the proletarian revolution can begin—if it ever does begin anywhere according to their theories !—only in countries of advanced industrial development, and that the chances of a victory for socialism in such countries are increased in proportion to the extent of their industrial development. Furthermore, they deny the possibility of a victory for socialism taking place in one country alone, especially if that country be at a stage of backward industrial development. Now Lenin, already during the days of the great war, basing his contention upon the law of the irregular development of imperialist States, contraposed this theory of the opportunists by his own theory of the proletarian revolution, which is : that socialism can be victorious in one country alone even when that country is in a condition of backward capitalist development.

We all know that the October revolution entirely confirmed Lenin's theory.

How does Comrade Trotsky's theory of " permanent revolution " stand in relation to Lenin's theory of the proletarian revolution ?

Let us consider Trotsky's work entitled *Our Revolution*, published in 1906. Here we read :

> In the absence of direct State support on the part of the European proletariat the Russian working class will not be able to keep itself in power and to transform its temporary rule into a stable socialist dictatorship. No doubt as to the truth of this is possible.

What do these words signify ? That the victory of socialism in one country alone (in Russia, for the nonce) is impossible without the " direct State support . . . of the European proletariat ". Which is to say that so long as the European proletariat has not won to power, no victory is possible.

Is there anything in common between this ".theory " and Lenin's thesis of the possibility of a victory for socialism taking place " at the outset in a small number of capitalist countries, nay even in one alone " ?

Obviously, nothing at all !

We admit that Trotsky's pamphlet was written at a time (1906) when it was difficult to determine the character of our revolution, and the views expressed therein do not entirely correspond to the writer's views at a later date. Let us consider, therefore, another of Trotsky's pamphlets, *The Program of Peace*, which was published on the eve of the October revolution, 1917, and, revised in 1924, was included in his book entitled *1917*. In this essay, Comrade Trotsky criticises the Leninist theory of the proletarian revolution, and contraposes the slogan of the United States of Europe. He asserts that socialism cannot secure a victory in one isolated country, that a victory can be secured only as a result of the triumph of several European States (let us say Great Britain, Russia, and Germany) grouped together as the United States of Europe. He confidently maintains that " a victorious revolution in Russia or in Great Britain is impossible without the revolution in Germany : and vice versa ". He goes on to say :

> The only concrete and historical objection to the slogan of the United States of Europe was formulated by the " Sozialdemokrat " [the chief newspaper of the bolsheviks at that date, and published in Switzerland]. Here we read : " Irregularity in political and

economic development is the supreme law of capitalism ". From this the "Sozialdemokrat" concludes that socialism may be victorious in one country alone, and that, consequently, it was not necessary to make the dictatorship of the proletariat dependent in each country upon the inauguration of the United States of Europe. It is an indisputable fact that the development of capitalism is irregular. But this irregularity is, itself, irregular! Certainly the degree of capitalist development is not the same in Great Britain, in Austria, in Germany, and in France. Nevertheless, in comparison with Africa or Asia, these countries represent capitalist "Europe" ripe for the social revolution. No country can afford to "wait" for the others to join in the struggle; this is an elementary truth which it is well to reiterate, so that the idea of simultaneous international action be not replaced by the idea of international postponement and inaction. Without awaiting the others, we have to begin and to continue the struggle on a national scale, urged on by the conviction that our initiative will set the ball rolling in other lands. Should this not happen, it would be futile to expect (and historical experience no less than theoretical considerations are there to prove the contention), for instance, that revolutionary Russia could hold its own in face of a conservative Europe, or that a socialist Germany could be maintained in isolation in the midst of a capitalist world. (Trotsky, *Collected Works*, Russian edition, vol. iii., part I., pp. 89–90.)

As will be seen, we have here, once more, the theory that the triumph of socialism must take place simultaneously in the leading countries of Europe. This theory conflicts with the Leninist theory of revolution and the victory of socialism in one country.

It goes without saying that in order to achieve the *complete* victory of socialism, in order to provide a *full* guarantee that the old order shall not be re-established, the combined efforts of the proletarians of many lands are needed. There can be no doubt that, if our revolution had not been supported by the European proletariat as a whole, the Russian proletariat could not have withstood the concerted attacks of its enemies. In like manner, without the cooperation of the Russian proletariat, the revolutionary movement in western Europe would not have been able to develop as rapidly as it has since the advent of the dictatorship of the proletariat in Russia. Of course we need support. But what do we mean when we speak of the support of our revolution by the western European proletariat? When the sympathy of the European workers has been won, when they come forward to scotch the interventionist plans of the imperialist States, can we say that this amounts to a true and serious aid? Certainly, we can! In the absence of such support, in the absence of such aid, not only on the part of the European workers but also on the part of the workers in colonial and other oppressed lands, the dictatorship of the proletariat in Russia would have been in a sorry plight. The sympathy and help from the workers beyond the Russian frontiers, together with the strength of the Red Army and the readiness of the Russian workers and peasants to defend their socialist homeland even to the death, sufficed to ward off the imperialist onslaughts and to win enough security for the serious work of reconstruction. Is this sympathy likely to grow or to diminish? Without doubt, it is growing. Are the conditions in Russia such as will not only favour the organisation of a socialist economy in that country, but will likewise be helpful to the forward movement of the workers in western Europe and promote the liberation of the oppressed peoples of the East? Yes. The seven years of proletarian dictatorship in Russia speak eloquently to the fact. Can it be denied that a mighty upward movement in the realm of labour has already begun in Russia? Certainly not.

What, in view of all this, is the significance of Comrade Trotsky's contention that revolutionary Russia cannot hold its own against conservative Europe?

First of all, Trotsky does not understand the inner strength of our revolution; secondly, he does not grasp the incalculable importance of the moral support to the Russian revolution contributed by the workers of the West and by the peasants of the East; in the third place, he is not aware of the cancer which is gnawing at the vitals of imperialism.

Carried away by his criticism of Lenin's theory of the proletarian revolution, Comrade Trotsky unconsciously deals himself a knock-out blow in his pamphlet *The Program of Peace*, which was first published in 1917 and subsequently reissued in 1924.

Maybe, however, that this pamphlet likewise no longer represents Trotsky's views? Let us, therefore, consider some of his more recent writings, those written after the victory of socialism in one country alone, i.e. in Russia. We will take the Postface (1922) to the new edition of his *Program of Peace*. This is what he writes:

TWO PECULIARITIES

In my *Program of Peace* I repeat at frequent intervals my conviction that the proletarian revolution cannot be brought to a victorious conclusion in one country alone. This affirmation may seem to conflict with five years' experience in Soviet Russia. Such a conclusion would, however, be erroneous. The fact that a workers' State, in spite of its isolation and the backwardness of its development, has withstood the attacks of a world in arms, demonstrates the amazing strength of the proletariat, and goes to prove that the proletariat in other, more advanced countries, when it rises, will accomplish veritable marvels. But though we have, as a State, been able to withstand political and military attacks, we have not yet succeeded in building up a socialist society, indeed we have not even begun doing so yet. . . . So long as the bourgeoisie rules in the other European States, we are obliged (in order to fight against economic isolation) to enter into agreements with the capitalist world; at the same time we can truthfully say that such agreements may, in the long run, help in the healing of this or that wound in the body economic, and may help us to go forward a pace or so; but a steady rise of socialist economy in Russia will not be possible until *after the victory* [1] of the proletariat in the leading countries of Europe. (Trotsky, *Collected Works*, Russian edition, vol. iii., pp. 92–93.)

Thus does Trotsky, in his obstinate endeavour to save the theory of " permanent revolution " from irrevocable ruin, come into conflict with realities.

No matter what we may do, we have " not yet succeeded " in building up a socialist society; nay more, " we have not even begun " doing so! Some of us, it appears, were nourished upon the hope of " agreements with the capitalist world ", though these agreements, too, were incompetent to yield satisfactory results, seeing that " a steady rise of socialist economy " will remain impossible so long as the proletariat has not been victorious in " the leading countries of Europe ".

Since there is as yet no victory of the proletariat in western Europe, the Russian revolution has the alternative choice of rotting as it stands or of degenerating into a bourgeois State.

Trotsky has his own good reasons for speaking, during the last couple of years, of " the degeneration " of our Party.

He had his own good reasons last year when he foretold " the end " of our country.

How can we reconcile this strange outlook with Lenin's

[1] Italicised by Stalin.

contention that, by means of the New Economic Policy, we shall be able " to build the foundations of a socialist economy " ?

How are we to reconcile this " permanent " despair with Lenin's words when he writes :

> Henceforward socialism is no longer a question of the far-off future, no longer an abstraction, no longer an object of distant veneration. . . . We have brought socialism into our everyday life, and it behoves us to take our bearings. This is our task to-day, this is the task of our epoch. In conclusion, I may be allowed to state my conviction that, no matter how difficult the task may be, no matter how novel it may seem when compared with the tasks of former days, no matter the difficulties its accomplishment may face us with, we shall, all together, cost what it may, perform this task, not in a day, but in the course of years, so that out of the Russia of the New Economic Policy shall arise a socialist Russia. (*Works*, Russian edition, vol. xviii., part II., p. 108.)

How, again, are we to reconcile Trotsky's " permanent " despair with this other passage from Lenin's writings ?

> In actual fact, all the means of large-scale production are in the hands of the State, and the powers of State are in the hands of the proletariat ; there is the alliance of this same proletariat with the many millions of middle and poor peasants ; there is the assured leadership of these peasants by the proletariat ; and so on, and so forth. Have we not already, here and now, all the means for making out of the cooperatives (which, in the past, we treated as trading concerns, and which, even to-day, we have a certain justification for treating similarly under the new economic policy), out of the cooperatives alone—have we not all the means requisite for the establishment of a fully socialised society ? Of course we have not yet established a socialist society ; but we have all the means requisite for its establishment. (*Works*, Russian edition, vol. xviii., part II., p. 140.)

It is obvious that Trotsky's views concerning " permanent revolution " do not and cannot harmonise with Lenin's theory of the proletarian revolution. Nay more ! Lenin's theory of the proletarian revolution is the exact opposite of Trotsky's theory of " permanent revolution ".

Lack of faith in the strength and capacity of our revolution, lack of faith in the strength and capacity of the Russian proletariat—these are the foundations of the theory of " permanent revolution ".

Hitherto it has been usual to draw attention to only one

aspect of the theory of " permanent revolution ", namely the lack of faith in the revolutionary possibilities of the peasant movement. Now we must supplement this by drawing attention to another aspect, namely the lack of faith in the strength and the capacity of the Russian proletariat.

In what way does Trotsky's theory differ from the prevalent theory of the mensheviks, a theory which holds that the victory of socialism in one country (and especially in a backward country) is not possible unless a victory of the revolutionary forces has already been achieved in the leading countries of western Europe?

In essence, the two theories are identical.

There can be no doubt that Comrade Trotsky's theory of " permanent revolution " is a variety of menshevism.

Recently, in the columns of our Russian newspapers, certain wrong-headed diplomatists have endeavoured to show that the famous theory of " permanent revolution " is quite compatible with Leninism. They admit that this theory did not apply to the posture of affairs in 1905. But Trotsky's mistake consists in the fact that he anticipated, that he tried to apply to the posture of affairs in 1905 certain principles which were then not applicable. In the course of time, however, and notably in 1917, when the revolution had taken a firm hold, they continue, Trotsky's theory is quite in order. It goes without saying that the leading figure among these diplomatists is Comrade Radek. Here is what he writes:

> The war created an abyss between the peasants (who were yearning for land and peace) and the petty-bourgeois parties; the war brought the peasants under the leadership of the working class and its vanguard, the party of the bolsheviks. Then the possibility arose of establishing, not the dictatorship of the working class and the peasantry, but the dictatorship of the working class supported by the peasantry. The theory which Rosa Luxemburg and Trotsky put up against Lenin in 1905 [the theory of permanent revolution] became, in actual fact, the second stage of historical development. (Cf. " Pravda ", February 21, 1924.)

This passage is full of false implications.

It is not true that, during the war, " the possibility arose of establishing, not the dictatorship of the working class and the peasantry, but the dictatorship of the working class supported by the peasantry ". In reality, the February (March) revolution of 1917 realised the dictatorship of the proletariat and of the peasantry combined in a peculiar fashion with the dictatorship of the bourgeoisie.

It is not true that the theory of " permanent revolution " (which Comrade Radek is loath to mention by name) was elaborated by Rosa Luxemburg and Trotsky in 1905. The theory is actually the work of Parvus and Trotsky. Now, ten months after publishing his article in " Pravda ", Radek deems it advisable to correct his mistake in order to take Parvus to task concerning the theory of " permanent revolution ". (See Radek's article on Parvus which appeared in " Pravda ".) But justice demands that Radek should have brought Parvus' fellow sinner, Comrade Trotsky, to book.

It is not true that the " permanent revolution ", which was thrust aside in 1905, became a correct theory in " the second stage of historical development ", i.e. during the October revolution. The whole growth of the October revolution goes to prove the bankruptcy of this theory, and the impossibility of reconciling it with the fundamental principles of Leninism.

Neither rhetoric nor diplomacy can mask the cleavage between the theory of " permanent revolution " and Leninism.

3. SOME CHARACTERISTICS OF THE TACTICS OF THE BOLSHEVIKS DURING THE PERIOD OF PREPARATION FOR THE OCTOBER REVOLUTION

IF we are to have a clear understanding of the tactics adopted by the bolsheviks during the period of preparation for the October revolution, we must study some of the more salient characteristics of those tactics. This is made all the more necessary since, in the numerous pamphlets dealing with bolshevik tactics, these characteristics are often ignored.

What are these characteristics?

First Characteristic. If we are to believe Comrade Trotsky, there were but two stages in the history of the preparation for the October revolution: the period of scouting, and the period of insurrection. What, according to Trotsky, was the demonstration in April 1917?

> The April demonstration, which took a more leftward trend than had been expected, was a kind of scouting expedition which was intended to sound the state of mind of the masses and the relationship of the masses to the majority of the soviets.

And what again, according to Trotsky, was the July demonstration in 1917?

> On this occasion, too, the affair was no more than a scouting expedition, though on a larger scale, marking a new stage in the movement and a higher degree of development.

Needless to say that the June demonstration in 1917, organised by the pressure of our Party, must with even more justice, if we are to accept Comrade Trotsky's estimate, be qualified as being no more than a " scouting expedition ".

Thus it would appear that, as early as March 1917, the bolsheviks already had a political army of workers and peasants ready for action; and if these troops were not sent to the assault either in April, or in June, or in July of that year, this was because the scouts had nothing satisfactory to report.

This naïve conception of the political tactics of our party

is nothing but a confusion between the ordinary tactics of the military arm and the revolutionary tactics of the bolsheviks.

As a matter of fact, all these demonstrations were the outcome of the spontaneous pressure of the masses, who swarmed into the streets in order to demonstrate their indignation against the war.

The role of the Party was to give form and guidance to the spontaneous action of the masses, to give a lead in conformity with the rallying cries of the bolsheviks.

The bolsheviks had not, nay they could not have had in March 1917, a political army ready to put into the field. They certainly laboured at the creation of such an army (and by October 1917 their forces were ready for action). But it was during the struggles and class collisions which took place between April and October that this army was formed. Every demonstration was turned to account, the one in April together with those in June and July; the municipal elections, both general and local, were made use of; the encounter with Korniloff was taken advantage of; the capture of the soviets had its effect; no opportunity was missed. The political army is not the regular army. The military chief goes to the wars with ready-made troops; but the party has to recruit its men during the struggle, in the course of the clashes betwixt class and class, slowly, while the masses become aware by their own experience of the truth of the slogans and the correctness of the policy launched by the Party.

It is not to be denied that each demonstration threw a light on the underlying relationships of power, that each demonstration was a kind of scouting expedition. But the scouting expedition was not the motive of the demonstration, it was nothing but a result of the mass action.

Lenin, in his analysis of the events which took place on the eve of the October revolution, and comparing them with those of April to July, writes :

> The situation is not the same as on April 20th to 21st, June 9th, and July 3rd, for then we had to do with a spontaneous upheaval, which we, as a Party, did not lay hold of (as on April 20th), or which we held back and turned into a peaceful demonstration (as on June 9th and July 3rd). In those days we were fully aware that the soviets were not yet on our side, that the peasants still believed

that Liber, Dan, and Chernoff were pointing to the right road, that the peasants had not yet accepted the bolshevist way, the way of insurrection. Consequently, we knew that the majority of the people had not rallied to us, and that, therefore, insurrection would be premature. (*Works*, Russian edition, vol. xiv., part II., p. 284.)

It is obvious that a " scouting expedition " alone cannot lead us far.

What we are faced with is, not a scouting expedition, but the following considerations :

(1) During the period of preparation which resulted in the October revolution, the party, in all its activities, was relying upon the spontaneous onrush of the revolutionary mass movement.

(2) By thus relying on this spontaneous demonstration of the masses, the Party secured for itself the exclusive leadership of the revolutionary movement.

(3) This leadership made it possible for the Party to organise the political army of the masses for the October rising.

(4) Such a policy could have no other result than that of placing all the preparations for the October insurrection under the leadership of one Party, the Party of the bolsheviks.

(5) The consequence was that, after the October revolution, political power fell into the hands of one party exclusively, namely the Party of the bolsheviks.

We see, then, that the main factor in preparing for the October days was that the preparations were made under the leadership of one party, the Communist Party. This is the fundamental characteristic of the October revolution, the fundamental characteristic of bolshevist tactics in the period of preparation.

Need we point out that, in the absence of this characteristic, the victory of the dictatorship of the proletariat during an imperialistic epoch would have been impossible ?

Herein consists the difference between our October revolution and the French revolution of 1871. In the latter the leadership of the revolution was shared by two parties, neither of which could be called a communist party.

Second Characteristic. We have seen that the preparations for October were made under the guidance of one party, the Party of the bolsheviks. But in what way did the Party exercise its leadership, what were the measures taken by the Party ?

It isolated the parties of the essers and the mensheviks, considering these the most dangerous groups during the period of revolutionary fulfilment.

What is the basic rule of strategy according to the theory of Leninism? It is the recognition of the following points:

(1) During the period of revolutionary fulfilment, the parties of the compromisers become exceedingly dangerous, for, in effect, they are supporters of the enemies of the revolution.

(2) In order to overthrow the enemy (be that enemy a tsar or the bourgeoisie) it is essential, first of all, to isolate these parties.

(3) Consequently, during the period of preparation, our main work lies in isolating these parties from the masses, and in detaching the masses from their allegiance to such parties.

During the period of conflict with tsarism, during the period of preparation for the bourgeois-democratic revolution (1905-1906), the liberal-monarchist party, the party of the constitutional democrats (cadets), was dangerous because in reality its members supported tsarism. Why? Because this party was a party of compromises, a party trying to conciliate tsar and people (i.e. the peasantry as a whole). In those days our Party acted correctly in directing most of its blows against the cadets, for, had we not succeeded in isolating the cadets, we could never have brought about a breach between tsarism and the peasantry, and, without such a breach, we could not count on the victory of the revolution. There were many who were unable to understand this characteristic of bolshevist strategy, who, consequently, nicknamed the bolsheviks "cadet eaters", and reproached them for running after a red herring instead of getting on with the fight against the real enemy, tsarism. But such accusations merely served to show how little the bolshevist strategy had been understood, a strategy which demands the isolating of the parties of the compromisers in order to facilitate and speed up the victory over the chief foe.

Without such a strategy the leadership of the proletariat in the bourgeois-democratic revolution could never have been established.

During the period of preparation for October, the centre of gravity of the fighting forces was shifted. The tsar had been dethroned. The party of the cadets, from being a party of conciliation, had become the governing, the dominating power of imperialism. The struggle was no longer one between tsar and people, but between bourgeoisie and proletariat. During this period, the democratic petty-bourgeois parties of the essers and the mensheviks were the danger point, for they were, as an actual fact, the supporters of imperialism. Why? Because these parties were, at that time, parties of compromisers, parties of conciliation between imperialism and the toiling masses. Quite naturally, it was against them that the bolsheviks aimed their most formidable blows: for, had we not succeeded in isolating the essers and the mensheviks, we could not have been sure that the toiling masses would break away from imperialism; and, in default of such a breach, we could not count on a victory for the soviet revolution. There were many who failed to grasp the significance of this characteristic of the bolshevist tactic, who accused the bolsheviks of harbouring "excessive hatred" against the essers and the mensheviks, and of "forgetting" the main issue. But the whole period of preparation for October speaks eloquently in favour of the bolshevist tactics, showing that on such tactics alone depended the triumph of the October revolution.

The salient characteristic of this period was the growth of revolutionary feeling among the labouring peasant masses, their loss of faith in the social revolutionaries and the mensheviks, their break-away from these, their rallying to the proletariat as the only united revolutionary force capable of securing peace for the homeland. The history of this period centres round the struggle between the essers and the mensheviks, on the one hand, and the bolsheviks, on the other, for the capture of the peasant masses. The outcome of this contest was decided by the period of coalition, by the period of Kerensky's rule, by the refusal of the essers and the mensheviks to confiscate the lands of the big proprietors, by the endeavours of the essers and the mensheviks to keep the war agoing, by the July offensive on the western front, by the reestablishment of the death penalty in the army, by the Korniloff rising. The outcome of the struggle was all in favour of the bolshevist strategy. For, had the bolsheviks not been successful in isolating the essers and the mensheviks, it would have been impossible to overthrow the imperialistic government and thereby to find an issue out of the war. The policy of isolating the essers and the mensheviks was sound.

Thus, the isolating of the parties of the mensheviks and the essers was the foundation of the bolshevist leadership during the period of preparation for October. Here we have the second characteristic of the bolshevist tactics.

Had not these tactics been adopted, the alliance between the working class and the labouring masses of the peasantry would have been impossible of achievement.

Quaintly enough, Comrade Trotsky makes no mention of this characteristic of bolshevist tactics in his *Lessons of October*.

Third Characteristic. The leadership of the party during the period of preparation for October tended towards securing the isolation of the essers and the mensheviks from the masses, tended towards detaching the masses from their allegiance to these parties. But how did our Party secure its end ? In what form ? By means of what slogans ? The end was achieved in the form of a revolutionary movement of the masses, moving forward under the watchword : " All power to the soviets ! " The goal was won in the fight to change the soviets from organs of mass mobilisation into organs of insurrection, organs of power, into the apparatus of the new proletarian State structure.

Why did the bolsheviks single out the soviets as the chief organisational lever capable of dislodging and isolating the mensheviks and the essers, of furthering the proletarian revolution, and of leading the workers in their millions to victory, to the establishment of the dictatorship of the proletariat ?

What are soviets ?

Lenin, in September 1917, described them as :

> the new State apparatus, whose first function is to instal the armed force of the workers and peasants, though this armed force is not, like the old-time standing army, separate from the people, but is intimately linked up with the people. From the military point of view, this force is infinitely stronger than the erstwhile armies, and cannot be replaced by any other force. In the second place, this apparatus inaugurates such close and indissoluble, such easily controlled and renewed, links with the masses, with the majority of the people, as have never yet existed in any State apparatus. Thirdly, this apparatus, thanks to its being an elected body whose members can be replaced at the will of the people without any bureaucratic formalities, is far more democratic than any hitherto extant apparatus of State. Fourthly, it creates a solid link with the most varied occupations, thus facilitating the introduction of far-reaching reforms without bureaucratic formali-

ties. Fifthly, it gives a form to the organisation of the vanguard, i.e. of the most class-conscious, most energetic, most advanced section of the oppressed classes, of the workers and peasants, thus proving itself to be an apparatus by whose aid the vanguard of the oppressed classes may raise, instruct, educate, and sweep along after itself, the whole gigantic mass of these classes which had hitherto remained outside the orbit of political life, outside the orbit of history. Sixthly, it provides the possibility of uniting the advantages of parliamentarism with those of immediate and direct democracy, that is to say, of uniting in the persons of the elected representatives of the people both legislative and executive functions. In comparison with bourgeois parliamentarism, this is an enormous advance in democracy, an advance weighty with worldwide historical significance. . . . If the creative powers of the revolutionary classes had not given birth to the soviets, the prospects of a proletarian revolution in Russia would have been hopeless; for the proletariat would certainly not have been able to maintain itself in power had it had to rely upon the old apparatus of State, and to fashion a new apparatus all in a moment was out of the question. (*Works*, Russian edition, vol. xiv., part II., pp. 228–230.)

Here we have the reasons why the bolsheviks singled out the soviets. They looked upon the soviets as the basic organisational link which would greatly facilitate the organisation of the October revolution and the creation of a new and powerful apparatus for the proletarian State.

The slogan " All power to the soviets ", from the point of view of its inner development, passed through two stages. The first stage went on until the defeat of the bolsheviks in July ; the second stage began after the Korniloff rising had been crushed.

During the first stage the watchword betokened a rupture of the coalition between mensheviks and essers on the one hand and cadets on the other (for in those days the soviets were social revolutionary and menshevist), and freedom for the struggle of parties within the soviets, a freedom which made it possible for the bolsheviks to conquer the soviets and to change the composition of the Soviet government by means of a peaceful development of the revolution. Such a system is, of course, not the dictatorship of the proletariat. But it undoubtedly facilitated the conditions indispensable to the establishment of the dictatorship, for, by placing the mensheviks and essers at the head of things and forcing them to carry out their anti-revolutionary program, the bolsheviks' plan hastened the exposure of the true nature of these pinchbeck heroes, and precipitated their isolation, their severance from the masses. The defeat of the bolsheviks in July interrupted this development by giving the advantage to the counter-revolutionary cadet generals and throwing the essers and the mensheviks into the arms of these. This situation of affairs forced the bolsheviks temporarily to withdraw the slogan " All power to the soviets ", and to await a resurgence of the revolution before sounding the rallying cry again.

The defeat of Korniloff opened the second stage. Once more the watchword, " All power to the soviets ", was launched. But it no longer meant quite the same thing as during the first stage, for now it signified a complete rupture with imperialism and the seizure of power by the bolsheviks, seeing that the majority in the soviets had become bolshevist; it signified that, by the road of insurrection, the revolution could pass directly to the dictatorship of the proletariat; nay more, it signified the organisation and the State inauguration of the dictatorship of the proletariat.

The tactic whereby the soviets were transformed into organs of governmental power was of inestimable value in that it severed the millionfold masses of those who labour from the shackles of imperialism, proved that the essers and the mensheviks were the tools of imperialism, and set the feet of the masses on the direct road to the dictatorship of the proletariat.

Thus, the policy of transforming the soviets into an organ of governmental power, in so far as it was the prime method for isolating the parties of the compromisers from the masses and led to the triumph of the dictatorship of the proletariat, was the third characteristic of the bolshevist tactic during the period of preparation for the October revolution.

Fourth Characteristic. The picture would be incomplete if we did not ask ourselves how and why the bolsheviks succeeded in changing their slogans into slogans for the masses, stirring these masses to action ; how and why the bolsheviks were able to convince, not only the advance guard and the majority of the working class, but likewise the majority of the people, that the bolshevist policy was sound.

To ensure that the revolution shall be victorious, that it shall surge up from the very heart of the people, that it shall sweep

TACTICS OF THE BOLSHEVIKS

along in its wake the millionfold masses of the nation—it is not enough for the Party to launch accurate slogans. Another condition is essential: the masses themselves must be convinced by their own experience of the correctness of the slogans. Only then do the slogans of the Party become the slogans of the masses. Only then does the revolution become, in very truth, the people's revolution. One of the characteristics of bolshevist tactics during the period of preparation for October was that the bolsheviks were aware of the ways and the by-ways along which, in the most natural manner in the world, the masses could be led to adopt these slogans, along which the masses could be led to the very threshold of the revolution. Thereby the masses came to understand the correctness of the slogans, to control them, to test them in the light of experience. In other words, one of the characteristics of bolshevist tactics is that the bolsheviks do not confuse Party leadership with mass leadership, that they draw a clear line between these two kinds of leadership, and that their tactic thus becomes a science not only of Party leadership but likewise of mass leadership.

The summoning and the dispersal of the Constituent Assembly was a striking example of the application of this characteristic of bolshevist tactic.

The bolsheviks had, as early as April 1917, launched the watchword, "The Soviet Republic". It is a matter of common knowledge that a Constituent Assembly is a bourgeois parliament, and is thus in fundamental contradicion with the concept of a Soviet Republic. Why was it that the bolsheviks, who were striving to set up a Soviet Republic, simultaneously demanded from the Provisional Government the summoning of the Constituent Assembly ? Why did the bolsheviks not only take part in the elections to this body, but themselves convene the Assembly ? How did it come to pass that, one month before the insurrection, the bolsheviks admitted the possibility of a temporary combination of Soviet Republic with Constituent Assembly ?

Here are the answers to these questions :

(1) The idea of the Constituent Assembly enjoyed wide popularity among the masses of the population.

(2) The rallying cry for the immediate convocation of the Constituent Assembly facilitated the exposure of the counter-revolutionary nature of the Provisional Government.

(3) In order to compromise the idea of the Constituent Assembly in the eyes of the masses, it was necessary to confront these masses with the Assembly itself, to bring them with their demands for land, for peace, for Soviet power, to the very walls of the Assembly chamber, and thus to put them in the presence of an actual, a living, Constituent Assembly.

(4) Only by such means, by their own experience, could the masses learn the true nature, the counter-revolutionary nature, of the Constituent Assembly, and the need for its dissolution.

(5) This naturally presupposed the possibility of a temporary combination of Soviet Republic with Constituent Assembly as one of the means for doing away with the Assembly.

(6) Had such a combination been realised (on the understanding that all power was in the hands of the soviets), it would have meant nothing else than the subordination of the Constituent Assembly to the soviets, its transformation into a dependency of the soviets, and, ultimately, its painless death.

We need hardly point out that, had it not been for this policy of the bolsheviks, the dissolution of the Constituent Assembly would not have been so easy a task, and the subsequent campaign of the essers and the mensheviks under the slogan " All power to the Constituent Assembly " would not have come so ignominiously to grief.

Lenin writes in this connexion :

> We took part in the elections to the Russian bourgeois parliament, to the Constituent Assembly, in September and November 1917. Was our tactic right or wrong ? . . . Were not we, the Russian bolsheviks, in September and November 1917, more than any communists of western Europe, entitled to believe that, as far as Russia was concerned, parliamentarism, from the political point of view, had seen its best days ? We were certainly entitled to our belief. It is not a question of knowing whether bourgeois parliaments have been a long while in existence or a short while, but of knowing whether the broad masses of the workers *are ready* (ideologically, politically, practically) to adopt the soviet order of government and to do away with (or allow others to do away with) the bourgeois-democratic parliament. It is a well-established and undeniably historical fact that in Russia during September and November 1917 the working class in the towns, together with the soldiers and the peasants, as a result of all kinds of specific conditions, were ready and more than ready to adopt the soviet regime and to do away with even the most democratic of bourgeois

TACTICS OF THE BOLSHEVIKS

parliaments. Yet the bolsheviks did not boycott the Constituent Assembly. Far from it. They took part in the elections to that body, not only before, but likewise after the seizure of political power by the proletariat. (*Works*, Russian edition, vol. xvii., pp. 148–149.)

Why did the bolsheviks not boycott the Constituent Assembly? Because, writes Lenin:

> Even a few days before the establishment of the Soviet Republic, even *after* its establishment, participation in a bourgeois-democratic parliament cannot be harmful to the revolutionary proletariat; nay more, participation makes it easier for the proletariat to prove to the backward masses why such parliaments deserve to be broken up, facilitates this break-up, and drives another nail into the coffin of bourgeois parliamentarism. (*Works*, Russian edition, vol. xvii., p. 149.)

Typically enough, Comrade Trotsky, who does not understand this characteristic of bolshevist tactic, speaks banteringly of the theory as " Hilferdingery ".

He does not understand that the toleration of a combination of Constituent Assembly and Soviet Republic (provided always that the watchword of insurrection is current and that the victory of the soviets is probable), in conjunction with the convocation of the Assembly, is a genuinely revolutionary tactic which has nothing in common with Hilferding's tactic aiming at the transformation of the soviets into dependencies of the Constituent Assembly. The mistakes of some of our comrades in regard to this question do not warrant Trotsky's disparagement of Lenin's and the Party's perfectly justifiable attitude concerning the possibility of realising, in certain circumstances, " a combined form of government ". (Cf. *Works*, Russian edition, vol. xiv., part II., p. 275.)

Comrade Trotsky does not understand that had it not been for the original policy of the Party in regard to the Constituent Assembly, the bolsheviks would not have succeeded in winning over to their side the millionfold masses of the people and that, had they not rallied these masses to their side, the October rising would never have developed into a revolution sending its roots far and wide among the people.

It is interesting to note that Comrade Trotsky quizzes me for making use of such words as " people ", " revolutionary democracy ", and so forth, in my article. He maintains that the use of such expressions ill becomes a Marxist.

Comrade Trotsky is apparently unmindful of the fact that Lenin (who was surely a Marxist !) already in September 1917, a month before the victory of the dictatorship, was writing of " the need for an immediate transference of all power into the hands of the *revolutionary democracy*, led by the revolutionary proletariat ". (Cf. *Works*, Russian edition, vol. xiv., part II., p. 139.)

Nor, apparently, does Comrade Trotsky remember that Lenin (who was surely a Marxist !)—quoting from a celebrated letter written by Marx to Kugelmann in April 1871, wherein we read that the breaking up of the bureaucratic and military State machine is the preliminary condition of all genuinely popular revolutions on the Continent—expresses himself without equivocation when he says :

> What deserves special attention is Marx's extremely profound observation that the destruction of the bureaucratic and military State machine is " the preliminary condition of all genuinely popular revolutions ". This concept of a " popular " revolution seems strange on the lips of Marx, and Russian followers of Plehanoff and the mensheviks (these disciples of Struve, who would fain pass themselves off as Marxists) might well consider Marx's use of such a word as " a slip of the tongue ". They distort Marxism until in their hands it assumes a pitiful, liberal complexion ; until nothing exists for them beyond the antithesis between bourgeois revolution and proletarian revolution—and even this antithesis is an extraordinarily petrified affair in their minds. . . . On the continent of Europe in 1871, the proletariat nowhere constituted a majority of the population. A " popular " revolution, which actually rallied the majority of the population, could be described as " popular " only if it comprised the proletariat and the peasantry. These two classes, even in those days, were " the people ". Both these classes have this in common, that the " bureaucratic and military State machine " oppresses them, crushes them, exploits them. To break this machine, to destroy it, that is the true aim of the " people ", the majority of the people, the workers and the greater part of the peasants, that is the " preliminary condition " of a free alliance between the poorer peasants and the proletariat. Without such an alliance, a stable democracy is impossible and the social transformation is impossible. (*Works*, Russian edition, vol. xiv., part II., pp. 327-328.)

We cannot afford to forget Lenin's words.

To sum up. The fourth characteristic of the bolshevist tactic during the period of preparation for October, the most important means for rallying the masses to fight in the ranks of the party, is to convince the masses, through their own experience, of the correctness of the Party slogans, thereby leading them to the revolutionary position.

I fancy I have said enough to explain the characteristic traits of this tactic.

4. THE OCTOBER REVOLUTION AS PRELUDE TO THE WORLD REVOLUTION

THE prevalent theory which maintains that the victory of the revolution must take place simultaneously in all the leading countries of Europe, the theory which denies the possibility of a victory for socialism in one country alone, has proved itself to be a figment, a stillborn contention. The history of the proletarian revolution in Russia during the last seven years, instead of speaking in favour of the theory, speaks against it. The theory cannot be accepted as a scheme for the development of the world revolution; it conflicts with the facts we have before our very eyes. As a rallying cry, the theory is even less acceptable. First, it shackles rather than sets free the initiative of the individual countries which (in consequence of certain historical conditions) possess the power of independently breaking through the capitalist front; secondly, instead of spurring on each separate country to take up the offensive against capitalism, it leads these countries passively to await the moment when the " general catastrophe " will take place; and thirdly, it cultivates, among the proletarians of the various countries, a mentality of indecision à la Hamlet, a doubt as to whether the workers of other lands will stand shoulder to shoulder with them in the fight; whereas what is needed is a mentality of revolutionary decision. Lenin is perfectly right when he contends that the triumph of the proletariat in one country alone is true to " type ", that only in " rare and exceptional " cases can the " revolution take place in several countries at once ". (*Works*, Russian edition, vol. xv., pp. 466-467.)

But the Leninist theory is not confined to this aspect of the question. It also envisages the theory of the development of the world revolution. The victory of socialism in one country is not an end in itself; it must be looked upon as a support, as a means for hastening the proletarian victory in every other land. For the victory of the revolution in one country (in Russia, for the nonce) is not only the result of the unequal development and the progressive decay of imperialism; it is likewise the beginning and the continuation of the world revolution.

The roads leading to the world revolution are not so straightforward as they were wont to appear in days gone by when there had as yet been no victory of the revolution in a single land, and when a fully-fledged imperialism (which marks the advent of the socialist revolution) was still in the womb of time. A new factor has come to the fore: the variations in the rate of the development of capitalist countries, under the conditions that are created by a developed imperialism, conditions which lead inevitably to wars, to a general weakening of the capitalist front throughout the world, and to the possibility of achieving the victory of socialism in individual countries. Another new factor has come to the fore: the huge area of the U.S.S.R., lying betwixt West and East, betwixt the very heart of international financial exploitation and the arena of colonial oppression, a vast region whose mere existence would suffice to revolutionise the whole world.

These are but two of the factors we have to bear in mind when we are considering the roads which will lead to the world revolution.

Formerly, we were wont to believe that the revolution would develop by way of the regular " maturing " of the elements of socialism, and that the more developed, " more advanced " countries would take the lead. This outlook must now be greatly modified. Lenin writes :

> The system of international relationships has become such that a European country, Germany to wit, is now subject to other States, subjugating States. On the other hand, a number of States (and, as it happens, the oldest States of the West), by the very fact that they came out victors in the great war, were placed in a position to utilise their victory by making a few insignificant concessions to the oppressed classes, concessions which nevertheless serve to retard the revolutionary movement among these classes, and which create a semblance of " social peace ".
>
> At the same time a number of eastern countries (India, China, etc.), as the result of the imperialist war, have been definitively forced out of the traditional rut. Their development is taking the same course as that of the capitalist world in general. The ferment which is at work in Europe is at work in the East likewise. It is now obvious to every one that the lands of the East have entered the path of development along which other countries

have travelled, a path which can lead to no other goal than a world-wide capitalistic crisis. . . .

The capitalist countries of western Europe will accomplish their evolution towards socialism . . . in a different manner than we had expected. They will not accomplish it by means of the methodical " maturing " of socialism in these lands, but through the exploitation of some of these States by others (the exploitation of the first State to be defeated during the imperialist war), and through the exploitation of the whole of the East. Thanks to the first imperialist war, the East has definitively been drawn into the revolutionary movement, has definitively been swept into the vortex of the worldwide revolutionary movement. (*Works*, Russian edition, vol. xviii., part II., pp. 135-136.)

If we add to this the fact that, not only are the conquered countries and the colonial lands being exploited by the victors, but some of the victorious countries are being financially exploited by the more powerful victors such as the United States and Britain ; that the antagonisms prevalent among these countries are the most vital factors in causing the disintegration of world imperialism ; that, in addition to the aforesaid antagonisms, there are others, and very profound ones, developing within the frontiers of each of these countries ; that all these antagonisms are accentuated and rendered more acute by the existence of the great Soviet Republic—if we take all these facts into consideration, then we have a more or less complete picture of the peculiarity of the international situation.

What is most likely to happen is that the world revolution will develop in such a way that a certain number of additional countries will cut themselves adrift from the comity of imperialist States, and that the proletariat of these countries will be supported in this revolutionary act by the proletariat of the imperialistic States. We see that the first country to achieve this separation, the first victorious revolutionary country, has already won the support of the workers, of the labouring masses in general, in other lands. Without this support that country could not have held its own. Undoubtedly, this support will grow and strengthen as time goes on. Further, the very development of the world revolution, the very process of separating a number of additional countries from the imperialist States, will be all the quicker and more thoroughgoing in proportion as socialism shall have struck root in the first victorious country, in proportion as that country

PRELUDE TO THE WORLD REVOLUTION

shall have transformed itself into the base whence the development of the world revolution can proceed, in proportion as that country shall have become the crowbar getting a solid pry and setting the whole structure of imperialism rocking.

If it be true that a definitive victory of socialism in the first country to win its freedom is not possible without the combined support of the proletarians of several lands, then it is no less true that the world revolution will develop with greater speed and completeness in proportion as the help given by the first liberated country to the workers and labouring masses of all the other lands shall be more effective.

In what ways should this help find expression?

In the first place, the proletariat of the victorious revolutionary country "must do its utmost to develop, support, and awaken the revolution in all other countries". (Lenin, *Works*, Russian edition, vol. xv., p. 502.)

Secondly, the "victorious proletariat" of one country,

> having expropriated the capitalists and having organised socialist production, would rise against the remainder of the capitalist world, winning over to its cause the oppressed classes in other lands, inciting them to revolt against the capitalists, and even, when needs must, having recourse to armed intervention against the exploiting classes and their States. (Lenin, *Works*, Russian edition, vol. xiii., p. 133.)

Characteristically enough, such help on the part of the victorious country not only hastens the victory of the proletarians in other lands, but, by the very fact of hastening this victory, it ensures the final victory of socialism in the first country where the proletarian revolution has triumphed.

It is more than likely that, in the course of the development of the world revolution, there will come into existence—side by side with the foci of imperialism in the various capitalist lands and with the system of these lands throughout the world—foci of socialism in various Soviet countries, and a system of these foci throughout the world. As the outcome of this development, there will ensue a struggle between the rival systems, and its history will be the history of the world revolution.

> A free union of nations under socialism cannot be achieved without a more or less prolonged and fierce struggle on the part

of the socialist republics against the backward States. (Lenin, *Works*, Russian edition, vol. xiii., p. 133.)

The worldwide significance of the October revolution lies not only in the fact that it was the first step taken by any country whatsoever to shatter imperialism, that it brought into being the first little island of socialism in the ocean of imperialism, but likewise in the fact that the October revolution is the first stage in the world revolution and has set up a powerful base whence the world revolution can continue to develop.

We see, therefore, that those who, forgetting the international character of the October revolution, declare the victory of the revolution in one country to be simply and solely a national phenomenon, are wrong. No less wrong are those who, while recognising the international character of the October revolution, are inclined to look upon it as something passive, destined simply to receive aid from without. In actual fact, not only does the October revolution need the support of the revolution in other lands, but the revolution in these other lands needs the support of the October revolution in order to hasten and push forward towards the day when world imperialism shall be for ever overthrown.

December 17, 1924.

WORK OF THE FOURTEENTH CONFERENCE OF THE COMMUNIST PARTY OF THE SOVIET UNION

(REPORT TO THE PARTY OFFICIALS IN MOSCOW ON MAY 9, 1925)

COMRADES! It does not seem to me necessary to examine in detail the resolutions adopted by the Fourteenth Conference of our Party. We should only be wasting time. Enough to bring out the basic ideas which run like a red thread through all these resolutions. This will enable us to emphasise the fundamental conclusions arrived at in these resolutions, and will thus facilitate their future study.

Taking the resolutions as a whole, we see that the manifold questions dealt with can be arranged in six main groups. Group 1 deals with the international situation. Group 2 is concerned with the immediate tasks of the communist parties in capitalist countries. Group 3 discusses the immediate tasks of the communist elements in colonies and dependencies. Group 4 treats of the future of socialism in our own country in relation to the extant international situation. Group 5 envisages our party policy in the rural areas, and the tasks facing our party leaders under the new conditions. Group 6 considers the vital nerve of our industrial life, namely, the metallurgical industry.

1. THE INTERNATIONAL SITUATION

WHAT are the new and special characteristics in the international situation which are capable of determining the essential features of the present attitude of affairs ?

One characteristic is the fact that (within recent times, and so pronouncedly as to leave its imprint on the international situation) the revolution in Europe has suffered a set-back, that we have entered a period of calm (to which we have given the name of " the temporary stabilisation of capitalism "), and that, at one and the same time, we are witnessing the growth of economic development and political power in the Soviet Union.

What do we mean when we say that the revolution has suffered a set-back, has entered a period of calm ? Is not this the beginning of the end of the world revolution, the liquidation of the proletarian revolution throughout the world ? Lenin told us that, once the proletariat had triumphed in our own land, a new epoch would begin, the epoch of the world revolution, an epoch full of conflicts and wars, of flow and ebb, of victories and defeats, an epoch which would, in the end, lead to the victory of the proletariat in the chief capitalist countries. But if the revolution in Europe has begun to decline, must we not conclude that Lenin's theory of a new epoch, the epoch of world revolution, is out of date ? Does this not mean that the proletarian revolution in the West is no longer a question of practical politics ?

Nothing of the kind !

The epoch of world revolution constitutes a new stage in the revolution, it covers a whole strategic period which may occupy years or even decades. In the course of this period there will occur, nay, must occur, ebbs and flows in the revolutionary tide. Our revolution passed through two stages in the course of its development, two strategic periods, and then, after October, passed into a third stage, a third strategic period. The first stage lasted more than fifteen years, from 1900 to 1917. Our aim in those days was to overthrow tsarism and to bring about the victory of the bourgeois-democratic revolution. During this period we witnessed many an ebb and flow in the revolutionary tide. In 1905, there was a rise in the tide. This was followed by a temporary lull. From 1907 to 1912, the revolution was at low-water mark. Then, events in the Lena gold fields (where, on April 17, 1912, the workers' organised attempts to secure better conditions were drowned in blood) led to an outburst of angry demonstrations, of protests among the workers all over Russia. This marked a rise in the tide of the revolutionary movement, which was, during the war, succeeded once more by an ebb. The month of February 1917 witnessed a fresh flow of the tide, which led to a victory of the people over tsarism by means of the triumph of the bourgeois-democratic revolution. Each time the tide ebbed, the defeatists asseverated that the revolution was at an end. For all that, the revolution won through to victory in February 1917 (March, new style), in spite of the alternations of the tides.

The second stage in our revolution dates from February 1917. The main objectives during this stage were: the ending of the imperialist war; the overthrow of the bourgeoisie; the victory of the dictatorship of the proletariat. This stage, or strategic period, covered eight months. These eight months were months of serious crisis in the revolutionary movement, for the war and the general ruin resulting from the war spurred on the revolution and precipitated its advance. These eight months of revolutionary crisis must be regarded as equivalent to at least eight years of normal constitutional development. This strategic period, like those which preceded it, was not characterised by a continuous upward trend of the revolutionary surge (as not a few are inclined to imagine!); on the contrary, it had its ebbs and flows just as other similar periods had before it. During this period we had the mighty surge of revolutionary feeling in the July demonstrations. The tide then ebbed for a while, after the bolsheviks had suffered a defeat. Then came the Korniloff putsch. This was followed by a renewed rise in the revolutionary tide, which reached high-water mark in the victory of the October revolution. After the July set-back, our defeatists chattered about the "liquidation" of the revolution. Nevertheless, at the end of a period of trial and difficulty, the proletarian dictatorship was successfully established.

Since the October victory we have been living in the third strategic period, the third stage of the revolution, during which our objective is the overthrow of the international bourgeoisie. It is difficult to foresee how long this period will last. Certainly it will cover a goodly span of time, and we shall witness a succession of ebbs and flows in the revolutionary tide. For the time being, the international revolutionary movement is in the declining phase; but, in view of manifold causes which I shall discuss anon, this decline will yield place to an upward surge which may end in the victory of the world proletariat. If, however, it should not end in victory, another decline will set in, to be followed, in its turn, by yet another revolutionary surge. Our defeatists maintain that the present ebb in the revolutionary tide marks the end of the revolution. They are mistaken now just as heretofore, during the first and the second stage of the revolution, when every decline in the revolutionary movement signified for them a defeat of the revolution.

Such are the oscillations within each stage, within each strategic period, of the revolution.

What do these oscillations signify? Do they, perhaps, signify that Lenin's theory concerning the epoch of world revolution is fallacious or in the way of being proved so? Of course not! These oscillations serve merely to show that the revolution does not develop along a straight, continuous, and upwardly aspiring line, but along a zigzag path, by means of a forward and a backward march, an ebb and a flow in the tide; these advances and retreats temper the revolutionary fighters and prepare them for the final victory.

Such is the historical significance of the present condition of reflux in the revolutionary movement, such the historical meaning of the prevailing calm.

But this reflux or ebb is only one aspect of the affair; for, side by side with the ebb in the European revolutionary tide, outside Russia we have the marvellously rapid growth of economic life in the Soviet Union and the development of its political power. In other words, we are faced, not only with the stabilisation of capitalism, but, simultaneously, with the stabilisation of the Soviet system of society. Thus we are witnessing two stabilisations: a temporary stabilisation of capitalism; and the stabilisation of the Soviet regime. A temporary equilibrium or balance has been established between these two stabilisations. This equilibrium is the characteristic feature of the present international situation.

What is the stabilisation of capitalism ? Is it not, rather, a stagnation ? And if the stabilisation is in reality a stagnation, can we apply the term to the condition of affairs in Soviet Russia ? No ; stabilisation is not stagnation. Stabilisation consists in the strengthening of the actual situation in a given country, and its further development. World capitalism has not only strengthened its present positions ; it has gone further and has taken a step forward, widening its sphere of influence and piling up more and more wealth. It is not true that capitalism is incapable of further development, that the theory (advanced by Lenin in his book *Imperialism*) of the decay of capitalism excludes the possibility of a further evolution of capitalism. Anything but ! In his book *Imperialism*, Lenin shows that the temporary advance of capitalism is but a preparation for the progressive decay of capitalism.

Thus we have two rival stabilisations. On the one hand we find capitalism stabilising itself, consolidating its position, continuing its development. On the other hand we find the Soviet system stabilising itself, consolidating its position, and marching forward to victory.

The question is, which of these two powers is going to triumph over the other ?

How is it that one stabilisation can march shoulder to shoulder with the other ? Because capitalism is no longer sole master of the world. Because the world is now divided into two camps : one of these camps is occupied by capitalism under Anglo-American leadership ; the other is occupied by socialism under the leadership of the Soviet Union. Because, finally, the international situation will be determined by the relationships of power between these two hostile camps.

The characteristic trait at the present moment is, therefore, not only the stabilisation of capitalism and of the Soviet regime, but also that these respective forces have attained to a temporary equilibrium, an equilibrium which is slightly in favour of capitalism and slightly disadvantageous to the revolutionary movement. For there is no denying the fact that the present state of calm, when compared with the upward swing of the revolution that preceded it, is a set-back, even though a momentary one, for socialism.

What is the difference between these two stabilisations ? Whither do they lead ?

The stabilisation of the capitalist regime, the temporary strengthening of capitalism, cannot but lead to an intensification of the antagonisms innate in capitalism (*a*) between the imperialist groups in the various countries, (*b*) between the workers and the capitalists of each land, (*c*) between imperialism and the colonial peoples of every country.

But stabilisation under the Soviet regime, which strengthens socialism, will necessarily lead to a minimising of antagonisms and to an improvement of relations, (*a*) between the proletariat and the peasantry of our country, (*b*) between the proletariat and the colonial peoples of oppressed lands, (*c*) between the dictatorship of the proletariat and the workers throughout the world.

Capitalism cannot develop unless the exploitation of the working class is intensified, unless the large majority of the workers is kept in a condition bordering on starvation, unless the oppression of colonies and dependencies is intensified, unless conflicts and shocks occur between the various imperialistic groups of the bourgeoisie. But the Soviet system and the dictatorship of the proletariat can develop only by constantly raising the material and cultural level of the working class, by the ceaseless improvement in the position of the workers in the Soviet Union, by bringing the workers of all countries more closely together, by rallying the peoples in colonies and dependencies to the revolutionary movement of the proletariat. The development of capitalism means nothing more than the impoverishment and misery of the vast majority of working folk, together with the creation of a privileged position for an infinitesimal number of workers who have been corrupted by the bourgeoisie. The development of the dictatorship of the proletariat will entail a continuous improvement in the wellbeing of the immense majority of the workers.

Thus the development of capitalism cannot help but lead to conditions which intensify its inherent contradictions. Nor can capitalism solve these contradictions.

Were it not for the irregular and spasmodic development of

capitalism, thanks to which the various capitalistic countries come into conflict with and wage war upon one another in their endeavour to acquire colonial possessions; if capitalism could develop without having to export capital to lands of backward economic life, lands whence raw materials are obtainable, lands of cheap labour power; if, instead of being sent abroad, the surplus capital accumulated in the great cities were devoted to a serious development of agriculture and to effecting an improvement in the material conditions of the peasantry; if, finally, this surplus were used to raise the general standard of life of the working class—then there would be no question of an intensification of the exploitation of the working class, of a pauperising of the peasantry under the capitalist system, or of a fiercer oppression of the peoples in colonies and dependencies, or of conflicts and wars between capitalist lands.

But were these things so, capitalism would no longer be capitalism!

As a matter of fact, capitalism cannot develop without intensifying its own inherent contradictions, and thereby heaping up the factors which will help to destroy it.

On the other hand, the dictatorship of the proletariat cannot continue to develop without creating the factors which will raise the level of the revolutionary movement in every land, and thereby prepare the way for the final victory of the proletariat.

Such are the differences between the two stabilisations.

Such are the reasons why the stabilisation of capitalism can be neither lasting nor secure.

Let us now consider the stabilisation of capitalism from a concrete, a practical point of view.

In what ways does the concrete, the practical, stabilisation of capitalism find expression?

In the first place, it finds expression in the fact that, for the nonce, the United States of America, Britain, and France have succeeded in coming to an understanding as to how and to what extent they will despoil Germany. Their agreement in this matter has come to be known as the "Dawes plan". May we look upon this understanding as likely to endure? Certainly not! For it was brought about without consulting those most interested in the bargain, namely the German people. Further it has inaugurated a twofold oppression of the German nation:

oppression by its own bourgeoisie; and oppression by alien bourgeoisies. We should surely have to believe in miracles were we to fancy for a moment that a highly cultured nation like the German nation, that a well educated proletariat like the German proletariat, could consent to suffer such a twofold yoke without endeavouring to throw it off, to break the oppression by a series of widespread revolutionary upheavals. Even such a seemingly reactionary event as the election of Hindenburg leaves no doubt in our minds that the temporary understanding among the Entente powers against Germany is not likely to endure and is in fact ludicrously unstable.

The second way in which the stabilisation of capitalism has found concrete expression is in the fact that British, American, and Japanese capitalists have temporarily come to an agreement as to the allotment of their spheres of influence in China, and as to the best methods for the exploitation of that vast field for the investment of international capital. Can such an agreement prove a lasting one? Once again, certainly not! The contracting parties are already squabbling, and they will fight to the death over the division of the spoils. Further, the pact was concluded without the knowledge of the Chinese people, which has neither wish nor inclination to submit to the laws of alien robbers. Does not the growth of the revolutionary movement in China prove that the machinations of alien imperialists are already condemned by the Chinese, here and now?

Thirdly, the stabilisation of capitalism has found expression in the fact that the imperialist groups of more advanced countries have agreed, for the time being, not to interfere in the exploitation and oppression of " their " respective colonial possessions. Are we to believe that this agreement is likely to be a lasting one? Nothing of the kind! Each group of imperialists is endeavouring, and will continue its endeavours, to grab a portion of its rivals' possessions. Furthermore, the policy of oppression carried on by the groups of imperialists serves merely to strengthen and to steel the revolutionary spirit of the colonial peoples, thereby hastening the advent of the revolution. The imperialist governments are trying to " placate " the peoples of India, to " subdue " the peoples of Egypt, to " tame " the Moroccans, to bind the Indo-Chinese and the Indonesians hand and foot; and they make use of every imaginable device to achieve their ends.

Maybe they will secure certain temporary " results " ; but we can safely say that in the long run their machinations will fail.

A fourth manifestation of capitalist stabilisation may take the form of an alliance of the imperialist groups in the more advanced countries in order to make a concerted attack upon the Soviet Union. Let us suppose that this actually happens. Let us suppose that they do succeed in creating a united front against the Soviet Union and that they make use of every known craft and guile to secure their aim—as, for instance, the forgeries manufactured in connexion with the Sofia cathedral outrage. Should we be entitled to look upon such an alliance against the Soviet Union or such a stabilisation as enduring or likely to bear fruit ? For my part, I should say not. Why ? Because the immediate effect of any such alliance would be to rally the whole of our country as one man to the defence of the Soviet Union, thus making of Russia an even more impregnable fortress than in the days when she was attacked by the armies of fourteen States. Let us but recall Churchill's threat at the time of that general onslaught. The mere utterance of the threat was enough to rally the whole country around the Soviet power in order to repel the rapacious imperialists. Furthermore, a campaign against the Soviet Union would kindle the fires of revolution in many a land, and these foci of revolt would be a menace in the rear of the imperialistic armies, disintegrating them and demoralising them. There is no shadow of doubt that such centres of revolution have multiplied considerably of late, and that they bode no good to imperialism. In addition, we may say that Soviet Russia is no longer isolated, seeing that the workers of the West and the oppressed peoples of the East have become our allies. Should the imperialist governments embark upon a war against the Soviet Union, this war would undoubtedly rally the workers of the capitalist countries and the peoples in colonial lands to the aid of the Soviet Union against the armies of imperialism. I do not need to stress the fact that, should an attack on Russia materialise, we should be prepared to use any and every means in order to open the floodgates of revolution throughout the world. The leading personalities in capitalist countries cannot deny that we have had some experience in this domain !

Such are the facts and the considerations which go to prove

that the stabilisation of capitalism is not likely to endure, and that this stabilisation itself calls into being certain conditions which will lead to the disintegration of capitalism. On the other hand, we see that the stabilisation of the Soviet regime leads to a continuous accumulation of factors tending to consolidate the dictatorship of the proletariat, to spur forward the revolutionary movement in other lands, and to bring about the victory of socialism.

The antithesis is, fundamentally, one of principle ; for capitalist stabilisation and sovietist stabilisation are the respective expressions of the antithesis between two economic systems and governments—the capitalist system on the one hand and the socialist system on the other.

To one who has not grasped this antithesis, the true basis of the present international situation will for ever remain unintelligible.

The foregoing is a general picture of the international situation to-day.

2. IMMEDIATE TASKS OF THE COMMUNIST PARTIES IN CAPITALIST COUNTRIES

I NOW pass to the second group of questions.

The present situation of the communist parties in capitalist lands is influenced by the fact that the flow in the revolutionary tide has given place to an ebb, that the period of storm has been followed by a period of calm. It behoves us to make the most of this period of calm in order to consolidate the communist parties, to bolshevise them, to convert them into genuine mass parties finding their best supporters among the trade unionists, to group the working elements belonging to non-proletarian classes (and, in especial, the peasantry) around the proletariat, and to educate the proletariat in the spirit of the revolution and of the dictatorship of the proletariat.

I shall not enumerate all the immediate tasks which lie before the communist parties of western lands. These tasks will be readily understood by those who read the resolutions concerning this matter, and in particular the one passed by the enlarged executive of the Comintern after the question of bolshevisation had been discussed. I shall content myself with an examination and an elucidation of the fundamental task now confronting the communist parties of the West, shall be satisfied with a general discussion of the problem, whose solution will greatly facilitate the solution of all the other urgent problems.

What is this fundamental task?

It is the creation of intimate ties between the communist parties and the trade unions; the development of the campaign for unity among the trade unions, and the successful termination of that campaign; the insistence that every communist shall belong to an appropriate trade union; the systematic propaganda among trade unionists in favour of forming a united front against capitalism. These activities will create the conditions which will make it safe for the communist parties to rely upon the support of the trade unionists.

Unless this task is fulfilled it will be impossible for the communist parties to become genuine mass parties; nor can conditions be prepared which will speed the victory of the proletariat.

The trade unions and the communist parties of the West are not what they are in Soviet Russia. The mutual relationships between the unions and the communist parties of the West are by no means as intimate as those existing between the unions and the Communist Party in our own land. Our Russian trade unions were born later than the Party, and they grew up around the Party of the working class. Trade unions did not exist in Russia, and the Party had therefore to carry on the industrial struggle simultaneously with the political struggle of the working class; the Party had to take the lead in strikes both large and small. This mainly accounts for the exceptional prestige enjoyed by our Party among the workers before the February revolution, at a time when trade unions existed merely here and there in an embryonic state. Real trade unions did not come into being until after the February (March) revolution of 1917. By October in the same year we possessed well-organised trade unions which wielded considerable authority among the workers. Lenin recognised already in those days that, without the support of the trade unions, it would be impossible to inaugurate and to maintain the dictatorship of the proletariat. The greatest development of the Russian trade unions did not take place until after the seizure of power and, more especially, after the introduction of the New Economic Policy. There can be no doubt that, at the present day, the trade unions constitute one of the main buttresses of the dictatorship of the proletariat. The most characteristic feature of trade-union development in Russia is that these industrial organisations grew up and consolidated themselves in the wake of the Party and around the Party, in an atmosphere of mutual friendship.

In western Europe the picture is totally different. Trade unions were formed and underwent extensive development long before working-class political parties came into existence. Instead of the trade unions growing up round the parties, it is the parties which have grown out of the unions. In the field of industrial struggle, the struggle which touches the workers most closely, the place was preempted, so to speak, by the trade unions. Thus the political parties were forced into the parliamentary arena, a fact which necessarily exercised a powerful influence upon the nature of their work and upon the authority they could wield over the workers. Precisely because the political parties appeared in the West after the trade unions, because the trade unions were formed before the parties and became the main strongholds of the proletariat in its struggle against capitalism —for this very reason, the political parties (in so far as they are autonomous and lack anchorage in the trade unions) have been forced into the background.

If, therefore, the communist parties wish to become mass parties capable of setting revolution afoot, they must create intimate ties between themselves and the trade unions, and must find support in these industrial organisations.

Were these characteristics of the situation in the West to be ignored, the communist movement would, most certainly, be shipwrecked.

Yet there are in the West certain "communists" who will not grasp these characteristics, who continue to utter their antiproletarian and antirevolutionary slogan: "Come out of the unions!" The communist movement in the West has no greater enemy than such so-called communists and others of their kidney. These worthies think that they can "attack" the trade unions from without, and they look upon the industrial organisations of the workers as "enemy entrenchments". They cannot see that by adopting such tactics they induce the workers to look upon them as the enemy. These folk cannot understand that, be they good or be they bad, the trade unions are, for the rank-and-file worker, his citadel, his stronghold, whence will come support in the fight for wages, for shorter hours of labour, and so forth. Such "communists" do not grasp that their tactics, far from facilitating communist penetration among the masses, hinder this work and hamper it.

The rank-and-file worker will say to such a "communist": "You are attacking my fortress, you wish to destroy the work which it has taken me decades to build, because, so you say, communism is better than trade unionism. I don't know. Perhaps you are right in your theoretical speculations concerning communism; 'tis not for me, a simple worker, to judge. But one thing I do know: that I possess my trade-union fortress; that my union leads me forth to the fight; that my union has defended me, well or ill, against the onslaughts of the capitalists;

and that he who tries to destroy my fortress is endeavouring to destroy the work of my own hands. Cease attacking my fortress, come into the unions, work in the unions for five years or more if need be, help us to better the unions and to strengthen them. If you do this I shall have a chance of seeing what kind of a chap you are. If you prove to be a stalwart I shall have no hesitation in supporting you." And so on, and so on.

Such is the attitude of the average trade unionist towards those who advocate the policy of leaving the unions.

He who has not grasped this characteristic in the psychological make-up of the rank-and-file worker in western Europe, understands nothing about the present situation of the communist parties.

What constitutes the strength of social democracy in the West?

The fact that it has its main support in the trade unions.

What constitutes the weakness of our communist parties in the West?

The fact that they are not yet intimately linked up with the trade unions, and that certain communist elements do not wish to be linked up with the existing industrial organisations of the workers.

It therefore behoves the communist parties of the West, here and now, to develop and to carry to a successful conclusion the campaign in favour of trade-union unity; to see to it that every communist, without exception, shall become a member of an appropriate trade union, there to work patiently and systematically for the solidarity of the working class in its fight against capitalism. By such means, the communist parties will win over the trade-union movement to their support.

This is what we mean when we speak of a campaign in favour of trade-union unity.

This is what is meant by the resolutions of the enlarged executive of the Comintern concerning the immediate tasks of the communist parties of the West.

3. IMMEDIATE TASKS OF THE COMMUNIST ELEMENTS IN COLONIES AND DEPENDENCIES

I PASS, now, to consider the third group of questions.

Here are the new facts in this connexion:

(*a*) The ever-increasing export of capital from countries of high capitalistic development to those of backward development (an export which favours capitalist stabilisation), leads to the growth of capitalism in colonial lands, to its expansion at a continuously quicker rate, thus bringing about the disruption of the old forms of social and political relationships, and creating new ones in their stead.

(*b*) The proletariat of these lands is growing and will continue to grow at an accelerated speed.

(*c*) The revolutionary movement of the workers, and revolutionary crises, are growing and will continue to grow apace in these colonies and dependencies.

(*d*) At the present moment, the wealthier and more powerful stratum of the native bourgeoisie, which dreads revolution far more than imperialism, favours compromise with the imperialists rather than the liberation of the motherland from the foreign yoke. Thus they betray their country to the advantage of imperialism. (Consider, for instance, Hindustan, Egypt, etc., in this connexion.)

(*e*) In view of such facts, the rescuing of these lands from the oppression of imperialism can only be accomplished by an attack upon the native bourgeoisie.

(*f*) It follows from the foregoing considerations that the immediately actual question in these colonial and dependent lands is the creation of ties between the workers and the peasants under the leadership of the proletariat—just as was the case in Russia before the revolution of 1905.

It has hitherto been customary to speak of the East as a homogeneous whole. Such an estimate is no longer possible, for there are colonies where capitalism has taken root, others where capitalism is in course of development, others, again, where capitalism is in a backward stage. In none of these lands can precisely the same tactics be adopted.

Until quite recently, the nationalist movement has been looked upon as a combined effort towards freedom, sweeping every element of the community (reactionary bourgeois and revolutionary proletarian alike) into the current of revolt against those who had turned their native land into a colony or a vassal State. Now that the nationalist bourgeoisie has split into a revolutionary section and an antirevolutionary section, the picture of the nationalist movement has a different aspect. Side by side with the revolutionary elements in the nationalist movement, there are now consolidating themselves, within the bourgeoisie, certain conciliatory and reactionary elements which would rather conclude a pact with foreign imperialism than fight for the emancipation of their native land.

Hence the need for the communist elements in the colonies to combine forces with the revolutionary elements of the bourgeoisie, and, above all, with the peasantry, in a concerted attack upon imperialism and the bourgeois compromisers in their midst, in order, under the leadership of the proletariat, to march forward to a genuine revolutionary struggle for emancipation from the yoke of imperialism.

A considerable number of colonial lands are on the eve of their 1905, so to speak.

It is, therefore, essential to gather the more advanced workers of such lands into a united communist party capable of taking the lead in the oncoming revolution.

In 1922, writing about the ripening revolutionary movement in colonial lands, Lenin said :

> The actual " victors " in the recent imperialist war have not the strength to vanquish a small and weak country like Ireland, they have not even the strength to set their own financial and monetary house in order. What, then, can they do in Hindustan and in China, where the people are in a ferment ? Here they have a population of seven hundred million to deal with. Were we to include the peoples living in other Asiatic countries and in outlying parts where the population is quasi-Asiatic, more than half the population of the world would be concerned. In these lands, without a halt and with ever-increasing speed, their 1905 is approaching. But, whereas the Russian revolution of 1905 could, anyway at the outset, function in isolation, that is to say, without incontinently sweeping other countries into the current, the revolution which is now smouldering in India and in China is already becoming linked up with the general revolutionary struggle, with the world

wide revolutionary movement, with the international revolution. (*Works*, Russian edition, vol. xviii., part II., p. 74.)

The colonial lands are on the eve of their 1905—such is the conclusion to be drawn from the present situation in the colonies.

This is the meaning of the resolutions adopted by the enlarged executive of the Comintern concerning the problem of colonies and dependencies.

4. FUTURE OF SOCIALISM IN THE SOVIET UNION

Now we shall examine the fourth group of questions.

So far we have dealt with the resolutions passed by our conference, at which strictly Comintern problems are discussed. It is time to pass to the consideration of questions which are the special concern of the Communist Party of Russia. Such an examination will show us the link between the problems of our Russian homeland and those outside our borders.

What is likely to be the effect of the stabilisation of capitalism upon the future of socialism in the Russian Union? Must we not consider it as the end, or the beginning of the end, of socialist construction in our land?

Will it be possible to upbuild socialism in our technically and industrially backward country, if capitalism continues in being for a more or less lengthy period in other lands?

Can we feel safe from intervention, and, consequently, from a restoration of the old regime, so long as we are surrounded by capitalist States wherein capitalism, for the nonce, is stabilised?

Such questions inevitably arise in connexion with the new international situation; we cannot evade them.

In our own Soviet country we are faced by two conflicts. At home, there is the antagonism between proletariat and peasantry; and, in relation to the foreign world, there is the antagonism between ourselves as a socialist State and all the lands where capitalism is still dominant.

Let us consider these two conflicts.

No one will deny that certain antagonisms do actually exist between our proletariat and the Russian peasantry. We need but recall what took place, and is still taking place, in connexion with the policy concerning prices for agricultural produce, in connexion with the campaign for reducing the price of manufactured goods, and so on, in order to realise the crude actuality of these antagonisms. Two basic classes exist at present in Russia: the proletariat and the peasantry, the latter being a class of private owners. Here we have quite sufficient cause for antagonism. The problem resolves itself into this: can we overcome the antagonism at present existing between the proletariat and the peasantry? When we ask ourselves the question: " Shall we be able to upbuild socialism by our own unaided efforts? ", by implication we are really asking, " Can we overcome the antagonisms between proletariat and peasantry? "

Leninism enables us to answer in the affirmative. We can reconcile the conflicting interests of proletariat and peasantry. We can upbuild socialism, and we shall upbuild it shoulder to shoulder with the peasants, and under the leadership of the working class.

What reasons have we for venturing on such an answer?

Besides the antagonisms existing between proletariat and peasantry, there exists likewise a certain community of interests in the fundamental questions which concern the historical evolution of the two classes. This community of interests outweighs, or at all events can outweigh, the extant antagonisms, and constitutes the basis, the foundation, of the alliance between the workers and the peasants.

What is this community of interests?

There are two paths along which agricultural methods can develop: the path of capitalism, and the path of socialism. The capitalist path leads by way of the impoverishment of the majority of the peasantry to the enrichment of the upper strata of the urban and rural bourgeoisies. The socialist path leads to a systematic betterment in the standard of life among the majority of the peasantry. The peasantry, just like the proletariat, is particularly interested in striving that the development of husbandry shall proceed along the socialistic path. Only through such a development can the peasants hope to be rescued from poverty and from semi-starvation. Needless to say that the dictatorship of the proletariat, thanks to which the essential threads of economic life are in the hands of the workers' government, must do its utmost to ensure that agricultural development shall enter upon the socialist path. The peasants, for their part, are vitally interested in that prospect.

Thus there is community of interests between proletariat and peasantry, a community of interests which outbalances existing antagonisms.

This is the reason why Leninism teaches us that we can and must build up a fully developed socialist society shoulder to shoulder with the peasantry, must build it up upon the foundation of the alliance between the workers and the peasants.

That is why Leninism teaches us that, by utilising the community of interests already existing between proletariat and peasantry, we can and must, by our own unaided strength, overcome the antagonisms which at present tend to sow dissension between workers and peasants.

Not all our comrades are agreed upon this point of Leninist theory. Comrade Trotsky, discussing the conflict of interests between proletariat and peasantry, writes :

> The antagonisms which appear under a workers' government in a backward land where the vast majority of the population is made up of peasants can only be solved in the international arena, the arena of the proletarian world revolution. (Cf. Preface to *1905*.)

In other words, we are not capable of solving or overcoming the conflict of interests between proletariat and peasantry in our own country and with our own unaided strength ; we cannot do so, says Trotsky, unless there is a world revolution. Only, therefore, as the outcome of a world revolution can we at long last begin to upbuild socialism.

It is obvious that Trotsky's theory has nothing in common with the theories of Leninism. Comrade Trotsky writes elsewhere :

> In the absence of direct State support on the part of the European proletariat, the Russian working class will not be able to keep itself in power and to transform its temporary rule into a stable socialist dictatorship. No doubt as to the truth of this is possible. (Cf. *Our Revolution*, Russian edition, p. 278.)

Which is tantamount to saying that we may as well cease to dream of keeping the workers in power for any lengthy period unless the western European proletariat has won to power and can offer us its support !

Again, we read :

> It would be futile to expect . . . that, for instance, revolutionary Russia could hold its own in face of a conservative Europe. (Trotsky, *Collected Works*, Russian edition, vol. iii., part I., pp. 80–90.)

Comrade Trotsky would thus not only deny us the possibility of upbuilding socialism; but likewise he maintains that we shall not be in a position, even for a short while, to keep ourselves in power so long as we are faced by a reactionary Europe. And yet we have made good up till now and have repulsed the furious attacks of a reactionary Europe!

One more quotation from Trotsky:

> A steady rise of socialist economy in Russia will not be possible until after the victory of the proletariat in the leading countries of Europe. (Trotsky, *Collected Works*, Russian edition, vol. iii., part I., pp. 92–93.)

Nothing could be more explicit!

I have quoted these extracts in order to juxtapose them with certain quotations from Lenin's writings. I propose to lay bare the very core of this question concerning the possibility of establishing a fully developed socialist society in a country where the dictatorship of the proletariat prevails, even though such a country be surrounded by capitalist lands.

First of all I will give you a relevant passage from Lenin's works. In the year 1915, while the imperialist war was still raging, Lenin wrote:

> Irregularity in economic and political development is an invariable law of capitalism. It is, therefore, possible for socialism to triumph at the outset in a small number of capitalist countries, nay even in one alone. The victorious proletariat in such a land, having expropriated the capitalists and having organised socialist production, would rise against the remainder of the capitalist world, winning over to its cause the oppressed classes in other lands, inciting them to revolt against the capitalists, and even, when needs must, having recourse to armed intervention against the exploiting classes and their States. . . . For a free union of nations under socialism cannot be achieved without a more or less prolonged and fierce struggle on the part of the socialist republics against the backward States. (*Works*, Russian edition, vol. xiii., p. 133.)

Expressed in other words this passage would run: A country where the dictatorship of the proletariat had been established, even though it be surrounded by capitalist States, is capable, by its own unaided strength, of solving the antagonisms between proletariat and peasantry; it can and must upbuild socialism, inaugurate a socialist economic system, organise an armed force which will be able to march forward to the help of the proletariat in other countries where the struggle against capitalism is in full swing.

This is the fundamental theory of Leninism as concerns the victory of socialism in one country alone.

Lenin said much the same thing in his speech upon the electrification of Russia, when he addressed the Eighth Congress of Soviets at its meeting in 1920:

> Communism is the Soviet power plus the electrification of the country. Unless we instal electrical plants throughout the land, Russia will remain a country of middle peasants. This fact needs to be well rammed home. We are weaker than capitalism, not only from an international point of view but likewise from a national, a homeland, point of view. All this is common knowledge. We ourselves are conscious of it; but we shall see to it that our economic base (at the present time represented by the middle peasantry) shall be transferred to large-scale industry. Only by means of electrification, only when our industry, our agriculture, our transport system, have been grounded upon the technical basis of modern large-scale industry, shall we achieve our final victory. (Lenin, *Works*, Russian edition, vol. xvii., p. 428.)

Lenin is well aware of the technical difficulties which beset our path; yet he does not draw the absurd inference that a "steady rise of socialist economy in Russia will not be possible until after the victory of the proletariat in the leading countries of Europe". On the contrary, he considers that we, unaided, can overcome the difficulties and gain a decisive victory, that is to say inaugurate a full and adequate socialist system.

A year later, in 1921, Lenin wrote:

> If we can secure ten to twenty years of amicable relationships with the peasantry, then we can count upon a victory on an international scale (even if the other proletarian revolutions now in course of preparation should be slow to come). (Rough draft of a pamphlet to be entitled *The Food Tax*. This draft was published in the "Bolshevik", No. 7, 1925.)

We see that Lenin is fully conscious of the political difficulties which confront us in our endeavour to upbuild socialism; but he does not conclude from this that "in the absence of political support on the part of the European proletariat the Russian working class will not be able to keep itself in power".

FUTURE OF SOCIALISM IN SOVIET UNION 241

On the contrary, he considers that by means of an equitable policy in regard to the peasantry we can compass a victory " on the international scale ", i.e. realise a complete socialist system.

What is an equitable policy in regard to the peasantry? Such a policy depends entirely upon ourselves as the Party which is at work upon the upbuilding of socialism in Russia.

Lenin said as much in 1922, with even greater precision. In his pamphlet *Cooperation* he writes:

> In actual fact, all the means of large-scale production are in the hands of the State, and the powers of State are in the hands of the proletariat; there is the alliance of this same proletariat with the many millions of middle and poor peasants; there is the assured leadership of these peasants by the proletariat; and so on, and so forth. Have we not already, here and now, all the means for making out of the cooperatives (which, in the past, we treated as trading concerns, and which, even to-day, we have a certain justification for treating similarly under the New Economic Policy), out of the cooperatives alone—have we not all the means requisite for the establishment of a fully socialised society? Of course we have not yet established a socialist society; but we have all the means requisite for its establishment. (*Works*, Russian edition, vol. xviii., part II., p. 140.)

We possess, therefore, under the dictatorship of the proletariat, all the requisites for the upbuilding of a fully socialised society, if we can overcome the internal difficulties—and it is understood that we can and must overcome them by our own unaided strength.

Could anything be clearer?

Lenin is opposed to the contention that the relatively backward economic condition of Russia would make it impossible for that country to realise socialism. He shows that such a theory is incompatible with the theory of socialism.

> This argument is nothing more than a patter which its expounders learned off by heart during the period when western European social democracy was developing. It consists of the sapient declaration that Russia is not ripe for socialism, that the objective conditions for the inauguration of a socialist society do not as yet exist in Russia. (*Works*, Russian edition, vol. xviii., part II., pp. 118–119.)

Were this true, there would have been no sense in our seizing power in October 1917 and bringing about the revolution. For if, on one pretext or another, we exclude the possibility and the necessity of upbuilding a fully socialised system of society in Russia, then the October revolution has no meaning. He who denies the possibility of inaugurating socialism in one country alone, must, if he be logical, likewise deny the expediency of the October revolution. Again : one who has no faith in the October revolution, cannot admit the possibility that socialism will make good in a country which is encircled by capitalist States. The relationship between scepticism in regard to the October revolution and the negation of the possibility that socialism can be inaugurated in our land is patent to all men's eyes. Lenin quizzically remarks :

> I know that there are some wise and reverend seniors, who esteem themselves wonderfully clever—even call themselves socialist—sand who declare that power should not be seized until such time as the revolution shall have broken out in every land. They overlook the fact that by such assumptions they are severing themselves from the revolution and throwing in their lot with the bourgeoisie. To wait until the toiling masses can make a revolution on the international scale would be to entrench oneself in passivity. Such a tactic would be the climax of absurdity. (*Works*, Russian edition, vol. xv., p. 287.)

So much for the first kind of contradictions, the antagonisms or conflicts within our own borders, conflicts relating to the possibility or impossibility of upbuilding socialism in a land surrounded by capitalist States.

Now let us consider the second kind of contradictions, the antagonisms and conflicts arising between our country (in so far as it is a socialist land) and the other countries (in so far as they are capitalist lands).

So long as our country is surrounded by capitalist lands, there will always be the danger of intervention on the part of the capitalist States ; so long as such a danger threatens, we have also the risk of a restoration of the old order being effected.

Can such dangers be fully averted by the unaided efforts of a single land ? No ! Even if that country be one where the dictatorship of the proletariat has been installed, it cannot guarantee itself against the danger of intervention. A *full* guarantee against intervention, the *final* victory of socialism, is only possible on the international scale, as a result of the concerted efforts of the proletariat in a number of lands, or rather, as a result of the *victory* of the proletariat in several countries.

What is the meaning of the phrase " final victory of socialism " ?

It means that there really exists a full guarantee against any attempt at intervention and, consequently, against any attempt at a restoration of the old order. A serious attempt at restoration of the old order can only be made if substantial help from abroad be forthcoming, if international capitalism rally to the aid of the would-be restorers. Consequently, if the workers in other lands champion the cause of the Russian revolution, and, still more, if they secure a victory (even if such a victory should be gained in but a few countries), this would serve as a guarantee against intervention and restoration, and would go far towards securing the final victory of socialism. Lenin writes :

> So long as our Soviet Republic remains isolated on the fringe of the capitalist world, it would be fantastical and utopian to hope . . . for the disappearance of this or any other danger. So long as such fundamental antagonisms exist, just so long will the dangers exist likewise, and we cannot run away out of range of them. (*Works*, Russian edition, vol. xvii., pp. 408–409.)

Elsewhere, again, Lenin says :

> We are living, not merely in one State, but in a system of States ; and it is inconceivable that the Soviet Republic should continue to exist interminably side by side with imperialist States. Ultimately, one or the other must conquer. (*Works*, Russian edition, vol. xvi., p. 102.)

That is why Lenin writes :

> A decisive victory can only be achieved on an international scale, and by the combined efforts of the workers of all lands. (*Works*, Russian edition, vol. xv., p. 287.)

Such is the nature of the antagonisms of the second kind.

To confuse the first set of antagonisms (which it is quite within the competence of a country to dispel on its own initiative) with the second set of antagonisms (which can only be dispelled by the combined efforts of the proletariat in many lands) is to be guilty of a superlative blunder in regard to the Leninist theory, is to be an incurable opportunist and a hopeless nincompoop.

Last January I received a letter from a comrade which illustrates to perfection the condition of intellectual muddle which prevails in regard to the question of the victory of socialism in one country alone. He writes:

> You tell me that, according to Leninist theory . . , socialism can make good in one country alone. Unfortunately I have not been able to discover any references, in the relevant passages of Lenin's works, to the victory of socialism in one country alone.

The misfortune is, not that this comrade (whom I consider one of our most promising young students of communism) should not have found " any references, in the relevant passages of Lenin's works, to the victory of socialism in one country alone ". He'll find them some day! The unfortunate thing is that he has confounded the contradictions, the antagonisms and the conflicts, within the Russian borders, with those outside our frontiers; thus he has lost his way in a maze. Let me read you my answer to this comrade's letter:

> It is not a question of *complete* victory, but simply of a victory; one which will comprise the ending of landlordism and capitalism, the seizure of power, effective resistance to imperialist onslaughts, and the inauguration of a socialist economy. The proletariat of one country is quite competent to achieve all these things. But complete security from attempts at restoration can only be won through the combined efforts of the proletarians of several countries. It would have been idiotic to postpone the revolution in Russia in the belief that the victorious Russian proletariat (benefiting by the active sympathy of proletarians in other lands, though these foreign proletarians had not as yet made a successful revolution themselves) could not make headway against a conservative Europe. Such an outlook is not Marxism; it is opportunism, pure and unalloyed. If this theory were correct it would prove Lenin to be wrong when he declares that we shall transform the Russia of the New Economic Policy into a socialist Russia, and that we have everything we need for the upbuilding of a fully socialised society. . . . Our practical policy would be imperilled were we to countenance the tendency to regard a victorious country as something passive, only able to mark time until the victorious proletariat of other lands can hasten to its aid. Let us admit that five years, perhaps ten years, will elapse before the proletariat of the West can make a victorious revolution; let us presume that the Russian republic, all this while, continues to exist and to organise a socialist economy under the aegis of the New Economic Policy. Can you imagine for a moment that our country will do nothing more

than tread water during these five or ten years, instead of swimming steadily forward, instead of devoting itself to the inauguration of a socialist economy? We need but ask the question, to be immediately aware of the dangers which beset the path of those who deny the possibility of a socialist victory in one country alone. But does it follow that the victory will be complete, decisive? No, of course not. So long as the capitalist encirclement persists, so long will the danger of intervention ever be at the gates. (January, 1925.)

Such is the light in which the question of the future of socialism in Russia appears when we consider the resolution adopted by the Fourteenth Conference of our party.

5. PARTY POLICY IN THE RURAL DISTRICTS

I WILL now pass to an examination of the fifth group of questions.

Before dealing with the resolutions of the Fourteenth Conference wherein our Party policy in the rural areas is discussed, I would like to say a few words concerning the clamour that was raised in the bourgeois press in regard to our own Party criticism of the mistakes we made in our rural campaign. The bourgeois press jubilantly declares that such frank admission of our mistakes is a sign of the weakness of the Soviet power, a sign of decomposition and decay. Needless to say that all this noise is nothing but falsehood and deception.

Self-criticism is a sign of strength and not a sign of weakness. Only a strong party, a party that has struck deep roots, a party marching forward to victory, can risk such a pitiless critique of its own inadequacies; the Communist Party of Russia is a party of this kind, and it has been in the past, and will continue to be in the future, a ruthless critic of its own shortcomings. The bourgeois quidnuncs judge us according to their own standards. They fear the light of day, and are careful to conceal the truth from the people; they mask their deficiencies behind a veil of seeming prosperity. They naturally think that we communists, too, should hide the truth from the people. They fear the light, because even a modicum of free criticism in respect of their own deficiencies would be enough to destroy to its foundations the whole edifice of the capitalist order. That is why they believe that when we communists permit ourselves free scope for self-criticism it is a sign that we are on our last legs. These worthies, both bourgeois and social democrats alike, can only judge us by their own standards. Parties which cling to the past, parties which are doomed to disappear, such parties have good grounds for dreading the light, for being afraid of criticism. But we have no reason to be scared by daylight, by free criticism, for our Party is forging upward and onward to victory. This is why the self-criticism which has been in full swing for some months now is a sign of the utmost strength of our Party and not a sign of weakness, a sign of consolidation and not of disintegration.

Enough of this! Let us turn to consider the question of our policy in the rural districts.

What new developments are to be observed in the country areas in response to the new situation at home and abroad?

Four main points emerge.

(1) The change in the international situation and the slowing down of the revolutionary tempo, make it essential that we should adopt gentle (if slower!) methods in dealing with the peasantry, so as to enlist this class for the work of upbuilding socialism, to make the peasantry cooperate with us in organising a socialist economy.

(2) The growth of economic life in the countryside and the process of differentiation among the peasantry, make it essential that we should do away with any vestiges of war communism which still linger superfluous on the stage.

(3) The awakening of the peasants and their active participation in political life, make it necessary to change the old methods of guidance and management in the rural areas.

(4) The recent elections to the soviets have shown beyond question that in many districts the middle peasants are siding with the rich peasants against the poor peasants.

In view of these new facts, what should be the main line of action in the villages?

Certain comrades, aware of the differentiation going on in the countryside, have come to the conclusion that the policy of the Communist Party should be an intensification of the class struggle. Such is not at present our main task. This policy would not be correct. It is nothing but empty chatter, nothing but a parrot-like repetition of the whilom menshevik songs out of the whilom menshevik opera!

Our main task is not to kindle the class war in the villages. Our main task to-day is to rally the middle peasants around the proletariat, once more to win them over to our side. Our main task is to create intimate bonds between ourselves and the broad masses of the peasantry, to raise the cultural and material standard of the peasant's life, and to place the feet of these peasant masses on the road leading towards socialism. Our main task is to upbuild socialism shoulder to shoulder with the peasantry under the leadership of the working class; for only under such leadership can we guarantee that the economic organisation of the country will be carried out along socialist paths.

Here we have in a nutshell the most important tasks of our party in relation to the rural areas.

It would not be amiss to recall Lenin's words penned at the time when the New Economic Policy was being introduced—words which have lost none of their actuality during the lapse of years.

> The essential point is to set a far larger and mightier mass in motion than ever before. This can only be done if we join hands with the peasantry. (*Works*, Russian edition, vol. xviii., part II., p. 71.)

And again :

> We must create close bonds between ourselves and the peasant masses, between ourselves and the tillers of the soil ; we must begin to march forward—maybe by fits and starts, beyond question much more slowly than we had hoped—but at all events involving the whole mass in this forward movement. Then a moment will come when the movement will rush forward with a speed such as we to-day cannot imagine in our rosiest dreams. (*Works*, Russian edition, vol. xviii., part II., pp. 29-30.)

Consequently it behoves us to set our hands to two main tasks in the villages.

First we must see to it that the peasant economy shall become a part of the general economic system of the Soviet Republic. In former days, town and country went their several ways, following independent but parallel processes of development. Then came the rise of capitalism, and the capitalists wanted to include the peasant economy within the capitalist orbit. But this inclusion was effected by impoverishing the masses of the peasantry and enriching the upper stratum of the peasant class. The process was peculiarly well fitted to bring about the revolution ! After the victory of the proletariat, the inclusion of the peasant economy in the general economy of the Soviet Union can be achieved by the creation of conditions likely to favour the development of the national economy on the basis of a gradual and continuous improvement in the lot of the major portion of the peasantry. This process is diametrically opposed to the process inaugurated by the capitalists in the days before the revolution.

How can the peasantry be drawn into the general current of Soviet economic development ? By means of the cooperatives. By means of cooperative credit, agricultural cooperatives, distributive cooperatives, and productive cooperatives.

Such are the ways and means through which the peasantry will slowly, but surely, be drawn into the current of the general system of socialist construction.

In the second place, we must gradually and systematically do away with the old methods of administration and leadership in the rural areas, and infuse fresh life into the soviets, transforming them into genuinely elective institutions, and building up the foundation of soviet democracy throughout the countryside. Lenin told us that, for the majority of the workers, the dictatorship of the proletariat was the highest type of democracy. He insisted that this highest type of democracy could only be introduced after the seizure of power by the proletariat, when the proletariat was in a position to consolidate its gains. We are now entering upon the phase of the consolidation of the Soviet power, and the seeds of Soviet democracy have been sown. Caution is needed ; we must not speed along too quickly ; at each step we must gather round the Party the innumerable active elements from the ranks of the non-Party peasantry.

If we are successful in the first of these tasks (i.e. the inclusion of the peasant economy in the general system of the Soviet economy), we shall be able to harness the peasantry and the proletariat to the selfsame chariot of socialist construction ; in this event, our second task (i.e. the introduction of Soviet democracy and the infusion of new life into the soviets among the rural population), if successful, will enable us to improve our State apparatus, to link it up with the mass of the people, to make it clean and honest, simple and cheap, and thereby to facilitate the transition from the dictatorship of the proletariat to a Stateless society, to the communist commonwealth.

Such are, in broad outline, the resolutions concerning our party policy in the rural areas adopted by the Fourteenth Conference of the Communist Party of Russia.

It follows that the Party will have to modify its method of leadership in the countryside.

Certain party members maintain that, since we have Nep and since capitalism is becoming temporarily stabilised, our task should be to carry on unbendingly, both in the Party and in the State apparatus, until a general smash-up occurs. I consider that this would be a dangerous and wrongheaded policy. What we need now is not to carry on unbendingly, but to show a maximum of elasticity both in policy and in organisation, a maximum of elasticity both in political and organisational leadership. In the absence of such elasticity, we shall not be able, in the present complicated situation of affairs, to keep our place at the helm. We need the utmost elasticity in order to keep the Party at the helm and to guarantee that the leadership shall remain in the hands of the Party.

Furthermore, it is necessary that communists should abandon certain outrageous methods of administration. We must not be content with having only one way of dealing with the peasantry. When a peasant does not understand what we are driving at, we should exercise patience and explain the matter to him; we must succeed in convincing him. To achieve this end we must spare neither time nor energy. It is obviously far easier simply to issue orders and then to sit tight and wait until they are carried out. That is what our district executives are so apt to do! But the easiest and simplest course of action is not always the best. Not long ago, a village nucleus secretary was asked by the representative of the provincial committee why there were no newspapers in the district. The answer was: "Why should we bother about papers? We are more peaceful and in better case without them. If the peasants once start reading the papers, they'll be asking us questions, and then there'll be no end to the shindy!" This secretary called himself a communist! I need hardly say that such a communist is a veritable curse.. What we have to realise is that without "shindies" we cannot lead; without newspapers it is even more difficult to do so. Let us grasp this truth, let us hammer it into our heads. Only thus can we secure the Party and the Soviet power in their leadership of the rural areas.

At the present day, in order to lead adequately, we must know how to manage and administer economic life, we must understand economics. It no longer suffices to make fine speeches about "world politics", Austen Chamberlain, or Ramsay MacDonald. The period of economic reconstruction is at hand, and only those who are well grounded in the economics of agriculture, who are capable of giving good and practical advice to the peasant, who can help the peasant in organising the work of cultivation, only such as these are fit for leadership. The duty of communists in the rural areas to-day consists in making a study of agricultural science, in setting up intimate ties between themselves and agricultural life, in making themselves acquainted with all the detail work of farming processes. Lacking these essentials, it would be futile to contemplate becoming leaders in the rural districts.

It is no longer possible to make use of the old methods of leadership in the rural districts, now that the level of peasant activity in the political field has risen. This political activity needs to be guided into the channels of Soviet organisation; it must assume the Soviet form. He who labours at putting new life into the soviets and rallying around the party the pick of the peasantry, such a one is a true leader.

Nor can we be satisfied with the old methods of leadership in the rural areas, now that there is increased economic activity in the villages. This economic activity should be canalised through cooperation, should assume the cooperative form. He alone is capable as a leader who creates a cooperative social life in the villages.

Such are, broadly speaking, the concrete and practical tasks facing the Party leadership in the rural areas.

6. THE METALLURGICAL INDUSTRY

I WILL now consider the last group of questions dealt with by the Fourteenth Conference of our Party.

What is the new and peculiar characteristic in the economic development of Soviet Russia ?

It is that we do not estimate boldly enough in the industrial sphere, for here our achievements always put our estimates to shame.

The Russian budget furnishes a striking illustration of this fact. You will remember that, during the course of one half-year, we had to readjust our budget three times in consequence of the rapid increase in our receipts. In other words, our disbursements did not keep pace with our receipts ; thus the treasury was replenished by a considerable surplus. This shows that the springs of our economic life are welling forth copiously, so copiously, indeed, that the forecasts of our financial experts are completely upset. It also proves that we are living through a period of rapid industrial development, on no less extensive a scale, if not on a greater scale, than took place in the United States immediately after the civil war of 1861–1865.

The most notable manifestation in this connexion is the growth of our metallurgical industry. Estimated in pre-war currency, metallurgical production last year amounted to 191,000,000 roubles. In November of the same year our estimates for the budgetary year 1924–1925 amounted to 273,000,000 roubles (pre-war currency). Owing to the unlooked for growth in our metallurgical industry we had to modify our plans and increase the budget to 317,000,000 roubles. Again, in April, this once more proved to be too low a reckoning, and we raised the estimate to 350,000,000 roubles. To-day we are told that this sum is still too small, and we shall have to increase it to 360,000,000 roubles and more.

This means that our metallurgical production is twice as large this year as it was last, and I do not include in this increase the extensive growth of our petty industry, our means of transport, our coal and other combustible production, and so forth.

THE METALLURGICAL INDUSTRY

Thus, so far as the organisation of industry is concerned, so far as the foundations of socialism are concerned, we have already entered the broad highway of expansion. In speaking of the metallurgical industry (which is after all the mainspring of industry in general) we are entitled to say that the period of stagnation is passed, and that the industry is now rapidly advancing. Comrade Dzherzhinsky is right when he declares that our country can and must become one of those in which the metallurgical industry occupies a premier place.

I need hardly stress the tremendous significance of these facts in relation to the development of our country and in relation to the world revolution.

From the point of view of internal development, the expansion of our metallurgical industry is of vast importance, for it signalises the growth of all our industries, of the whole of our economic life. The metallurgical industry lies at the root of industry in general. In the absence of a well-developed metallurgical industry, we cannot hope to set going our petty industry, our transport, our coal and combustible production, our electrical installations, or our agriculture. The growth of our metallurgical industry is the gauge of the growth of our industry in general, of our whole economic system.

Lenin, writing of "heavy industry", by which he mainly meant metallurgical industry, said:

> We know that a good harvest does not suffice for the wellbeing of Russia—any more than an ample production of petty wares providing the peasants with articles of consumption is sufficient. What we need, in addition, is heavy industry. Many years of hard work will have to be devoted to putting it on its feet. . . . If we are not successful in saving our heavy industry, if we cannot reorganise it, we shall not be able to upbuild any kind of industry. Lacking this, we are doomed to disappear, so far as being an independent country is concerned. (*Works*, Russian edition, vol. xviii., part II., p. 95.)

When we turn to consider the international significance of the growth of our metallurgical industry, we realise that this significance is incalculable. For its amazing growth proves that, under the dictatorship of the proletariat, the workers are not only capable of destruction but also of construction, that they are competent to build up with their own hands a new industry and a new society freed from the exploitation of man by man. To be able to do this in actual fact (and not merely to theorise about it in books) is to contribute in no small degree to the success of the world revolution, to make it secure and final. The constant stream of workers coming from the West to visit our country, is not a chance phenomenon. It has an agitational and practical value which is of enormous significance for the development of the revolutionary movement throughout the world. The workers who come to visit Russia look eagerly into every nook and cranny of our factories and workshops. They do not trust what is written in books; they want to see for themselves, to judge from the evidence of their own eyes as to the capacity of the proletariat for the upbuilding of a new industry and a new society. Once these workers are convinced of this fact, you may be sure that the cause of the world revolution will go forward by leaps and bounds. Lenin writes:

> For the moment, it is through our economic policy that we shall bring the greatest influence to bear upon the world revolution. All the workers in every land . . . have their eyes fixed upon the Russian Soviet Republic. . . . In this country, the struggle assumes an international complexion. If we can accomplish our task, we shall surely and definitively celebrate our triumph on an international scale. It is for this reason that questions relating to economic reconstruction are of such exceptional importance to us. Along these lines of industrial development, we must march upward and onward if we are to be victorious; our progress will be slow but continuous, without haste and without halt. (*Works*, Russian edition, vol. xviii., part I., p. 282.)

Such is the international significance of the expansion of our industry in general, and the growth of our metallurgical industry in particular.

There are about four million industrial workers in Russia at the present day. A small number, it is true. Still, that number is sufficient to start the building of the socialist edifice and to organise the defence of our country against attack by the foes of the proletariat. But we cannot rest content with this small number of industrial workers. We need from fifteen to twenty million proletarians; we need the electrification of the more important parts of our country; we need the organisation of agriculture on a cooperative basis; we need the highest possible development of our metallurgical industry. Then no

THE METALLURGICAL INDUSTRY

imaginable dangers need scare us. Then we shall conquer on an international scale.

The historical significance of the Fourteenth Conference of the Russian Communist Party is that it clearly traces the route by which we need to travel if we are to attain this splendid goal.

The route thus indicated is the right one; it is the Leninist path; it is the road leading to victory.

THE NATIONALIST QUESTION IN YUGOSLAVIA

SPEECH TO THE YUGOSLAV COMMITTEE OF THE E.C.C.I.
ON MARCH 30, 1925)

COMRADES!

I DO not feel that Comrade Semich has fully understood the way in which the bolsheviks envisage the nationalist question. Neither before nor after the October revolution have the bolsheviks separated this question from the general question of revolution. The fundamental essence of the bolshevist outlook on the nationalist question is that the bolsheviks have always considered this problem in a revolutionary way.

Comrade Semich has quoted Lenin. We are told that Lenin favoured the settlement of the nationalist question by the constitutional method. Semich would imply that Lenin looked upon the nationalist question as a constitutional one, i.e. not as a question of revolution but as a question of reform. In this, Comrade Semich is wrong. Lenin never had any "constitutional" illusions. We need but read his works to be convinced of this. If Lenin mentioned the word "constitutional" in this connexion, it was because he was considering a constitution that had arisen as the outcome of a revolution; he did not seek a solution of the nationalist question along a constitutional road but along a revolutionary one. We in Russia certainly have a "constitution", and this constitution contains paragraphs relating to the question of nationalities. But our constitution was not brought into being by means of a transaction with the bourgeoisie; it was born out of the victory of the revolution.

Comrade Semich then referred to my own pamphlet on the nationalist question, written in 1912. He tried to find a justification (though an indirect one) for his point of view by quoting from that work. His endeavour was fruitless. Nowhere in this pamphlet did he or could he find the least allusion to warrant his "constitutional" solution of the nationalist question. In confirmation of this, I would draw Comrade Semich's attention to a passage in the pamphlet where I contrast the Austrian solution of the problem (constitutional method) with the Russian Marxists' solution of the problem (revolutionary method). Here is what I wrote:

> The Austrians hope to realise the "liberty of nationalities" little by little, by means of petty reforms. They regard the

granting of national autonomy as an effective measure; they have no hopes of a radical change, of a democratic movement for freedom. Such an idea never enters the circle of their vision. The Russian Marxists, on the other hand, consider that the freeing of nationalities is part of the question of a fundamental change, they link it up with the democratic movement for liberation, for they have no reason to rely upon reforms. This essentially modifies the matter from the viewpoint of the probable fate of the various nationalities in Russia.

This seems to me perfectly clear.

It does not express my own personal outlook, but the general outlook of the Russian Marxists who have always considered the nationalist question to be inseparably linked up with the general question of revolution.

This problem had two phases. The first phase was before the October revolution, the second followed that revolution. During the first phase, the nationalist question was part of the general question of the bourgeois-democratic revolution; that is to say, it formed part of the question of the dictatorship of the proletariat and the peasantry. During the second phase, the problem assumed wider dimensions. It became a question of colonies, it transformed itself from a question of home policy into a question of worldwide policy. Then it had to be considered as part of the general question of the proletarian revolution (as an element in the question of the dictatorship of the proletariat). In both phases, as is evident, the question was envisaged from a purely revolutionary angle.

In my opinion, Comrade Semich has not understood this in its entirety. That is why he wants to treat the national question as a constitutional one—which is equivalent to saying that he looks upon it as a question of reform.

Having made this initial mistake, he follows it up with another. Comrade Semich is loath to consider the nationalist question as, essentially, a question of the peasantry. (I do not say "a question of agriculture" but "a question of the peasantry". My use of the latter phrase is deliberate, for these two questions, agriculture and peasantry, cover different ground.) Of course the nationalist question is not to be identified with the peasant question, for the latter is only a part of the former. In addition to the peasant question, the nationalist question includes such problems as national culture, national statecraft, etc. Nevertheless, the peasant question lies at the root of the nationalist question, constitutes its quintessence. That is the reason why the peasantry forms the main army of the nationalist movement; without this army of supporters, there could be no powerful nationalist movement at all. This is what we have in mind when we say that the nationalist question is, in essence, a peasant question. It seems to me that, by refusing to accept this formula, Comrade Semich shows that he underestimates the intrinsic strength of the nationalist movement and that he fails to grasp the profoundly popular and profoundly revolutionary nature of its appeal. Such a lack of understanding, such an underestimation, constitute a grave danger; for, in practice, they imply an underestimation of the potential might which lies at the heart of (let us say) the stir among the Croats who are struggling for national emancipation; and this underestimation is a menace to the Yugoslav communists, for it brings further complications in its wake.

Such, then, is Comrade Semich's second error.

A third error is his endeavour to deal with the nationalist question in Yugoslavia as though it were quite unconnected with the international situation and the probable course of events in Europe. Starting from the fact that at the present moment there is no serious movement for independence among the Croats and the Slovenes, Comrade Semich reaches the conclusion that the question of the right of nations to constitute themselves into independent States is of academic interest only, having no roots in actual life. This is, obviously, a mistaken point of view. Even if we admit that, for the moment, the question has no actuality, yet, in the event of war breaking out, it would become very actual indeed. It would become equally actual if a revolution were to take place. War is bound to break out sooner or later, and sooner rather than later; such is the inevitable trend of imperialism.

When, in 1912, we Russian Marxists were drafting our first program concerning the nationalist question, there was no serious movement for national independence in any region of the tsarist empire. Nevertheless, we deemed it necessary to include in our program an item dealing with the right of nations to self-determination, the right of every national minority to sever itself from the State to which it is attached and to form itself into an independent realm. Why did we do this? Because we based our program not merely upon events as they were then, but upon events which were in course of preparation in the general system of international relationships; because we reckoned, not only with the present, but likewise with the future. We knew that if any nationality were to arise and demand its separation from a given State, we Russian Marxists would rally to its support. Comrade Semich, in the course of his speech, quoted freely from my pamphlet on the nationalist question. Here is what I wrote about the independence and self-determination of nationalities:

> The growth of imperialism in Europe is not a chance matter. Europe has become too cramped a hunting ground for capital, which is seeking fresh pastures in other continents; is looking out for new markets, for cheap labour, and for a new fulcrum. But this leads to complications abroad, and to wars. It is conceivable that circumstances at home or abroad may lead this or that nationality within the Russian empire to raise the question of its independence, and to answer the question to its own advantage. In such a case the Marxists would be the last to raise any objections to these aspirations.

This was penned in 1912. Both during the war and afterwards, and in especial after the triumph of the dictatorship of the proletariat in Russia, the course of events was to prove the correctness of this thesis.

All the more should we take into account such possibilities in Europe in general, and in Yugoslavia in particular, seeing that the revolutionary nationalist movement is becoming ever more acute in the subjugated lands, and seeing that the revolution has triumphed in Russia. We have also to remember that Yugoslavia is not a fully independent country, that she is wedded to certain imperialistic groups, and that, consequently, she cannot wholly escape the influence of the great forces that are at work beyond her borders. If a national program for Yugoslavia is to be satisfactorily drawn up (and this is precisely the work it is incumbent on us to do) we have to remember that this program must take other things into consideration besides what is happening here and now. We shall have to consider the events which are in course of preparation, and the inevitable issue of extant international relationships. Hence it seems to me that the question of the right of nations to self-determination is a living and vital question, one full of actuality.

A few words now about the nationalist program. It should be based upon a definite view concerning a soviet revolution in Yugoslavia, that is to say, the theory that unless the bourgeoisie is overthrown and the victory of the proletariat achieved, the nationalist question cannot be satisfactorily solved. Of course there are exceptions to this rule. For instance, in 1905, Norway separated herself from Sweden without striking a blow—an event which Lenin dealt with in detail in one of his articles. But this separation took place before the war. Besides, the circumstances were exceptionally favourable. After the experiences of the war and the Russian revolution, such cases are not likely to occur again. Their occurrence is, indeed, so rare, that from a practical point of view we need hardly take such a possibility into consideration. For this reason it is necessary to base our program upon the theory of revolution.

Furthermore, it is imperative that we should include in the program an item concerning the right of nations to self-determination, and even their right to form themselves into a separate State. I have already told you why, under existing circumstances at home and in the international arena, this point is of the utmost importance.

Finally, the program should include an item dealing with the territorial autonomy of those nationalities in Yugoslavia which do not deem it necessary to separate themselves from that country. It is quite wrong to think that such a contingency will not arise. After the victory of the revolution in Yugoslavia, it may well be that, just as happened in Russia, certain nationalities will not desire to cut themselves loose and form independent States. It behoves us, therefore, to introduce a special item concerning autonomy, an item which will envisage the possibility of transforming the State of Yugoslavia into a federation of national, autonomous States based upon a soviet regime.

Thus those nationalities which should desire to sever their connexion with the States to which they are at present attached, could do so ; and, on the other hand, those nationalities which desired autonomy as part of a federation of States could attain the goal of their desires likewise.

To avoid all misunderstanding, let me add that the right to

separation does not mean an *obligation* to form a separate State. Any nationality may take advantage of this right ; contrariwise, any nationality can forgo the right if such is its wish. This lies with the said nationality to decide. Some of our comrades would make the exercise of this right obligatory, and would force the Croats, for instance, to form a separate State. That is a false contention, and must be rejected. We must not confound a right with an obligation.

The " Bolshevik," No. 7, 1925.

POLITICAL TASKS OF THE UNIVERSITY OF THE PEOPLES OF THE EAST

(SPEECH TO THE STUDENTS OF THE UNIVERSITY ON MAY 18, 1925)

COMRADES!

FIRST of all I would like to congratulate you on the fact that you are celebrating the fourth anniversary of the founding of the Communist University of the Peoples of the East. I need hardly say that you have my best wishes for success in the difficult task your university has shouldered, the task of training communists for work in oriental lands.

I want, furthermore, to claim your indulgence in that I have so seldom paid you a visit. I know that I should have come more often. But what can I do? I am up to my eyes in work, and there has literally been no possibility of visiting you more frequently.

Let us proceed at once to an examination of the political tasks which confront the University of the Peoples of the East.

On analysis, we find that there is a certain duality in the composition of this university. Fifty nationalities and racial groups find a home under its roof. Still, the students are all children of the East. And yet these statements do not give us an adequate picture, a clear and complete description. There are, in fact, two distinct groups of students at the university. One group is made up of those who came to us from Soviet lands in the East, from lands which had thrown off the imperialist yoke, from lands where the workers had overthrown the bourgeoisie and had seized the reins of power. The other group is composed of those who have come to us from colonial and vassal lands, from lands where capitalism is king, where the yoke of imperialism is as strong as ever it was, where the peoples have still to win their independence and clear out the imperialists.

Thus we have, as it were, two Easts, living different lives and developing under different conditions.

This twofold grouping of the students must of course leave its mark upon the work of the university. It explains why the university has one foot on Soviet ground and the other foot on the soil of the colonies and dependencies.

Two tasks, therefore, confront the university. One task is

to train up citizens competent to minister to the needs of the Soviet republics of the East. The other task is to train up citizens competent to minister to the needs of the toiling masses in the colonial and vassal lands of the East.

Let us examine these two tasks separately.

1. TASKS OF THE UNIVERSITY IN THE MATTER OF THE SOVIET REPUBLICS OF THE EAST

In what way do these countries, these republics, differ from colonial and dependent lands?

(1) These republics are freed from the yoke of imperialism.

(2) They are developing and consolidating themselves as national units, not under the aegis of the bourgeois regime, but under the aegis of the Soviet power—a fact unprecedented in history, but, nevertheless, a fact.

(3) Though these republics are but slightly developed from the industrial point of view, they can count upon the support of the industrial proletariat of the Soviet Union.

(4) Having thrown off the yoke of foreign colonisers, protected by the dictatorship of the proletariat in Russia, and being themselves members of the Soviet Union, these republics can and must participate in the work of upbuilding socialism in our country.

The fundamental task is to help the workers and peasants of these republics to take a hand in the establishment of socialism in our land; and (conforming to the special circumstances of life in each republic) to create and develop conditions which will quicken this movement of participation.

The following tasks are, therefore, to be immediately undertaken by all active workers in the Soviet East.

(1) The creation of industrial foci in all the Soviet republics of the East. These foci will become rallying points around which the peasants can group themselves side by side with the proletarians. As you are already aware, this work has been set afoot, and its development will run parallel with the economic growth of the Soviet Union. We are assured of success in this direction, even if it takes time to achieve, for we know that these republics are rich in raw materials of many kinds.

(2) The development of agriculture and, above all, of irrigation. This work, too, as you know, has been begun in Transcaucasia and in Turkestan.

(3) The support and advancement of cooperation among the

broad masses of the peasants and artisans. This is the most trustworthy way of ensuring the entry of the Soviet republics of the East into the general system of Soviet economic reconstruction.

(4) The creation of closer ties between the soviets and the masses; care that these soviets, by the composition of their membership, shall be truly representative of the respective nationalities. By such means we shall inaugurate a Soviet national State in close touch with the toiling masses, and understood by these same masses.

(5) Encouragement of the respective national cultures; inauguration of a wide network of courses of lectures; schools for elementary education and for professional training where the teaching shall be given in the appropriate native languages; these measures will help in forming communist battalions and technical experts recruited from among the native populations.

The accomplishment of these tasks will greatly facilitate the work of socialist construction in the Soviet republics of the East.

There is talk of "model" Soviet republics of the East. What is a "model" republic? A model republic is one which honestly and conscientiously performs all its tasks, thereby rallying the workers and peasants of neighbouring colonial and vassal lands into the movement towards their own emancipation.

I said a moment ago that the soviets must create close ties between themselves and the toiling masses of their respective republics, that they must become national soviets. What does this mean and how are we to set about the task in practice? It seems to me that the recent delimitation of the Turkestan frontier is an excellent example of how to set about creating closer ties with the masses. The bourgeois press sees only a "bolshevist trick" in this delimitation of frontiers. Yet it ought to be clear that there is no trickery in the matter. Our one desire is to satisfy the deeply rooted aspirations of the Turcoman and Uzbek masses, which are eager to manage their own affairs. Before the revolution, both these countries were divided up among various khanates and States, and were an easy prey to exploitation by the wielders of power. The time has now come when these snippets of land can be united to form independent States, when the toiling masses of Uzbekistan and Turkestan can realise their aspirations towards self-government. The most important result of the recent delimitation of frontiers in Turkestan has been the welding together of these detached portions of land to form independent States. If, subsequently, these States enter the Soviet Union as fully qualified members having equal rights with all the other States in the federation, this merely signifies that the bolsheviks have found the clue to the aspirations of the toiling masses in the East, and that, throughout the whole world, the Soviet Union is the only voluntary federation of the toiling masses of various nationalities. In order to reunite partitioned Poland, the bourgeoisie has had to enter upon a series of wars. In order to reunite disintegrated Turkestan and Uzbekistan, the communists have needed but a few months of peaceful propaganda.

That is the way to bring the masses into contact with the administrative apparatus; the way to make the masses of workers participate in the life of the soviets.

In so far as we are successful in carrying out this policy we shall know that our line of action is the right one.

I mentioned earlier that the national cultural level of the oriental masses would have to be raised. What is a national culture? How are we to make a national culture compatible with a proletarian culture? Lenin, in pre-war days, said that we had two cultures: bourgeois culture, and proletarian culture. He maintained that the bourgeois cry of "national culture" was a reactionary one, that it tended to infect the minds of the workers with the virus of nationalism. How are we to reconcile the development of national cultures, the inauguration of schools where the teaching is carried on in the native tongue, and the creation of communist cadres from among the indigenous populations—how are we to reconcile this line of action with the upbuilding of socialism, with the upbuilding of a proletarian culture? Are we not enmeshed in contradiction? Of course not! We are now engaged upon the task of upbuilding a proletarian culture. There's no denying that! But proletarian culture (which is socialist at bottom) can assume different forms and different means of expression according to the various dispositions of the peoples participating in the work of socialist construction, according to their language, their local customs, and so forth. The culture may have a national form and a proletarian content. Such is the general culture towards which socialism gravitates. Proletarian culture, far from hindering national culture, actually provides the latter with a content. On the other hand, national culture, far from hindering proletarian culture, actually provides it with a form. So long as the bourgeois held the reins of power, the catchword of "national culture" was no more than a bourgeois slogan helping to consolidate nationalities under the aegis of the bourgeois system. But when the proletariat seized power, this catchword of "national culture" became transformed into a proletarian slogan aiming at the consolidation of nationalities under the aegis of the Soviet power. He who has not grasped the difference of principle between these two situations will never understand Leninism, and will therefore never be able to contemplate the nationalist question from the Leninist point of view.

Certain persons (Kautsky, for instance) talk of the creation of a language common to all mankind, a language which will, by degrees, replace all other languages during the period of socialism. Personally, I am rather sceptical on this point. Hitherto experience has shown the theory to be a fallacious one. The socialist revolution, far from cutting down the number of languages that claim to be something more than dialects, languages that demand a place in the world, has actually increased the number; for, by arousing the broad masses of humanity, by leading them to take an interest in political life, socialism has stirred up a veritable hive of hitherto unknown or quasi-unknown nationalities. Who ever realised that tsarist Russia harboured no fewer than fifty nationalities and ethnic groups within its borders? By breaking the chains of a series of forgotten peoples and nationalities, the October revolution has breathed into them a new life and new possibilities of development. It is customary to speak of "India" as a homogeneous whole. Yet, when the revolution breaks out in Hindostan, many hitherto ignored nationalities will emerge from their seclusion, will come forward, each with its own language and its own distinctive racial culture. As for the participation of the various nationalities in the general proletarian culture, this much is pretty certain, that such participation will take place in conformity with the language and the customs of each national participant.

Not long ago I received a letter from some Buriat comrades.

They asked me to explain the important and complicated question of the relationship between the culture of mankind as a whole and the cultures of the various nationalities. Here is what they wrote:

> We beg you to explain the following questions which are very serious ones for us, and very difficult for us to answer. The aim of the Communist Party is to establish one universal culture throughout the world. How do you conceive of the transition from the national cultures of the various autonomous republics to the one universal culture for all humanity? How will peculiarities of the various national cultures (language, customs, and so forth) be assimilated?

What I said a moment ago could very well serve as answer to these comrades. They wish to know how the assimilation of various nationalities into the wide stream of proletarian culture will take place. Undoubtedly, certain nationalities may be and should be absorbed into the general culture. History is punctuated with such assimilations. This process of absorption of minor stocks tends to promote the development of more powerful races, for partial assimilation is the result of a general process of national growth. It follows that the possible assimilation of certain isolated nationalities does not run counter to our theory, but, on the contrary, confirms it. Proletarian culture in no wise excludes, but fosters national cultures, just as these latter round off and enrich the proletarian culture of mankind.

Such, in broad outline, are the immediate tasks confronting the comrades of the Soviet republics of the East.

Such is the nature, such the content of these tasks.

The present period of intense economic activity and of fresh concessions to the peasantry must be turned to good account in order to hasten the performance of these tasks and thereby to facilitate the participation of the Soviet republics of the East (essentially agricultural countries) in the general work of upbuilding socialism in the Soviet Union.

We are told that the new policy in regard to the peasantry (short-term leases, employment of wage labour, etc.) is retrogressive. There is some truth in the contention! None the less, the Soviet power and the Communist Party still retain their preponderant position and influence. Stable currency, industry and transport rapidly developing, credit system more and more consolidated (by the judicious assigning of credit, or by the withholding of credit, this or that stratum of the population may be raised or degraded in the most inconspicuous way possible !)—all these constitute, for the proletarian dictatorship, reserves thanks to which a withdrawal on part of the front may facilitate the preparation of a general advance. That is why concessions made by the Party to the peasantry may, at a given moment, help rather than hinder the work of inducing the peasantry to participate in the upbuilding of socialism.

What may this signify for the Soviet republics of the East ? It furnishes the active workers in these republics with a new weapon which will lighten the task of bringing them into the general current of Soviet economic development, and will hasten this desirable achievement.

Such is the link between the Party policy in the rural areas and the immediate tasks confronting the active workers in the Soviet East.

Consequently, the duty of the University of the Peoples of the East in regard to these eastern republics is to train its students in such a way as to ensure their maximum efficiency in carrying to a successful issue the tasks I enumerated earlier.

The University cannot cut itself off from everyday life. It is not and must not be allowed to become an institution standing aloof from common experience. It must strike deep roots into the realities of existence. It cannot, therefore, afford to ignore the immediate tasks confronting it in respect of the Soviet republics of the East. It must ever keep these things in view, while forming the contingents destined for work among the peoples of these republics.

In this connexion I may mention two deviations in the practice of the active workers in the Soviet East. If the University hopes to form contingents of truly revolutionary workers it will have to guard against these two deviations.

One of these deviations is the excessive simplification of the tasks I have summarised, and the endeavour to apply mechanically to these eastern lands, lying on the outskirts of the Soviet Union, methods of economic organisation which are admirably adapted to the conditions at the centre of the U.S.S.R. but which run counter to the developmental situation of these eastern republics. Comrades who stray into this path have failed to understand two things. First of all they have not realised that conditions at the centre and conditions on the periphery are far from being identical; in the second place, they have not realised that the Soviet republics of the East do not form one homogeneous whole, that certain among them, for instance Georgia and Armenia, have reached a high stage of national development, that others, such as Chechnya and Kabardia, are on a much lower plane of national integration, and that others, such as Kirghizistan, stand midway between the two extremes. These comrades do not understand that unless one adapts the work to local conditions, if one fails to take into account all the peculiarities of the various countries, the upbuilding of a really solid and stable structure is impossible. Those who wander off into the byways are cutting themselves adrift from the masses and are becoming nothing better than left-wing phrasemongers. The University of the Peoples of the East must wage ruthless war against this undue simplification.

The second deviation consists in exaggerating local peculiarities, in forgetting the common bonds which link up these eastern republics with the industrial regions of the Soviet Union, in ignoring the tasks imposed by socialism, in working in a spirit of narrow and purblind nationalism. Those who are guilty of this deviation are little concerned with the internal organisation of their country, preferring to leave this to the natural course of events. They look upon " foreign " politics, the extension of the frontiers of their republic, litigation with neighbouring republics, filching territory from the people next door, as of greater importance than the internal organisation of their country. Thus, I need hardly say, they delight the bourgeois nationalists of their country. Worse still, those who stray into this path are breaking away from socialism, and are tending to become bourgeois nationalists themselves. The University of the Peoples of the East must fight tooth and nail against this latent nationalism.

Such, then, are the tasks which must be undertaken by the University of the Peoples of the East in regard to the Soviet republics of the East.

2. TASKS OF THE UNIVERSITY IN THE MATTER OF COLONIES AND DEPENDENCIES IN THE EAST

I WILL now examine the second question, which concerns the tasks of the University of the Peoples of the East in relation to the colonial and vassal lands of the Orient.

What is the difference between these lands and the Soviet Republics of the East?

In the first place, the people in these countries live under the yoke of imperialism, and develop under the aegis of imperialism.

Secondly, the revolutionary crisis in these lands is far more acute because of the double yoke imposed upon them, on the one hand by their own bourgeoisie, and on the other hand by the bourgeoisie of foreign countries.

Thirdly, in certain of these lands (India, for instance) the capitalist system is developing rapidly and is creating a native proletariat.

Fourthly, as the revolutionary movement progresses, the national bourgeoisie in each colonial or dependent land, tends to divide into two sections, a petty-bourgeois section, which is revolutionary, and a great-bourgeois section, which aims at compromise. The former continues the revolutionary struggle; the latter makes common cause with the imperialists.

Fifthly, confronting the imperialist coalition there is formed another coalition, the coalition of workers and revolutionary petty bourgeois. This is an anti-imperialist coalition aiming at the complete liberation of the country from the yoke of imperialism.

Sixthly, the question of proletarian leadership, and the question of enabling the masses to shake off the influence of that section of the nationalist bourgeoisie which would fain compromise with the powers-that-be, are questions of ever-increasing actuality in these lands.

Seventhly, the last-named fact greatly facilitates the linking up of the nationalist movement for the liberation of these countries with the proletarian movement in the more advanced countries of the West.

At least three deductions are possible from these seven points of difference.

(1) The liberation of colonial and vassal lands from the yoke of imperialism is not possible save by a victorious revolution. Independence does not come as a gift!

(2) If the advent of revolution is to be hastened, if complete independence of capitalistically developed colonies and dependencies is to be achieved, the compromising section of the bourgeoisie must be isolated, its influence upon the revolutionary section of the bourgeoisie must be annulled, the leadership of the proletariat must be ensured, and the advanced elements in the working class must be organised in an independent communist party.

(3) No lasting victory is possible in these lands unless the movement for their liberation is effectively linked up with the proletarian movement of the more advanced countries of the West.

The fundamental task of the communists in the colonies and dependencies is to make these deductions the starting point of their revolutionary work.

What, then, are the immediate tasks confronting the communists in these lands?

In earlier days it was customary to look upon the colonial lands of the East as a homogeneous entity. This outlook no longer corresponds to the actual state of affairs. To-day, there are no fewer than three categories of colonial and vassal lands. First of all there are the countries (like Morocco, for instance) where there is no proletariat, or so small a proletariat as not to be worth mentioning; countries where industrial life is extremely backward. Secondly, there are countries (like China and Egypt, let us say) where manufacturing industry is little developed, and where the proletariat is, comparatively speaking, not very numerous. Thirdly, there are countries (like India) which are fairly well developed from the capitalist point of view, and possess a proletariat which has attained noteworthy proportions.

It is obvious that each of these countries will need separate treatment.

In Morocco, for instance, the native bourgeoisie has as yet had no reason for splitting up into a revolutionary and a compromising section. The communists should, therefore, do everything to promote the creation of a united nationalist front capable of fighting against imperialist encroachments. A separation of the communist elements from the general movement for emancipation to form a communist party can take place in these lands only in the course of the struggle against imperialism, and more especially after that struggle has been waged to a successful conclusion.

In such countries as Egypt and China, where the native bourgeoisie is already split into a revolutionary section and a compromising section, but where the compromisers have not yet made common cause with imperialism, the communists are faced by other tasks than the formation of a united nationalist front against imperialism. They will have to transcend the policy of the united nationalist front, and adopt the policy of forming a revolutionary coalition between the workers and the petty bourgeois. This coalition may find expression in the creation of a single party whose membership will be drawn from among the working class and the peasantry, after the model of the Kuomintang. But such a party should be genuinely representative of the two component forces, the communists and the revolutionary petty bourgeois. This coalition must see to it that the half-heartedness and duplicity of the great bourgeoisie shall be laid bare, and that a resolute attack shall be made upon imperialism. The formation of such a party, composed, as we have seen, of two distinct elements, is both necessary and expedient, so long as it does not shackle the activities of the communists, so long as it does not hamper the agitational and propagandist freedom of the communists, so long as it does not prevent the proletariat from rallying round the communists, so long as it does not impair the communist leadership of the revolutionary forces. But the formation of such a party is neither necessary nor expedient unless all these conditions are forthcoming ; otherwise the communist elements would become absorbed into the bourgeois elements and the communists would lose their position as leaders of the proletarian army.

Somewhat different is the situation of affairs in a country like Hindustan. Here we find, not only that the native bourgeoisie is severed into a revolutionary fraction and a compromising or reformist fraction, but, in addition, that on all important issues the reformist fraction has already rallied to the side of imperialism. This section of the native bourgeoisie dreads revolution more than it hates imperialism, it is more concerned about its money bags than about the interests of the fatherland; it is the wealthiest and most influential class in the national community, and it has wholeheartedly thrown in its lot with the irreconcilable enemies of the revolution, has made common cause with the imperialists against the workers and peasants of its native land. The revolution cannot be victorious unless this alliance is broken. If we are to break it, we must concentrate our attack upon the reformist section of the native bourgeoisie, must expose its treachery, must withdraw the toiling masses from its influence, and must systematically prepare the way for the leadership of the proletariat. In other words, the proletariat of such lands as Hindustan must be trained to become the leader in the movement for national emancipation, whilst the bourgeoisie and its spokesmen must gradually be dislodged from the leadership. The aim, therefore, must be to create a revolutionary, anti-imperialist coalition, and to ensure that, within this coalition, the role of leader shall be played by the proletariat. The coalition may (there are alternative possibilities) take the form of a single, united party of workers and peasants voicing a joint program. But the advanced communist elements will need to insist upon the independence of the Communist Party in such lands, for the proletariat cannot be prepared for its task as leader, nor can the proletarian leadership be realised, by any other than the Communist Party. Yet the Communist Party may, nay must, openly cooperate with the revolutionary section of the native bourgeoisie, if it is to succeed in isolating the compromising and reformist section, and in rallying the masses of the urban and rural petty bourgeoisie to the fight against imperialism.

To sum up. The immediate tasks confronting the revolutionary movement in colonial and vassal lands where capitalism is well developed are as follows :

(1) To win over the best elements among the workers to the cause of communism and to form independent communist parties.

(2) To set up a nationalist and revolutionary coalition of workers, peasants, and revolutionary intellectuals, as a counterpoise to the coalition of the great bourgeoisie with the imperialists.

(3) To guarantee that the leadership of the revolutionary coalition shall be in the hands of the proletariat.

(4) To free the urban and rural petty bourgeoisie from the influence of the reformist native bourgeoisie.

(5) To secure the linking up of the national liberationist movement with the proletarian movement of advanced countries.

We see, therefore, that the tasks facing the communists in the colonial and vassal lands resolve themselves into five groups.

These tasks, considered in the light of the present international situation, are of exceptional importance. For the moment the salient characteristic of the international situation is that the revolutionary movement has entered a period of calm, of truce. What is the meaning of this state of calm ? It means that the pressure on the workers of the West has been redoubled, that the oppression of colonial lands is more ruthless, and that, above all, the attacks upon Soviet Russia (the standard bearer of the revolutionary movement) have been reinforced. The imperialists have already begun preparing their onslaught against the Soviet Union. The campaign of calumny embarked upon at the time of the rising in Esthonia, the campaign against the U.S.S.R. in connexion with the explosion in the Sofia cathedral, the general and continuous campaign against Soviet Russia carried on in the columns of the capitalist press—one and all are the prelude to an offensive. Public opinion is thus to be prejudiced against Soviet Russia ; these campaigns constitute, as it were, a clearing of the ground as a preliminary to more drastic action ; they are meant to create a " moral justification " for intervention. The future alone can tell what will be the results of these campaigns, and whether the imperialists will venture upon a serious offensive. One thing is obvious, that these attacks foreshadow nothing but evil to the colonial peoples. The preparation of a counter-offensive by all the forces of the revolution as an answer to the probable onslaught of the imperialists is, therefore, an urgent question of the day, and cannot be postponed.

It is for this reason that a systematic endeavour to accomplish the more urgent tasks in colonial and vassal lands is of such prime importance to the revolutionary movement.

In view of the foregoing considerations, we may ask what is the mission of the University of the Peoples of the East in relation to the colonies and dependencies ? The University must study all the special characteristics of the revolutionary development in these lands, it must educate the students coming from these countries, must educate them in such a way as to be sure that they will be able to fulfil all the tasks enumerated above.

The University of the Peoples of the East has opened its doors to about ten groups of students from these multiform colonial lands. We all know how eager these comrades are for light and knowledge. The University must see to it that the students shall become genuine revolutionists, equipped with all the theories and all the practical experience of Leninism, and capable of accomplishing the immediate tasks facing the movement for national emancipation, not as the outcome of fear, but thanks to the promptings of conviction.

Here it is well to draw attention to two deviations into which the militant workers in these lands are liable to stray, and against which it is essential to fight with the utmost resolution if genuinely revolutionary troops are to be created.

First of all, the *revolutionary* possibilities of the nationalist movement for emancipation must not be *underestimated*; on the other hand, the likelihood of a united national front comprising *all* the elements in colonies and dependencies must not be over-stressed, or looked forward to regardless of the conditions of the modes of life and the degrees of development in these regions. This is a deviation to the right which threatens to set back the revolutionary movement, and to merge the communist elements into the general welter of the national bourgeoisie. The University must combat this straying from the path with the utmost determination.

In the second place, the *revolutionary* possibilities of the nationalist movement for emancipation must not be *overestimated*, nor must the importance of the alliance between the working class and the revolutionary bourgeoisie against the imperialists be underestimated. The Javanese communists seemed to suffer from this deviation when they, recently and quite wrongly, raised the slogan "All power to the soviets" in their country. This is a deviation to the left which threatens to sever the Party from the masses, and to transform it into a clique. A resolute fight against the deviation is essential if truly revolutionary battalions are to be formed in the colonial and vassal lands.

Such, in broad outline, are the political tasks facing the University of the Peoples of the East in relation to the workers in the Soviet republics and the colonial lands of the East.

We may hope that the University of the Peoples of the East will be able to accomplish these tasks creditably.

THE NATIONALIST QUESTION ONCE MORE

(COMMENT ON SEMICH'S ARTICLE)

COMRADE SEMICH is to be congratulated in that, after the discussion in the Yugoslav committee, he has been able to publish an article fully endorsing the outlook of the delegation from the Communist Party of Russia to the Comintern. But it would be incorrect to assume on the strength of this article that there were no differences of opinion between the delegation from the Communist Party of Russia and Comrade Semich, either before or during the discussion in the Yugoslav committee of the Comintern. Yet Comrade Semich seems desirous of giving this impression, since he endeavours to prove that the differences of opinion on the nationalist question were no more than misunderstandings. He is, unfortunately, mistaken. He states in his article that the polemic carried on against him was founded upon " a series of misunderstandings " which arose " solely " from the fact that his speech at the Yugoslav committee was " not translated in full ". It would appear, then, that the whole blame must fall upon the shoulders of the translator, who, for some reason, failed to translate Comrade Semich's speech in full. In the interests of truth, I must declare that Comrade Semich's statement does not accord with the facts. It would have been better had Comrade Semich quoted the relevant passages from his speech in support of his contentions. (The full report of the speech to the Yugoslav committee is among the archives of the Comintern.) For reasons best known to himself, he has not thought proper to do so. I have, therefore, been forced to undertake this task—a far from pleasant one!—in Comrade Semich's place, for it is absolutely essential that the matter should be thrashed out.

This is all the more imperative seeing that, in spite of Comrade Semich's wholehearted espousal of the views advanced by the delegation from the Communist Party of Russia, not a few points still remain to be cleared up.

In my speech to the Yugoslav committee (see above, p. 257), I dealt with three questions upon which there was divergence of opinion. (1) The means for solving the nationalist problem. (2) The social content of the nationalist movement in the present historical epoch. (3) The role of the international factor in the nationalist question.

As concerns the first of these questions, I said that I did not feel that Comrade Semich had "fully understood the way in which the bolsheviks envisage the nationalist question", that he separated the nationalist problem from the general problem of revolution, and that he had thus entered a road which would lead him to an attempt to solve the nationalist question by "constitutional" methods.

Is this correct?

I leave the judgment to the readers of the following passage from Semich's speech to the Yugoslav committee (March 30, 1925).

> Is it possible to solve the nationalist question by constitutional methods? Let us confine ourselves at the outset to a theoretical statement of the problem. We will suppose that a given State, X, shelters within its borders three distinct nationalities, A, B, and C. These three nationalities express a wish to live in one and the same State. What is the upshot? Nothing more than the internal ordering of this State. That is a constitutional question. In our imaginary instance, the nationalist question is nothing more than a question of constitutional adjustment. . . . If, in this hypothetical case, we can reduce the nationalist question to one of constitutional adjustment, we must admit, as I have always insisted, that the right of peoples to self-determination (even up to the point of to their breaking away and setting up independent States) is an indispensable prerequisite to the solution of the constitutional question. Solely in this sense do I conceive the constitutional question.

Comment is superfluous! It is obvious that those who look upon the nationalist question as an integral part of the general question of the proletarian revolution, will never be willing to look upon it as a mere matter of constitutional adjustment. Only those who can sever the nationalist question from the general question of the proletarian revolution, can, like Semich, be content to regard it as no more than one element of the constitutional question.

In Comrade Semich's speech we find an assertion that the right of nations to self-determination cannot be acquired without a revolutionary struggle. He says: "It is plain that such a right cannot be acquired save by a revolutionary struggle. Such rights cannot be won by parliamentary methods, but only by revolutionary mass action." What is the meaning of "revolutionary struggle" and "revolutionary ... action"? Are "revolutionary struggle" and "revolutionary ... action" equivalent to the overthrow of the dominant class, to the seizure of power, to the victory of the revolution as the prerequisite to a solution of the national question? Of course not! We have to do with two totally different things: for to consider the victory of the revolution to be the essential prerequisite to a solution of the national question is not at all the same as to regard "revolutionary ... action" and "revolutionary struggle" as the preliminary conditions for the solution of the national question. Nor, we may note in passing, are "revolutionary struggle" and "revolutionary ... action" incompatible with constitutional and reformist methods. The decisive factor in determining the character of a party (whether it be a revolutionary party or a reformist party) is not "revolutionary action" taken by itself, but the political aims and tasks in whose accomplishment the party turns such revolutionary struggles to good account. After the dissolution of the first duma in 1906, the Russian mensheviks suggested the organisation of a "general strike" and even of an "armed insurrection". This did not make them any less menshevik! What was their purpose when they advocated such a step? It was certainly not to overthrow tsarism and to organise for the complete victory of the revolution. They wanted merely to "exercise pressure" upon the tsarist government in order to win reforms, to obtain a widening of the "constitution", and to bring about the summoning of an "improved" duma. Their "revolutionary action" was for the reform of the old conditions while leaving power in the hands of the ruling class. This is the constitutional method. Revolutionary action undertaken with a view to breaking the old order, to overthrowing the ruling class, is a different thing altogether. In this case such action sets our feet upon the road leading to the complete victory of the revolution. As is plain, the difference is fundamental.

Hence I consider that Comrade Semich, by referring to the "revolutionary struggle" while in the same breath he reduces the national question to one of constitutional adaptation, himself confirms my statement that he "has not fully understood the way in which the bolsheviks envisage the national question". He has not grasped that the national question must not be considered as an isolated phenomenon but as one which is indissolubly intertwined with the question of the victory of the revolution, that it is part of the general question of revolution.

Though I have dwelt rather emphatically on this point, I do not mean to imply that I have said anything new anent Comrade Semich's mistake. Far from it! At the Fifth Congress of the Communist International, Comrade Manuilsky, referring to this same error, declared:

> In his pamphlet, *The National Question in the Light of Marxist Theory* and in a series of articles published in "Radnik", the organ of the Communist Party of Yugoslavia, Comrade Semich declares that a campaign for the revision of the constitution is the most immediately practical task now incumbent upon the Communist Party of Yugoslavia. In this way, he restricts action on behalf of the right to self-determination within purely constitutional limits.

Comrade Zinovieff, too, referred to this same error during the sittings of the Yugoslav committee:

> Only one thing is missing in Comrade Semich's picture: the revolution! The national question is a revolutionary problem, not a constitutional one.

It is not possible that all these comments upon Comrade Semich's error can be fortuitous and totally without foundation. No smoke without fire!

So much for Comrade Semich's fundamental mistake.

His other mistakes arise from his initial misconception.

Now as to the second of the questions upon which there is a divergence of opinion. In my speech to the Yugoslav committee I said (see above, p. 260) that Comrade Semich " is loath to consider the nationalist question as, essentially, a question of the peasantry ".

Was I right?

Read the following passage from Comrade Semich's speech to the Yugoslav committee, and judge for yourselves.

> What is the social significance of the nationalist movement in Yugoslavia?—The social significance consists in the rivalry between Serbian capitalism, on the one hand, and Croat and Slovene capitalism on the other.

Nobody will deny the part played by these rival groups of capitalists. But it is equally undeniable that a person who contemplates the social significance of a nationalist movement from the angle of the rivalry between competing groups among the bourgeoisies of the various nationalities, cannot consider the national question as essentially a peasant question. What is the essence of the nationalist question, now that, from being a local question concerning the peoples dwelling within one particular State, it has become a worldwide question, a question of the struggle of the colonial and vassal peoples against imperialism ? The essence of the nationalist question consists at present in the fight of the masses in the colonies and dependencies against financial exploitation, against political enslavement, against the destruction of the subordinate national cultures by the bourgeoisie of the ruling nationality. Under these circumstances, what importance can be attached to the rivalry between competing groups among the bourgeoisies of the various nationalities ? That rivalry has no decisive importance ; in certain cases, even, its importance is practically nil. Obviously what is of importance here is, not the fact that the bourgeoisie of one nation can beat the bourgeoisie of another nation by means of competition, but the fact that the imperialist group of the ruling nationality exploits and oppresses the masses, and above all the peasant masses, of the colonies and dependencies, and that by oppressing and exploiting these masses the imperialists spur them on to the struggle against imperialism, and make them the allies of the proletarian revolution. The nationalist question cannot be considered as, in essence, a peasant question, if we contemplate it only from the angle of the rivalry among the bourgeoisies of the various nationalities. Nor, on the other hand, can we believe that the social significance of the nationalist question lies in this rivalry between competing bourgeoisies, if we consider the nationalist question as, essentially, a peasant question. There is no earthly sign of resemblance between these two formulas.

Comrade Semich refers to a passage in my pamphlet, *Marxism and the Nationalist Question*, written towards the close of 1912. Herein we read that " the nationalist struggle is a struggle of the middle classes among themselves ". Comrade Semich would seem to be quoting this passage in justification of his formula concerning the social significance of the nationalist movement in contemporary historical conditions. But the above-mentioned pamphlet was written before the imperialist war, at a time when the nationalist question had not yet assumed, in the eyes of the Marxists, a worldwide significance, and when the basic demands of the Marxists concerning the right to self-determination was considered to be, not a part of the proletarian revolution, but a part of the bourgeois-democratic revolution. It would be absurd to deny that, since the date when the pamphlet was written, there has been a fundamental change in the whole international situation. Who can be so blind as not to see that the war and the Russian revolution have converted the nationalist question from being a part of the bourgeois-democratic revolution into being a part of the proletarian-socialist revolution? In October 1916 Lenin wrote an article entitled, *Results of the Discussion concerning the Right to Self-Determination*. Herein he declared that the essential point of the nationalist question in general, and of the right to self-determination in particular, was that they had ceased to be parts of the democratic movement, and had become vital constituents of the proletarian movement, of the socialist revolution. I will refrain from citing other works on the nationalist question, whether by Lenin or by any other spokesmen of communism in Russia. Let the above quotation suffice. In view of these later pronouncements on the matter, what value can we attach to Comrade Semich's reference to a pamphlet by myself written at the time of the bourgeois-democratic revolution in Russia? Have we not now entered upon a new epoch, bringing with it a new historical situation? Have we not entered upon the epoch of the worldwide proletarian revolution? Comrade Semich quotes without giving due attention to time and space! He does not take the actual situation of affairs into his reckoning, and thereby he breaks the most elementary rules of dialectic. He cannot see that what may be perfectly apt and true in one historical situation, may be completely false when applied to another. In my address to the Yugoslav committee (see above, p. 260) I drew attention to the fact that the bolsheviks have always considered that there were two phases in the development of the nationalist question in Russia. The first phase was before the October revolution. At that time, when the bourgeois-democratic revolution was in progress, the nationalist question formed part of the general question of the democratic movement. The October revolution marked the beginning of the second phase, when the proletarian revolution was in progress and the nationalist question became an essential element in the proletarian revolution. Need we draw attention to the supreme importance of this distinction? Yet I fear that Comrade Semich has not yet clearly recognised the full significance of this distinction between the two phases of development in the nationalist question.

This is the reason why I consider that Comrade Semich, by endeavouring to base the nationalist movement on the rivalry among the competing bourgeoisies of the various lands instead of taking the peasantry as his basis, " shows that he underestimates the intrinsic strength of the nationalist movement, and that he fails to grasp the profoundly popular and profoundly revolutionary nature of its appeal " (see above, p. 261).

Such is the position with regard to Comrade Semich's second error.

In his speech to the Yugoslav committee, Comrade Zinovieff criticised Semich's mistaken judgments in precisely the same terms as myself. To quote his very words:

> Comrade Semich is at fault when he declares that the peasant movement in Yugoslavia is under the leadership of the bourgeoisie and that it is therefore not a revolutionary movement. (Cf. " Pravda ", No. 83.)

Is it just by chance that these words should coincide with mine? Certainly not!

Let me repeat: There is no smoke without fire.

Now as to the third question upon which there is a divergence of opinion. I maintained that Comrade Semich endeavoured " to deal with the nationalist question in Yugoslavia as though it were quite unconnected with the international situation and the probable course of events in Europe ". (See above, p. 261.)

Is this so?

Undoubtedly! For nowhere in his speech did Comrade Semich give the slightest hint that the present international situation is, especially in the case of Yugoslavia, an extremely important factor in the solution of the nationalist question. What Comrade Semich has not taken into account is that Yugoslavia came into being thanks to a conflict between two great imperialist coalitions, and that Yugoslavia cannot escape the influences now at work in the imperialist States which surround her. Semich declares that he can very well imagine that changes will take place in the international situation which will make the nationalist question a matter of practical politics. But, in view of existing international relationships, such a declaration is altogether insufficient. We are no longer concerned with the fact that certain modifications may, in a more or less remote future, occur in the international situation so as to place the nations' right to self-determination in the forefront of practical politics. Bourgeois democrats, did they happen to consider it expedient, might very well recognise that for themselves! This is not at present our concern. A choice of two things confronts us. Either the question of national self-government, i.e. the modification of existing frontiers in Yugoslavia, is merely an appendage to the national program, or else it lies at the very root of that program. One thing is certain. The question of self-determination cannot at one and the same time be an appendage and a foundation of the national program launched by the Communist Party of Yugoslavia. Yet I fear that Comrade Semich is still inclined to consider the right of nations to self-government as no more than a possible appendage to the national program.

This is why I maintain that Comrade Semich separates the nationalist question from that of the international situation, and that, in consequence, the right to self-government, i.e. the right to change the present frontier line of Yugoslavia, is for him an academic or theoretical problem and not one of practical politics.

So much for Comrade Semich's third error.

Comrade Manuilsky said almost the same thing at the Fifth Congress of the Communist International. I quote from his report:

> The fundamental premise for such a method of dealing with the national question as Comrade Semich proposes is that the proletariat must accept the bourgeois State as it exists within the frontiers which have been set up by violence and war. (Cf. the " Bolshevik ", Nos. 11 and 12, 1925.)

Can we look upon this accordance of views as purely fortuitous? Certainly not!

Once more I repeat: No smoke without fire.

QUESTIONS AND ANSWERS

(SPEECH AT SVERDLOFF UNIVERSITY ON JUNE 9, 1925)

COMRADES!

You have submitted certain questions to me in writing, ten in all. Here is the first.

I

What measures and what conditions are necessary for the strengthening of the smychka,[1] *the alliance between the working class and the peasantry, during the period of proletarian dictatorship, in the event of the Soviet Union not receiving the support of the social revolution of the western European proletariat in the course of the next ten or fifteen years?*

This question seems to me to cover the ground of all the other questions you have asked me. I shall, therefore, deal with it only in a general way, and shall not attempt to answer it exhaustively. Of course, I wish to leave enough to be said in answer to the other nine!

In my opinion, the resolutions passed by the Fourteenth Conference of the Russian Communist Party furnish an ample reply to this question. Herein we read that the main guarantee for the strengthening of the smychka is a correct policy in regard to the peasantry.

What is a correct policy in regard to the peasantry?

It consists in the carrying out of a series of economic, administrative, political, cultural, and educational measures calculated to strengthen the smychka.

Let us consider what can be done in the economic field.

The first step is to put an end to the survivals of war communism in the rural districts. Next we must introduce a rational system for the fixing of prices, both of agricultural and of industrial products, thereby ensuring the rapid growth of industry and agriculture and the disappearance of the so-called

[1] See footnote to p. 26.

"scissors ".[1] Then the sum total of the agricultural tax will have to be reduced, and the tax will have to be gradually transformed into a local tax contributing to the local budget instead of as at present to the State budget. Further, the wide masses of the peasantry must be drawn into the cooperative movement, and, above all, into the agricultural and credit cooperatives, so that the peasants may likewise play their part in upbuilding socialism. Tractors as a means for revolutionising agricultural technique and for creating cultural foci in the rural areas, must be introduced in large numbers. Finally, the electrification scheme must be carried out, for this will draw the town and countryside together, and will help to break down existing antagonisms.

Such, in the realm of economic life, is the road along which the Party must travel if it wishes to ensure a satisfactory alliance between town and countryside.

I wish to draw your special attention to the matter of transferring the agricultural tax from the State budget to the local budgets. At first sight, such a transference may seem rather strange. Nevertheless, it is a fact that the agricultural tax is becoming more and more an affair of local politics; soon it will become completely so. Two years ago, the agricultural tax contributed the main, or almost the main, revenue to our State budget. Now it is no more than an insignificant part of our State revenue. The budget for this year [1924–1925] has been calculated at two-and-a-half milliards of roubles. The agricultural tax will yield at best 250 to 260 millions of roubles this year, that is to say at least 100 millions less than in the foregoing twelve months. Not a very large return, you will agree! And in proportion as the State budget grows, the contribution from the agricultural tax to the State revenue will diminish. Further, from the 260 millions which it is reckoned will accrue to State revenue this year from the agricultural tax, 100 millions, i.e., more than a third, are to be transferred to the local budgets. Why should this be done? Because of all existing taxes the agricultural tax is the one that is best suited to the satisfying of local needs. The local budgets will undoubtedly grow. This growth will largely be due to the

[1] In 1922–1923, when there was a growing disproportion between the falling prices of agricultural produce and the rising prices of manufactured articles the term "scissors" was applied to this state of affairs. The "scissors" were said to be closing or opening,, according as the disproportion diminished or increased.—E. and C. P.

absorption of the revenue from the agricultural tax, which will have to be turned to the best account for the satisfaction of local needs. Such a development is all the more certain seeing that the main revenue of the State is already derived, and will to an increasing degree be derived from State enterprises, from indirect taxes, and the like.

It is, therefore, more than probable that the yield from the agricultural tax will be transferred from the State budget to the local budgets, and such a transference will be both necessary and appropriate if we are to strengthen the bonds between workers and peasants.

Now let us turn to consider the administrative and political measures which will facilitate the union of town and countryside.

We shall have to make Soviet democracy a reality both in the towns and the rural areas; we shall have to put new life into the soviets by simplifying the State machinery, making it cheaper and more healthy, morally speaking, by clearing out the bureaucratic elements and the bourgeois disruptive forces; we shall have to create the most intimate bonds between the State apparatus and the masses. Such is the road the Party must travel if it is to be successful (in the administrative and political field) in consolidating the workers' and peasants' alliance—the smychka.

The dictatorship of the proletariat is not an end in itself. It is a means, a path leading to socialism. What is socialism ? It is a stage on the way from a society dominated by the dictatorship of the proletariat to a society wherein the State will have ceased to exist. In order to realize the transition, it behoves us to overhaul the State apparatus in such a way that it will guarantee the transformation of a society dominated by the dictatorship of the proletariat into a Stateless society, a communist society. In order to achieve this end, we have adopted the following rallying cries : put new life into the soviets; make soviet democracy in town and village a living reality; hand over the administration to the best elements of the working class and of the peasantry. But without the active collaboration of the masses we shall not be in a position to improve the State apparatus, to make a clean sweep of the bureaucratic and disintegrating elements, and to make the machinery of government near and dear to the masses. We cannot secure the active and steadfast collaboration of the masses unless we induce the best elements among the workers and peasants to play a direct part in the administrative organs, unless we create intimate bonds which shall link up the State apparatus with the lowest sections of the labouring masses.

What distinguishes the soviet apparatus of State from the bourgeois apparatus?

The bourgeois apparatus of State functions from above, stands as it were over the masses; thus it stands apart from the population, separated from the masses by an insurmountable barrier, and its whole spirit is alien to the broad masses of the population. On the other hand, the soviet apparatus of State merges with the masses; it does not and cannot stand over the masses, for if it did so it would forfeit its soviet character; it dare not alienate itself from the masses, for if it did so it would cease to enrol the millionfold masses under its banner. Here we have one of the chief differences between the soviet apparatus of State and the bourgeois apparatus of State.

In his pamphlet, *Will the Bolsheviks retain Power?*, Lenin says that the 240,000 members of the Communist Party will certainly be able to govern the country in the interests of the poor and against the wealthy, seeing that they are in no way less competent than the 130,000 landowners who in former days governed the country in the interests of the wealthy and against the poor. Misinterpreting these words, certain comrades have come to believe that the *State apparatus* can be satisfactorily worked by a few hundred thousand Party members, and that these will amply suffice to govern a huge country like Russia. It is because of this confused way of thinking that they would fain identify the Party with the State. This is a fatal error, and a grotesque distortion of Lenin's thoughts. When Lenin mentioned the 240,000 Party members, he did not mean they could adequately supply the needs of the Soviet State apparatus in respect either of numbers or of general capacity. Quite the contrary! In the composition of the soviet apparatus of State he included, in addition to the Party members, the million electors whose votes were cast for the bolsheviks on the eve of the October revolution; he declared that, by bringing the masses to participate in the daily work of governmental administration, we could multiply the personnel of our State apparatus tenfold. He wrote:

> These 240,000 are backed by a million votes cast by the adult population, for, as is confirmed by recent experience in Europe in

general and in Russia in particular (recall the August elections to the Petrograd municipal council), thus may we reckon the relationship of the numbers of votes cast in favour of the Party members and the numerical strength of the Party itself. We are, therefore, already possessed of a " State apparatus " consisting of a million persons whose loyalty to the socialist State is based upon conviction and not upon the fact that they will receive a goodly bundle of bank-notes every 20th day of the month ! Nay more, we have a marvellous means for increasing tenfold, at one swoop, the number of participants in our apparatus of State, a means which has never been used and never could be used by a capitalist State. This marvellous means consists in bringing the workers, in bringing the poor classes of the population, into the everyday work of government. (Cf. *Works*, Russian edition, vol. xiv., part II., p. 236.)

How shall we succeed in " bringing the workers, in bringing the poor classes of the population, into the everyday work of government " ?

This will be effected by the initiative of our mass organisations, by commissions and committees of every conceivable kind, by conferences and delegate meetings ; all these will come into being as an outcome of the activities of the soviets, of the trade unions, of the factory and workshop committees, of the cultural institutions, of the Party organisations, of the Youth organisations, of the various cooperative associations, and so forth and so on. Our comrades often fail to see that around the basic organisations, such as the Party, the soviets, the trade unions, the Communist Youth, that around the organisations catering for the army, women, education, and what not, there is a veritable ant-heap of independent organisations, commissions, and committees, comprising millions of non-Party workers and peasants, an ant-heap of persons who, by their daily, toilsome, inconspicuous and silent labour are building the foundations and creating the very life of the Soviet State, are tapping the sources whose waters will vivify and strengthen the Soviet State. Without these organisations, whose active members run into millions of persons, and whose work brings them into close contact with our soviet and Party organisations, the maintenance and the development of the Soviet power, the administration and government of so vast a country as Russia, would be impossible. The soviet apparatus of State does not consist only of soviets. In the fullest meaning of the terms, it is composed of the soviets together with the organisations whose millionfold membership consists of Party and non-Party groups of every kind, which link up the soviets with the " lowest " strata, which merge the State apparatus with the masses, and which, little by little, are breaking down every barrier between the State apparatus and the population.

This is how we shall increase " tenfold " the numbers of those engaged in running the State apparatus ; in this way we shall bring it into close contact with the masses, making the workers sympathetic towards it, cleansing it of the relics of bureaucracy, merging it with the masses, and thus preparing the way for the transition from a society dominated by the dictatorship of the proletariat into a Stateless society, into a communist society.

This is what lies at the root of the slogans concerning the vivification of the soviets and the realisation of Soviet democracy. Such are the chief means whereby we shall strengthen the smychka, the bond between town and countryside in the administrative and political activities of the Party.

As to the means for strengthening the smychka in the field of culture and education, I shall not waste time in an extensive study of these, for they are obvious and widely known, and need no further elucidation. I shall confine myself to giving the merest sketch of the main line of advance in this field of work for the immediate future. First of all, we must create the conditions for the realisation of compulsory elementary education throughout the whole area covered by the U.S.S.R. This is a reform of enormous importance. If we are successful in carrying it through, we shall have gained a splendid victory, not only on the educational front, but likewise on the political and economic fronts. This reform will be the prelude to a mighty awakening among our people. But it will cost hundreds of millions of roubles ; it will necessitate the creation of an army of teachers numbering something like half a million. Nevertheless, we must carry out this reform in the very near future, if we mean to raise the cultural level of our people. We shall carry it through, never fear !

If the stabilisation of capitalism should last for a long time, by what degenerations will our Party be threatened?

Does any such danger of degeneration exist?

The danger is, or, rather, the dangers are, real enough, and they exist quite independently of the stabilisation of capitalism. The stabilisation of capitalism makes them more tangible, that's all. In my view there are three main dangers to reckon with:

(a) The danger of losing sight of the socialist goal which is the aim of all the work of reconstruction in our country; this danger, therefore, is an intensification of the tendency to relinquish the conquests of the revolution.

(b) The danger of losing sight of the international revolutionary goal—the danger of a short-sighted nationalism.

(c) The danger that the Party may lose its position as leader, and, therewith, the possibility of the Party becoming no more than a tailpiece to the State apparatus.

We will begin by an examination of the first of these dangers.

This danger is characterised by a lack of faith in the inner forces of our revolution; by a lack of faith in the union between the workers and the peasants, and in the leading part played by the working class within this union; by a lack of faith in the possibility of transforming " Nep Russia " into " Socialist Russia "; by a lack of faith in the victory of socialist construction in our country.

This is the cast of mind of those who would fain relinquish the gains of the October revolution; it points the way to degeneration and decay; for it leads to an abandonment of the principles and the aims of the revolution, and to the degradation of the proletarian State into a bourgeois-democratic State.

The mainspring of this frame of mind, the reason for its appearance within our Party, is to be accounted for by the growth of the bourgeois influence over the Party since the introduction of the New Economic Policy, and the life-and-death struggle between the capitalist and the socialist elements in the economic life of the Soviet State. The capitalist elements are not content to wage war in the economic field, but are endeavouring to transfer the fight into the ideological realm of the proletariat. They are trying to undermine the faith of the less stable elements in the Party, to inspire them with misgivings as to the possibility of upbuilding socialism in Russia, to infect them with scepticism in regard to the socialist goal of all our striving. Nor can we fail to see that these endeavours have not been wholly barren.

"How can such a backward country as ours hope to realise a fully socialist society?" This is a sample question asked by such an infected "communist". "The condition of our productive forces does not warrant our setting up such a utopian objective. Let's be jolly glad that we can hold on somehow! How can we venture to think of socialism just now? Let's do what we can, and hope for the best. . . . ."

Others hold forth after the following manner: "We have already fulfilled our revolutionary mission by bringing about the October revolution. Now everything depends upon the international revolution, for, unless the proletariat of western Europe makes a successful revolution, we in Russia cannot hope to upbuild socialism. As a matter of fact, there isn't any more work in Russia for a revolutionist to put his hand to. . . ." We all know that in 1923, on the eve of the revolutionary events in Germany, some of our young students wanted to throw away their books and make tracks for Germany. They maintained that there was nothing left in Russia for a revolutionist to do, and that their duty now was to relinquish their studies and go to Germany, there to help in the revolution.

Both these specimens of "communists" deny the possibility of realising socialism in Russia. They have the same outlook as that of the so-called "liquidators", the frame of mind of those who would fain relinquish the gains of the October revolution. The only difference is that the former group cloaks its "liquidationism" in fine phrases about the "theory of productive forces" (by a delicious irony Milyukoff, in his journal "Poslednie Novosti", has recently congratulated these "communists" on being "serious Marxists"!), whereas the latter group cloaks its "liquidationism" in left-wing phraseology and in "terribly revolutionary" utterances concerning the world revolution.

Let us, for the sake of argument, admit that there is no further work for a revolutionist to set his hand to in Russia, that there is no possibility of upbuilding socialism in our country unless the revolution is victorious in other countries, and that the triumph of socialism in the more advanced countries may be postponed for another ten or twenty years. Are we to suppose that in our country, surrounded as it is with capitalist States, the capitalistic elements in our economic life will cease their life-and-death struggle with the socialistic elements, and will await the victory of the world revolution with folded arms ? The absurdity of such a question is obvious on the face of it. But what then can our " serious Marxists " and " terrible revolutionists " set about doing ? They will have to drift with the stream and ultimately become nothing better than commonplace bourgeois democrats !

We can't have it both ways. Either our country must be looked upon as the base of operations for the world revolution, either we have (as Lenin says) all that is needful for the upbuilding of a fully socialised society (in which case we can and must upbuild this society and trust in a complete overthrow of the capitalistic elements within our economic life) ; or our country cannot be considered the base of operations for the world revolution, we do not possess the necessary adjuncts for the upbuilding of socialism, and therefore cannot possibly inaugurate a socialist society (in which case, should the victory of socialism in other lands delay its coming, we shall have to reconcile ourselves to witnessing the progressive ascendancy of the capitalistic elements in our country, together with the decomposition of the Soviet power and the decay of the Party).

Make your choice !

Scepticism in regard to the possibility of our upbuilding socialism in Russia leads to " liquidationism ", to the relinquishment of the gains of the October revolution, to decay and degeneration.

Our Party must, here and now, set itself to fight against the danger of liquidation ; this fight is all the more urgent at the present time in view of the temporary stabilisation of capitalism.

Now let us turn to the second danger.

The distinguishing marks of this danger are a lack of trust in the international proletarian revolution ; a lack of faith in its victory ; the adoption of a sceptical attitude of mind towards the liberationist movements in colonial and vassal lands ; the failure to understand that, in default of the support of the worldwide revolutionary movement, our country cannot make an effective stand against world imperialism; the inability to grasp the fact that the victory of socialism in one land alone cannot be definitive (seeing that such a country has no guarantee against capitalistic intervention) until the revolution has triumphed in at least a few other countries; the absence of that modicum of internationalism which leads us to understand that the victory of socialism in one land alone cannot be an end in itself, but is merely a means which can be utilised for the development and growth of the revolutionary movement in other lands.

Should we follow this road, we should land ourselves in a quagmire of nationalism, degeneration, and the complete surrender of the international policy of the proletariat. Those who are attacked by this sickness look upon our country, not as part of a whole which goes by the name of " the international revolutionary movement ", but as the alpha and omega of this movement. Such folk imagine that the interests of all other countries should be sacrificed to the interests of our country.

Must we rally to the support of the Chinese movement for national emancipation? Wherefore? Won't that be risky? Won't it embroil us with other lands? Would it not be better for us to create " spheres of influence " in China, acting in this matter in concert with other " advanced " powers, and to pull off a deal which shall be to our advantage? A useful step, and no risks to run. . . . Rally to the support of the liberationist movement in Germany? Is it worth our while? Would it not be better to come to an agreement with the Entente concerning the treaty of Versailles, and to reap a nice little reward for ourselves in the process? Keep up friendly relations with Persia, Turkey, Afghanistan? Is the game worth the candle? Would it not be better to set up the whilom " spheres of influence " with one or the other of the great powers? And so on, and so forth.

Here we have a new kind of nationalist cast of mind, one which tends to relinquish the foreign policy of the October revolution, and to create a medium for the culture of the bacteria of degeneration.

We said that the origins of the first danger were to be found in the growth of bourgeois influences in the home policy of the Party, and in the life-and-death struggle between the capitalistic and socialistic elements in our economic life. The origins of the second danger are to be found in the growth of bourgeois influences in the foreign policy of the Party, and in the struggle of the capitalist States against the dictatorship of the proletariat. The pressure exercised by the capitalist States upon the Soviet Union is tremendous, and the officials who are working in our Commissariat for Foreign Affairs are not always able to withstand this pressure, but are tempted to adopt the line of least resistance, to enter the path leading to nationalism, this line of retreat seeming to them the best way of avoiding international complications.

Now it is abundantly clear that the first proletarian State can retain its position of standard bearer of the international revolutionary movement only on condition that it retains a consistently internationalist outlook and promulgates the foreign policy of the October revolution. It is equally obvious that the adoption of the line of least resistance and of a nationalistic viewpoint in the domain of foreign affairs will lead to the isolation and the decay of the country where the proletarian revolution gained its first victory.

Thus we see that the lack of an international revolutionary outlook threatens us with nationalism and with dissolution.

This is why the fight against the danger of nationalism is a matter of such urgency for the Party.

Finally, let us consider the third danger.

Here we are confronted by a lack of faith in the inner forces of the Party and its capacity for leadership; by the tendency of the State apparatus to weaken the leadership of the Party and to free itself from the latter; by the failure to understand that in the absence of the guidance of the Communist Party there can be no dictatorship of the proletariat.

This danger threatens from three directions.

First of all, the classes which should be led have suffered a change; the workers and peasants are no longer the same as they were during the period of war communism. In those days, the working class was declassed and scattered, the peasants were a prey to fear lest the landowners should return as the result of a defeat of the revolution in the course of the civil war. At that time the Party was the only concentrated force, guiding affairs in a purely militaristic fashion. To-day the situation is very different. War is at an end; and, consequently, the immediate danger which rallied the toiling masses around the Party no longer exists. The proletariat is reunited and reanimated; it has risen to a higher level both materially and intellectually. The peasantry, too, has attained a higher level and has developed since those days. The political activity of both these classes has increased and will continue to increase. Military methods of government are no longer possible. It behoves us to introduce the utmost elasticity into our leadership; to study with the minutest care the needs and aspirations of the workers and peasants; and to attract into the Party all those workers and peasants who have signalised themselves by their activity and intelligence in the field of politics. Of course, we cannot expect to acquire all these things betwixt night and morning! Hence there is a discrepancy between what the Party ought to do and what the Party actually does at the given moment. Thus there is a danger of weakening the leadership which has been assumed by the Party, the danger of forfeiting the communist guidance of the masses.

In the second place we have to recognise that in recent days, during the period of economic development, the apparatus of State and the organisations catering for the social life of the people have grown considerably, and become increasingly strong. Trusts and syndicates, trade and credit institutions, administrative, political, cultural, and educational organisations, and, finally, every kind of cooperative, have grown and expanded, and have absorbed hundreds of thousands of new participants (non-Party workers for the most part) into their ranks. But the State apparatus has not only grown numerically. Its power and its influence have increased likewise. And as the apparatus grows in importance, its pressure on the Party will be more and more felt, it will more and more endeavour to take the leadership out of Party control, it will more and more resist Party influence. We must effect a regrouping of forces and must reallot the work of the leaders within the apparatus of State, so as to guarantee the Party leadership in the new situation with which we are faced. I need hardly say that such a move cannot be carried out at one stroke. Hence arises the danger that the apparatus of State may break loose from the Party.

Thirdly, the work itself has become more complicated and varied. Here I am speaking of the actual work of reconstruction upon which we are engaged. New fields of activity have opened out both in town and countryside. Consequently, the task of leadership has assumed more concrete forms. We were wont to speak of leadership " in general ". To speak thus to-day is merely phrase-mongering. What is needed now is a concrete, a thoroughly practical leadership. The period we have just passed through produced a sort of wiseacre, a type of Party worker who had a ready answer for any kind of question relating to theory or practice. This type must yield place to a new type of Party worker, one who is versed in some special aspects of his work. To be an efficient leader, we must know the science of leadership, must study this science conscientiously, patiently, perseveringly. Leadership in the rural areas necessitates a knowledge of agriculture, of cooperation, of the policy of the government in relation to prices ; it demands a knowledge of the laws which bear directly upon life in the villages. Leadership in the towns necessitates a knowledge of industry, of the life of the workers, of their demands and aspirations ; it implies a knowledge of cooperation, trade unionism, working folks' clubs, and so forth. Unfortunately, such knowledge cannot be acquired in a twinkling ! If the Party leadership is to become worthy of the Party itself, the quality of the Party membership will have to be raised. Quality must henceforward be deemed the highest asset for Party membership. But the process of raising the quality of our membership must needs be slow. Old habits are difficult to uproot ; and routinism, rather than expert knowledge, is, unhappily, still apt to guide the management of our Party organisations. This explains why the alleged leadership so often degenerates into a grotesque accumulation of absolutely futile orders, why " leadership " becomes no more than an empty word, leading to nothing and leading nobody. Party leadership and the Party prestige are very seriously threatened by the dangers arising from such a state of affairs.

There is ground enough here to make it quite plain that by depriving the Party of its position as leader of the masses, that same Party is threatened with disintegration and decay. Prompt steps to counteract this danger are absolutely essential.

3

How is the fight against the kulaks [1] to be waged successfully without kindling the class war?

The author of this question, so it seems to me, has tried to be too concise. His endeavour to abridge has led him to choose his words badly. What class war is here in question? If it refers to the class war in the countryside as a general phenomenon, then I would draw attention to the fact that the proletariat does not wage this war against the kulaks alone. The antagonisms between the proletariat and the peasantry as a whole—what have we here but a class struggle, though it is a class struggle of a peculiar and unusual kind? The proletariat and the peasantry are the two main classes of our present-day community. Between these two classes certain antagonisms exist which may, in the course of time, disappear, but which here and now are very much alive and give rise to conflicts between the two classes.

When we consider the relationship between town and countryside, between proletariat and peasantry, it seems to me that the class war in Russia is proceeding along three main lines.

(a) The struggle between the proletariat as a whole (represented by the State) and the peasantry in connexion with the fixing of maximum prices for industrial and agricultural products, in connexion with standardising taxation, and so forth.

(b) The struggle between the proletariat as a whole (represented by the State) and the rural bourgeoisie or kulaks in connexion with the reduction of the prohibitive prices fixed by speculators for agricultural products, in connexion with the transference of the main burden of taxation on to the kulaks, etc.

[1] The Russian peasants comprise three main categories: 1. *rich peasants*, or *kulaks*, whose farms are large, and who employ wage-labour; these form a "rural bourgeoisie"; the village money-lenders and liquor-sellers under the old regime were also termed "kulaks": 2. *middle peasants*, who work their holdings themselves, with the aid of their families, but do not usually employ wage-labour: 3. *poor peasants*, who have very small holdings, or none at all, being mainly agricultural labourers (for wages) and half-peasants or semi-proletarians (who work in the towns at certain seasons).—E. and C. P.

(c) The struggle between the poor peasants, and more especially the farm labourers, and the kulaks.

We may consider these three aspects of the class struggle as three fronts differing in importance and in the nature of the issues that are being fought. Our attitude towards the various forms of the struggle along these fronts should, therefore, vary accordingly.

Let us examine the matter in greater detail.

First Front. In consequence of the mediocrity of our industrial development and the impossibility of raising loans wherewith to set it on a secure footing, the proletariat (represented by the State) has enacted a number of important measures for the defence of our industry against foreign competition, and with a view to expanding it in such a way as to advantage the whole of our national economy, including agriculture. These measures are: State monopoly of foreign trade, agricultural tax, State purchase and sale of agricultural produce, an all-embracing plan for the development of our national economy. The measures are based upon the idea of nationalisation of the chief branches of industry, transport, and credit. The results from an application of these measures have been as anticipated. They put a stop to the fall in the prices of industrial commodities, and to the rise in the excessively high price of agricultural produce. Nevertheless, it is obvious that the peasants, who have no option but to buy industrial commodities and to sell their agricultural products, will endeavour to buy cheap and to sell dear. In addition, the peasants would like to see the agricultural tax abolished, or, at least, to see it reduced to an absolute minimum.

Here we have a definite cause for a struggle between proletariat and peasantry.

Is the State in a position to renounce the above-mentioned measures? No, it is not. Such action on the part of the State at this juncture would ruin our industries, disrupt the proletariat as a class, change our country into an agrarian dependency of the industrially advanced lands, and frustrate the whole of the achievements of our revolution.

Is it to the interest of the peasantry as a whole that these measures should be abolished? Certainly not; for if these measures were abolished it would mean the triumph of the capitalist trend, which in its turn would mean the impoverishment of the majority of the peasants and the enrichment of a handful of wealthy persons, of capitalists. Who would venture to maintain that the peasantry desires its own impoverishment, that it desires to see our country turned into a colony, that it has not been keenly interested in the development of our economic system along socialist lines?

We here have a definite ground for an alliance between proletariat and peasantry.

Does this mean that our industrial institutions, relying on the State monopoly, are in a position to force up the prices of commodities to the disadvantage of the peasant masses and, in the long run, to the disadvantage of industry itself? No such thing! Industry would be the first victim of such a policy. It would then become impossible to transform our industry from the hothouse plant it was but yesterday into the healthy and flourishing concern it promises to be in the future. Hence our campaign in favour of a reduction of the prices of manufactured goods, and for raising the productivity of labour—which has had a fair measure of success.

Further, is it possible that our institutions for the purchase and sale of wares, relying on the State monopoly, can so reduce the price of agricultural products as to ruin the peasantry, to damage the best interests of the proletariat and the peasantry, and thereby to prove disastrous to our economic life as a whole? Most certainly not! Such a policy would ruin our industry, for it would disorganise the home market, and would hinder the flow of agricultural supplies to the workers. This lies at the root of our campaign against the "scissors". That campaign, too, has yielded good results.

Finally, can our local and central institutions, relying on the law concerning the agricultural tax, and profiting by their right to collect the taxes, be allowed to regard the law as something enacted for all time, as giving them power, in the execution of their duties, to demolish the granaries, or to pull the roofs off the houses of the penniless taxpayers, as happened in certain districts in the Tambov province? Of course, such behaviour is preposterous. High-handed measures of this kind undermine the peasants' trust in the proletariat and in the State. That is why the Party has set about reducing the agricultural tax, giving it a more or less local character, setting our fiscal system in order, and putting an end to the abuses which have arisen here and there in connexion with the collection of the taxes. These measures have, as you know, partly achieved their end.

Thus we see that, primarily, there is a community of interest between proletariat and peasantry, so far as fundamentals are concerned, for both these classes are equally interested in the triumph of socialism in our economic life. Hence is born the alliance between the proletariat and the peasantry. But this community of interests is contraposed by an antagonism of interests between the two classes in current affairs. Hence arises a struggle within the alliance, a struggle which is, nevertheless, largely neutralised by the preponderant influence of the community of interests, so that the antagonisms will ultimately pass away. Then the workers and the peasants will no longer be separate classes; they will have become working folk in a classless society. There are ways and means for overcoming these antagonisms. We must maintain and strengthen the alliance between the proletariat and the peasantry, for this is in the best interest of both the allies. Not only do we possess the ways and means, but we have already put them to good use, applying them successfully to the complicated situation created by the introduction of the New Economic Policy, and by the temporary stabilisation of capitalism.

Does it follow from the foregoing considerations that we should fan the flames of the class war on this front? No, it does not. Quite the contrary! From all that I have just said, it follows that we must use every means in our power to moderate the struggle on this front, to settle the differences by means of agreements and concessions on the part of both antagonists, and, above all, to prevent the struggle from becoming embittered, or from degenerating into violent conflicts. This is precisely what we are doing. Our task is all the easier because the community of interests which unites the peasantry with the proletariat is far stronger and more profound than are the antagonisms which separate them.

As you see, we must sedulously avoid kindling the class war on this front.

Second Front. Here the combatants are the proletariat (represented by the State) and the rural bourgeoisie or kulaks. The class struggle in this case assumes just as special a form as it did in the case of the fight on the *First* Front.

With a view to giving the agricultural tax a specifically income-tax character, the State has thrown the burden of it upon the shoulders of the kulaks. But the kulaks respond by trying to wriggle out of paying their contribution and by using all their influence in the villages with a view to shifting the burden on to the shoulders of the middle and poor peasants.

In its fight against soaring prices and in its endeavour to stabilise wages, the State is forced to take measures of an economic nature. These measures aim at fixing a just price for agricultural produce, a price which shall in every way meet the needs of the peasants. The kulaks respond by buying up the harvest of the middle and poor peasants, and by thus amassing huge reserves, which they store in their barns. They do not, forthwith, send these goods to market, for they know that the " corner " they thus establish will lead to an artificial rise in prices, and that large profits will accrue to the successful speculator. You will remember that in certain provinces the kulaks succeeded in forcing up the price of corn to eight roubles per pood [1 pood = about 40 lbs.].

The class war on this front, with its special characteristics, and in a more or less veiled form, arises from such causes as I have enumerated.

At first sight it might seem that the policy of intensifying the class war on this front would be sound. This supposition is, however, quite false. Here, likewise, it is not to our interest to accentuate the class struggle. We can and must avoid provocation, and all the complications such provocation might entail.

We must put fresh life into the soviets, win over the middle peasants, and organise the poor peasants within the framework of the soviets. Thereby the main burden of taxation will be thrust on to the shoulders of the kulaks, and the broad masses of the peasantry will be relieved from the weight of taxation. Excellent results have already been achieved by the measures we have adopted to carry out these plans.

It is imperative that the State should have at its disposal a sufficient reserve of food, so as to be able to bring pressure to bear upon the market, to have the power of intervening when necessary, to keep prices at a level which is acceptable to the working masses, and thus to scotch the machinations of the rural speculators. Recently, as you know, tens of millions of poods have been utilised for this purpose. Here, likewise, we have secured very gratifying results. Not only in such towns as Leningrad, Moscow, and Ivanovo-Voznesensk, and in such areas as the Donetz coalfield, were we able to keep down the price of grain, but in many other districts we forced the kulaks to capitulate and to put their corn reserves on the market.

Of course, we cannot always arrange these matters as we should like. It is possible that, in certain cases, the kulaks will take the law into their own hands and themselves fan the flames of class war, will transform the struggle into something resembling an attack by brigands or an insurrectionary movement. In such an event the policy of kindling the class war would not be our policy but the kulaks' policy, it would be a counter-revolutionary policy. The sufferings entailed by the carrying out of such a policy (one, mark you, directed against the Soviet State) would fall upon the kulaks, who would have to pay dear for the step they had taken.

You will see that on this front, too, a deliberate kindling of the class struggle is out of the question, as far as we are concerned.

Third Front. The combatants on this front are the poor peasants (more especially the agricultural labourers) and the kulaks. The State is not directly concerned. This front is not so extensive as the other two. But the class war is obvious and open here, whereas it is more or less veiled on the other fronts.

On the third front, there is direct exploitation of wage-labour or semi-wage-labour by the peasant proprietor. It would, therefore, be unsuitable if we embarked upon a policy of mitigating or of moderating the fight. What we have to do is to organise the poor peasants for the struggle against the kulaks, and ourselves to act as leaders in the fight.

But, you will ask, is not this "kindling the class war"? Not at all! When we speak of kindling the class war, we do not talk of the organisation and leadership of an unavoidable struggle, but, rather, of the artificial and deliberate stimulation of struggle where struggle is better avoided. Do we need to have recourse to artificial means now that we have the dictatorship of the proletariat, and now that the Party and the trade unions have absolute freedom of action? Of course not.

The policy of kindling the class war is, as we see, just as inept on this front as on the other two.

So much for the third question.

You will have no difficulty in realising that the question of the class struggle in the rural areas is not quite so simple as might appear at first sight.

Is the slogan " Workers and Peasants' Government " a practical one, or is it merely used for the purposes of agitation?

This question seems to me a somewhat strange one.

The way in which the question is phrased would seem to imply that the Party is capable of launching slogans which are out of touch with reality, and which are used in order to favour some sly move or the other (a move which the questioner, heaven only knows why, chooses to christen " agitation "). This would mean that the Party is capable of issuing watchwords which have no scientific justification. Is there any truth in the implication? Of course there is none! A party capable of acting thus would not be long for this world, and would deserve to vanish like a soap-bubble, and never be heard of again. Our Party would not then be the Party of the proletariat, a Party pursuing a scientifically sound policy. It would be no more than a flake of spume floating on the surface of the political seas.

By its character, its program, and its tactic, our government is a proletarian, communist, workers' government. No amount of quibbling can obscure this fact. Our government cannot have two programs at one and the same time; cannot have a proletarian program and some other program as well. Our government's program and its practical labours are proletarian and communist; and, so far as there is any meaning in words, our government is, therefore, proletarian and communist.

Does this imply that our government is not likewise a workers' and peasants' government? There is no such implication. Our government, though proletarian by its program and its practical labours, is at the same time a workers' and peasants' government.

How do you account for this?

Because the fundamental interests of the bulk of the peasantry are identically the same as those of the proletariat.

Because, consequently, the interests of the peasants find complete expression in the program of the proletariat, in the program of the Soviet State.

Because the Soviet Government is buttressed by the alliance

of the proletariat with the peasantry, an alliance based upon the community of their fundamental interests.

Because, finally, in the organs of government and in the soviets, there are not only workers but peasants as well, striving shoulder to shoulder against the common foe, striving for the realisation of socialism—peasants labouring alongside the workers and under the leadership of the workers.

That is why the slogan " Workers' and Peasants' Government " is not a mere " agitational " slogan. It is a revolutionary slogan of the proletariat, and finds its scientific justification in the communist program.

5

Some comrades interpret our policy towards the peasants as an extension of democracy for the peasantry, and as a modification in the character of the ruling power in our land. Is this interpretation correct?

Is it a fact that we are extending the scope of democracy in the rural areas?
Yes.
Is this a concession to the peasantry?
Undoubtedly.
Is this concession very great, and is it consonant with the constitution?
I do not consider that the concession amounts to much, and it in no way conflicts with our Soviet constitution.
What, then, are we modifying, and what, precisely, does this concession amount to?
We are modifying our methods of work in the countryside because the old methods were no longer satisfactory under the new conditions of rural development. We are modifying the routine hitherto prevailing in the villages because this routine was seriously hampering the smooth working of the smychka [1] and was hindering the efforts of the Party members to rally the peasantry around the proletariat.
In many districts hitherto it has been quite usual to find a small group of persons at the head of affairs and governing the villages. These people were as often as not on far more friendly terms with the powers-that-be in the provincial capital or in the district town than they were with the peasants under their charge. Such rural administrators were prone to look for guidance to their superior officials and kept their eyes so fixed on these that they had no glance to spare for the population in the village. They did not feel themselves answerable to the villagers, to the electors, but to the officials in the district town or in the capital of the province. They failed to understand that those in high places are only links in the chain which welds the entire population

[1] See footnote to p. 26.

together, and that if one link should break, be it never so lowly and insignificant, the whole chain will fall to pieces. The result has been a loss of control, and arbitrary actions on the part of the administrators, who have calmly taken the law into their own hands. This has given rise to discontent and grumbling on the part of the villagers. As you are aware, we were obliged, in such circumstances, to arrest and imprison quite a number of presidents of rural committees and members of Party nuclei. We are determined to put an end to this state of things in the villages, to deal with this abuse in so resolute a manner that it will never rear its head again.

In many rural districts, the elections to the soviets have not hitherto been genuine elections. They have been nothing better than bureaucratic acts on the part of small groups of administrators who, fearful of losing their positions of power, have, by chicanery and by exerting undue pressure upon the electors, forced " deputies " of their own choosing into the governing bodies. The consequence was that the soviets ran the risk of becoming transformed from institutions which were near and dear to the masses into institutions which were alien to the masses, and the guidance of the peasants by the workers (a leadership which is the very basis and the strength of the dictatorship of the proletariat) was threatened with destruction. The Party was, therefore, compelled to demand fresh elections to the soviets. The new elections showed that, in many districts, the electoral procedure was a relic from war communism, and it behoved us to see that so outworn and harmful a procedure should be completely abolished. We set to work with a will, and have accomplished this very necessary task.

That is what lies at the root of our concession to the peasantry, what lies at the root of the extension of democracy in the rural areas.

The concession is needed, not only by the peasantry, but likewise by the proletariat, for it strengthens the proletariat, it enhances the prestige of the proletariat in the countryside, and it increases the peasants' trust in the proletariat. The aim of the concessions and the compromises is, in the long run, to consolidate the power of the proletariat.

What, for the moment are the limits of our concessions ?

These limits were fixed by the Fourteenth Conference of the

Russian Communist Party and by the Third Soviet Congress of the U.S.S.R. You know that they are not very wide, and do not exceed the boundaries about which I have just been speaking. But it does not follow that they must for all eternity remain as they are at present. Far from it. As our national economy develops, as the economic and political power of the proletariat becomes ever more consolidated, as the revolutionary movement in the West and in the East progresses, as the international situation of the Soviet State improves, so, proportionally, will our concessions assume a wider scope. Lenin, in the year 1918, spoke of the need for " extending the Soviet constitution to the whole population in proportion as the resistance of the exploiters is broken ". (*Works*, Russian edition, vol. xv., p. 161.) Here there is talk of extending the constitution so as to include the whole of the population, the bourgeoisie not excepted. The words were spoken in March 1918. Yet from that date till the day of his death five years went by, and Lenin never once uttered a syllable as to the desirability of carrying out such a measure. Why was this ? Because the time was not yet ripe. No one will doubt but that a day will come when we can put the measure into execution. We must wait till the situation of the Soviet Republic both a home and abroad has become solidly established.

It is for these reasons that, although we can look forward to the time when a further extension of democracy can be introduced, we deem it necessary for the nonce to restrict our democratic concessions within the limits prescribed by the Fourteenth Conference of the Communist Party of Russia and by the Third Soviet Congress.

Do these concessions modify the character of the ruling power in our land ?

Not in the least.

Do these concessions introduce into the system of the dictatorship of the proletariat any modifications which could lead to weakening of that system ?

Certainly not.

Far from being weakened, the dictatorship of the proletariat takes on a fresh lease of life directly the soviets become active and the pick of the peasantry plays its part in the work of administration. The leadership of the peasantry by the proletariat is not only upheld when the scope of democracy is extended ; it acquires additional strength, for the further extension of democracy creates an atmosphere of trust, a feeling of confidence in the proletariat. This is, after all, in so far as we are concerned with the relationship between the peasants and the workers, the prime essential of the dictatorship of the proletariat.

Those comrades err who declare that the concept of the dictatorship of the proletariat is thoroughly elucidated by reducing it to a concept of force. This dictatorship does not consist exclusively of force. It implies, in addition, the assumption of the role of leadership on the part of the working masses in respect of the non-proletarian classes. It further signifies the upbuilding of the socialist economy, a type of economy which is superior to the capitalist economy, and is more productive than that economy. To sum up, the dictatorship of the proletariat is :

(1) The exercise of force, a force which is unfettered by legal restrictions, in regard to the capitalists and landowners.

(2) The leadership of the peasantry by the proletariat.

(3) The upbuilding of socialism, in respect of society as a whole.

Not one of these aspects can be ignored without distorting the concept of the dictatorship of the proletariat. Only by considering the three aspects as a united whole are we able to get a complete and finished picture of the concept of the dictatorship of the proletariat.

Does the Party's new policy in regard to soviet democracy cause any kind of deterioration in the system of the dictatorship ?

No ; quite the contrary ! The new policy strengthens the system of dictatorship. As far as force is concerned—and the Red Army is the embodiment of force in our system—I need hardly point out that the realisation of soviet democracy in the rural areas will inevitably lead to an improvement in the lot of the Red soldier and will wed him with yet closer bonds to the Soviet power for the simple reason that the main bulk of our army is composed of peasants. If we now turn to consider the question of leadership, we must realise that by putting new life into the soviets, we are facilitating the task of leadership, consolidating it in the hands of the proletariat by strengthening the trust which the peasants have placed in the workers. Finally, in respect of the upbuilding of socialism, the Party's new policy cannot but render this work easier, for it will consolidate the alliance between the proletariat and the peasantry, an alliance without which the realisation of socialism would be impossible.

There is but one conclusion to be drawn from the foregoing exposition, namely, that by giving concessions to the peasantry at the present time, we strengthen the proletariat and consolidate its dictatorship without changing the character of its power by a hair's breadth.

Is our Party, influenced in its actions by the present stabilisation of capitalism, making any concessions to the right-wing deviation in the Communist International? If so, is this tactical manœuvre really necessary?

This question is obviously the outcome of our pact with the group led by Shmeral and Zapototsky, a pact directed against the right-wing elements in the Communist Party of Checko-Slovakia.

I do not consider that our Party has made any concessions whatsoever to the right-wing of the Communist International. On the contrary. The entire session of the enlarged executive of the Comintern was devoted to the isolation of the right-wing elements of the International. You need but read the resolutions anent the Checko-Slovakian Party and anent bolshevism to realise that the shafts of the enlarged executive were all aimed at the right-wing elements in the Communist International.

In view of this, it would be absurd to talk of concessions being made by our Party to the right wing of the Comintern.

As a matter of fact, Comrades Shmeral and Zapototsky are not authentic right-wingers. They do not support the platform of the right, the platform adopted by the Brünn comrades. It would be more correct to say that they hesitate between embracing the tenets of Leninism and throwing in their lot with the right-wingers. Their trend is slightly in favour of the second alternative. Their behaviour at the sittings of the enlarged executive was characteristic. Under the pressure of our criticism, on the one hand, and under the menace of a split negotiated by the right wing on the other, they rallied to our side, to the side of the Leninists, and undertook to work in concert with the Leninists against the right-wing elements. They are greatly to be congratulated on the line they have taken. Was it not our duty to meet these hesitant comrades half-way as soon as they began to rally to the Leninist side, as soon as they began to yield ground to the Leninists in opposition to the right-wingers? Of course we could do no otherwise. It would indeed be a strange and sad thing were there those among us who were incapable of grasping the most elementary principles underlying the bolshevik tactic. Facts are there to prove that the policy adopted by the Comintern in regard to the Communist Party of Checko-Slovakia has been amply justified. Are not Comrades Shmeral and Zapototsky fighting shoulder to shoulder with the Leninists against the right wing? Have not the Brünn elements in the Checko-Slovakian Party already been isolated?

" That's all very well," I can hear some of you say, " but is it going to last?" I don't know, and I refuse to pose as a seer. All I can say with certainty is that, so long as Shmeral and his followers continue to fight against the right wing, so long will our pact with them hold: and that as soon as there is a change of feeling among Shmeral and his followers, the pact will no longer have any validity for us. But this question does not at present arise. The fact which is of interest to us is that the agreement entered into for the fight against the right wing has strengthened the Leninists, and has furnished them with fresh possibilities of sweeping the waverers along in their train. That is the thing that matters at this juncture, and not conjectures as to the future vacillations of Comrades Shmeral and Zapototsky.

There are some people who think that Leninists must support every left-wing braggart and neurasthenic, that Leninists are always and in all circumstances to be the spokesmen of the left wing among the communists. This is not true. We belong to the left wing only in relation to the non-communist parties of the working class. But we have never undertaken to be " more left than any one else ". This is what Parvus advocated at one time, and his wrong-headedness earned him a rebuke from Lenin. Among communists there is neither a left wing nor a right wing: we are Leninists and nothing else. Lenin knew what he was about when he fought simultaneously against the left-wing deviation among the communists and against the right-wing deviation. He had good grounds for penning one of the finest of his pamphlets, *Left-Wing Communism, an Infantile Disorder*.

I hardly think the comrades would have asked the sixth question if they had given timely consideration to this latter circumstance.

In view of the weakness of Party organisation in the rural areas, is there not a risk that, as soon as we start the campaign in furtherance of our new policy, the antisoviet agitation in the villages will undergo consolidation and find more concrete expression?

We certainly do run such a risk. When we launch the slogan, " New life to the soviets ! " we fully realise that in future the elections to these bodies will take place unhampered by restrictions, and that there will be the utmost freedom of electoral propaganda. Naturally enough, the antisoviet elements will not let slip so admirable an opportunity as this opening affords, and they wi l doubtless launch a fresh attack against the Soviet power. Herein lies the danger referred to above, and a practical demonstration of the risks involved was recently given during the elections in Kuban, in Siberia, and in Ukraine. The danger is enhanced by the weakness of our village organisations in many districts, and by the interventionist tactics of the imperialist powers.

What are the causes which give rise to this danger ?

There are at least two causes.

(1) The antisoviet elements have an inkling that there has recently been a certain transference of sympathies in the rural areas, and that this transference of sympathies is all in favour of the kulaks. In a number of districts, the middle peasants have turned towards the kulaks for support. The state of things could merely be surmised before the elections ; after the elections there was no denying the fact. That is the main reason for fearing that the antisoviet agitation in the villages may become an organised campaign.

(2) In many places our concessions to the peasantry have been interpreted as a sign of weakness on the part of the Soviet State. Since the elections, therefore, the reactionaries in the villages have raised the war-cry : " Press harder ! " Though this cause of danger is less vital than the previous one, nevertheless it helps to reinforce the antisoviet agitation in the countryside.

What we communists have got to understand is that, *as far*

as the rural areas are concerned, we are passing through a period of struggle to win over the middle peasants. The middle peasantry must, at all cost, be rallied to the side of the proletariat. Should we fail in this endeavour, the antisoviet agitation in the villages will grow stronger and more threatening, and the new Party policy will only succeed in advantaging the reactionaries.

Another thing we must bear in mind is that, if the new Party policy is to be successful in winning over the middle peasantry, we shall have to apply it through the soviets, through the cooperatives, by means of government loans, by transferring the agricultural tax to the local budgets, and so forth. Administrative pressure will merely serve to foil our campaign. We shall have to convince the middle peasants of the correctness of our policy by utilising the political and economic methods lying to our hand. Only by precept and example shall we be able to attract them into our camp.

Finally, we have to remember that our new Party policy is not intended to put fresh life into the antisoviet agitation! It is being run in order to inspire the soviets with renewed vigour, in order to attract the peasant masses, in order to make it abundantly clear that, far from denying the possibility of a struggle with the antisoviet elements, our adoption of the new line of action means that we foresee that such a struggle is inevitable. Further, if these antisoviet elements raise the cry, " Press harder ", in the conviction that the government's concessions to the peasantry imply weakness on the part of the State, and if the counter-revolutionaries turn these concessions to account for the furtherance of their agitation against the Soviet republic, then it remains for us to prove to them that the Soviet power is strong, and to remind them of the prison cells which are ready for their reception!

The danger arising from antisoviet propaganda in the countryside will certainly be destroyed root and branch if we set to with a will and carry out our work satisfactorily.

Is it not to be feared that, owing to a growth of the influence of non-Party elements, non-Party fractions will be organised within the Soviets?

The answer in this case can only be a conditional one. The danger does not arise until those who belong to no party have begun to contemplate the possibility of themselves taking over the functions of the Party, substituting themselves for it. But there is no danger so long as the influence of more or less organised non-Party elements grows merely in those places where the Communist Party has not yet penetrated. This applies in the case of the trade-union organisations in the towns, and in the case of non-Party associations of a more or less sovietist character in the countryside.

Whence does this danger arise?

Characteristically enough, the danger does not exist, or hardly exists at all, within the ranks of the working class. How is this to be accounted for? By the fact that a numerous contingent of active, non-Party proletarians has always rallied round the Party, surrounding it with an atmosphere of confidence, and linking it up with the working-class masses.

No less characteristic is the fact that this danger is peculiarly acute among the peasantry. Why should this be so? Because the Party is weak in the rural areas; because it has not rallied to its side a large contingent of active non-Party peasants which could serve as a link between the Party and the broad masses of the peasantry. It seems to me that nowhere do we so urgently need a goodly number of active non-Party workers as among the peasantry.

There is but one way out of this difficulty. If we are to prevent the non-Party peasant masses from getting hopelessly out of touch with the Party, from perhaps becoming antagonistic to the Party, we shall have to create around the latter a large contingent of active non-Party peasants.

But such a contingent is not formed all at once, or even in the course of a couple of months. This contingent from among the backward peasant masses will be recruited in the course of time, in the course of our daily work among these masses, and while we are endeavouring to put new life into the soviets and to interest the peasants in cooperatives as a form of public social work on behalf of the common weal. It behoves us, therefore, to change our method of approach, to accost the non-Party peasant as an equal, to treat him as a brother whom we trust. We cannot expect to be treated with confidence by persons whom we treat with distrust. Lenin has told us that the relationship between the Party members and those who do not belong to the Party must be one of "mutual trust". Do not let us forget this injunction. The primary need in the formation of a large contingent of active peasants which shall rally around the Party, is the creation of an atmosphere of mutual confidence between the Party members and the non-Party elements.

How is this condition of mutual trust to be achieved? Certainly not by trying to rush matters, or by issuing commands. It can be achieved, as Lenin said, only by a process of "mutual testing" as between Party and non-Party elements in the course of practical everyday work. At the time of the first Party purge, the Party members were scrutinised as to fitness by non-Party elements, and this had most excellent results, for it created an unusually good atmosphere of trust around the Party. Lenin, commenting on the results of the first Party purge, said that the practice of mutual testing as between Party and non-Party workers should be extended to all the fields of our labours. In my view, it is highly important that we should be reminded of Lenin's advice, and proceed forthwith to act on it.

Thus we see that by exercising the rights of mutual criticism and mutual scrutiny in the course of our everyday work, we shall succeed in creating an atmosphere of mutual confidence as between Party members and non-Party elements. This is the path for the Party to travel along if we are to avoid the danger of estranging the non-Party elements from the Party influence, and if we are to be successful in creating a large contingent of active peasants which will rally around the Party organisations in the rural areas.

In the absence of aid from abroad, shall we be able to supply and to increase the capital necessary for carrying on our large-scale industries?

There are two ways of interpreting this question.

It may mean by " aid from abroad " the immediate help of the capitalist States, in the form of credits or a loan, which loan would be the indispensable prerequisite for the development of Soviet industry.

On the other hand, the " aid from abroad " may refer to the help which the Western European proletariat, on the morrow of its victorious revolution, will be prepared to give the U.S.S.R., which help, in its turn, would constitute the indispensable factor in the organisation of socialist economy.

The answer would, of course, differ according to the interpretation of the question. I will deal successively with both of the issues involved, in the order given above.

Seeing that our country is encircled by capitalist States, is it possible for our large-scale industry to develop unless we obtain credits from abroad?

Yes, such a thing is possible. Of course, there will be tremendous difficulties to overcome, tremendous trials to go through. But, all obstacles notwithstanding, we shall succeed in the end in making our industrial life a flourishing one, even if we cannot obtain credits from abroad.

Hitherto the founding and the development of powerful industrial States has been achieved by three methods.

First, by grabbing and pillaging colonies. Great Britain's development took this line. Her buccaneers and freebooters of old cut themselves out possessions in every quarter of the globe. For two hundred years and more " supplementary capital " was wrung out of these lands in order to advantage the home industries, and in the end Great Britain became the " workshop of the world ". This method is out of the question for us, seeing that colonial conquest and spoliation are incompatible with the principles underlying the Soviet system.

NINTH QUESTION

Next there is the method of military conquest and the exaction of large indemnities, to be paid by the conquered land to the victor. Germany provides an example of this method. After having beaten France in the Franco-German War of 1870, an indemnity amounting to five milliards of francs was extorted from the French people. With the money, Germany proceeded to develop her manufacturing industry. This method in its essence is much the same as the first method, and is equally uncongenial to us seeing that it, too, conflicts with the principles upon which the Soviet State is founded.

The third method consists in making concessions and advancing loans to countries in a backward stage of development from the capitalist point of view, and thereby making such lands more or less the vassals and slaves of the creditor States. Such, for instance, was the case of tsarist Russia. By granting concessions to the western powers and by receiving loans, Russia became degraded to a semi-colonial position. This would not, however, have prevented her from, in due course, achieving independent industrial development, aided, naturally, by a number of more or less " successful " wars, and by the plunder of not a few of her neighbours. This method, likewise, is obviously not a possible one for a Soviet State. We did not fight world imperialism during three long years in order merely to achieve such an end. We did not carry on the civil war for three years in order, on the morrow of our victory, voluntarily to place our necks beneath the imperialist yoke.

It would be quite wrong to suppose that, for practical purposes, one of these three methods is exclusive of either or both the others. A State may quite well adopt one of the methods, and then change over to one of the others. This has been the course of history in the United States of America. The reason is that, despite their superficial difference, all these methods have something in common which assimilates them to one another, and sometimes enables them to merge into one another. All three methods lead to the foundation of capitalist industrial States, all three imply the influx of " supplementary capital " from abroad, be it acquired as it may, as an indispensable condition in building up such a State. But we should fall into yet greater confusion were we, on account of these common attributes, to merge one method into the other, to identify one with the other, for we have to realise that they are three distinct methods for the creation of capitalist States, and that each method leaves its imprint on the special character of the State to which it gave rise.

What, then, is the Soviet State to do? We have seen that the old methods for promoting the industrial development of a country run counter to our principles. Further, we know that the influx of capital from abroad is only possible if we agree to accept a position of dependence in regard to our creditors.

There remains a new method of development, one that has not yet been fully considered by other countries. This method consists in developing our industries without resorting to foreign loans, without attracting capital from beyond our borders. This method was suggested by Lenin in his article, *Less, but Better*.

> We must endeavour to build up a State wherein the workers will maintain their leadership over the peasantry, will continue to enjoy the peasants' confidence, and will exercise the most rigid economy. . . . We must construct our apparatus of State with the utmost frugality. . . . If we can keep the leadership of the peasantry in the hands of the workers, we shall be able, by exercising the maximum economy in running the State machine, to ensure that any savings (however small) can be placed at the disposal of our large-scale industry, or they may go towards the electrification scheme, or what not. . . . Then only shall we be able to change horses, as it were . . .; to exchange the sorry screw of pinching and scraping bequeathed to us by an impoverished land where the vast majority of the population is of peasant origin, for the fine steed of large-scale industry, electrification, utilisation of watercourses, the construction of the Volkhov electric power station, etc.—the horse whose rider can be no other than the proletariat. (*Works*, Russian edition, vol. xviii., part II., p. 138.)

Our country has already adopted this method. We shall have to persevere along the same road if we are to develop our large-scale industry and convert our land into a powerful, industrial, proletarian State.

The bourgeois States have not explored this path, it is true; but that does not imply that it is not a practicable path for a proletarian State to pursue. A course of action which is impossible, or nearly impossible, for a bourgeois State to adopt, may be eminently suitable for a proletarian State. The proletarian State enjoys certain advantages which bourgeois States do not or cannot enjoy. Nationalised industry, transport, and credit ; State monopoly of foreign trade ; home trade regulated by the State—all these are new sources from which " supplementary capital " can flow, and this supplementary capital can be utilised for the development of our industries. No bourgeois State has ever had such springs to tap as these. As you are well aware, the proletarian State is making good use of these and similar sources of supplementary capital in the upbuilding of our industrial economy, and we can already show very satisfactory results along these lines.

That is why, despite difficulties and trials, a proletarian State can adopt methods which it would be out of the question for a bourgeois State to employ.

Besides, the present position of affairs, when we cannot obtain capital from abroad unless we submit to the most degrading conditions, will not last for ever. A little stream of foreign capital is already flowing into our country, and, doubtless, with the continued growth and stabilisation of our national economy, this stream will steadily increase in volume.

That is how matters stand as far as the first interpretation is concerned.

Now we shall consider the second.

Is the upbuilding of a socialist economic order in Russia possible unless the triumph of socialism has first of all been achieved in the more important European countries, and in default of such aid as a victorious western proletariat could furnish in the way of technical knowledge and equipment ?

Before discussing this matter (which, by the way, I have already touched upon at the outset of my speech) I should like to dispel one very widespread misconception which has arisen in connexion with the question. Certain comrades are prone to confound the question of the " redintegration and enlargement of the basic capital requisite for the running of our large-scale industry ", with the question of upbuilding a socialist economic order in U.S.S.R. Is such an identification possible ? No, certainly not. Why ? Because the former question is far narrower in scope than the latter. Because the question of increasing the primary capital utilised for the running of large-scale industry is no more than part of our national economy, and the industrial part at that ; whereas the question of the upbuilding of a socialist economy touches the whole of our economic life, that is to say, this question includes both manufacturing industry and agriculture. Because the problem of realising socialism is a problem concerning the organisation of economic life as a whole, it is a problem concerning the proper coordination of industry and agriculture; whereas the question of the expansion of industrial capital hardly touches this problem at all. Industrial capital may be redintegrated or increased without in any way solving the question of upbuilding socialism. A socialist society is a fellowship, a productive and consumptive cooperative, formed jointly by the workers engaged in industry and in agriculture. If, in this association, industry be not intimately linked up with agriculture, which provides the raw materials of manufacture and furnishes us with food, while in its turn absorbing the products of industry—if, let me repeat, industry be not intimately linked up with agriculture, then we shall never be able to establish a socialist society.

That is why the question of the relationships between industry and agriculture, between proletariat and peasantry, is of such superlative importance in the upbuilding of a socialist economy.

That is why the question of the re-equipment of our factories and the expansion of our industrial capital should not be confused with the question of socialist construction.

Well now, is it possible for us to upbuild socialism in our country unless there is, first of all, a socialist victory in other lands, and unless we can receive technical and material aid directly from the western proletariat?

This is not only possible, but necessary and inevitable. We are already building up socialism by developing the nationalised industries, by linking up industry with agriculture, by introducing cooperation into the countryside, by including peasant economy in the general system of Soviet economy, by instilling new life into the soviets and merging the wide masses of the population into the apparatus of State, by creating a new culture and a new social order. While travelling along this road, we shall undoubtedly meet with many difficulties and be beset by countless trials. A victory of socialism in the West would certainly render our task easier to perform. But this victory of socialism in western Europe will not come as speedily as we might wish. Besides, the difficulties that beset our path are not insurmountable. Have we not already overcome some of them?

I have referred to all this at the outset of my speech. At an earlier date I touched on the same theme in my *Report to the Party Officials in Moscow* (supra, pp. 216 et seq.). Earlier still, I dealt with the same question in the preface to my book *Towards October* (supra, pp. 179 et seq.). I said that the refusal to believe in the possibility of upbuilding socialism in our land amounted to "liquidationism", a surrender of the gains of the October revolution, and that this outlook must inevitably lead to the degeneration of the Party. I need not repeat what I have had occasion to say so often before. I will, therefore, refer you to Lenin's works, where you will find abundant material in elucidation of this subject.

All I want to say upon the matter now is a few words anent the history of the question and its significance in relation to the Party.

Leaving aside the discussion which took place during the years 1905-1906, the question of socialist reconstruction was first adequately discussed during the imperialist war, in the year 1915. Lenin was the first to formulate the question when he penned his thesis on *The Possibilities of a Victory for Socialism in one Country alone*. (See *Works*, Russian edition, vol. xiii., p. 133.) This was the period when the bourgeois-democratic revolution was being transformed into the socialist revolution. Comrade Trotsky disputed the soundness of Lenin's thesis, saying: "It is impossible to hope that revolutionary Russia, for instance, can hold its own against conservative Europe. . . ."

In 1921, after the experiences of the October revolution and the civil war, the question was again placed on the agenda, and the upbuilding of socialism was vigorously debated in the Party. The New Economic Policy had just been introduced, and certain comrades were inclined to look upon that policy as a shirking of our socialist duties, as a renunciation of the work of socialist construction. In his pamphlet, *The Food Tax*, Lenin describes the New Economic Policy as a necessary measure for linking up our industrial economy with our agricultural economy, as a prelude to laying the foundations of a truly socialist economy, as a means for the successful edification of a socialist order. This was penned in April 1921. In January 1922, Comrade Trotsky wrote the preface to his book, *1905*. It is an answer, of a sort, to Lenin's pamphlet, and upholds a totally different point of view concerning the upbuilding of socialism in our land. Here is what Trotsky writes :

> The contradictions inherent in the position of a workers' government functioning in a backward country where the large majority of the population is composed of peasants, can only be liquidated on an international scale, in the arena of a worldwide proletarian revolution.

A year later (1922) we are again faced by two opposing statements on this identical subject.

One is uttered by Lenin in his *Address to the Moscow Soviet*, and runs :

> A Socialist Russia will arise out of the Russia of the New Economic Policy.

The other is to be found in the postface to Trotsky's *Program of Peace*. Here we read :

> The real growth of the socialist economy in Russia can take place only after the victory of the proletariat in the more important countries of Europe.

Another year elapsed, and then, shortly before his death, Lenin returned to the question in his article *Cooperation*, which appeared in May 1923. Here it is stated that, so far as the Soviet Union is concerned, we have everything necessary for the upbuilding of a fully socialistic society.

We see that the problem of upbuilding socialism in our country is one of the most important questions confronting our Party. Since Lenin so often came back to the question, it is obvious that he looked upon it as one of fundamental importance to our Party tactics.

Since then, the growth of our economy, the intensification of the struggle between the socialist and the capitalist elements within that economy, and, above all, the temporary stabilisation of capitalism, have rendered the problem of socialist construction even more acute.

Why is this question of such vital importance from the point of view of Party tactics ?

Because it touches the scope of our work, raises the whole question of the aims and objects of our socialist construction. We cannot upbuild anything unless we have a knowledge of the ultimate aim of our work; no step forward is possible unless we know where we are to place our feet. This question of the scope of our work is of especial moment for our Party, seeing that we have always had a clear and precise aim towards which we have striven. Are we building under the sign of socialism, in the hope of bringing the work to a triumphant finish? Or are we constructing haphazard, blindly, in order that, "while awaiting the advent of the worldwide socialist revolution", we may dung the soil for a bourgeois-democratic harvest? This is, for the nonce, one of the most important questions. We cannot hope to be successful in our constructive work if to the clear and precise question we do not furnish an equally clear and precise answer. Thousands of Party members, of trade unionists, of cooperators, of workers in our industrial and cultural institutions, of Red Army soldiers, of Young Communists, have appealed to us and have demanded to know precisely what the aim of our work may be, what the thing is which we are supposed to be upbuilding. Woe betide the leaders who cannot or will not give a clear and precise answer, who shuffle, who refer the questioners from pillar to post, thus infecting these eager enquirers, who would fain be busily engaged in the active work of upbuilding socialism, with the caries of their own intellectualist scepticism.

One of the great merits of Leninism is that nothing is left to chance. There is, for Leninists, a definite aim, towards which their constructive work must unfailingly be directed; they have all the prerequisites for a successful issue to their endeavours to upbuild a fully socialised order of society.

Such are the possibilities in regard to the upbuilding of socialism.

It is quite another question when we come to consider how we can turn this possibility into a certainty, for that does not entirely depend upon us. It depends upon the relative strength or weakness of friends and foes abroad. We shall achieve our end if we are left in peace to get on with the building, if we are given a breathing space, if no serious attempt at intervention takes place; or if, supposing that such intervention does take place, it proves abortive, if the strength and power of the international revolutionary movement and the strength and power of our own land are mighty enough to render such an attempt at intervention fruitless. On the other hand, we shall not be able to upbuild a socialist economic order if an intervention on the part of our enemies proves successful.

Kindly expound the main difficulties which in consequence of the stabilisation of capitalism and the delay in the coming of the world revolution, confront us in our Party and our Soviet work; and more especially be good enough to deal with the difficulties arising in the relationships between our Party and the working class, and between the working class and the peasantry.

It seems to me that, if I confine myself to a discussion of the most important, there are five difficulties. One result of the stabilisation of capitalism has been to render them somewhat more acute.

1. The first difficulty arises from the danger of intervention. This does not mean that we are menaced by intervention at this very moment, that the imperialist powers are ready and able to attack our country. For that to be possible, imperialism would have to be at least as powerful as it was on the eve of the great war. You are well aware that this is not the case. The history of the war in Morocco, and that of the intervention in China, which are merely dress rehearsals for future wars and interventions, gives definite indications that imperialism is weakened. Thus there is no urgent danger of intervention. But so long as we are encircled by capitalist States, there will be a persistent tendency on their part to attack us. This constant menace compels us to maintain an army and a fleet for our defence, and the upkeep of these forces runs us into an expenditure amounting to hundreds of millions of roubles per annum. The absorption of so much money into the military and naval arm necessitates a curtailment of expenditure in other fields, such as the domains of economic and cultural development. Were it not for the constant threat of intervention, we could utilise these sums for the strengthening of our industries, for the improvement of our agricultural processes, for the inauguration of compulsory elementary education, and so on, and so forth. The danger of intervention hampers our constructive work, and gives rise to this initial difficulty.

The overcoming of this difficulty does not rest entirely with us ; it can be overcome only by an effort on our part in conjunction with the revolutionary workers of other lands.

2. The second difficulty arises from the antagonisms between the proletariat and the peasantry. I have already discussed these antagonisms, when dealing with the class struggle in the rural areas, and I need not repeat all those arguments here. Conflicts arise over the price of agricultural produce on the one hand, and the price of industrial commodities on the other, they arise in connexion with the agricultural tax, with the administration in the country districts, and so on. The danger in this case is the possibility of a rupture in the alliance between the working class and the peasantry, the possibility of weakening the leadership of the proletariat over the peasantry.

What distinguishes this difficulty from the foregoing one is that we can overcome it by utilising our own internal strength. By starting the campaign in favour of our new policy in the countryside we shall be able to conquer this difficulty.

3. The third difficulty arises from conflicts of national interests within the frontiers of the U.S.S.R., conflicts between the " centre " and the " outliers ", due to disparity in economic and cultural development. Let us take it that the political antagonisms have been settled, there remain the cultural and, more especially, the economic antagonisms to deal with. These cultural and economic antagonisms are only now becoming manifest, and the work of settling them is all to be done. The danger is twofold. First of all there is the danger of high-handed procedure and arbitrary commands on the part of the bureaucracy at the centre. These officials seem incapable of exercising tact and consideration in their dealings with the republics of the various nations comprised in the Union, they do not even seem to wish to do so. Consequently, the second danger arises, mistrust is engendered, and the outlying republics and autonomous regions become estranged from the centre. We shall have to fight against both the dangers, and more especially against the first, if we are to find a satisfactory solution of the difficulties arising out of the question of nationalities within the Soviet Union.

Just like the second difficulty, this difficulty likewise is capable of being overcome by our own exertions, within the U.S.S.R.

4. This difficulty consists in the possibility of the State apparatus breaking loose from Party control, the possibility of

the Party losing its position of leadership in respect of the State apparatus. I discussed this danger in connexion with the possible degeneration of the Party, and I do not need to enlarge upon it further. The danger is kept alive by the presence of bureaucratic and bourgeois elements in the State apparatus, and is enormously increased as a result of the expansion and the growing importance of that apparatus. Our task is to reduce the State apparatus as far as possible, to clear out all bureaucratic elements and all bourgeois influence, to assign Party members to the nodal points in the State apparatus, and to see to it that the apparatus of State is thus subjected to the Party leadership. This difficulty, too, we can solve on our own initiative.

5. This difficulty arises from the possibility of the Party organisations and the trade unions being cut off from the working-class masses, thereby causing the needs and aspirations of the masses to be ignored and neglected. The danger is engendered and develops thanks to the preponderant influence of certain bureaucratic elements in the Party organisations and in the trade unions, not excepting the Party nuclei and the factory committees. This danger has become more threatening recently as a result of the watchword, " Turn your face to the villages ! " The summons resulted in concentrating the attention of our members in these organisations upon the peasantry. Many comrades failed to grasp that, while facing towards the peasantry, it behoved them not to turn their backs upon the proletariat, that the new slogan could not be realised in fact save through the proletariat, and that by neglecting the needs and aspirations of the workers we run the risk of severing them from the Party and the trade-union organisations.

What are the signs and portents which may warn us of the advent of this danger ?

First there will be a loss of sensitive appreciation, a lack of attention, on the part of those who run the Party and trade-union organisations, in relation to the needs and aspirations of the working-class masses ; secondly, there may be a failure to realise that the workers have acquired a heightened sense of their own dignity, that they are increasingly aware that they are the ruling power, that they can no longer tolerate bureaucratic methods on the part of Party and trade-union officials ; thirdly, there may be a failure to understand that one cannot issue frivolous and ill-begotten orders to the workers, that, indeed, the day for "orders" is passed, and that now we must see to it that we win the confidence of the whole working class and attract it towards the Party; fourthly, there may be a failure to see that, before wide-reaching reforms (such as the introduction of the three-spindle system in the textile industry) can be introduced, reforms which affect the lives of great masses of workers, we have to launch a campaign among the workers on behalf of the new measures, have to call conferences and so forth for the elucidation of such measures, etc.

Should any of these dangers materialise (and, as we know, they have materialised quite lately in the textile industry), then it is to be feared that the Party and trade-union organisations will become severed from the broad masses of the workers, and conflicts will occur in our factories.

Such are the characteristics of the fifth difficulty.

If we are to overcome this difficulty, we must clear all the bureaucratic elements out of our Party and trade-union organisations, we must see to it that the composition of the factory and workshop committees is thoroughly overhauled, we must put new life into the industrial conferences, we must transfer the centre of gravity of Party work into the nuclei in the large industrial enterprises, and we must assign the best among our Party members to these nuclei.

Let us pay more heed to the needs and aspirations of the working-class masses, let us ponder their demands! Less bureaucratic red tape in the practical labours of our Party and trade-union organisations! Let us be more sensitive and more considerate to the workers' feeling of class dignity! Such are the tasks which it behoves us to lay our hands to here and now.

TASKS OF THE UNION OF YOUNG COMMUNISTS

(AN ANSWER TO THE QUESTIONS PROPOUNDED BY THE EDITORIAL BOARD OF " KOMSOMOLSKAYA PRAVDA ", THE ORGAN OF THE YOUNG COMMUNISTS)

(MAY, 1925)

I

What are the chief duties incumbent upon the Union of Young Communists in view of the existing international and internal position of the Soviet Union?

The question is propounded in too general a form, and therefore the answer can only be made in general terms. The present international and internal situation of the Soviet Union makes it incumbent upon the Union of Young Communists to support both by word and deed the revolutionary movement of the oppressed classes of all countries, and also to support the struggle of the proletariat of the Soviet Union to upbuild socialism and to ensure the freedom and independence of the proletarian State. It follows, therefore, that the Union of Young Communists will only be able to fulfil this task if it is guided in all its work by the directives given by the Communist International and by the Communist Party of Russia.

II

What tasks are incumbent upon the Union of Young Communists in connexion with the danger of liquidationism (the loss of the perspective of socialist construction), nationalism (the loss of the perspective of the international revolution), and degeneration of the role of the Party as leader—that is to say in connexion with those dangers to which attention was drawn in Questions and Answers?

To put the matter briefly, the tasks incumbent upon the Union of Young Communists in this domain consist in educating our young workers and young peasants in the spirit of Leninism. What do we mean when we speak of educating young folk in the spirit of Leninism? We mean, first of all, impressing upon them that the victory of socialist construction in our country is necessary and possible. We mean, in the second place, doing our utmost to strengthen their conviction that our workers' State is the offspring of the international proletariat; that it is the base whence the revolution in all countries will develop; that the final victory of our revolution is the concern of the international proletariat. We mean, in the third place, that our young folk must be inspired with confidence in the leadership of the Communist Party of Russia. Within the Union of Young Communists there must be created an educational organisation competent to carry on the education of our young folk along the lines above indicated.

Young communists are active in all domains of socialist constructive work: in industry; in agriculture; in the cooperatives; in the soviets; in the educational organisations; etc. It is essential that every official in the Union of Young Communists should invariably associate his daily work with the perspective of the upbuilding of a socialist society. It is essential that he should understand how to carry on his daily work in this spirit, and with a view to the realisation of this perspective.

Young communists are active among the workers and peasants of the various nationalities. The Union of Young Communists constitutes, in a sense, a special International. In this matter, not only does the national composition of the Union play a part, but it is likewise important that the Union of Young Communists is directly affiliated to the Communist Party of Russia, which is one of the most important sections of the proletarian international. Internationalism is the fundamental idea which permeates the activity of the Union of Young Communists. It is upon this idea that its strength depends. The spirit of internationalism must always be kept active in the Union of Young Communists. The successes and the failures in the struggle of the proletariat of our country must be associated, in the minds of the Young Communists, with the successes and the failures of the international revolutionary movement. It is essential that the Young Communists should learn that our revolution must not be regarded as an end in itself, but as a means and an aid towards the victory of the proletarian revolution in all lands.

The Union of Young Communists is not, formally speaking, a section of the Party organisation. Nevertheless, it is a communist organisation. This means that the Union of Young Communists, without being in the formal sense a Party organisation of the workers and peasants, has to carry on its activities under the leadership of the Party. The important thing is that the confidence of the young folk in the Party, and the leadership of the Party in the Union of Young Communists, shall be ensured. Young Communists must always bear in mind that the most important part of the work of the Union of Young Communists is to ensure that the Party shall keep the lead. Young Communists must never forget that in default of such a leadership, the Union of Young Communists will not be able to fulfil its fundamental task, that of educating the young workers and the young peasants in the spirit of the dictatorship of the proletariat and of communism.

III

How, at the present time, should we approach the problem of the expansion of the Union of Young Communists? Should we, in the main, continue the policy of trying to enlist as members the greatest possible number of young urban workers, young rural workers, and young poor peasants, together with all the best of the young middle peasants; or should we make it our main object to consolidate and to educate the young folk who are already enrolled as members of the Union?

These aims should not be presented as alternatives. Both of them must be simultaneously pursued. Certainly it is essential to enrol as many as possible of the young town workers and also the best elements among the poor peasants and the middle peasants.

At the same time, it is equally important to see to it that the new members of the Union of Young Communists shall be properly trained by the officers of the Union, and shall be assimilated by the Union. The strengthening of the proletarian core of the Union is the most important among the immediate tasks of that body. In the carrying out of this task lies the guarantee that the Union of Young Communists will maintain the right direction. But the Union of Young Communists is not solely an organisation of the young urban workers. It is an organisation of both the young workers and the young peasants. Consequently, while striving to strengthen the proletarian core of its membership, the Union must see to it that the best elements among the young peasants shall be enrolled as members, and that there shall be a firm alliance between the proletarian core and the peasant section of the Union of Young Communists. In default of this, the leadership of the young peasants by the proletarian core in the Union will be impossible.

IV

Some of the provincial committees of the Union of Young Communists, following the example of the women's delegate meetings, have set to work upon the organisation of delegate meetings of the non-Party peasant youth. The purpose of these meetings is stated to be to bring the active elements among the young peasants, and especially among the young middle peasants, under the leadership of the Union of Young Communists. Is such a line of action correct? Does it not involve the danger that these delegate meetings may degenerate into sort of non-Party unions of young peasants, which might set themselves up in opposition to our Union of Young Communists?

In my opinion, such a course of action is a mistaken one. My reasons for this opinion are as follows.

First of all, the tactic in question masks a dread of the middle peasants, implies an endeavour to keep the young middle peasants at a distance, a determination to fend them off. Is such an attempt a right one? Obviously not. We must not fend off the young middle peasants. On the contrary, our aim must be to bring them closer to the Union of Young Communists. Only by such a policy will it be possible to lead the young middle peasants to repose confidence in the workers, to repose confidence in the proletarian core of the Union of Young Communists, to repose confidence in our Party.

In the second place, there can be no doubt that special delegate meetings of the young middle peasants existing side by side with the Union of Young Communists would, in view of the present revival of activity among all the groups of the peasantry, inevitably incline towards the transformation of these delegate meetings into a special Union of Young Middle Peasants. In existing circumstances, this special Union would necessarily tend to set itself in opposition to the Union of Young Communists. There would be a danger that, as the upshot of these trends, the Union of Young Communists would be severed in twain—into a union of young urban operatives and a union of young peasants. Can we afford to ignore such a danger? Certainly not. Is there any need for such a severance, at the present juncture, under the existing circumstances of our development? Certainly not. On the contrary, what we need to-day, is not the fending off of the young peasants, but the cementing of a close association between them and the proletarian core of the Union of Young Communists. We do not need severance, but a firm alliance.

In the third place, the formation of delegate meetings of the young middle peasants cannot be justified by reference to the fact that there are delegate meetings of working women and peasant women. We must not confound under one head the young workers and young peasants, who have their special organisation in the form of the Union of Young Communists, and the working women and peasant women, who have no special organisation of their own. Nor must we confound the young middle peasants with the working women who form a part of the working class. The organisation of delegate meetings of the young middle peasants is dangerous to the Union of Young Communists, whereas the organisation of delegate meetings of working women and peasant women does not involve any sort of danger to any one, for the reason that there does not at present exist any kind of permanent organisation of working women and peasant women similar to the Union of Young Communists.

That is why I consider that there is no ground for the organisation of special delegate meetings of the young middle peasants in connexion with the Union of Young Communists.

I consider that the Sixth Congress of the Union of Young Communists was right when it decided that in the rural districts it would be content with bringing into existence all accessory organisations, such as educational circles, agricultural groups, etc., as satellites of the Union of Young Communists.

V

Is it possible for the officials of the Union of Young Communists, under present conditions, to combine their practical activities with a thorough study of Marxism and Leninism? What ought the Young Communist organisations and the individual Young Communists to do in this direction?

First of all let me say a word or two about Marxism and Leninism. The question is formulated in such a way as to suggest the possibility that Marxism and Leninism are two distinct things, that one might be a Leninist without being a Marxist. But there is absolutely no ground for such a view. Leninism is not Leninist doctrine minus Marxism. Leninism is Marxism of the epoch of imperialism and the proletarian revolution. In other words, Leninism includes all that Marx taught, with the addition of Lenin's contribution to the Marxist treasury— a treasury which necessarily includes all that Marx taught (the doctrine of the dictatorship of the proletariat, the peasant problem, the nationalist problem, the Party, the problem of the social roots of reformism, the problem of the most important deviations from communism, etc.). It would be better, therefore, to formulate the question differently, speaking of Marxism or Leninism (the two being fundamentally one and the same), and not to speak of Marxism " and " Leninism.

In the second place, there can be no doubt that without a combination of the practical work of the officials of the Young Communist League with a satisfactory theoretical grounding of the same officials (the study of Leninism), there can be no rational communist activity within the Union of Young Communists. Leninism is the generalisation of the experience of the revolutionary movement of the workers of all lands. This experience is the guiding star which lights the path of all practical revolutionists in their daily activities and gives them their direction. Practical revolutionary workers cannot be sure that they are working along the right lines unless they take the before-mentioned experience into account. They will be groping in the dark unless they study Leninism, unless they make Leninism their own, unless they are prepared to combine their practical work with the necessary theoretical grounding. That is why the study of Leninism is an indispensable prerequisite for the transformation of the existing body of officials of the Union of Young Communists into a genuinely effective Leninist body of officials, who will be competent to train up the millions upon millions of young communists in the spirit of the dictatorship of the proletariat and of communism.

But is such a union of theory and practice possible in existing circumstances, and in view of the fact that the officials of the Union of Young Communists are so mightily overworked? Yes, it is possible. No one will deny that there are great difficulties in the way. Yet it is possible because it is necessary, because unless this requisite is fulfilled it will be impossible for the officials of the Union of Young Communists to become a genuinely Leninist body. We must not be weaklings who run away from difficulties and look for something easier to do. Difficulties exist in order that we may fight against them and overcome them. The bolsheviks would certainly have gone under in their fight against capitalism if they had not learned how to overcome difficulties. The Union of Young Communists has undertaken a great task. That is why its members must concentrate their energies in order to overcome the difficulties in their path.

Patient and methodical study of Leninism—that is what the officials of the Union of Young Communists need if they themselves are to train up the millionfold masses of young folk in the spirit of the proletarian revolution.

"Pravda," November 29, 1925.

POLITICAL REPORT OF THE CENTRAL COMMITTEE TO THE FOURTEENTH CONGRESS OF THE COMMUNIST PARTY OF THE SOVIET UNION

(MAY, 1925)

COMRADES! During the last two weeks you have been able to listen to various members of the Central Committee and the Political Bureau, who have given you reports concerning the activities of the Central Committee during the interval between the Thirteenth and the Fourteenth Party Congress. They were detailed reports, and were thoroughly sound on the whole. I do not think there is any reason for recapitulating these reports. It will be enough if I devote myself to the discussion of some of the questions arising out of the activities of the Central Committee of our Party during the interval between the Thirteenth and the Fourteenth Congress.

As a rule, a report upon the activity of the Central Committee begins with an account of the foreign political situation. I shall follow that practice here.

I. THE INTERNATIONAL SITUATION

The essential and novel feature in our foreign political relationships, the circumstance which is fundamental to all that has happened during the period under consideration, is that between our country (the country where socialism is being upbuilt) and the countries of the capitalist world there has been established a sort of provisional equilibrium of forces. There is now, as it were, a kind of " peaceful cohabitation " between the land of the soviets and the lands where capitalism prevails. What seemed at first as if it were only to be a short breathing space after the war, has become a whole epoch of comparative repose. That is why there is an equilibrium of forces ; that is why there is a period of " peaceful cohabitation " between the bourgeois world and the proletarian world. The foundation of this state of affairs is formed by the internal weakness of world capitalism, on the one hand, and the growth of the revolutionary labour movement, on the other ; and especially by the growth of our own forces, the forces of the U.S.S.R.

How are we to account for the weakness of the capitalist world ? That weakness finds its explanation in the insuperable antagonisms within the capitalist world, antagonisms which dominate the whole international situation. These contradictions, these conflicts and antagonisms, are insuperable for capitalist countries, and can only be overcome in the course of the development of the proletarian revolution in the West.

What are these contradictions, these conflicts and antagonisms ? They can be classified in five groups.

The first group of antagonisms consists of those between the proletariat and the bourgeoisie in capitalist countries. The second group of antagonisms consists of those between imperialism and the liberationist movement in colonies and dependent countries. The third group of antagonisms consists of those between the victorious and the conquered countries after the imperialist war, antagonisms which inevitably tend to become intensified. The fourth group of antagonisms consists of those which have arisen among the victorious States, and which will

THE INTERNATIONAL SITUATION

also inevitably become intensified. The fifth and last group of antagonisms consists of those which have developed between the U.S.S.R. and capitalist countries as a whole. The trend of the foreign policy of our country, the foreign political situation in which the Soviet Union is placed, is determined by the conflicts and antagonisms belonging to these five groups.

Comrades! Unless we make a careful study of the nature and the growth of these antagonisms, we cannot understand the present position of our country. That is why a brief consideration of them forms a necessary part of my report.

1. Stabilisation of Capitalism

We begin, then, with the first group of antagonisms, the antagonisms between the proletariat and the bourgeoisie within capitalist countries. We are concerned here with the following basic phenomena.

(*a*) Capitalism is emerging out of the chaos in production, trade, and finance which resulted from the war; here and there it has already emerged from that chaos. In the Party we are accustomed to speak of this as the partial or temporary stabilisation of capitalism. What does this mean? It means that production and commerce in capitalist countries, which for a time (during the post-war crises in the years 1919 and 1920) had sunk to a terribly low level, have now begun to revive, while the political power of the bourgeoisie has been more or less re-established. This means that capitalism has temporarily overcome the chaos which prevailed shortly after the war.

As far as Europe is concerned, the following figures show the change.

In comparison with the state of affairs during the year 1919, production in all the more advanced countries of Europe has either increased (reaching, in places, a figure amounting to from 80 to 90 per cent. of the pre-war production), or else it has remained unaltered. Only in England have some of the branches of production remained at a very low level. Generally speaking, if we consider Europe as a whole, production and commerce have increased, though they have not yet attained the pre-war level. As regards the production of grain, in England this amounts to from 80 to 85 per cent. of the pre-war production ; in France, 83 per cent. ; and in Germany 68 per cent. The increase of grain production has come very slowly in Germany. In France it is not increasing at all ; and in England it is declining. These losses are compensated by the import of grain from America. Coal production in Britain during the year 1925, reached 90 per cent. of the pre-war level ; in France, 107 per cent. ; in Germany, 93 per cent. The production of steel was, in Britain, 98 per cent. of the pre-war production ; in France, 102 per cent. ; in Germany, 78 per cent. The consumption of cotton in Britain is now 82 per cent. of the pre-war consumption ; in France, 83 per cent. ; in Germany, 81 per cent. British foreign trade has an unfavourable balance, and amounts to 94 per cent. of the pre-war trade ; in Germany, there has been a small increase since 1921, but there the foreign trade likewise has an unfavourable balance ; in France, foreign trade is at 102 per cent. of the pre-war level. Taking European trade as a whole, we find that in the year 1921 it was 63 per cent. of the pre-war level ; now, in the year 1925, it has reached 82 per cent. of the pre-war level. In these countries, the budgets are balanced at the cost of a terrible burden of taxation. Fluctuations of exchange still continue as far as some of the European countries are concerned, but the chaos of a few years ago no longer exists.

Speaking generally, we may say that the post-war economic crisis in Europe is over, and that production and commerce are tending to regain the pre-war level. One European country, France, has already excelled the pre-war level both in respect of commerce and industry ; another, Britain, is more or less stationary, and has not yet reached pre-war figures.

(b) Instead of the revolutionary flood tide which was noticeable during the years of the post-war crisis, we now see, in central and western Europe, an ebb in the revolutionary movement. This means that the question of the conquest of power, the question of the seizure of power by the proletariat, has, in western and central Europe, been postponed from to-day's agenda until to-morrow's. A period of revolutionary impetus, a period in which the movement is rapidly progressive, advancing so eagerly that the Party can hardly keep pace with it (such a period as we had in Russia in 1905 and again in 1917), will come by-and-by. But at the moment there is no impetus ; we are in a transient period of ebb tide ; a period in which the proletariat is collecting its forces. It is one in which notable results are being achieved, in which new forms of the movement are becoming manifest, in which trade unionism is making rapid advances. It is one of profound revolutionary significance, in this sense, that a union between the labour movement of the West and the labour movement of the Soviet Union is being consolidated ; and in this sense, that the English labour movement is becoming more revolutionary, that the Amsterdam International is decaying, and so on. I repeat, we are passing through a period in which strength is being gathered, a period which will be of immense significance for the coming revolutionary activities. This is the period in which it is incumbent upon the various communist parties to gain control of the mass organisations of the proletariat (the trade unions, etc.), and to give the go-by to the social democratic leaders, just as we ourselves did in the years 1911 and 1912.

(c) The centre of financial power in the capitalist world, the centre of the financial exploitation of the world as a whole, has been shifted from Europe to America. Hitherto, France, Germany, and England were the centre of the financial exploitation of the world. Now, we cannot say this without reserves. The United States of America has become the main centre of the financial exploitation of the world. This country is developing rapidly in all directions, in respect alike of production and commerce and the accumulation of capital. Let me give a few figures. The production of grain in North America has transcended the pre-war level, being now 104 per cent. of what it was before the war. The production of coal amounts to only 90 per cent. of the pre-war production, but the falling off in the production of coal is more than compensated by the enormous increase in the production of petroleum, so that the American petroleum production is now 70 per cent. of that of the whole world. The production of steel is 147 per cent. above the pre-war level. The national income amounts to 130 per cent. of what it was before the war. Foreign trade stands at 143 per cent. above the pre-war level, and is much in favour of the United States as against European countries. Of the total gold reserves in the world (amounting to 9 milliards), 5 milliards are in America. The U.S. currency is the most stable of all the currencies in the world. As regards the export of capital, the United States is almost the only power which is exporting capital to an increasing extent. France and Germany export very little capital, and England is exporting far less capital than of yore.

(*d*) The temporary stabilisation of European capitalism to which I have previously referred has been mainly effected with the aid of U.S. capital, and at the cost of the financial subordination of Europe to the U.S. In proof of this, it is enough to adduce the figures of the indebtedness of the European nations to America. The total amount of these debts is more than two-and-a-half milliards sterling. These are State debts, and do not include the large sums invested by private American capitalists in European undertakings. What do these facts signify ? They signify that the stabilisation of capitalism on the continent of Europe has been effected by means of an influx of capital from the United States and, to a lesser degree, from Britain. At what cost ? At the cost of the financial subordination of Europe to America.

(*e*) Europe, therefore, in order to be able to pay the interest on these vast sums, has been compelled to increase the burden of taxation, and to make the condition of the workers very much worse than it was before. These processes are already going on. At the present day, when the paying off of the debts and the payment of interest have as yet been hardly begun, we find that (in Britain, for example) taxation has risen from 11 per cent. of the national income in 1913 to 23 per cent. in 1924. In France, it has risen from 13 per cent. of the national income to 21 per cent.; and in Italy, from 13 per cent. to 19 per cent. Of course the burden of taxation will become still heavier in the near future. Consequently, the material condition of all the toilers of Europe, and especially of the industrial operatives, will grow steadily worse, and the working class will inevitably become more and more revolutionary. Indications of this growth of revolutionary sentiment are obvious alike in Britain and on the continent of Europe. When I say this, I am thinking of the obvious leftward movement of the European working class.

Such are the fundamental facts indicating that the temporary stabilisation of capitalism in Europe is but a specious stabilisation resting upon an extremely insecure foundation.

It is likely enough that production and commerce in western

and central Europe may attain the pre-war level. But we should be wrong were we to infer from this that capitalism will thereby regain the pre-war degree of stability. That degree of stability will never be regained by European capitalism. Why not? First of all, because Europe has achieved its temporary stabilisation at the cost of financial subordination to the United States. This involves an enormous increase in the burden of taxation, an inevitable deterioration in the condition of the workers, and a general spread of revolutionary sentiment. In the second place, because there are numerous other influences, to which I shall return, contributing to make the present stabilisation uncertain and transient.

Taking a comprehensive view of this first group of antagonisms, we are entitled to draw the general conclusion that the circle of leading States which are in a position to exploit the world financially has grown much smaller than it was in the days before the war. In those days, Britain, France, Germany, and to some extent the United States, were the chief exploiters; now, as I said, the circle has been much restricted. The predominant financial exploiter of the world, and therefore the most influential creditor, is the United States. Britain is no more than the chief assistant of that country. This does not yet signify that continental Europe (apart from Russia) has been reduced to the status of a colony. The European countries, while continuing to exploit their own colonies, have themselves become financially dependent upon the United States, so that they in their turn are exploited by America, and will be exploited yet more thoroughly. That is why we are entitled to say that the circle of leading financial exploiters has been greatly narrowed, whereas the circle of the exploited States has expanded.

There you have one of the reasons why the present stabilisation of European capitalism is based upon such an insecure foundation.

2. Imperialism, Colonies, and Half-Colonies

We now come to the second group of antagonisms, the antagonisms between imperialist countries and colonial countries.

The basic facts in this domain are these: the development of manufacturing industry and of the proletariat in the colonies, a development which went on during the war and is continuing during the post-war period; the rise in the cultural level, in general, and the growth of national intelligence, in particular; the appearance of a nationalist revolutionary movement in the colonies, and the general crisis affecting the world dominion of imperialism; the liberationist struggle in India and Egypt against British imperialism; the wars of liberation in Syria and Morocco against French imperialism; the war of liberation in China against British cum Japanese cum American imperialism; the growth of the labour movement in India and in China, and the growing importance of the part played by the native working class in the nationalist revolutionary movement.

As a result of these changes, the great powers are threatened with the loss of their most important hinterland, the colonies. In this respect, the stabilisation of capitalism is in a very bad way indeed, for the revolutionary movement in the oppressed countries, growing step by step, is beginning here and there to take the form of open warfare against imperialism (as in Morocco, Syria, and China), while the imperialists are obviously becoming incapable of keeping " their " colonies under control.

It is often said, especially by bourgeois writers, that the bolsheviks must be to blame for the accentuation of the crisis in the colonies. The accusation does us too much honour! Unfortunately, we are not as yet strong enough to give all the colonial countries direct aid in their struggle for liberation. The cause lies deeper. The main cause (there are, of course, others) is that European countries, having to pay interest to America, find it necessary to increase the intensity of oppression and exploitation in the colonies and dependencies, thus intensifying the crisis in these countries, and strengthening the revolutionary movement there.

All this tends to weaken the position of the imperialists very seriously indeed. Even though, as far as the first group of antagonisms is concerned, European capitalism has been partially stabilised, so that the question of the seizure of power by the proletariat is no longer one of immediate practical politics —nevertheless the crisis in the colonies has attained a climax, and in quite a number of them the question of driving out the imperialists has become actual.

3. Conquerors and Conquered

Next we have to consider the third group of antagonisms, the conflicts between the victorious and the conquered countries.

The basic facts in this domain are as follows. After the peace of Versailles, Europe was split into two camps: the camp of the conquered countries (Germany, Austria, and others); and the camp of the victorious countries (those of the Entente together with the United States). Next, we have to notice that the victorious countries, instead of attempting (as in the early days of the peace) to throttle the conquered countries by the occupation of territory (as in the case of the Ruhr), adopted a new method, the method of financial exploitation, which was applied primarily to Germany and secondly to Austria. This new method finds expression in the Dawes plan, whose consequences are only now beginning to become apparent. In the third place, the Locarno conference, which is supposed to have made an end of the antagonisms between victors and vanquished, has in reality, despite all trumpetings, done nothing in the way of abolishing these conflicts. Indeed, it has served merely to intensify them.

The essential significance of the Dawes plan is that Germany is to pay, in instalments, a round sum amounting to 130 milliards of gold marks to the Entente. The results of the Dawes plan are already becoming manifest in the worsened economic position of Germany, in the collapse of numerous enterprises, in the growth of unemployment, and so on. The essence of this precious scheme, drafted in America, is that Europe is to pay off its indebtedness to America at the cost of Germany, that country having to pay indemnities to Europe; but since Germany cannot produce out of nothing the vast amounts required, she must receive a number of free markets which are not yet occupied by the other capitalist countries, so that there she can create new energy and new blood for the payment of the indemnities. Apart from a number of comparatively insignificant markets, America has our Russian market in view. According to the Dawes plan, the Russian market is to be left to Germany, so that Germany may be able to extort something out of this market and therefore have something to pay the indemnities to the rest of Europe, which, in its turn, will then be able to pay its debts to the United States. The whole plan is very beautifully constructed—on paper. But it reckons without the host, implying as it does for the German people a double pressure, the pressure of the German bourgeoisie upon the German proletariat, and the pressure of foreign capital upon the German people as a whole. No one will venture to say that this double pressure can fail to have its effect upon the German people. That is why I believe that this part of the Dawes plan is pregnant with the German revolution. The Dawes plan was conceived in order to pacify Germany, but it will inevitably lead to a revolution in Germany. The second part of the plan, that based upon the design that Germany shall extort from the Russian market the money to be paid to the rest of Europe, is likewise a reckoning without the host. Why do I say this? I say it because we in Russia have no intention of allowing ourselves to be transformed into an agrarian dependency of any other country, not even of Germany! We shall produce for ourselves the machinery and the other means of production we need. In assuming that we shall allow our country to become an agrarian dependency of Germany, the Dawes plan, I repeat, is reckoning without the host. The idol has feet of clay.

Such is the Dawes plan.

As far as Locarno is concerned, this is nothing more than a continuation of Versailles, and has only been designed to " maintain the status quo ", as the diplomatists say. It is designed to maintain that position of affairs wherein Germany is a conquered country and the Entente is a group of conquering powers. The Locarno conference was intended to give a legalist sanction to this arrangement. The new frontiers of Germany, frontiers devised to favour Poland and France, are to be maintained. Germany is to forfeit her colonies, is simultaneously to be tied hand and foot, to be stretched on a Procrustes' bed, and to devote herself to the payment of 130 milliards of gold marks. To believe that Germany, an expanding and progressive country, will content herself with such a situation, is to believe in miracles. If in earlier days, after the Franco-German war, the Alsace-Lorraine question (one of the most crucial of the conflicts of the time) was a main factor in bringing about the recent imperialist war, what guarantee have we that the peace of Versailles and its sequel, the Locarno conference (establishing legal sanctions for depriving Germany of Upper Silesia, creating the Danzig corridor, and alienating Danzig itself; for depriving Ukraine of Galicia and west Volhynia; for depriving White Russia of its western portion; for depriving Lithuania of Vilna)—what guarantee is there that this treaty, which breaks up a number of States into fragments and taps new sources of conflict, will not suffer the same fate as that experienced by the treaty which, after the Franco-German war, tore away Alsace and Lorraine from France?

There is no guarantee, nor can there be a guarantee.

If the Dawes plan is pregnant with the German revolution, Locarno is pregnant with European war.

The British conservatives wish, at one and the same time, to maintain the status quo as far as Germany is concerned, and to lead Germany into the field against the Soviet Union. Are they not asking rather too much?

They talk of pacifism, of peace between the European States. Briand and Austen Chamberlain embrace one another, what time Stresemann is overflowing with complimentary utterances about England. All this signifies nothing. We know from the history of Europe that treaties embodying fresh groupings of forces with an eye to a new war have always been termed " peaceful treaties ". Treaties are arranged which will inevitably lead to war; yet the signing of them is always effected to the accompaniment of the pipings of peace. There has never been any lack of false apostles of peace. Let me remind you of the incidents that followed the Franco-German war. Germany had been victorious in this war; France had been conquered. Bismarck was then extremely anxious to maintain the status quo, this meaning the state of affairs which had come into being after Germany had gained the victory over France. In those days Bismarck was in favour of peace, because this peace guaranteed him a number of privileges as compared with France. France, too, was in favour of peace, for a time at least, until she had recovered from the disastrous effects of the war. At this date, when all were preaching peace, and when the false apostles of peace were singing hymns about Bismarck's peaceful designs, Germany and Austria entered into a treaty, a pre-eminently peaceful treaty, which subsequently became one of the foundations for the imperialist war that began in August 1914. I am referring to the treaty between Austria and Germany in the year 1879. Against whom was this treaty directed? Against Russia and France. What was the substance of the treaty? Listen: " In view of the fact that a drawing together of Germany and Austria-Hungary cannot be a menace to any one, but is well adapted to consolidate the European peace established by the Berlin stipulations, Their Majesties "—this meaning the German emperor and the Austrian emperor—" have decided to enter into an alliance of peace and mutual defence ". Do you hear? A drawing together of Germany and Austria for the sake of the peace of Europe! The treaty was described as a " peace alliance "—and yet all historians are agreed that this treaty was a direct precursor of the imperialist war which began in August 1914. The outcome of the treaty was the signing of another treaty, that between Russia and France during the years 1891–1893. Of course this treaty, likewise, was a peace treaty! What were its terms? It was to the effect that " France and Russia, both inspired by the determination to maintain peace, have come to the following agreement " What agreement? The nature of the agreement was not openly stated, but was specified in a secret clause to the effect that in the event of a war against Germany, Russia was to supply 700,000 soldiers and France, if I am not mistaken, 1,300,000 soldiers.

Both of the before-mentioned treaties were officially described as peace treaties, designed to promote friendship and to guarantee the tranquillity of Europe.

In due sequence, six years later (1899) came the Hague peace conference, where the question of the limitation of armaments was discussed. This happened at the very time when, as an outcome of the Franco-Russian treaty, members of the French general staff were visiting Russia in order to elaborate plans for military operations in the event of war, and when Russian general staff officers were visiting France in order to work out the details for the future invasion of Germany. At the time of the Hague conference, too, the general staffs of Germany and Austria were putting their heads together in order to work out the best scheme for an attack by Austria and Germany on their neighbours in the West and in the East. While these manœuvres and countermanœuvres were going on behind the scenes, the

Hague conference assembled in 1899. At The Hague, peace was extolled to the skies, and lying and eloquent speeches were made anent limitations of armaments.

Here we have an example of the incomparable hypocrisy of bourgeois diplomacy, in which preparations for a new war are conducted under the cover of paeans to peace.

In view of the recent history of Europe, have we any reason to believe in the genuineness of the peace hymns sung in honour of the League of Nations and of Locarno? Certainly not. Nor can we trust the good faith of Chamberlain and Briand when they embrace one another, or the honesty of Stresemann when he overflows with compliments to Britain. On the contrary, we believe that Locarno is a plan for the regrouping of forces in view of a new war, and is not designed to promote peace at all.

Of considerable interest is the part played by the Second International. The leaders of the Second International do their utmost to persuade the workers that Locarno is an instrument of peace, that the League of Nations is a shrine of peace, that the bolsheviks must not be admitted to the League of Nations because they are opposed to peace, and so on, and so on. What does all this clamour, raised by the Second International, amount to in view of the facts I have just been recording, especially the facts relating to the various treaties entered into not long after the Franco-German war, treaties that were described as peace treaties when they were in reality war treaties? What does the attitude of the Second International towards Locarno signify? It signifies that the Second International is not merely an organisation for bringing about the bourgeois demoralisation of the working class, but also an organisation which aims at finding moral justification for all the injustices of the Versailles treaty. It signifies that the Second International wants to play jackal to the Entente, that it is an organisation which, by its activities, by its noisy clamour on behalf of Locarno and the League of Nations, wants to provide a moral justification for all the injustices and all the acts of oppression which are perpetrated under the sign of the treaty of Versailles and under that of the conference of Locarno.

4. CONFLICTS BETWEEN THE VICTORIOUS COUNTRIES

I come, now, to the fourth variety of antagonisms, the conflicts between the victorious countries. The basic facts may be summarised by saying that, notwithstanding a coalition of a sort between Britain and America (the essence of which is an understanding between Britain and the United States that the interallied debts are not to be annulled), the conflict of interests between Britain and the United States is steadily becoming intensified. One of the most important contemporary problems, as far as the great powers are concerned, is, to-day, the petroleum problem. The United States produces about 70 per cent. of all the petroleum produced in the world, and it consumes more than 60 per cent. of all that is consumed throughout the world. In respect, therefore, of this raw material, which is absolutely vital to the economic and military activity of the great powers, the United States is always and everywhere coming into conflict with Britain, and encountering the resistance of Britain. If we study the activities of the two most important petroleum firms in the world, Standard Oil and the Shell concern, the former representing the United States and the latter Britain, we see that all over the world, wherever there are oil wells, these two companies are fighting one another. It is a fight between America and Britain. For this petroleum question is absolutely vital. The power which can command most petroleum will have the upper hand in the next war. The control of the commerce and industry of the world depends upon the control of petroleum. Now that the navies of the most advanced countries are coming more and more to depend upon petrol-driven motors, mineral oil is absolutely essential to the great powers in their struggle for world dominion alike in peace time and in war time. That is why there is a life-and-death struggle between the oil companies of Britain and America—a struggle which is not always fought in the open, but which goes on unceasingly beneath the surface, as we can learn from the history of the conflict between Britain and the United States in this matter. Enough to recall the various notes which Hughes, when American minister for foreign affairs, addressed to England in relation to this matter of petroleum. The fight, then, is sometimes masked and sometimes open. It goes on in South America, in Persia, in the oil regions of Rumania and Galicia, all over the world. I shall not refer, here, to the important conflict of interests between Britain and the United States in China. Enough to remind you that a masked struggle is going on in that part of the world also—though America's behaviour is far more subtle, and is not characterised by the brutality of the colonial methods of which the British are so fond. On the quiet, none the less, the United States is trying to get the better of Britain in China, wants to drive the British out of China, and to get all the rich pickings there for herself. Naturally, the British capitalists cannot be expected to remain indifferent to these manœuvres.

I will not go further into the question of the conflicts of interests between France and Britain, the conflicts arising out of the dispute for the dominant position on the continent of Europe. But that there is such a dispute is generally known. It is likewise obvious that the conflicts of interest between Britain and France do not concern only this matter of leadership on the Continent, but also relate to colonial questions. Rumours have been current in the press that Britain was privy to the organisation of the wars against French imperialism in Syria and Morocco. I have no documentary evidence bearing upon this matter, but for my own part I am inclined to believe that there may be good reason for the assertion.

Nor shall I speak at any length of the conflicts of interest between the United States and Japan, which are also a matter of common knowledge. Any one who had cognisance of the last manœuvres of the American navy in the Pacific Ocean, and of the manœuvres of the Japanese navy, must have realised the purpose underlying these manœuvres.

Finally I must refer to the amazing growth of armaments in the countries that were victorious in the great war. I am talking about the victors, about the oppositions among the victors. These victors speak of themselves as allies. It is true that the United States was not a member of the Entente, but the United States joined with the Entente in fighting Germany. Well, these allies are now arming themselves with all possible speed. Against whom are the equipments directed? Before the great war, the Entente countries used to say that their armaments were intended as a defence against Germany, that Germany was armed to the teeth, was a menace to the peace of the world. So be it; but how about post-war conditions? Germany no longer exists as an armed power. Germany has been disarmed. None the less, armaments are growing to an unprecedented extent in the victorious countries. What, for instance, is the explanation of the incredible increase in the French air fleet? Why should there be such an immense increase in the British navy and in the British air fleet? How are we to explain the enormous increase in the United States navy and in the Japanese navy? Whom and what do these "allied" gentry fear, now that they have jointly conquered and disarmed Germany? What are they afraid of, and why do they equip themselves for war? What has become, too, of the pacifism of the Second International, which goes on talking about peace, and fails to see (or pretends not to see) that the "allies", who officially term one another friends, are arming frenziedly against a "non-existent" enemy? What has the League of Nations done, what has the Second International done, to hinder the crazy increase in armaments? Do they not all know that when such a rivalry of armaments continues, "the guns go off of themselves"? You will vainly expect an answer from the League of Nations or from the Second International. The real reason is that the conflict of interests among the victorious countries is becoming intensified, that a clash of arms is inevitable, and that, foreseeing the next war, the rivals are equipping themselves with all their energies. I do not exaggerate when I say that the peace between the victorious countries is not a friendly peace but an armed peace—one which carries within itself the germs of war. What is now going on in the victorious countries reminds us strongly of the situation that existed before war broke out in 1914. Then, likewise, there was a condition of armed peace.

The rulers of Europe are trying to hide this fact by raising a pacifist clamour. I have already explained how much this pacifism is worth, and how much meaning must be attached to it. The bolsheviks have been asking for disarmament ever since the days of Genoa. Why do not the leaders of the Second International and the other pacifist chatterers support our proposals?

The growth of armaments, evidencing the existence of irreconcilable conflicts among the victorious States, shows that the stabilisation, the partial stabilisation, of capitalism which Europe has effected at the price of its enslavement, cannot possibly last, for the antagonisms among the victorious nations are increasing (to say nothing of the antagonisms between the victorious countries and the conquered countries).

5. The Capitalist World and the Soviet Union

I now come to the fifth series of antagonisms, the conflicts between the Soviet Union and the capitalist world.

The basic fact in this connexion is that there no longer exists a worldwide capitalist system. Now that a Soviet country has come into existence, now that the Russia of the old regime has been transformed into the Soviet Union, worldwide capitalism has ceased to exist. The world has been severed into two camps, the imperialist camp and the anti-imperialist camp. That is the first thing we have to note.

The second fact to which attention must be drawn in this connexion is that the two most important capitalist countries, Britain and the United States, present themselves as an Anglo-American alliance leading the other capitalist countries. On the other hand, at the head of the various countries which are dissatisfied with imperialism, and carry on a life-and-death struggle against it, is our country, the Soviet Union.

The third point I have to make is that two dominant and mutually antagonistic poles of attraction have come into existence, so that, the world over, sympathies are diverging towards one pole or the other: the sympathies of the bourgeois governments tending towards the British-American pole, and the sympathies of the workers of the West and of the revolutionists of the East tending towards the Soviet Union pole. Britain-America is attractive in virtue of its wealth, for in this quarter loans are obtainable. The Soviet Union is attractive in virtue of its revolutionary experience, in virtue of the experience gained in the struggle for the liberation of the workers from the yoke of capitalism and for the liberation of the oppressed nations from imperialist oppression. You see why there is a trend of the sympathies of the workers of Europe and of the revolutionists of the East towards our country. You know what a stay in

Russia means to a worker from central or western Europe, or to a revolutionist from one of the oppressed countries; you know how such pilgrims come to us in crowds, and you know how keen is the sympathy towards our country felt by trusty revolutionists all over the world. There are two camps; two poles of attraction.

My fourth point is that there is a characteristic difference between the internal condition of these respective camps. In the capitalist camp, there is no unity of interests, no adequate centrifugal force promoting consolidation. Within the capitalist camp there is a conflict of interests, a tendency towards disruption, a fight between victors and vanquished, a conflict among the victors, a dispute among all the imperialist countries for colonies and opportunities of making profits—so that stabilisation in this camp cannot possibly be permanent. In our country, on the other hand, we have a healthy and persistently strengthening stabilisation, a growth of economic prosperity, a steady advance in the work of socialist construction, so that throughout our camp there is going on a continual process of consolidation among the discontented elements and strata, alike of the West and of the East, around the proletariat of Soviet Russia. They all throng to join forces with the Soviet Union.

Over there, in the capitalist camp, dissension and disintegration prevail; here, in the socialist camp, consolidation is advancing, and there is an ever-growing unification of interests against the common foe, against imperialism. Such are the fundamental facts which I have to adduce regarding the fifth group of antagonisms, the antagonisms between the capitalist world and the Soviet world.

I should like, Comrades, to lay special stress upon the way in which the revolutionary and socialist elements all over the world are being attracted towards the proletariat of our country. In this connexion, I am thinking of the labour delegations which come to Soviet Russia. These delegations make the most careful study of all the details of our constructive work, wishing to convince themselves that we are able, not only to destroy the old, but also to create the new. What is the significance of these labour delegations, these pilgrimages of workers to our country, which have inaugurated a new phase in the development of the labour movement in the West? You have heard, Comrades, how the leaders of the Soviet State have received the British labour delegation and the German labour delegation. Did you notice that the comrades who held the leading positions in the various branches of administration, did not content themselves with merely giving the members of the labour delegations general information about this point or that, but treated the visitors as persons to whom they themselves were, so to speak, accountable? I was not in Moscow at the time, but I read in the newspapers how Comrade Dzherzhinsky, the head of the Supreme Economic Council, gave a report of this kind to the German labour delegation. That is something new and peculiar in the life of our country, a matter which deserves close attention. I read, likewise, that the chiefs of our petroleum industry, Kossior in Grosny, and Serebroffsky in Baku, did not give the labour delegation such casual information as is given to an ordinary tourist, but treated these favoured visitors as if they had been chief inspectors entitled to receive formal reports. I read, further, that all our supreme authorities, the Council of People's Commissaries, the Central Executive Committee, and the local executive committees of the Soviets, regarding the labour delegates as persons empowered by the working class of the western world to make a friendly and brotherly inspection of our constructive work and our labour State, were all prepared and eager to give such thoroughgoing reports.

What do all these facts show, Comrades? They show two things. First of all that the working class of Europe, or at least the revolutionary section of the European working class, regards our State as its own child; and that the working class sends its delegations to us, not out of idle curiosity, but in order to learn what is really going on in Russia, and because it feels morally responsible for everything that we do here. In the second place, these facts show that the revolutionary section of the European proletariat, inasmuch as it adopts our State and regards it as its own child, is accepting the duty of defending Soviet Russia, and, if necessary, fighting on behalf of Soviet Russia. Can you think of any other State, however democratic, which would submit itself to the fraternal supervision of labour delegations from other countries? There is no other such State anywhere in the world. Only our State, the State of the workers and peasants, is able to do such a thing. Inasmuch as we show this enormous amount of confidence in the labour delegations from other lands, our own country is gaining the full confidence of the working class of central and western Europe. This confidence is worth far more to us than any loans, for the confidence of the European workers in our State is the most important antidote to intervention. That is the basis of those changes in the relationships between our State and the western proletariat, the changes which have taken place, or are in the course of taking place, because of the pilgrimages of the workers to Soviet Russia. That is the novelty which many have overlooked, but which is now decisive; for if the European working class regards us as part of itself, as its own child, for which it accepts moral responsibility; if it accepts the obligation of defending our State in the event of capitalist intervention; if it is ready to defend our interests against the capitalists—what does that signify? It means that our forces are growing day by day and hour by hour. It means that the weakness of capitalism is growing day by day and hour by hour. For no country can, in these times, carry on a war without the workers. If the workers refuse to make war against our republic, if they regard our republic as their own child whose fate is of supreme importance to them, then a war against our country becomes impossible. That is the true meaning of these pilgrimages to Soviet Russia, the pilgrimages which have taken place and will continue to take place, the pilgrimages we must support with all our forces, for they are a pledge of solidarity, a pledge of the consolidation of the friendship between the workers of our country and the workers of the West.

It may be well, here, to say a few words about the great number of the delegations which have visited our country. Not long ago, at the Moscow Conference, I heard a comrade ask Comrade Rykoff: "Don't all these delegations cost us too much money?" Comrades, no one ought to talk like that. We must not talk like that about the labour delegations that come to Soviet Russia. It is a scandal to do so. We must not grudge any expense, or shun any sacrifice, which can encourage the workers of the West to send delegations here, so that they can convince themselves that the Russian working class, having achieved the conquest of power, is competent, not only to destroy capitalism, but also to upbuild socialism. The workers of the West, or at any rate many of them, are still inclined to believe that the working class cannot get along without the bourgeoisie. This erroneous belief is the chief malady of the working class in central and western Europe, and has been inoculated into the workers there by the social democrats. We shall not grudge any sacrifices which may enable the working class of the West to convince itself, through the testimony of its delegations, that the working class of Soviet Russia, which has achieved the conquest of power, is competent not only to destroy the old regime, but likewise to upbuild socialism. We shall not grudge any sacrifices to make it possible for the workers of the West to convince themselves that we occupy a unique position as a workers' State, and that it is worth their while to fight on behalf of this State, that it is worth their while to defend Soviet Russia against attacks upon it by the capitalists of their own lands. We shall not grudge any sacrifices that may have such an effect. (Applause.)

Three kinds of delegations have visited us: delegations of intellectuals, teachers, etc.; delegations of adult workers, about ten in number; and delegations of young workers. The total number of delegates and excursionists who have visited our country is about 550. Sixteen other delegations are still expected, their coming having been registered by the Central Executive of the Trade Unions. We shall welcome these delegations as we welcomed others, in order to consolidate the ties between the working class of our country and the working class of the West, and in order thereby to set up a barrier against all the possibilities of intervention.

That is the sum total of the antagonisms which are eating like a canker into the heart of capitalism.

What is the upshot of these contradictions and antagonisms? What do they prove? They prove, as I said at the outset of my report, that the capitalist world is being disintegrated by a number of internal antagonisms, which are paralysing it; that, on the other hand, our world, the socialist world, is steadily growing stronger. That is the upshot of the provisional equilibrium which has been established; the war against us has come to an end, and there has ensued a period of " peaceful cohabitation " of the Soviet State with the capitalist States.

I shall now refer to two additional facts which have contributed to the replacement of the period of war by the period of " peaceful cohabitation ".

The first of these is that the United States does not at the present moment wish for any war to take place in Europe. Substantially, America says to Europe : " I have lent you many milliards. If you want any more money, and if you do not want your exchanges to crash, you had better keep the peace among yourselves. Be good children. Get on with your work, earn money, and pay the interest on your debts ". This advice may not be absolutely decisive in its effect, but obviously, in the circumstances, it will have a certain amount of influence upon Europe.

My second point is that, owing to the victory of the proletarian revolution in our country, a vast domain, with very extensive markets and enormous supplies of raw materials, has been detached from the capitalist system. Obviously this must have had a considerable effect upon the economic condition of Europe. The loss of one-sixth of the world, the loss of the markets and the sources of raw material of the sometime Russian empire, signifies for capitalist Europe a restriction of production and a profound disturbance. If the European capitalists are not to be wholly cut off from our markets and from our sources of raw material, they must be content, for a time, to accept a " peaceful cohabitation " ; and experience has shown that stabilisation of the capitalist economy of Europe cannot be secured without access to our markets and to our sources of raw material.

6. Foreign Situation of the Soviet Union

The before-mentioned factors have brought about the establishment of a certain equilibrium of forces as between the socialist camp and the capitalist camp. Thanks to them, the war against the Soviet Union has been followed by a breathing space, during which, as Lenin phrased it, " a kind of collaboration " with the capitalist world has become possible to us. In this phase, and as an outcome of all the influences I have been describing, various capitalist powers have " recognised " Soviet Russia, and more will do so in the near future.

I need not enumerate the States which have " recognised "

us. As far as the leading countries of the capitalist world are concerned, I think that the United States is the only one which still refuses to recognise us in any way. Nor shall I give any details about the commercial treaties entered into between Germany and Soviet Russia, between Italy and Soviet Russia, etc., after recognition had taken place. Nor, again, shall I say much about the development of our foreign commerce, which has notably increased of late. (The United States, which supplies us with cotton, is especially interested in our foreign trade; so are Britain and Germany, which import grain and other agricultural produce from Soviet Russia.) Enough, here, to say that the current year is the first since the period of " peaceful cohabitation " began in which we have been able to enter into comprehensive trading relationships with the capitalist world.

Of course this does not mean that all causes of tension are over; that there will be no conflict of claims and counter-claims between our State and the States of the western world. You know that the western world wishes us to pay the tsarist debts. Europe has not forgotten these debts, perhaps will never forget them; certainly will not forget them soon. We are told that our pre-war debts to western Europe amounted to six milliards, and that the war debts amounted to seven milliards, this making a total debt of thirteen milliards. If we allow for the fall in exchange, and if we subtract the amount claimed by the border States, there remains an indebtedness of seven milliards to the States of western Europe. You know that, according to Comrade Larin's calculations, our counter-claims, representing the damage done to us by Britain, France, and the United States as a consequence of their intervention in the days of the civil war, amount to something like fifty milliards, so that we are owed at least five times as much as we can be supposed to owe on account of the tsarist debts (exclamation by Larin: " We shall get the lot back ! "). Comrade Larin says that we shall some day get the lot back. (Laughter.) If we take a more modest estimate, such as that made by the People's Commissariat for Finance, our counter-claims amount to not less than twenty milliards. You see that, even on the lower reckoning, the balance is very much in our favour. (Laughter.) But the capitalist countries refuse to accept our figures, and according to them we are still their debtors.

On the ground of these conflicting calculations, there is friction in our negotiations with the capitalists, and we often come to a standstill. That is what took place during the negotiations with Britain, and it will probably happen during the negotiations with France.

What is the attitude of the Central Committee in this matter?

The attitude of the Central Committee has been unchanged since we were negotiating with Ramsay MacDonald about a treaty. We cannot repeal the law of the year 1918 annulling the tsarist debts. We still take up our stand upon this law. We cannot declare null and void the decrees that we promulgated at that time, and which, in Soviet Russia, have given a legal sanction to the expropriation of the expropriators. We take our stand upon these laws now, and shall continue to do so in the future. But we are not disinclined, when we enter into practical negotiations with Britain and France, to make certain exceptions in the matter of the old tsarist debts, in this sense, that we are willing to pay a little if we shall get something in return. We are not unwilling to satisfy the sometime holders of private property in Russia by giving them concessions, but only on the proviso that these concessions are not made upon servile conditions. We found it possible, upon such a basis, to come to an understanding with MacDonald. The idea underlying the British negotiations was that the war debts were in fact annulled. It was for this very reason that the treaty was quashed just when it seemed that matters had been satisfactorily arranged. By whom was it quashed? Unquestionably by the United States. Although the United States was not taking any overt part in the negotiations between Rakoffsky and MacDonald; although MacDonald and Rakoffsky had come to terms upon the draft for a treaty, although this draft treaty offered a way out of the difficulty for both parties, and was more or less conformable to the interests of both parties—the United States thought fit to give Britain " advice " upon the matter, the reason being that the draft treaty embodied the idea of the annulment of the war debts, and America could not tolerate this precedent, which might have led to the loss of the many milliards owed to America by Europe. That was why the negotiations for a treaty came to nothing.

None the less we still take our stand to-day upon the stipulations of the draft discussion between Rakoffsky and MacDonald.

Certain questions of foreign policy have become pressing while I was actually engaged in drafting this report. They are extremely delicate and controversial questions, concerning the relationships between our government and western European governments. There are two of these to which I wish to draw particular attention. First of all comes the question which has so frequently been raised by the British conservatives, and is still being raised by them, the question of propaganda. The second is the question of the Communist International.

We are charged with carrying on a special propaganda against imperialism, in Europe, on the one hand, and in colonies and dependencies, on the other. The British conservatives declare that it is the Russian communists who are destroying the power of the British empire. I should like to explain here that all this is pure nonsense. We do not need to organise any special propaganda, either in the West or in the East, now that the workers' delegations have been to visit us, now that the members of these delegations have studied the situation in our country, and have carried back tidings about this situation to all the countries of the West. We need no other propaganda than this, which is the best, the strongest, and the most effective propaganda on behalf of the Soviet system and against the capitalist system. (Applause.) We are charged with carrying on propaganda in the East. I maintain that that, likewise, is nonsense. We do not need to carry on any special propaganda in the East, for we know that our whole State system is built upon the foundation of the brotherly collaboration of the various nationalities which make up our country. Every Chinese, every Egyptian, every Indian, who comes to Soviet Russia and stays there for six months or so, has an opportunity of convincing himself that our country is the only one which understands the soul of the oppressed nations, which understands how to organise a genuine collaboration between the proletarians of the nationality which used to rule and the proletarians of the nationalities which used to be oppressed. We need no other propaganda and no other agitation in the East. Enough that the delegations which come to us from China, India, and Egypt, in order to study Soviet conditions for themselves, should diffuse tidings about our regime throughout the world. That is the best and the most effective form of propaganda.

But there does exist a power competent to destroy the British empire, and one which certainly will destroy it. I mean the British conservatives. That is the force which will inevitably lead the British empire to ruin. Enough to remind you of the policy which the British conservatives have been carrying on since they became the government. What did they begin with? Their first step was to make themselves masters of Egypt; then they increased the oppression in India; and then they undertook intervention in China. Such is the policy of the conservatives. Whose fault is it if the English ruling class is incapable of any other policy? Surely it is easy to understand that the British conservatives, if they continue to work along those lines, will, as surely as two and two make four, succeed in destroying the British empire.

Now, a few words about the Comintern. In the West, the hirelings of the imperialists and the manufacturers of forged letters spread reports to the effect that the Comintern is an organisation composed of conspirators and terrorists; that the communists travel through western countries and organize conspiracies against the European governments. Among other outrages, the explosion in the Sofia cathedral is attributed to the communists. Let me reiterate a fact which should be known to every civilised human being unless he is an utter ignoramus or a paid agent. Let me explain that communists never have had and never will have anything to do with the theory and the practice of individual outrages; that communists never have had and never will have anything to do with the theory and the practice of conspiracies against individual persons. The theory and the practice of the Comintern is based upon the idea of organising a revolutionary mass movement against capitalism. That is the true task of the communists. Only ignoramuses and idiots can confound conspiracies and individual acts of terrorisation with the policy of the Comintern, which is based upon the promotion of a mass movement.

Next, a few words about Japan. Some of our western opponents rub their hands and think: " In China, a revolutionary movement has begun; of course the bolsheviks have corrupted the Chinese people (for who else could corrupt a nation comprising four hundred million persons?), and the natural result of that will be that the Russians will soon find themselves at grips with the Japanese ". You know, Comrades, what nonsense that is. The forces of the revolutionary movement in China are immeasurable. They have not yet come into anything like full operation. The future will show how vast they are. The rulers of the West and the East, who do not see these forces, who do not make sufficient allowance for their strength, will find out when the time comes. We, as a State, cannot but take such forces into account. In our view, China is to-day in the same position as North America was when the separate colonies joined together to form the United States. China is faced by the same tasks as was Germany, when Germany achieved national unity; by the same tasks as was Italy, when that country achieved national unity and fought to secure liberation from foreign dominion. Right and justice are altogether on the side of the Chinese revolution. That is why the Chinese revolution, in its fight for the liberation of the Chinese people from the imperialist yoke, and in the struggle for the unification of China, has all our sympathy, and will continue to have all our sympathy. Those who fail to make due allowance for the forces of which I am speaking, will certainly lose. I believe that Japan will understand the necessity for taking into account the growing strength of the nationalist movement in China, a movement which will sweep away everything that checks its advance. Chang Tso Lin is coming to grief because he has not grasped the fact. He is also coming to grief because he has built his whole policy upon dissensions, upon making the relationships between Russia and Japan worse than before. Every general, every ruler belonging to the Manchurian group, who attempts to build upon dissensions between Russia and Japan, who tries to imperil the relationships between Russia and Japan, will certainly come to grief. He only will build upon a firm foundation whose policy is one which reckons with an improvement in the relationships between Russia and Japan, in a rapprochement between Russia and Japan. Only such a general, only such a statesman, will be able to consolidate his position in Manchuria, for we have no interests to serve by disturbing the relationships between ourselves and Japan. Our interests tend to promote a rapprochement between Russia and Japan.

7. Tasks of the Party

I have now to consider the tasks of our Party in relation to the international revolutionary movement and in relation to foreign policy of the Soviet Union.

What are the tasks of our Party as concerns the international revolutionary movement?

We must work along the following lines. First of all, we must do everything we can to strengthen the communist parties in the West, and to help these parties to win over the majority of the working masses. In the second place, we must intensify the struggle of the western workers to achieve trade-union unity, and to consolidate the friendship between the proletariat of the Soviet Union and the proletariat of capitalist countries. Important, in this connexion, are the working-class pilgrimages to which I have already referred. In the third place, we must establish and strengthen the alliance between the proletariat of our country and the liberationist movements in oppressed countries; for the people taking part in these movements are our allies in the struggle against world capital. In the fourth place, we must consolidate the socialist elements in our own country, in order to ensure that these elements shall be victorious over the capitalist elements, seeing that this victory will have a decisive significance in the way of promoting the revolutionary sentiments of the workers of all lands. Ordinarily, when the tasks of our Party in the domain of the international revolutionary movement are enumerated, the first three of the foregoing are mentioned, while the fourth task is forgotten. People are apt to forget that the struggle in our country is a struggle for the victory of the socialist elements over the capitalist elements; that the struggle for socialist construction in Russia has an international significance, because our country is the bulwark of the world revolution, and because our country is the main motive force of the international revolutionary movement. If the work of socialist construction in Russia proceeds at the proper pace, this will mean that, as regards the other three questions as well, we shall be able to carry on our work for the international revolutionary movement in accordance with the demands of the Party.

Now let us consider the tasks of the Party in the domain of the foreign policy of the Soviet Union.

First of all, we must carry on the struggle against new wars, the struggle to maintain peace and to secure the persistence of the so-called normal relationships towards capitalist countries. The basis of the policy of our government, of its foreign policy, is the idea of peace. The struggle for peace, the struggle against new wars, the disclosing of the true nature of all steps taken with the secret design of preparing for new wars, the disclosure of the true nature of such measures as would fain mask preparations for war beneath a pacifist flag (Locarno)—there you have our task. That is why we do not want to join the League of Nations. For the League of Nations is an organisation designed to mask preparations for war. As Comrade Litvinoff has rightly said, if we were to enter the League of Nations, we should only have the choice between hammer and anvil. Now, we neither wish to be a hammer for the weak nations nor yet an anvil for the strong ones. We are for peace; we are for the disclosure of the true nature of all measures tending to promote war, however peaceful they may pretend to be. Whether in the League of Nations, or at Locarno, they cannot deceive us by window dressing, nor yet frighten us by making a great noise.

In the second place, we must extend our commerce with the foreign world on the basis of the consolidation of the State monopoly of foreign trade.

In the third place, we must promote a rapprochement to the countries that were vanquished in the imperialist war; to those countries which, of all capitalist countries, have been most injured and wronged, and are therefore inclined to form an opposition to the dominant group among the great powers.

In the fourth place, we must join forces with the dependent and colonial countries.

Such are the tasks which the Party has at the present time to undertake in the domains of international relationships and the international labour movement.

II. INTERNAL SITUATION OF THE SOVIET UNION

COMRADES ! I come now to the second part of my report upon the activities of the Central Committee. This section of the report will deal with the internal situation of our State, and with the policy of the Central Committee in matters connected with the internal situation. Although figures relating to these matters have recently been published in the press, I shall have to give some figures here.

1. GENERAL ECONOMIC POSITION

Before we come to consider the figures, let me give you a general account of the directives by which our activity in the upbuilding of socialist economy is guided.

First Directive. Our constructive work, like all our other work, has to be carried on in a world which, outside Russia, is still capitalist. This means that the development of our economic life and our socialist construction takes place amid the antagonisms, amid the clashes, between our economic system and the capitalist system. These antagonisms cannot possibly be avoided. That is the framework within which the struggle between the two systems must go on, the struggle between the socialist system and the capitalist system. This signifies that our economy must be upbuilded, not only in opposition to the capitalist economy of the foreign world, but also in opposition to certain elements in our own country ; that it must be built up under stress of the conflict between the socialist elements and the capitalist elements in the U.S.S.R. itself.

From this it follows that we must upbuild our economy in such a way that our country shall not be transformed into an appendage of the capitalist world system ; that it shall not become a subordinate power enrolled in the general system of capitalist development ; that our economy shall not develop as a subsidiary part of world capitalism, but as an independent economic unity, mainly relying upon the home market, upon the interrelationships between our own manufacturing industry and our own peasant agriculture.

There are two alternative outlooks on this matter. One view is that our country will, for a long time to come, remain an agrarian country; that it will have to export agricultural produce and to import machinery; and that it will continue to work along these lines for many, many years. Such a view was recently expounded by Comrade Shanin. (Perhaps some of you have read his article in " Ekonomicheskaya Zhizn ".) According to this view, our country will never become a genuinely industrial country, or at any rate will not become such for a very long time. The growth of our manufacturing industry would be considerably restricted, and Soviet Russia, from being an economically independent entity based upon the home market, would become an appendage of the capitalist world system. Acceptance of such a view would mean the repudiation of our task of socialist construction.

The opposing view is that, so long as we are surrounded by capitalist States, we must devote all our energies to making our country remain an independent entity based upon the home market. We must see to it that our country shall be a centre of attraction for all those countries which, by degrees, will fall away from capitalism, and will enter the path of socialist economy. That line of development can only be followed if we develop our industries to the utmost, in a manner appropriate to the resources at our disposal. We emphatically reject the policy of transforming our country into an appendage of the capitalist world system. We advocate the path of socialist construction. That is, and will remain, the Party aim. It is our unquestioned duty to follow this line, so long as we are encircled by capitalist States.

But this position of affairs will continue only so long as our country is surrounded by capitalist countries. The position will be altered as soon as the revolution has taken place in Germany or in France, or in both these countries; as soon as socialist construction has begun there upon a higher technical foundation than exists in Russia. Then we shall be able to modify the policy of making our country an independent economic entity, and change over to a policy of incorporating our country into the general system of socialist development. Meanwhile, pending the revolution in France, or Germany, or both, we must maintain in Soviet Russia that minimum of independence in economic life which is essential as a safeguard against the economic subordination of Soviet Russia to the system of world capitalism.

Second Directive. We must continually bear in mind the peculiarities of Russian economic life, the differences between Soviet economy and the economy of capitalist countries. In capitalist countries, private capital rules; the mistakes which the individual capitalist trusts and syndicates make, the mistakes which the various groups of capitalists make, are corrected by the elementary tendencies of the market. Should over-production occur, there will be a crisis; and then, after the crisis, economic life will resume its normal course. If too much is imported, so that the balance of trade is unfavourable, the exchange begins to go wrong, inflation occurs, imports are restricted and exports are increased. All this takes place in the form of crises. No serious mistake, no extensive over-production, no grave disturbance of the balance between production and demand, can be corrected and done away with in capitalist countries otherwise than by crises. That is the way people live in capitalist countries. We cannot live in that way. In capitalist countries we see economic crises, commercial crises, financial crises, affecting individual capitalist groups. With us, it is different. Every serious arrest in trade or in production, every great mistake in the calculation of our economy, affects our economic system as a whole, and does not end with a partial crisis. Every crisis, whether a commercial crisis, a financial crisis, or an industrial crisis, can, in our country, very readily take the form of a general crisis affecting the country as a whole. That is why we need peculiar caution and exceptional perspicacity in our socialist construction. That is why we must be so farseeing in our economic development, make as few mistakes as possible, exercise prudence and foresight. Since, however, we are not particularly cautious, not exceptionally farseeing, not distinguished by a peculiar capacity for avoiding mistakes in the management of our economic life, and since we still have to learn our trade of socialist construction, we make mistakes, and shall doubtless make other mistakes in the future. Consequently, we need to build up reserves. We must organise our economic system in such a way that we shall be able to count upon reserves in order that we may safeguard ourselves against the results of our mistakes. Our work during the last two years shows that we are not immune from mischances or mistakes. In the domain of agriculture, a good deal turns, not only upon our economic sagacity, but also upon the forces of nature (failures of the crops, etc.). In manufacturing industry, again, a good deal turns, not only upon our economic leadership, but also upon the home market, which we do not as yet fully control. In foreign commerce, a good deal turns, not only upon ourselves, but also upon the behaviour of the western European capitalists. In proportion as our exports and imports increase, we tend to become more and more dependent upon the capitalist West, and we grow more and more sensitive to the blows our enemies can deliver upon us in this field. To protect ourselves against mischances and inevitable errors, we must see to it that we build up reserves.

We have no guarantees against a failure of the crops, and for that reason we need reserves in agriculture. In manufacturing industry, we have no guarantees against the mischances of the home market. It would be needless to insist that we, who have to live upon the means we can heap up here at home, must be extremely thrifty in the expenditure of these means. We must try to lay out every penny with the utmost care, and to devote our resources only to those enterprises which are absolutely indispensable at the moment under consideration. What has been said shows that reserves are essential in industry as well as in agriculture. We are not safeguarded against mischances in foreign trade (masked boycott, masked blockade, etc.). For this reason, likewise, it is necessary to have reserves.

Of course we can double the sums allotted to furnishing agricultural credits; but if we were to do this, we would not have the necessary reserves for the financing of industry; industry would greatly lag behind agriculture in its development; the production of manufactured articles would have to be restricted, with the result that the prices of these articles would rise, and the consequences would be disastrous. We might devote double the present sum to the development of industry. But this would bring about an unduly rapid tempo in the development of industry, so that, owing to the lack of a sufficiency of free capital, we should not be able to keep step with that development, and there would certainly be a fiasco—to say nothing of the fact that if we were to spend so much upon industry, there would be nothing left over for agricultural credits.

We might increase our imports twofold, especially the import of machinery, in order to hasten the growth of industry; but this, by making our imports greatly exceed our exports, would lead to an unfavourable balance of trade, and would disturb our exchange. This would mean an undermining of the foundations on which alone a carefully planned guidance and development of manufacturing industry is possible.

We might greatly increase exports, without paying heed to any other of the main constituents of our economic life. We might do this regardless of the condition of the home market. The consequence of such a policy would inevitably be to produce great complications in the towns, owing to an enormous increase in the prices of agricultural produce, this meaning a decline in real wages and a sort of artificially organised famine with all its disastrous consequences.

We might raise the wages of our workers, not merely to the pre-war level, but to a considerably higher figure. This would slow down the developmental tempo of our manufacturing industry, for the development of our industry in existing circumstances (lack of foreign loans, lack of credits, etc.) can only take place if we accumulate the amount of surplus profits necessary for the financing of industry. If we were to raise the wages of labour unduly, no such accumulation of surplus profits would be possible.

I have now explained to you the two main directives for reconstructive work, and can turn to consider the figures.

One more digression, first. Our economic system is a variegated one. We have five different economic forms. We have one economic form which may almost be described as a natural economy. I am thinking of those peasant economies in which production is only to a slight extent the production of commodities. The second economic form is commodity production in which production for the market plays a decisive part in the peasant economy. A third economic form is private capitalism, which is not yet dead, but has revived to a certain extent, and will, to a certain extent, continue to exist as long as the New Economic Policy remains in force. A fourth form is State capitalism, the form of capitalism which we have agreed to tolerate, and which we can control and keep within bounds to whatever extent the proletarian State thinks fit. Lastly, the fifth economic form is socialist industry, that is our State industry, where, in the process of production, there are not two hostile classes (proletariat and bourgeoisie), but only one class (proletariat).

I should like to say a few words about these five economic forms, for it would otherwise be difficult to understand the figures which I am about to adduce, or to grasp the developmental trends of our manufacturing industry. There is all the more reason for discussing these five economic forms, seeing that Lenin dealt with them at considerable length, showing us how, in our constructive work, we can best allow for the conflict between these various economic forms.

I should like, in especial, to say a few words about State capitalism, and also about State industry (which is a type of socialist industry), in order to dispel the misunderstandings and confusions which prevail in the Party concerning these questions.

Are we entitled to call our State industry a State-capitalist industry? No. Why not? Because State capitalism, even under the proletarian dictatorship, is an organisation of production in which production is carried on by two opposed classes: the class of exploiters, who own the means of production; and the class of exploited, who do not own any means of production. Whatever form State capitalism may adopt, it must be essentially capitalist if it is to be described as State capitalism. When Lenin analysed the nature of State capitalism, he was thinking mainly of concessions. Well, then, let us examine these concessions, and consider whether two classes are represented in the work of production. Yes, certainly, two classes are represented here: the class of the capitalists, the concessionaries, who are exploiters, and who, for the time being, own the means of production; and the class of the proletarians, who are exploited by the concessionaries. Here, obviously, we have nothing to do with socialism. It would not occur to any socialist to carry on a campaign on behalf of intensifying the productivity of labour in a concessionary undertaking, since every one knows that such an undertaking is not socialist, is alien to socialism.

Now consider another type of undertaking, a State enterprise. Is it State capitalism? No, it is not. Why not? Because in that enterprise there are not two classes represented, but only one class; the class of the workers, who own the means of production, and are not exploited, seeing that the maximum returns from the enterprise over and above the wages of labour are devoted to the further development of industry, that is to say to the improving of the position of the working class as a whole.

Of course, it may be contended that, none the less, we have not to do here with complete socialism, seeing that in the conduct of our enterprise there still persist vestiges of bureaucracy. That is true. All the same, State industry is a socialist form of production. There are two types of production: the capitalist type (to which State capitalism belongs), in which two classes are represented in production, in which production is carried on in order to make profits for capitalists; and another type, the socialist type of production, in which there is no exploitation, in which the means of production belong to the working class, and in which the enterprise is not carried on in order to make profits for a class alien to the workers, but in order to expand the industry for the general advantage of the working class as a whole. Lenin pointed out that our State enterprises are enterprises of a characteristically socialist type.

Here an analogy with our State could be drawn. Our State cannot be described as a bourgeois State. As Lenin said, it represents a new type of State, the proletarian State. Why do we say this? Because our State apparatus does not exist for the purpose of oppressing the working class, as is invariably the function of the State in all bourgeois States. In Soviet Russia, the function of the State is to free the working class from oppression by the bourgeoisie. That is why our State is a proletarian State, although even in the Russian Soviet State there still remain too many vestiges of the old regime. Lenin himself, the man who described our Soviet order as a typically proletarian State, expressed himself in very vigorous terms when he condemned the survival of vestiges of bureaucracy. Still, as he said again and again, in spite of these survivals our State conforms to the new proletarian type of State. We must distinguish between the essential type of the State, and the heritages from the old system which persist in it. In like manner, we must distinguish between the bureaucratic survivals in our State enterprises, on the one hand, and that form of production which we regard as socialist, on the other. Although in our State industries, in our economic apparatus generally, and in our trusts, mistakes are made, and bureaucracy persists, we are not therefore entitled to say that we have no socialist industry. If the survivals of the old order in our State industry justified the statement that our industry is not a socialist industry, then the survivals of the old regime in the Soviet State generally would entitle us to say that it is not a proletarian State. I could mention quite a number of bourgeois State apparatus which work better and more economically than our proletarian State apparatus. But this does not mean that our State apparatus is not proletarian; that, as far as its type is concerned, our State apparatus is not on a higher level than a bourgeois State apparatus. Why do I say this? Because a bourgeois apparatus of State, even if it should work better than ours, is working for the capitalists, whereas our proletarian State apparatus, even if it gets stuck in a rut sometimes, is still working on behalf of the proletariat and against the bourgeoisie.

We must not forget these differences of principle.

The same thing must be said regarding our State industry. Merely because there are defects, merely because there are survivals of bureaucracy, in the leading instruments of our State industry (defects and survivals which cannot be done away with twixt night and morning), we must not forget that our State enterprises are, in essence, socialist enterprises. In Ford's factories, for instance, all the work is done with great precision, and there is perhaps less peculation than in some of our State factories; but Ford's factories are working for the capitalists, are working for Ford, whereas our enterprises, where there is a good deal of peculation sometimes, and where the technique of the enterprise is often far from satisfactory, are none the less working for the proletariat.

These differences of principle, likewise, must not be forgotten.

Now let us turn to the figures relating to our economic system as a whole.

Agriculture. In the economic year 1924-1925, the gross production amounted to 71 per cent. of the pre-war production, that of the year 1913. In other words, in the year 1913, the gross agricultural product was valued at a little over 12 milliards of roubles; and in the year 1924-1925, at a little more than 9 milliards of roubles (pre-war currency). For the economic year 1925-1926, the data at present available show that there is likely to be a further increase in agricultural production, the estimate of the total value being 11 milliards of roubles, about 88 per cent. of the pre-war product. Our agriculture is, you see, on the upgrade.

Industry. If we take our industry as a whole, lumping together State industry, the concessions, and private industry, we find that the gross production in the year 1924-1925 attained a value of 5 milliards (pre-war roubles) as compared with 7 milliards for the year 1913. This is 71 per cent. of the pre-war production. The estimates for the current economic year lead us to expect an industrial production valued at $6\frac{1}{2}$ milliards, being about 95 per cent. of the pre-war production. Speaking generally, our industrial production is on the upgrade, and this year the increase in industrial production is more marked than the increase in agricultural production.

The question of electrification is of especial importance. In the year 1921, the State Electrification Commission drafted a plan in accordance with which, during the next ten or fifteen years, thirty electric power stations with a functional capacity of 1,500,000 kilowatts were to be built. The cost of inaugurating these was to be about 800,000,000 gold roubles. Before the October revolution, the functional capacity of the electric power stations in this country amounted to 402,000 kw. Up to now, we have completed new works with a total functional capacity of 152,350 kw.; and in the year 1926 other power stations are to be established with a functional capacity of 326,000 kw. If the work continues to be carried out at this rate, the U.S.S.R. electrification scheme will be completed within ten years, that is to say in the year 1932. Our electro-technical industry is growing proportionally with the electric power stations. For the year 1925-1926, the expected production is 165-170 per cent. of the pre-war production. I must point out, however, that the construction of great water-power works is demanding much larger sums than were originally estimated for. For instance, whereas the estimated cost of installing the Volkhov works was 24,300,000 " orientation " roubles, by September 1925 the cost had risen to 95,200,000 chervonets roubles, this being 59 per cent. of the amount expended for the building of the chief power stations, whereas the functional capacity of the Volkhov works is only 30 per cent. of the functional capacity of all the proposed works. The original estimate for the construction of the Zemo-Avchalsk power station was 2,600,000 gold roubles ; but the present estimates are for 16,000,000 roubles, of which 12,000,000 roubles have already been spent.

When we compare the production of the State industries and the cooperative industries (taken together) with the production of private industry, we find that in the economic year 1923–1924 the former were responsible for 76 per cent. of the total industrial production of the country ; in the economic year 1924–1925, State and cooperative industry produced 79·3 per cent. of the total production.

You see, then, that State and cooperative industry are gaining at the expense of private industry. According to the estimates for next year, the proportion of State and cooperative production will be 80 per cent., as compared to 20 per cent. contributed by private industry. Private industry is growing, but State and cooperative industry are growing quicker still.

When we compare the total amount of property concentrated in the hands of the State with the total amount in the hands of private enterprise, we find that in this domain, too, the proletarian State holds a predominant position, for it disposes of a capital fund of 11·7 milliards (reckoned in chervonets roubles), whereas private enterprise (chiefly in the form of peasant enterprises) can dispose of only a total of 7·5 milliards.

You see that the socialised property greatly exceeds non-socialised property in amount, and that the former is gaining at the expense of the latter.

Nevertheless, our social system as a whole cannot be described as either capitalist or socialist. It represents a transitional stage between capitalism and socialism. Although the extent of peasant production, based upon private property, is enormous, the proportion of production effected by socialist industry is increasing daily and hourly. Socialist industry is dependent upon concentration and organisation; socialist industry is able to take advantage of the fact that the dictatorship of the proletariat exists in this country; that transport, banking, and credit are in our hands: thus socialist industry gains a steadily increasing share in the total production of the country. It is advancing all the time, is subjugating private industry, is superseding all other economic forms. The destiny of the rural areas is that they will become subordinated to the towns, to large-scale industry.

That is the most important conclusion we have to draw as a result of a study of the characteristics of our system, of the share taken by socialist industry in production as compared with the share taken by private capitalist industry, and a study of the share taken by petty industry in the total production of the country.

Now a few words about the *budget*. You probably know that the budget has increased to 4 milliards of roubles. Reckoning in pre-war roubles, we find that our budget is no less than 71 per cent. of the State budget of pre-war times. If to the general State budget, we add the local budgets, in so far as these can be calculated, we find that our national budget is no less than 74·6 per cent. of the national budget of 1913. Characteristic of our budget is the fact that the proportion of revenue not derived from taxes is much greater than the proportion derived from taxes. This, likewise, shows that our economic system is steadily progressing.

The question how much profit has been made during the last year (1924) in our State and cooperative enterprises is of very great importance, seeing that this country is poorly supplied with capital, is one which does not receive any considerable foreign loans. We must carefully examine our industrial enterprises, our commercial enterprises, our banks, and our cooperatives, in order to learn what means are available for the further development of our industry. In the year 1923–1924, the centrally administered State industry and the metallurgical industries united in the Metal Trust yielded a profit of about 142 million chervonets roubles. Of this sum, 71 millions were handed over to the State treasury. In the year 1925, a profit of 315 millions has already been gained, and of this 173 millions are to be handed over to the State treasury, being 54 per cent. of the total profit.

INTERNAL SITUATION OF U.S.S.R.

The centrally administered State commercial undertakings gained a profit of about 37 million roubles in the year 1923-1924, of which 14 millions were handed over to the State treasury. In the year 1925, owing to the fall in prices, the profit was reduced to 22 millions. Of this sum, about 10 millions will be handed over to the State treasury. In foreign commerce, there was, during the year 1923-1924 a surplus of more than 26 million roubles, of which about 17 millions were handed over to the State treasury. For the year 1925, the profits of our foreign trade were 44 million roubles, of which 29 millions are to be handed over to the State treasury. According to the calculations of the People's Commissariat for Finance during the year 1923-1924, the banks made a profit of 46 million roubles, of which 18 millions were handed over to the State treasury. For the year 1924-1925 the profits of the banks are more than 97 millions, of which 51 millions are to be handed over to the State treasury. The consumers' cooperatives made during the year 1923-1924 profits amounting to 57 million roubles; and the agricultural cooperatives, profits amounting to 4 million roubles.

The figures I have just given represent less than the real profits. You know why that is. You know the way in which our economic institutions present their accounts, desiring, as they do, to keep as much as possible for the expansion of their undertakings! If the figures appear small to you (and they are really too small), you must remember that they are less than the true amounts.

Now a few words about the returns of our foreign commerce.

If we compare the total figures of our foreign commerce with those of the year 1913, we find that the foreign commerce of the year 1923-1924 amounted to 21 per cent. of what it was in pre-war days; and in the year 1924-1925, to 26 per cent. The exports for the year 1923-1924 were valued at 522 million roubles; the imports, at 439 million roubles; the total imports and exports, at 961 million roubles; the excess of exports over imports at 83 million roubles. In the year 1923-1924, exports exceeded imports. In the year 1924-1925, the exports amounted to 564 million roubles; the imports, to 708 million roubles; the total imports and exports, to 1,272 million roubles; and the excess of imports over exports, to 144 million roubles. You see that during this last year the balance of trade has been unfavourable.

Let us go more closely into this matter. In Soviet Russia, people are inclined to say that the excess of imports over exports for the economic year which has recently come to a close, was due to the fact that, owing to the partial failure of the crops, we had to import a great deal of grain during this year. Well, the import of grain amounted to only 83 millions, whereas the excess of imports over exports amounted to 144 millions. What, then, is the meaning of this excess of imports over exports? We have bought more than we have sold, we have imported more than we have exported, and this unfavourable balance of trade has affected our exchange. The directive issued by the Thirteenth Congress of the Party was to the effect that the Party must do everything in its power to ensure that the balance of trade should go the other way. I must admit that we all of us, Soviet instruments and Central Committee alike, made a great mistake in that we failed to follow this directive. No doubt, it was difficult to do so, but if we had set seriously to work we might at least have ensured that there should be a slight excess of exports over imports. Well, we made a mistake, and the Party Congress must set matters right. Indeed, the Central Committee, at a special session in November, did its utmost to rectify the blunder. After examining the figures relating to imports and exports, the Central Committee decided that next year the balance of foreign trade must be made favourable by at least 100 million roubles.

This is necessary, absolutely necessary, for such a country as ours, which has very little capital, into which there is a minimum export of capital from foreign countries; where a favourable balance of foreign trade must be maintained unless the value of our currency is to be gravely imperilled; and seeing that, without a stable currency, we cannot develop our manufacturing industry and our agriculture. You all know from experience how disastrous are the effects of fluctuations in the value of the currency. We must not return to that unhappy state of affairs, but we must do everything in our power to put an end to whatever may disturb the value of our currency

2. Industry and Agriculture

We now have to consider the circumstances which at the present time affect, and in the near future will continue to affect, the mutual relationships between our manufacturing industry and our agriculture.

(*a*) In the first place, Soviet Russia remains a predominantly agricultural country. The products of agriculture greatly exceed the products of industry. The most important fact about our industry is that its production is already approximating to that of pre-war days, and that the further development of industry presupposes a new technical basis, namely the provision of new machinery and the building of new factories. This is an extremely difficult task. If we are to pass from a policy of making the best possible use of our existing industries to a policy of establishing a new industrial system upon a new technical foundation, upon the building of new factories, we shall require a large quantity of capital. Since, however, there is a great lack of capital in this country, we have good reason to expect that in the future the growth of our industry will not proceed so rapidly as it has in the past. It is otherwise with agriculture. No one can say that all the existing possibilities of our agriculture have as yet been exhausted. In contrast with industry, our agriculture can advance rapidly on the basis of the existing technique. A mere raising of the cultural level of the peasants, the teaching of them to read and write, even such a simple measure as the proper cleansing of the seed they use, would suffice to increase the gross production of our agriculture by from 10 to 15 per cent. You can easily calculate what this would mean for the whole country. These possibilities already exist for our agriculture. That is why the further development of our agriculture does not encounter such technical difficulties as are encountered in the matter of the development of our industry. That is why the disproportion between the balance of manufacturing industry and the balance of agriculture will continue to increase in the next few years, seeing that our agriculture has a number of potentialities which have not yet been fully turned to account, but will be turned to account in the near future.

What tasks accrue in connexion with this circumstance?

(a) Above all, it is incumbent upon us to develop our large-scale State industry at all costs, and to overcome the difficulties which stand in the way. Next, we must do what we can to develop the local, the provincial soviet industries. Comrades, we cannot content ourselves with the development of our centrally administered industry, for the centrally administered industries, our centralised trusts and syndicates, cannot possibly satisfy the manifold needs of a population numbering 140 millions. To satisfy the multiform needs of so large a population, we must see to it that in every county, in every province, in every region, in every national republic, there shall be an active industrial life. Unless, in our work to promote economic development, we can arouse the local forces from their slumbers, unless we support local industries by all possible means, we shall never see in Soviet Russia that great blossoming of economic life of which Lenin used to speak. Unless we combine the interests and advantages of the centre with the interests and the advantages of the provinces, we shall not solve the problem of encouraging local initiative, or the problem of bringing about a rapid and general economic advance, or the problem of swiftly industrialising the country.

(b) Formerly, there was an over-production of fuel. Now, there is a fuel crisis, for industry is growing more rapidly than the supply of fuel. We are approaching the condition of affairs which prevailed in our country during the bourgeois regime, when there was a deficiency of fuel, and fuel had to be imported. In other words, the fuel balance does not correspond to the balance of industry and to the needs of industry. We must, therefore, rapidly increase our production of fuel, and must improve our technical methods of getting fuel, so that the development in this department shall keep pace with the general development of industry.

(c) There is a certain disharmony between the production of metals and the development of our general economic life. Taking the very lowest estimate of the need for metals and the maximum figures of the possible production of metals, we find that there is a deficiency in the production of metals amounting to tens of millions. Our economic life, and in especial our manufacturing industry, cannot develop properly in these circumstances. Consequently, special attention must be paid to this question. Metal is the foundation upon which our industry is built, and the production of metals must be made to keep pace with the development of industry in general and of transport in particular.

(*d*) There is a disproportion between the number of skilled workers and the development of our industry. Figures relating to this matter have been published in the press, but I will not reproduce them here, and will be content to say that for the year 1925–1926 our manufacturing industries will need 433,000 additional skilled workers. We can only hope to provide one fourth of that number.

(*e*) There is another trouble to which I must refer. The wear and tear of the rolling stock of our railways is excessive. The demand for rolling stock is so great that next year we shall be compelled to use our locomotives and carriages or trucks, not to 100 per cent. of their functional capacity, but to 120 per cent. or more! Thus, the fundamental capital of the People's Commissariat for Transport is being worn out, and this will lead to a catastrophe in the near future unless we take energetic measures to avert it.

3. COMMERCIAL PROBLEMS

Now I come to commerce. The figures show that in this domain, just as in that of industry, the share of the State, as compared with the share of the private capitalists, is increasing. The total internal trade before the war amounted annually to about 20 milliards, whereas the internal trade for the year 1923–1924 was about 10 milliards, or, to be precise, 51 per cent. of the pre-war trade; while for the year 1924–1925, it was about 14 milliards, or 71 per cent. of the pre-war trade. You see, then, that our home trade is obviously increasing. As regards the share of the State in this, for the year 1923–1924, it was 45 per cent., while that of the cooperatives was 19 per cent., and that of private capitalists 36 per cent. For the year 1924–1925, the share of the State was 50 per cent., that of the cooperatives, 24·7 per cent., and that of the private capitalists, 24·9 per cent. Thus the share of the private capitalists is diminishing and the share of the State and the cooperatives is increasing. If we divide the total trade into two parts, large-scale trading and small-scale trading, we note the same tendency. In large-scale trading, the share of the State was 62 per cent. in the year 1923-1924, and 68·9 per cent. in the year 1924-1925. The share of the cooperatives increased in the same years from 15 per cent. to 19 per cent. The share of the private capitalists in the same years declined from 21 per cent. to 11 per cent. In small-scale trading for the year 1923-1924, the share of the State was 16 per cent., and for the year 1924-1925 nearly 23 per cent. For the same two years, the share of the cooperatives in small-scale trading was 25·9 per cent. and 32·9 per cent., respectively. The share of the private capitalists for the same years was 57 per cent. and 44·3 per cent. Thus, whereas during the former year, the private capitalist still had the upper hand in the matter of small-scale trading, during the latter year the State and the cooperatives got the upper hand.

In the supply of raw materials and grain, there was likewise an increase in the share of the State and the cooperatives. For the year 1924-1925, in the case of oleaginous seeds, it was 65 per cent.; of flax, 94 per cent.; of cotton, nearly 100 per cent.; of grain, for the year 1923-1924, 75 per cent.; and for the year 1924-1925, 70 per cent. In this last case, there was, as you see, a slight falling off; but, speaking generally, there has been an unmistakable increase in the share of the State and the cooperatives in internal trade, both large-scale and small-scale.

If, in the matter of the grain supply, the share of the State (though still greatly preponderating over the share of the private capitalists) has fallen off a little, this must be ascribed to the mistakes that were made in the purchase of grain. Not only the Soviet organisations, but likewise the Central Committee has miscalculated in the purchase of grain, for it is the business of the Central Committee to watch over the Soviet organisations, seeing that the Central Committee is responsible for everything done by the Soviet organisations. The miscalculation was that, when we were drawing up our plans, we did not allow for the circumstance that the condition of the market this year differed from that of previous years. This year, for the first time, we entered the grain market without any sort of administrative pressure to back us up; the burden of taxation had been reduced to a minimum, so that the peasant and the State agent met one another for the first time in the market on equal terms. Our economic planning organisations did not allow for this circumstance, and they believed that prior to January 1, 1926, it would be possible to buy 70 per cent. of the quantity of grain required. We failed to allow for the fact that the peasants know very well what they are about in these matters ; that they are inclined to hold back wheat from the market, hoping for a rise, while bringing less valuable sorts of grain to market. As soon as we recognised our mistake, we changed our plans, and restricted the export of wheat. We also modified our import estimates. The new estimates for imports and exports, which are as yet only provisional, allow for a minimum of 100 millions.

4. Classes, their Activities, and their Mutual Relationships

The development of the economy of our country has led to an improvement in material conditions, especially in those of the working class. A rapid improvement in these conditions is now going on. Here are some figures. On April 1, 1924, according to the calculations of the People's Commissariat for Labour, the total number of workers (if all branches and varieties of industry are included, not excepting the workers in small-scale industry, the seasonal workers, and the agricultural labourers) was 5,500,000, of whom 1,000,000 were agricultural labourers, and 760,000 unemployed. On October 1, 1925, there were more than 7,000,000 wage workers, of whom 1,200,000 were agricultural labourers, and 715,000 unemployed. You see there is an unmistakable growth in the numbers of the working class.

The monthly average wage of the workers, reckoned in chervonets roubles, was in April 1924, 35 roubles per head, being 62 per cent. of the pre-war wage ; in September 1925, it was 50 roubles, or 95 per cent. of the pre-war wage. There are some branches of industry in which wages have risen above the pre-war level. The average real wage, estimated in commodity roubles, in April 1924 was 0·88 roubles per day ; in September 1925, it was 1·21 roubles. The average value of the daily production of a worker was 4·18 roubles in April 1924, and 6·14 roubles in the year 1925—reckoned in pre-war prices.

This is 85 per cent. of the pre-war productivity. If we follow month by month the relationship between the wage of labour and the productivity of labour, we see that an increase in the wage of labour goes hand in hand with the increase in the productivity of labour. But in June and July, we see that, notwithstanding the continued increase in the wage of labour, there is not so great a corresponding advance in the productivity of labour. The discrepancy is partly to be explained by the holidays, and partly by the entry of new workers (half-peasants) into the factories at this time.

Now I will say a few words about the *total sum paid in wages*. According to the People's Commissariat for Labour, the amount paid to industrial workers during the year 1923–1924 amounted to 808 millions, and in the year 1924–1925 to more than 1200 millions. For the year 1925–1926, the estimates are 1700 millions.

I need not here discuss the purposes of the *social insurance fund*. You are all familiar with these. I shall merely give general figures, to show how much the proletarian State is spending upon insurance. For the year 1924–1925, the total number of insured persons was 6,700,000, and in the year 1925–1926 will be 7,000,000. The average contributions for social insurance amounted for the year 1924–1925 to 14·6 per cent. of the total amount paid in wages ; for the year 1925–1926, according to the estimates, 13·84 per cent. of wages will go to these contributions. During the year 1924–1925, 422 millions were expended for these purposes ; according to the estimates for 1925–1926, the expenditure under this head will be 588 millions. I may mention, in this connexion, that at the close of the last financial year a surplus of 71 millions of the social insurance fund remained in the treasury.

Of course the increase in agricultural production has had an effect in improving the material condition of the peasantry. According to data in the hands of the State Planning Department, the consumption of the peasant population, the personal consumption, the percentage increase of this consumption, have increased more rapidly than the consumption of the urban population. The peasant has been better nourished, and has spent more both upon his farm and for his personal needs, than in the previous year. I should add that the proletarian State has given considerable assistance to the poor peasants and to the victims of the failures of the crops. The People's Commissariat for Finance reports that for the year 1924–1925 the amount spent in this way was 100,000,000 roubles. Items of this expenditure were : tax-remissions and insurance benefits, 60 millions ; relief after failure of the crops, 24 millions ; credits, 12 millions. The aid given to the victims of the failure of the crops in the year 1924 was carried out in areas with a population of more than 7 millions. A total sum of from 108 to 110 millions of roubles was spent in this way, 71 millions being provided by the State, and 38 millions by various public organisations and by the banks. In addition, a fund of 77 millions was established for combating the drought. There you have the data regarding the aid given by the proletarian State to the poor strata of the peasantry—inadequate aid, of course, but considerable enough to be worth mentioning here.

Socialist construction is impossible unless there is an improvement in the condition of the workers and the peasants. You see that this improvement is now going on.

Next I will say a few words about the increased activity of the masses. One of the most noteworthy and obvious features of our internal situation—a consequence of the improvement in the material condition of the workers and the peasants—is that there has been a remarkable increase in their political activity. They are beginning to examine our deficiencies far more critically, and to talk much more emphatically about the inadequacy of our methods. A period marked by a livening up of all the classes and all the social groups is beginning. This is manifest in the working class, in the peasantry throughout all its groupings, in the new bourgeoisie, in their agents in the rural districts (the kulaks), and in their representatives among the intelligentsia. These circumstances explain the change in our policy which found expression in the resolution passed at the Fourteenth Party Conference. The policy of livening up the soviets, of livening up the cooperatives and the trade unions, the concessions made to the peasantry in the matter of leases and wage labour, the material help given to the village poor, the policy of a lasting alliance with the middle peasants, the liquidation of the vestiges of war communism—these are the main features of the new policy of the Party in the rural districts. You know very well what sort of conditions prevailed in the villages at the close of the past and the beginning of the present year. The general dissatisfaction of the peasantry was on the increase, and here and there peasant risings were actually attempted. I need merely remind you of the rising in Georgia, and of a number of assaults upon the chairmen of district executive committees and upon the secretaries of our village nuclei. Such were the circumstances which led to the inauguration of a new Party policy in the rural areas.

Those have been the essential principles of the Party policy in relation to the peasantry during a period when there has been increased activity among the masses, and when their organisations have been reinvigorated—a policy which aims at the regulation of rural conditions, at increasing the authority of the proletariat and its Party in the rural areas, and at extending the alliance already existing between the proletariat and the poor peasants to include the middle peasants as well.

You know that this policy has been thoroughly justified by results.

5. Three of Lenin's Slogans on the Peasant Problem

Were we right in adopting this policy of an alliance with the middle peasants? What principles underlie the new policy? Did Lenin give us any pointers in the matter?

At the Second Congress of the Comintern a resolution on the peasant problem was adopted. This resolution declared that, during the epoch of the struggle for power, only the poor peasants could be the allies of the proletariat, and that the best that could be done with the middle peasants was to neutralise them. Is that statement correct? Yes, it is perfectly correct. Lenin wrote the resolution, intending it to apply to parties which were on their way to gain power. But ours is a party which has already secured power. There you have the essential difference. In the peasant problem, in the question regarding an alliance between the workers and the peasants, or between the workers and certain strata of the peasantry, Lenin put forward three distinct slogans, respectively corresponding to the three periods of the revolution. We have to grasp the nature of the transition from the first slogan to the second, and from the second to the third.

At an earlier date, when the bourgeois revolution was at hand, when we bolsheviks were for the first time formulating our tactics in relation to the peasantry, Lenin said : "We must enter into an alliance with the whole of the peasantry against the tsar and the great landowners, and we must neutralise the cadet (constitutional democrat) bourgeoisie." That was the slogan with which we entered into the bourgeois revolution, and were victorious. It was the first phase of our revolution.

Subsequently, when we came to the second phase, when the October revolution was at hand, Lenin uttered a new slogan, corresponding to the new situation : "An alliance of the proletariat with the poor peasants against all the bourgeois, while neutralising the middle peasants." That must be the watchword of those communist parties which are fighting for power. Even when they have already attained power, but have not yet consolidated their position, it is too soon for them to think of entering into an alliance with the middle peasants. The middle peasant is a man whose motto is : " Wait and see ". He watches out, till he discovers which party is the stronger ; he watches out, and not until we have gained the upper hand and have driven out the great landowners and the bourgeois, is he ready to enter into an alliance with us. Such is his nature as a middle peasant. That is why, during the second phase of our revolution, we could no longer have as our slogan an alliance of the workers with the peasantry as a whole, but only an alliance of the proletariat with the poor peasants.

Well, what happened at a later stage ? At a later stage, when we had consolidated our power, when we had repelled the onslaughts of the imperialists, and when we had entered upon the period of broadly conceived socialist construction, Lenin formulated a third slogan : "Alliance of the proletariat and the poor peasants with the middle peasants". This must be the watchword of the new period of our revolution, the period of broadly conceived socialist construction. It is sound, not merely because in this phase we can count upon the possibility of such an alliance, but also because, when we come to the upbuilding of socialism, we have to set to work, not merely with the aid of millions, but with that of dozens of millions of the dwellers in the countryside. Otherwise, the upbuilding of socialism will be impossible. Socialism is not something peculiar to the towns.

Socialism is such an organisation of economic life as can only be established by industry and agriculture working hand in hand upon the basis of the socialisation of the means of production. Socialism is impossible without a union between these two branches of economic life.

Such were Lenin's three slogans concerning the alliance with the peasantry. What Lenin said at the Second Congress of the Comintern was perfectly correct, applying as it did to a phase when the communists were only on the way towards power, or had not yet completely consolidated the power they have acquired, and in view of the fact that the middle peasants could only be neutralised by an alliance between the workers and the poor peasants. But after the workers have achieved the conquest of power, and have consolidated their position, after the work of socialist construction has begun and it has become necessary to invoke the assistance of dozens of millions of persons, an alliance of the proletariat and the poor peasants with the middle peasants is the only right method of advance.

This transition from the old slogan of "Alliance between the proletarians and the poor peasants", from the old slogan of the neutralising of the middle peasants, to the slogan of a firm alliance with the middle peasants, was effected at our Eighth Party Congress. Let me quote a passage from Lenin's speech made when he opened the congress. It runs as follows:

> The best representatives of the socialism of former days, those who believed in the coming of the revolution and were prepared to defend it in the theoretical field, used to speak of a *neutralisation* of the peasants—this meaning that we should aim at transforming the middle peasants into a social stratum which, if it did not actively support our proletarian revolution, would at least not disturb us in our work. This abstract theoretical formulation of the task is clear enough. *But it is insufficient.* We have now entered a *stage of socialist construction*, during which, guided by experience in the rural districts, we must in a concrete and detailed way elaborate the main rules and directives requisite *for the development of our relations to the middle peasants upon the basis of a firm alliance.*[1]

There you have the theoretical foundation for the Party policy, which, during the present historical period, is based upon a firm alliance with the middle peasants. If any one

---

[1] Italicised by Stalin.

INTERNAL SITUATION OF U.S.S.R.

wishes to confute these words of Lenin by referring to the resolution passed by the Second Congress of the Comintern (a resolution drafted by Lenin), let him say so in plain terms.

Such is the theoretical aspect of the problem. We must not take a fragment of what Lenin said or wrote; we must take the whole. Lenin formulated three slogans concerning the relationship to the peasantry: one at the time of the bourgeois revolution; another at the time of the October revolution; and a third after the consolidation of the Soviet power. Any one who fancies that these three slogans can be combined into a single generalised slogan is making a great mistake.

Turning from theory to practice, we find that, now that the October revolution has done its work, now that the great landowners have been driven out and the land has been parcelled among the peasants, Russia (as Lenin said) has been transformed more or less completely into a land of middle peasants. We see that, notwithstanding the process of differentiation which has been going on, the middle peasants now form the majority in the rural areas.

Of course a process of differentiation has been going on. Nothing else could be expected at the present time, under the New Economic Policy. But this process is going on very slowly. I recently read some directives which were supposed to have been issued by the Agitprop Department of the Leningrad Organisation of the Party. We are told that in tsarist days 60 per cent. of the peasants were poor peasants; and that now 75 per cent. are poor peasants. We are told that in tsarist days 5 per cent. of the peasants were rich peasants, or kulaks; and that now 8 or even 12 per cent. are kulaks. We are told that in tsarist days there were so-and-so many middle peasants; and that now there are fewer. I don't want to use strong language, but at any rate you must allow me to say that such figures are worse than a counter-revolution. How can any one who calls himself a Marxist perpetrate such absurdities, put them into print—worse still, in directives? As one of the members of the Central Committee, of course I share the responsibility for this incredible piece of stupidity! If in tsarist days, when the governmental policy was one of cultivating the development of kulaks, when there still existed private property in land and the free sale of land was permitted (circumstances which greatly promoted differentiation among the peasants), when the government did its utmost to promote differentiation, if then, nevertheless, there were 60 per cent. of poor peasants, how could it happen that under our proletarian government, when there is no private property in land, when the land can no longer be bought and sold, and when therefore there exists a definite obstacle to differentiation, when for two years there was a policy of trying to extirpate the kulaks root and branch (a policy which has not everywhere been completely abandoned), when the policy pursued by our credit institutions and by the cooperatives has been unfavourable to differentiation—how could it possibly happen that differentiation has gone further to-day, so that, as compared with tsarist times, there should be many more kulaks and many more poor peasants than formerly? How could persons who call themselves Marxists write such inconceivable absurdities? The whole thing is too ridiculous for words. (Laughter.)

The same remark applies to the unhappy grain balance sheet issued by the Central Statistical Board, compiled in June, according to which the rich peasants are supposed to control 61 per cent. of the marketable grain, while the poor peasants are said to have no surplus to sell, and the middle peasants have the remainder. The absurd thing is that a few months later the Central Statistical Board published some new figures, telling us this time that the rich peasants had, not 61 per cent., but 52 per cent. Quite recently, the Central Statistical Board has reduced the figure still further, from 52 per cent. to 42 per cent. Can any one base calculations upon such mutable figures as these? We should like to believe that the Central Statistical Board is a citadel of exact science; we should like to believe that no department can carry on its calculations and formulate its plans except upon the basis of the figures supplied by the Central Statistical Board. We hold the opinion that the business of the Central Statistical Board is to supply thoroughly objective material, uninfluenced by any sort of preconceived opinion, seeing that an attempt to juggle with the figures in accordance with some preconceived opinion is a crime. But how can any of us put faith in the figures of the Central Statistical Board if it does not believe in its own figures?

To put the matter in a nutshell: since, in consequence of

the agrarian revolution, the middle peasants have become the predominant element of the rural population, since (differentiation notwithstanding) the middle peasants constitute the majority in the countryside, and since our socialist constructional work and the Leninist cooperative scheme presuppose the enlistment of the great mass of the peasantry in these activities, our policy of an alliance with the middle peasants is the only sound one under the conditions of the New Economic Policy.

That is the practical aspect of the question.

Let us see how Lenin formulated our tasks at the time when he was introducing the New Economic Policy. I have before me his draft for the pamphlet *Taxation in Kind*. This draft contains an extremely clear formulation of his leading ideas on the subject:

> An increase in production is the fulcrum, the touchstone. . . . Consequently, our agricultural policy must concentrate upon the middle peasant, upon the diligent farmer, as the central figure of our economic revival. (The " Bolshevik," No. 7, 1925, p. 76.)

The foregoing words were penned by Comrade Lenin in the year 1921.

This idea, Comrades, formed the basis of the resolutions passed in April last year at the Fourteenth Conference of our Party. They formed the basis of the concessions then made to the peasantry.

What is the connexion between the resolutions passed at the Fourteenth Party Conference and the resolution concerning work among the poor peasants adopted by the Central Committee in October last year? (You will remember that the voting on this resolution, as in the case of the resolutions at the Party Conference, was unanimous.)

The main business at the plenary session of the Central Committee in October was to prevent the policy adopted at the April Conference, the policy of a firm alliance with the middle peasants, from being reversed by those in our Party who considered that this policy was unsound. Some of the members of our Party were declaring that the policy of a firm alliance with the middle peasants signified that the poor peasants were being forgotten, that the alliance with the middle peasants was being entered into at the expense of the poor peasants.

Absurd as it may seem, such views were put forward. Was the question of the poor peasants something new to us, when we met in October for the plenary session? Of course not. As long as there are poor peasants we must be in alliance with them. We knew this as far back as 1903, when Lenin's pamphlet *To the Poor Peasants* was published. Since we are Marxists, since we are communists, how can we have any other policy than that of relying upon the support of the poor peasants in the rural districts? Must we not still look to them for support? The question is not a new one; it could not be a new one for us either at the April Conference or in October at the plenary session of the Central Committee. If, none the less, the question of the poor peasants came up for consideration, this was because of the experience garnered during the recent elections to the soviets. What had happened? The soviets had shown increased vitality; soviet democracy had been introduced. For what purpose? Soviet democracy does not mean that the leadership of the working class is to be done away with. Soviet democracy cannot be a reality, cannot be a true proletarian democracy, unless the leadership of the proletariat and of its Party remains in force. What, then, is the meaning of soviet democracy subject to the leadership of the proletariat? It means that the proletariat must have its agents in the rural districts. From among what elements must these agents be recruited? From among the poor peasants. But in what condition were the poor peasants at the time when we began to reinvigorate the soviets? They were disintegrated; they were atomised. Not only to many among the poor peasants, but also to many communists, it seemed that the abandonment of the attempt to make an end of the kulaks, and the abandonment of the methods of administrative pressure, signified that the workers were ceasing to fight on behalf of the poor peasants, were ceasing to represent the interests of the poor peasants. Thereupon, the poor peasants, instead of carrying on their own organised struggle against the kulaks, began to whine in the most shameful manner.

What had we to do, in order to combat this mood? First of all, we had to carry out the resolutions passed at the Fourteenth Party Conference; we had to decide upon the best way of giving material assistance to the poor peasants, and then to provide this assistance to the best of our capacity. In the second place, we had to get to work upon the organisation of special groups or fractions of poor peasants, whose business it should be to carry on an open political campaign during the soviet elections, the cooperative elections, etc., so as to win over the middle peasants, and to isolate the kulaks.

In fulfilment of these aims Comrade Molotoff, having had three months' experience in the agrarian commission of the Central Committee, drafted his theses upon work among the poor peasants, and these theses were unanimously adopted at the plenary session of the Central Committee in October.

As you see, the resolution passed at the plenary session of the Central Committee in October was a direct continuation of the resolutions passed at the Fourteenth Conference.

The first thing was to state in concrete terms the amount of material assistance we were prepared to give, in order to improve the material condition of the poor peasants; the second thing was to see to the organisation of the poor peasants. This last is the new feature of our policy; and the idea of the organisation of groups of poor peasants is one for which we have to thank Comrade Molotoff.

What is the object of organising groups among the poor peasants? The aim of this organisation is to overcome the disintegration among the poor peasants; to make it possible for them, with the aid of the communists, to constitute themselves as an independent political force, capable of aiding the proletariat in the struggle against the kulaks and the struggle for the winning over of the middle peasants. The poor peasants are still dominated by the ideology of State pensioners. They put their trust in the G.P.U.,[1] in the authorities, in anything you please except themselves. They cannot make up their minds to put their own shoulders to the wheel. We must overcome this passivity, this pensioners' psychology, we must induce the poor peasants to stand upon their own feet; to organise themselves into groups, with the aid of the Communist Party and with that of the State; and to learn—in the soviets, in the cooperatives, in the peasant committees, and in all spheres of public activity in the rural districts—to carry on the campaign

---

[1] Should be "O.G.P.U." or imply the "Ogpu". The initials are those of the Russian words meaning the Department of State Political Administration.—E. and C. P.

against the kulaks. This campaign must be one of independent political organisation, not one consisting merely in appeals to the G.P.U. Thus only can the poor peasants be organised; thus only can they be transformed from being pensioners into being trustworthy supporters of the proletariat in the rural districts.

That was why the question of the poor peasants came up for discussion in October.

6. Two Dangers and Two Deviations in the Matter of the Peasants

As regards the peasant problem, there have been two deviations in our Party. One of these deviations takes the form of an underestimate of the danger to be apprehended from the kulaks; and the other takes the form of an overestimate of this danger, and of an underestimate of the importance of the middle peasants. I will not go so far as to say that these deviations involve us in mortal danger. A deviation is nothing more than a deviation; it is something which has not yet assumed a consolidated form. A deviation is the beginning of a mistake. Either we allow this development into a mistake to occur, which is very unfortunate; or else we nip the mistake in the bud, and then the danger is averted. A deviation is something which will only have the consequences of a mistake if we do not take effective action against it early enough.

First, a few words about the underestimate of the danger from the kulaks. People talk about a deviation in favour of the kulaks. That is absurd. Within the Party, there cannot possibly be deviations in favour of the kulaks. We are not concerned with a deviation in favour of the kulaks, but with a deviation in the direction of underestimating the danger from the kulaks. Even if there had not hitherto been any one ready to succumb to this danger, if there had not yet been any one to stray in the direction of this deviation, we should have to watch out for it, because development in Soviet Russia at the present time is characterised by a certain reinvigoration of capitalism, and a reinvigoration of capitalism necessarily arouses a certain amount of confusion in Party circles. On the one hand, our socialist industry is developing. There is a conflict between socialist industry and private capitalism. Which will gain the victory? At the present time, the socialist elements have the upper hand. We shall be able to bring pressure to bear both upon the kulaks and upon the private capitalists in the towns. Nevertheless, it is true that at the present time the kulaks are gaining strength, that we have not been able to get the better of them in the economic field. The kulaks are certainly gaining strength. Those who fail to recognise this, those who say that we are making bogeys of the kulaks, are exposing the Party to the danger of ceasing to watch out, are helping to disarm the Party in its fight against the kulaks, in its fight against capitalism—for the kulaks are the agents of capitalism in the rural areas.

There has been a good deal of talk about Bogusheffsky. Of course there is no ground for saying that Bogusheffsky has succumbed to a deviation in favour of the kulaks. His deviation is merely one in the direction of underestimating the danger from the kulaks. If Bogusheffsky had succumbed to a deviation in favour of the kulaks, he would have to be expelled from the Party; but as far as I know, no one has hitherto urged his expulsion. This deviation, this underestimate of the danger from the kulaks, is a deviation which prevents our keeping the Party in a state of readiness for the fight, is one which tends to disarm the Party in its struggle against the capitalist elements. As you know, the deviation in question has been condemned by a resolution of the Central Committee.

There is yet another deviation: an overestimation of the danger arising from the kulaks. Those who are panicstricken at the thought of this danger, are prone to scream: " Help, help, the kulak is coming ! " It is strange ! We introduced the New Economic Policy, knowing perfectly well that this involved a reinvigoration of capitalism, a reinvigoration of the kulaks, knowing perfectly well that the kulaks would raise their heads once more. Yet directly the kulaks so much as poke their noses round the corner, many of the comrades turn pale with fear, and shout: " Help ! Murder ! Police ! " So pitiable is their panic that they quite forget the middle peasants ! Nevertheless, our main task in the villages at the present time is to win over the middle peasants, to detach the middle peasants from the kulaks, to isolate the kulaks by entering into a firm alliance with the middle peasants. The comrades who are in a panic about the danger from the kulaks have forgotten this.

I think that these two deviations may be referred to the following causes :

The first deviation takes the form of underestimating the significance of the kulaks, and of the capitalist elements generally, in rural life. Those who succumb to this deviation contend that the development of the New Economic Policy is not leading to the reinvigoration of the capitalist elements in the villages ; they declare that the kulaks and the other capitalist elements are disappearing, or are already things of the past ; they deny that a process of differentiation is going on in the rural areas ; they insist that the kulak is a mere vestige, a wraith.

What is the upshot of this deviation ?

As it works out in practice, this deviation leads to a repudiation of the class war in the rural districts.

The second deviation consists in an exaggeration of the importance of the kulaks and of the other capitalist elements in the villages ; it takes the form of a panic fear of these elements. Those who succumb to this deviation deny that the alliance of the proletariat and the poor peasants with the middle peasants is possible or desirable.

Those who argue in this way assume that in the rural areas of Soviet Russia an unqualified restoration of capitalism is in progress ; that this process of capitalist restoration determines everything else that is happening ; that it is invading our cooperatives, wholly or mainly ; that, in consequence of this course of development, the differentiation in the rural areas must inevitably continue to increase ; that the two most antagonistic groups, the group composed of the kulaks and the group composed of the poor peasants, will continue to increase numerically year by year ; that the intermediate groups, those comprising the poor peasants, will become numerically smaller, will diminish year by year.

In practice, this deviation leads to fanning the flames of the class war in the villages, to a return to the policy of the committees of poor peasants, to the policy of trying to destroy the kulaks root and branch, that is to say, to a proclamation of the civil war within our country, and thus to the ruining of all our work of socialist construction. It leads, in the end, to the repudiation of Lenin's plans for developing cooperation, the plans which look forward to the incorporation of millions of peasant farms into the system of socialist construction.

You will ask which of the two deviations is the worse? That is not the right way of formulating the question. Both deviations are as bad as they can be, and we cannot say that one is worse than the other. If they continue to develop, they will be likely to break up the Party, to destroy it. Fortunately there are forces within our Party competent to check both these deviations in the germ. (Applause.) Although both the deviations are stupid, and although it is stupid to ask which of them is the worse, there is a different standpoint from which it behoves us to contemplate them. Which deviation is our Party best prepared to fight? That is the practical way of considering the question. Both the deviations are dangerous; both of them are bad; we must not waste time discussing whether one of them is worse than the other. But it is a practical necessity to discuss which of them we are best prepared to fight. If you were to ask whether the Party is better prepared to undertake a ruthless struggle against the kulaks, or (ignoring the kulaks for the time being) to enter into an alliance with the middle peasants, I believe that ninety-nine communists out of a hundred would say that the Party is better prepared to act on the watchword: " Let us go for the kulaks! " If we were to let these comrades have their way, the kulaks would promptly be stripped to the buff. As regards the rival policy, the policy of those who, instead of trying to destroy the kulaks out of hand, want to pursue the far more complicated plan of isolating the kulaks by entering into an alliance with the middle peasants —this is one which the comrades are by no means ready to accept. That is why I believe that the Party in its struggle against these two deviations, must concentrate its fire upon the second deviation. (Applause.) No preaching of Marxism or Leninism, however fervent, can enable us to hide the fact that the kulak is dangerous. A kulak is a kulak. A kulak is dangerous, however much Bogusheffsky says that he is a mere bogey. No quotations from our leading authorities will shake that belief. But the essential principle that we ought to enter into a firm alliance with the middle peasants, notwithstanding the fact that, in the resolution of the Second Congress of the

Communist International, Lenin advocated the neutralisation of the middle peasants, is one which can always be obscured by phrases about Leninism and Marxism. Here, there is ample opportunity for quotations from the masters; here, there is ample scope for every one who wishes to lead the Party astray; here is a chance for every one who wants to hide the truth that Lenin, when considering the relationships between the workers and the peasants, put forward, not one slogan, but three. Here all kinds of juggling with Marxism are possible, and that is why it behoves us to concentrate our fire in the attack upon the second deviation.

Such is the position of affairs in regard to the problem of the internal situation of the Soviet Union, of its economic life, of its industry and its agriculture, of the classes and their activity, of the reinvigoration of the soviets, of the peasantry, etc. I shall leave unconsidered certain other questions, which concern our State apparatus—which is growing in strength and importance, and which is showing an inclination to escape from the leadership of the Party (an escape which will not be permitted). I shall not discuss the bureaucracy of our State apparatus, were it only for the reason that the present report has already run to a considerable length, and because these questions are not new to any one in the Party.

7. Tasks of the Party

I now come to the tasks of our Party as concerns matters of internal policy.

In the domain of the development of the national economy, we have to work along the following lines :

(a) A further increase of production.
(b) The transformation of our country from an agricultural one into an industrial one.
(c) Making sure that the socialist elements of our economic life shall retain a decisive preponderance over the capitalist elements.
(d) Making sure that the Soviet Union shall remain sufficiently independent of the capitalist world.

(e) Increase in the proportion of the State revenue which is derived from other sources than taxation.

In the domain of industry and agriculture, we have to perform the following tasks:

(a) The development of our socialist industry upon the basis of a raising of the level of technique, the increase in the productivity of labour, the lowering of the cost of production, and the quickening of the turnover of capital.
(b) The supply of fuel and of metals and also the basic capital required for railway transport must be adapted to the growing needs of industry and of the country.
(c) The development of local soviet industries must be encouraged.
(d) Steps must be taken to increase the productivity of the soil, to improve the technique of agriculture, to industrialise agriculture, etc.

In the domain of commerce, we must undertake the following tasks:

(a) The extension of the qualitative improvement of the system of distribution (cooperatives of all kinds, State commerce, etc.).
(b) The greatest possible acceleration of the circulation of commodities.
(c) A lowering of retail prices; an increase in the preponderance of State trade and cooperative trade over private trade.
(d) Formation of a united front, and the establishment of a strict discipline, in the case of all the instruments of purchase.
(e) An increased trade with the foreign world, with guarantees to ensure that the balance of trade shall be a favourable one, this being an indispensable condition for the maintenance of a stable exchange, and a guarantee against inflation.

As regards economic planning, we must, above all, see to it that the necessary reserves shall be provided. In this connexion, let me say a word or two about one source of reserves, namely, vodka. A great many people seem to believe that we can upbuild socialism while we are wearing kid gloves. That is a great mistake, Comrades. If we cannot get any loans, if we suffer from a lack of capital, and if (furthermore) we do not wish to become the enslaved debtors of the western European capitalists or to grant concessions on the servile conditions which are proposed to us, then we must find other sources of income. It is better to do this than to become enslaved debtors. We have to make a choice between debt slavery and vodka. Those who think that socialism can be upbuilt by persons who wear white kid gloves are making a great mistake.

In the matter of the mutual relationships between the classes, we have the following tasks to perform:

(a) The promotion of an alliance of the proletariat and the poor peasants with the middle peasants.
(b) The safeguarding of the leadership of the proletariat in this alliance.
(c) The political isolation of the kulaks and of the urban capitalists, and their economic encirclement.

In the domain of soviet construction, there must be an energetic campaign against bureaucracy, with the enlistment of the broad masses of the workers in this struggle.

I should like to say a few words about the new bureaucracy, and about their ideologues, the " smenovehovstsy ".[1]

Their ideology is that of the new bourgeoisie, which is now growing, and which is gradually forming ties with the kulaks and with the intellectuals in the public service. The new bourgeoisie has created its own ideology, according to which the Communist Party will necessarily decay and the new bourgeoisie consolidate its forces. They hold that we bolsheviks, without being aware of the fact, are approaching the threshold of a democratic republic, will unawares cross this threshold.

---

[1] *Smenovehovstvo* is a compound word meaning " the change of the signposts ". The name " smenovehovstsy " was given to the members of a group of Russian writers, bourgeois émigrés for the most part, who, at the time of the introduction of the New Economic Policy, advocated an accommodation to the policy of the Soviet power. The leaders of the group are Klyushchnikoff and Ustryaloff.—E. and C. P.

Then, one fine day, we shall find ourselves in an ordinary bourgeois republic, established with the aid of a Napoleonic adventurer, perhaps a soldier, perhaps a civilian official.

Such are the characteristics of this new ideology, with which the intellectuals in the public service, and some who are in the house of our friends, strive to lead us astray. I shall not trouble to refute the foolish assertion that our Party will decay. It is waste of time to argue against absurdities. Our Party is not degenerating, and will not degenerate. It was constructed out of elements which are not likely to decay, and was constructed by a man who knew how to safeguard it against decay. (Applause.) The ideology of our members, young and old alike, is a steadily advancing one. We have the good fortune of being able to issue edition after edition of Lenin's works. People are reading them and are beginning to understand things. Not only the leaders, but also the rank-and-file members of the Party, are beginning to understand, and can no longer be humbugged. They will no longer be frightened by talk about the decay of the Party. They are able to judge for themselves. You can clamour as loud as you please : you can try to deafen us with quotations ; but the rank-and-file members of the Party, having listened to what you say, will judge for themselves, the works of Lenin in their hands. (Applause.) This is one of the main guarantees that our Party will not leave the road of Leninism. (Loud applause.) If, none the less, I have referred to the " smenovehovstsy ", it has only been to say a word or two in sufficient answer to their speculations upon a decay in our Party. Ustryaloff is the main founder of this ideology. He serves in our transport system, and is said to be an efficient civil servant. He can speculate about the decay of our Party as much as he likes, so long as he does his work properly. Here in Soviet Russia, Comrades, no one is forbidden to indulge in idle speculations. Ustryaloff may enjoy his fantasies as much as he pleases. What he has to remember is that, while speculating about the decay of the Party, he must go on providing water to drive our bolshevik mill. Otherwise he may have a bad time of it ! (Applause.)

III. THE PARTY

Now I come to the Party. Though I have postponed consideration of the Party until the end of my report, this is not because I consider it the least momentous factor of our development. On the contrary, I consider the Party at the end, because its work is the crown of the whole of our labours.

I have referred to the successes won by the dictatorship of the proletariat in the domains of home and foreign policy, in the domain of strategical manœuvres directed against the environing capitalist powers, and in the domain of socialist construction at home. These successes would have been unattainable unless our Party were fully equal to its tasks, unless it were developing in a healthy and vigorous manner. The importance of the Party as the guiding energy in all these things is immeasurable. The dictatorship of the proletariat does not run itself; it can only work thanks to the forces of the Party and under the guidance of the Party. But for the guidance of the Party, the proletarian dictatorship could not possibly continue in existing circumstances, when we are encompassed by hostile capitalist powers. Any weakening of the Party will inevitably and promptly result in a weakening of the proletarian dictatorship. That is why the bourgeois of all lands foam at the mouth when they speak of our Party!

This must not be supposed to imply that our Party is identical with the State. Nothing of the kind. The Party is the leading energy of our State. It is very foolish to maintain, as some comrades maintain, that the Political Bureau is the supreme organ of the State. This is not so. The assertion confuses the issues, and can only play into the enemy's hands. The Political Bureau is the supreme authority of the Party, and not the supreme authority of the State. Nevertheless, the Party is the supreme guiding energy in the State. The Central Committee and the Political Bureau are instruments of the Party. The State authorities must not be identified with the Party, although, in all fundamental questions alike of home and of foreign policy, the Party is the guide. Only because the Party is the guide have we been able to secure successes in our home and foreign policy. That is why the composition of the Party, its intellectual level, the strength of its membership, its capacity for laying down the directives for the upbuilding of the economic life of our State, the influence of the Party among the workers and among the peasants, and, finally, the internal condition of the Party, are questions of essential importance.

Let us first consider the composition of the Party. On April 1, 1924, the total membership of the Party without the Leninist levy was 446,000, including both Party members and candidates. Of these, 196,000, say 44 per cent., were workers; 128,000, say 28 per cent., peasants; 122,000, say 30 per cent., employees, etc. On July 1, 1925, the membership was 911,000, including both full members and candidates. Of these, 534,000, say 59 per cent., were workers; 206,000, say 24 per cent., peasants; 170,000, say 17 per cent., employees, etc. On November 1, 1925, the total membership was 1,025,000.

What percentage of the working class is enrolled in the ranks of our Party? In my report upon Party organisation to the Thirteenth Party Congress, I said that we had in Soviet Russia 4,100,000 workers, including agricultural labourers. I did not include in that estimate the workers in small-scale industry, for at that date their numbers could not be estimated, since social insurance had not yet been extended to them, and there were no statistics available. The figures given in that report related to January 1, 1924. Subsequently, when it became possible to procure statistics concerning the workers in small-scale industry, namely on July 1, 1924, it appeared that there were 5,500,000 workers in industry and agriculture; of these, 390,000 were enrolled in the Party, this being 7 per cent. of the whole working class. On July 6, 1925, the total number of workers was 6,500,000, of whom 534,000 were enrolled in the Party, this being 8 per cent. of the whole working class. On October 1, 1925, the total number of workers in agriculture and industry, including small-scale, medium-scale, and large-scale enterprises, was 7,000,000. Of these 570,000 were enrolled in the Party, being 8 per cent. of the working class.

I give you these figures in order to show you how foolish it is to talk of enrolling 90 per cent. of the whole working class in the Party within the next year or two.

Let us now consider the ratio between the membership of the Party and the number of the workers employed in large-scale industry. The number of those employed in large-scale industry, excluding the seasonal workers, but including both the State industries and the non-State industries (together with the armaments industries and the most important railway workshops), on January 1, 1924, was 1,605,000. At that date, there were 196,000 workers in the Party, this being 12 per cent. of the total number of workers in large-scale industry. If, now, we take the number of Party members working at the bench, and compare this to the total number of workers in large-scale industry, we find that on January 1st there were 83,000 Party members working at the bench, this being 5 per cent. of the total number of workers engaged in large-scale industry. All these figures relate to Jaunary 1, 1924. On June 1, 1924, 1,780,000 workers were employed in large-scale industry. In the Party at that time there were 390,000 workers, this being 22 per cent. of all the workers employed in large-scale industry. The workers at the bench enrolled in the Party at that date numbered 267,000, being 15 per cent. of all the workers in large-scale industry. On January 1, 1925, there were engaged in large-scale industry 1,845,000. The total number of workers enrolled in the Party at that time, whether working at the bench or otherwise, was 429,000, being 23·7 per cent. of all the workers engaged in large-scale industry; at the bench there were then working 302,000 members of the Party, being 16·5 per cent. of all the workers in large-scale industry. On July 1, 1925, there were 2,094,000 workers engaged in large-scale industry. The number of workers enrolled in the Party was 534,000, or 25·5 per cent.; the number of Party members working at the bench was 383,000, being 18·2 per cent. of all the workers in large-scale industry.

We see, then, when we consider the working class as a whole, that the number of workers enrolled in the Party increases more slowly than the number of all workers; but when we turn to large-scale industry, the picture is reversed. In large-scale industry the percentage of workers organised in the Party increases more rapidly than does the number of all the workers engaged in large enterprises. We must bear this in mind when we are considering the general composition of our Party, and when we are discussing the working-class core of the Party. To a predominant extent, the workers who are members in the Party are workers engaged in large-scale industry.

In view of these facts, is it possible to look forward, within a year or so, to transforming the Party membership in such a way that 90 per cent. of the members will be workers at the bench in large-scale enterprises? To expect this would be fantastical. Why? Because, when we have at the present time 380,000 Party members working at the bench, we should have, within a year, to raise the number of the Party members to 5,000,000, if the other Party members (in round figures 700,000) who are not working at the bench were to constitute only 10 per cent. of the Party membership. Comrades who talk of having 90 per cent. of the members of the Party drawn from among the workers in large-scale enterprises are making false calculations, and have got into a great muddle.

Is the influence of our Party increasing throughout the working class? It should hardly be necessary to prove that this is so. You know that our Party consists of carefully chosen members. In this respect, we have done what no party in the world has ever been able to do before. The fact that our membership is so carefully selected is what gives us an immeasurable influence in the working class, so that our Party has a monopolist position in the working class.

As regards the influence of our Party in the rural districts, the position is not so good. At the date of the Thirteenth Party Congress, the numbers of the rural population at ages from 18 to 60 was 53 millions; at the date of the Fourteenth Party Congress, it was rather more than 54 millions. At the time of the Thirteenth Congress, the number of communists in the village nuclei was 136,000, being 0·26 per cent. of the total adult rural population. At the time of the Fourteenth Party Congress, the number of peasant members of the Party was 202,000, this being 0·37 per cent. of the total adult rural population. The growth of our Party in the villages is a terribly slow one. I do not say that in this respect we ought to go ahead in seven-league boots, but the percentage of peasants enrolled in our Party is certainly far too small. Our Party is a workers' party. Workers will always preponderate in its membership. That is another way of saying that in this country the dictatorship of the proletariat is in force. On the other hand, it is clear that the dictatorship of the proletariat is impossible without an alliance between the workers and the peasants, and unless a certain percentage of the best elements from among the peasantry are enrolled in our Party, so as to give the Party a solid foundation in the villages. In this respect, the situation is at present by no means satisfactory.

Now let me consider the general growth of the intellectual level of our Party. As regards organisational problems, Comrade Molotoff will put in a report, so I need say very little about these questions. Still, I want to take this opportunity of pointing out that the intellectual level of the leading strata of the Party, old and young alike, has risen notably. As an example, let me remind you of the discussions which took place last year about Trotskyism. As you know, an attempt was then being made to effect a revision of Leninism, to bring about a change in the Party leadership—to swop horses while crossing a stream. You all know how resolutely the Party met these moves, which were really of a hostile character. What does this mean? It means that the Party is fully grown up, that its members are sure of themselves, that they are not afraid of discussion. Now, I regret to say, we have entered a period of new discussion. Still, I am convinced that the Party will quickly get through with this discussion, and that nothing serious will happen. ("Hear, hear" and applause.) Since I do not wish to introduce contentious matters, I shall say nothing about the way in which the Leningrad comrades behaved at their conference, and about the way in which the Moscow comrades reacted. I think that the delegates will themselves speak of this matter, and I shall draw up the balance in my reply to the discussion.

Comrades, I am approaching the end of my report. I have referred to our foreign policy, and to the antagonisms which are devastating the capitalist world. I have said that these antagonisms can only be liquidated by the proletarian revolution in the West.

I also referred to the antagonisms which determine the relationships between the Soviet Union and the capitalist States. I said that these States will endeavour to transform our country into an appendage of the capitalist system, and in this way to carry on a new kind of intervention. I added, that we shall be able to defend ourselves, counting upon the general support of the working class of the West, especially after the experience gained by the workers of the West in their frequent visits to Soviet Russia, and in their fraternisation with us. This fraternisation will cost the capitalists dear. We shall make headway against the antagonisms to which I am now referring. In the end we shall overcome the conflicts between the capitalist world and the socialist world—though not by our own unaided forces, for in this matter we shall need the assistance of the victorious proletarian revolution in a number of other countries.

I spoke, also, about the antagonisms between the capitalist and the socialist elements within our own country. I said that we can get the better of these antagonisms with our own unaided forces. One who does not believe this is a liquidator, a person who lacks faith in socialist construction. We shall overcome these antagonisms; we are ready to overcome them. Of course, the sooner help comes from the West, the better for us. If we get help from the West, we shall more speedily overcome these conflicts, shall all the sooner get rid of private capitalism root and branch, and bring about the complete victory of socialism, the upbuilding of a fully socialist society. But we shall not despair, even if we do not get any assistance from abroad; we shall not draw back from the task we have undertaken (applause); we are not afraid of difficulties. Those who are weary of the fight, those who dread difficulties, those who have lost their heads, had better give up their places to those who are still brave and steadfast! (Applause.) We are not the kind of people to be afraid of difficulties. We are bolsheviks, we have been steeled in the school of Lenin, we shall not run away, we shall look difficulties in the face and overcome them. ("Hear, hear" and applause.)

I referred, Comrades, to the successes and to the mistakes of our Party. We have made plenty of mistakes; in our foreign trade, in the matter of the provision of grain, and in other domains as well. Lenin has taught us not to be vainglorious. We will not be vainglorious. We have made a fair number of mistakes, but we have also secured successes. One thing, at any rate, we have achieved, a thing which no one can deprive us of. By our splended constructive work, by our vigorous bolshevist push on the economic front, by the successes achieved in this domain, we have shown the whole world that the workers who have conquered power are capable, not only of overthrowing capitalism, not only of destroying, but also of upbuilding a new society, of upbuilding socialism. This achievement, this plain demonstration, is a thing which no one can take away from us. It is the greatest and the weightiest of all our achievements to date. We have shown the working class of the West and the oppressed peoples of the East that the workers, who have hitherto throughout history only worked while the master class ruled, these workers, having conquered power, are competent to govern a great country, and to upbuild socialism even in the most difficult conditions.

What do the proletarians of the West need in order to win their way to victory ? Above all, they need faith in their own powers ; a conviction that the working class can get along without the bourgeoisie ; the conviction that the working class is competent, not only to destroy the old, but likewise to upbuild the new, to upbuild socialism. The main endeavour of the social democrats, the reformists, is to instil scepticism into the workers' minds, to make the workers doubt their own powers, doubt their capacity for winning by force a victory over the bourgeoisie. The significance of all our work, of all our constructive work, is that it serves as a demonstration to the working class in capitalist countries that they too will be able to get along without the bourgeoisie, and will be able unaided to build a new society.

The workers' pilgrimages to our country, the fact that the working-class delegations examine all the details of our constructive work and want to see everything with their own eyes—all this shows that the working class of capitalist countries is beginning (despite the efforts of the social democrats and other reformists) to believe in its own powers, and in the capability of the working class to upbuild a new society upon the ruins of the old.

I do not assert that we have achieved very much in the year to which my report relates. One thing, however, must be recognised : during this year the successes of our socialist constructive work have proved that the working class, after overthrowing the bourgeoisie and seizing power, is capable of reconstructing society upon a socialist foundation. That is an achievement of which no one can deprive us. It is an achievement of inestimable value. It signifies that we have given the workers of capitalist countries faith in their own powers, faith in their own impending victory. It signifies that we have given them a new weapon against the bourgeoisie. Their readiness to use this weapon is shown by the fact that the pilgrimages of the workers to our country are increasing in number. Once the workers of capitalist countries have acquired faith in their own powers, you may be certain that this is the beginning of the end of capitalism, and a sure sign that the victory of the proletarian revolution is at hand.

That is why I believe that our work at the construction of socialism is not vain. That is why I believe that this work will bring us victory all over the world. (Loud applause.)

IV. CONCLUDING WORDS AT THE CONGRESS

COMRADES! A number of questions have been sent in. I shall not try to answer them in detail, since the whole of my concluding words will be a systematic answer to these questions.

Nor do I intend to answer any personal attacks, for I am sure that the congress is in a position to understand the motives by which these attacks are instigated.

Nor shall I concern myself with those who have tried to make a " cave ", with those who have been meeting at Kislovodsk and have been intriguing against the Central Committee. That is their affair; they can combine and intrigue as much as they please. I shall merely point out that Comrade Lashevich, who here in the congress inveighed against intrigues, was himself one of the intriguers, and played a not inconsiderable part in the Cave of Adullam at Kislovodsk.

Now to the point.

1. SOKOLNIKOFF AND THE " DAWESATION " OF OUR COUNTRY

First a few rejoinders. I will begin with Comrade Sokolnikoff. He said in his speech : " When Stalin expounded two alternative outlooks, when he described two alternative lines of economic construction, he was leading us astray. He ought to have formulated these lines differently. He ought not to have spoken of the import of means of production, but of the import of finished commodities." I contend that this statement by Comrade Sokolnikoff shows him to be a supporter of the views put forward by Comrade Shanin. I mean that Comrade Sokolnikoff displays himself as a supporter of the Dawesation of our country. What was I talking about in my report ? Did I say anything there about the plan of imports and exports ? Of course not. Every one knows that at the present time we are compelled to import means of production. But Comrade Sokolnikoff makes a virtue of necessity, makes a principle, a theory, a perspective of development. That is where he is mistaken. I referred in my report to the two fundamental general trends of our economic construction. I wanted to show how, under the existing circumstances of the capitalist encirclement of our country, the independent economic development of our country could be guaranteed. I was speaking in my report about our general line, about our perspective, in this sense, that we must transform our country from an agricultural country into an industrial one. What is an agricultural country? It is one which exports agricultural produce and imports means of production, but does not itself construct these means of production (machines, etc.), or does so to a very small extent only. If we are to remain at this stage of development, in which we do not ourselves manufacture the means of production, but have to import them from abroad, then we cannot have any safeguard against the transformation of our country into an appendage of the capitalist system. That is why we must set to work in order to render ourselves capable of making our own means of production. Cannot Comrade Sokolnikoff grasp this elementary truth? That is all I was talking about in my report.

What does the Dawes plan demand? It demands that Germany shall secure the money requisite for the payment of indemnities from foreign markets, and especially from our Soviet market. Well, what does this signify? It signifies that Germany is to supply us with the means of production, that we are to import these means of production and to export agricultural produce. In this way, our manufacturing industry will tow in the wake of Europe. Such is the essence of the Dawes plan. In view of that fact I said in my report that the Dawes plan, as far as our country is concerned, is built on sand. Why did I say this? Because we have no inclination, for the sake of any other country (not even for the sake of Germany) to remain an agricultural land; because we want to manufacture our own machines and other means of production. The general line of advance must be to transform our country from an agricultural one into an industrial one, into a country capable of manufacturing the necessary means of production for itself. We must so arrange matters that the thoughts and endeavours of those who guide our economic life shall be mainly concerned with the transformation of our country from one which imports the means of production, into one that manufactures its own means of production. That is the main guarantee for the economic independence of our country. That will safeguard us against the risk that our country may become an appendage of capitalist countries. Comrade Sokolnikoff cannot grasp this elementary but illuminating fact. The authors of the Dawes plan would like us to restrict ourselves to the production of cotton, but we shall not be content with that. We want to produce, not cotton alone, but also the machines necessary for the production of cotton. They would like us to confine ourselves, so to say, to the production of motor-cars; but we shall not be content with that, for we want to produce, not only motor-cars, but also the machines used in making motor-cars. They would like us (to take yet another example) to be satisfied with manufacturing boots and shoes; but we, for our part, want to produce, not only boots and shoes, but also the machines which make them. That is the difference between the two general lines. It is one which Comrade Sokolnikoff apparently cannot grasp. To renounce following the line I have indicated is to renounce socialist construction; it means acceptance of the Dawesation of our country.

2. Kameneff and our Concessions to the Peasants

Next I will answer Comrade Kameneff. He says that by adopting the resolutions of the Fourteenth Party Congress (the ones relating to economic policy, to the livening up of the soviets, to the liquidation of the vestiges of war communism, to the legislation concerning agricultural leases and agricultural wage labour) we have made concessions, not merely to the peasantry at large, but to the kulaks, to the capitalist elements. Is that true? I maintain that it is false, that to say so is to calumniate the Party. I maintain that no Marxist would say anything of the kind, that only a liberal can do so.

What is the nature of the concessions we made at the Fourteenth Party Conference? Are these concessions within the confines of the New Economic Policy or not? Certainly they are within the confines of that policy. Did we expand the New Economic Policy in any way at the April conference? Let the opposition answer Yes or No. If we expanded that policy, why did they vote for the resolutions? Is it not agreed that we are all opposed to any extension of the New Economic Policy?

What, then, has happened? What has happened is that Comrade Kameneff is in a state of mental confusion; that the New Economic Policy permits of a free market, of capitalism, and of wage labour; and that the resolutions passed at the Fourteenth Conference are an expression of the New Economic Policy which was introduced under Lenin. Did Lenin know that the New Economic Policy would, to begin with, be turned to account mainly by the capitalists—by traders and by kulaks? Of course he knew. But did Lenin, when we introduced the New Economic Policy, maintain that thereby we were making concessions to speculators and to the capitalist elements, and not to the peasantry? No, he neither did say nor could have said anything of the kind. On the contrary, he always maintained that by permitting a free market, by tolerating capitalism, by introducing the New Economic Policy, we were making concessions to the peasantry in the interest of the maintenance and consolidation of our alliance with the peasantry—for the peasantry, under existing conditions, could not continue to exist without a free market, without a certain reinvigoration of capitalism. Inasmuch as, under existing circumstances, we could only maintain and consolidate our alliance with the peasantry by allowing freedom of trade, it was in this way that we had to lay the foundations of a socialist economy. That is the way in which Lenin treated the problem of concessions. In the same way must we treat the problem of the concessions made in April 1925. Allow me to read you Lenin's opinion about this problem. In his report upon taxation in kind, a report made to the secretaries of the Moscow nuclei, he explains the transition of the Party to the New Economic Policy in the following terms:

> I should like to spend a little time considering how this policy can be made to harmonise with the communist standpoint, and how it is that the Soviet Union, a communist power, is prepared to favour the development of a free market. Can we justify this from the communist standpoint? That we may be able to answer the question, we must make a careful examination of the changes which have taken place in the present economy. To begin with, the situation was characterised by a mass attack on the part of the peasantry against the rule of the landowners. The poor peasants and the kulaks marched shoulder to shoulder against the landowners, although, of course, the two sections had different motives; for the kulaks wanted to take the land away from the

landowners and thus to enlarge their own farms. Then the conflict of interests and aspirations as between the kulaks and the poor peasants came to light. In Ukraine, this conflict of interests is, even to-day, far more obvious than among us. The poor peasants were only to a very small extent able to take direct advantage of the wresting of the ownership of the soil from the great landowners, seeing that they (the poor peasants) did not possess the tools and other necessaries for this. Now we see that the poor peasants are organising, in order to prevent the kulaks from taking possession of the land which has been wrested from the landowners. Among us and in Ukraine the Soviet authority is supporting the committees of the poor peasants. What has been the result? *The result has been that the middle peasants have become the dominant elements in the rural districts.*[1] . . . The extremes of wealth and poverty among the peasants have been reduced, and the majority of the rural population has begun to approximate to the type of middle peasant. If we wish to increase the productivity of our peasant agriculture, we must make it our main business to take the middle peasants into account. *The Communist Party must guide its policy accordingly. . . . The change of policy towards the peasants is, therefore, to be explained by the fact that the situation of the peasantry has altered. The rural areas have become more " middle peasant " in character ; and if we wish to increase agricultural production, we must take this into account.*[1] (*Works*, Russian edition, vol. xviii., part I., pp. 195-196.—The report from which the above is quoted was made to the meeting of secretaries and nucleus leaders of the Communist Party of Russia in Moscow city and province, on April 9, 1921.)

In the same volume, on page 146, Lenin draws the following general conclusion :

> *We must accommodate the upbuilding of our State economy to the economy of the middle peasants*,[1] for we cannot refashion them in three years, nor yet in ten.

In other words, we have introduced a free market, we have allowed a certain revival of capitalism, we have introduced the New Economic Policy, in order to develop the productive forces of the country, in order to increase the amount of agricultural produce, in order to consolidate our ties with the peasants. That is the way in which Lenin looked at the question. He considered that our concessions which took the form of the New Economic Policy were made in the interests of our ties with the peasants.

[1] Italicised by Stalin.

Did Lenin know at that time that the New Economic Policy, the concessions to the peasants, would be turned to account by speculators, capitalists, and kulaks? Of course he knew. Does this mean that our concessions were, in essence, concessions to speculators and to kulaks? No, for the New Economic Policy in general and the freeing of the market in particular, were not turned to account by the capitalists and the kulaks alone, but also by the State and the cooperatives: for the State and the cooperatives are "traders" as well as the capitalists and the kulaks; and the State and the cooperatives, when they have learned how to trade, will get the upper hand over private trade (they are doing so already!) and they will thus cement the union between manufacturing industry and agriculture.

What does this mean? It means that the essential purpose of our concessions was to consolidate the ties between the workers and the peasants, and that has been their essential upshot.

Those who cannot understand this are not Leninists, but liberals.

3. Who have miscalculated?

My third rejoinder is made to Comrade Sokolnikoff. He said:

> The losses, the considerable losses, which we have sustained on the economic front since last autumn were due to the overestimation of our forces, to the overestimation of the degree of socialist maturity, to the overestimation of our capacity, of the capacity of the State, to carry on the whole national economy to-day.

This implies that the mistakes in the calculation of the supply of grain and the mistakes in our foreign trade (I am thinking of the unfavourable balance of trade for the economic year 1924–1925) were not due to blunders on the part of our regulative organs, but were the outcome of an overestimation of the socialist maturity of our economic life. It would seem, moreover, that Comrade Buharin must be mainly responsible for the trouble, seeing that Buharin's "school" has always been especially inclined to exaggerate the socialist maturity of our economic life.

Of course we can all let our fancy run in this way, and Comrade Sokolnikoff is fond of doing it. Still, there ought to be a limit. How can any one venture to talk such nonsense, and even to bring absolutely false charges at the Party Congress? Is not Comrade Sokolnikoff aware that at the beginning of November, in a special session of the Political Bureau, the problems of the grain supply and of foreign commerce were discussed, and that the mistakes of the regulating organs were rectified by the Central Committee—which, we are to suppose, likewise overestimated our socialist possibilities? How can any one talk such nonsense? Besides, what has all that to do with the "school" of Comrade Buharin, and with the person of Comrade Buharin? This is a fine way of shifting the blame from oneself on to some one else. Does not Comrade Sokolnikoff know that the shorthand report of the speeches at the sitting of the Central Committee, the speeches concerning the miscalculations, were sent to all the governmental committees? How can any one go against plain and well-known facts? There ought to be a limit to this sort of thing.

4. How Sokolnikoff Defends the Poor Peasants

My fourth rejoinder will likewise be made to Comrade Sokolnikoff. He said yesterday that, as people's commissary for finance, he made it is business, as far as he could, to ensure that our agricultural tax should have the characteristics of an income tax—but he was hindered in doing this, for he was not permitted to defend the poor peasants and to curb the kulaks. That is false, Comrades. When Comrade Sokolnikoff says this, he calumniates the Party. The question of the formal transformation of the agricultural tax into an income tax (I say, "the formal transformation", for in reality it is an income tax), this question was discussed at the plenum of the Central Committee in October, but no one except Comrade Sokolnikoff advocated that the question should be brought before the congress, seeing that it was not yet ripe for discussion at the Party congress. At that time, Comrade Sokolnikoff did not press his proposal. Now, however, it would seem that Comrade Sokolnikoff would like to turn this matter to account against the Central Committee —not, of course, in the interest of the poor peasants, but in the interests of the opposition. Since, therefore, Comrade Sokolnikoff thinks fit to speak here about the poor peasants, you will allow me to tell you something which shows what is the real standpoint of this advocate of the poor peasants. Not long ago, the people's commissary for finance, Comrade Milyutin, resolved to remit taxation in the case of the poor peasants whose tax amounted to less than 1 rouble. From the memorial sent in by Comrade Milyutin to the Central Committee, it was plain that the whole sum involved, the total return of this tax in the case of the poor peasants whose tax was less than 1 rouble, would amount to between 300,000 and 400,000 roubles, and that the cost of levying the tax was very little less than this figure. Well, what does Comrade Sokolnikoff, the advocate of the poor peasants, do ? He vetoes Comrade Milyutin's decision. The Central Committee receives, on this account, protests from fifteen provincial committees. But Comrade Sokolnikoff stands firm. Pressure was needed on the part of the Central Committee to make Comrade Sokolnikoff withdraw his veto upon the perfectly sound proposal of the people's commissary for finance. That is what Comrade Sokolnikoff calls the " defence " of the interests of the poor peasants. Yet, with such a burden upon his conscience, he has the impudence (to put it mildly) to level reproaches at the Central Committee. Strange behaviour, Comrades, very strange !

5. CONFLICT OF IDEAS, OR CALUMNY ?

Now one more rejoinder, the last one, which is a rejoinder to the compiler of the *Collection of Materials relating to disputed Questions.* Yesterday this recently printed *Collection* was distributed privately, to delegates only. In the *Collection*, we are told, among other things, that in April of the present year, when I received a delegation of village correspondents, I expressed myself in favour of the re-establishment of private property in land. It would seem that in " Bednota " the *Impressions* of a village correspondent to this effect were published, though I was unaware of the fact, and have never seen these *Impressions*. The first I heard about the matter was in October last. As long ago as April, the Riga telegraph agency (distinguished even among telegraph agencies by the zeal with which it disseminates falsehoods about Soviet Russia) communicated a similar item of information to the foreign press. Our comrades in Paris, who read the piece of news, telegraphed it to the people's commissary for foreign affairs, and asked for a contradiction. Thereupon I sent a message to Comrade Chicherin, requesting him to contradict it—if he thought it necessary to contradict every such stupidity, or every such piece of gossip (see the Archives of the Central Committee).

Were the compilers of the wonderful *Collection* aware of these facts? Of course they were. Why, then, do they continue to disseminate such nonsense about me? How can they, how can the opposition, sink so low as to adopt the methods of the Riga telegraph agency? (" Shame ! ")

Further, since I know the ways of these " cave-men ", since I know that they are capable of copying the methods of the Riga telegraph agency, I have sent a contradiction to the editor of " Bednota ". It is absurd that it should be necessary to contradict such balderdash, but, since I knew with whom I had to deal, I sent a contradiction. Here is what I wrote :

LETTER TO THE EDITOR OF " BEDNOTA "

Comrade Editor! I was recently informed that on April 5, 1925, " Bednota " published the *Impressions* of a village correspondent regarding my speech to a delegation of village correspondents. I did not read this at the time, but I find that I am described as sympathising with the idea of perpetuating the ownership of land for forty years and more, with the idea of private property in land and so on. Although this statement is so absurd that it ought not to need contradiction, I had perhaps better ask you to declare in your columns that the statement is utterly false, and has been invented out of whole cloth.

J. STALIN.

Do the comrades who made the *Collection* know about this letter? Certainly they do. Why, then, do they continue to disseminate gossip and falsehood? Is that the proper way of conducting a dispute? We are told that this is a conflict of ideas. Well, Comrades, I should not call it a conflict of ideas. In plain Russian, I should call it calumny.

Now let me pass on to questions of basic principle.

6. Nep

First, then, the question of Nep. I am thinking especially of Comrade Krupskaya, and her speech upon Nep. She said: " In essence, Nep is capitalism; capitalism tolerated on certain conditions; capitalism which the proletarian State holds in leash ". Is that a correct statement? Yes and no. It is perfectly true that we hold capitalism in leash, and that we shall continue to hold it in leash as long as it exists. But it is absurd to say that Nep is capitalism. It is absolutely absurd. Nep is a special policy inaugurated by the proletarian State; a policy which is based upon the toleration of capitalism, while keeping all the commanding positions in the hands of the proletarian State; a policy which is based upon the struggle between the capitalist and the socialist elements, upon the increasing predominance of the socialist elements over the capitalist elements; a policy which is based upon the victory of the socialist elements over the capitalist elements; a policy which is based upon putting an end to the existence of classes, upon the creation of the fundamentals of a socialist economy. One who fails to understand this transitional character of Nep, is deviating from Leninism. If Nep were capitalism, then the Russia of the New Economic Policy, the Russia of which Lenin spoke, would be a capitalist Russia. Is contemporary Russia really a capitalist country, rather than a country in a phase of transition from capitalism to socialism? Why, then, did not Lenin say simply: "*Capitalist* Russia will become socialist"? Why did Lenin use a different formula, saying: " The Russia *of the New Economic Policy* will become a socialist Russia "? Does the opposition accept Comrade Krupskaya's formula to the effect that Nep is capitalism, or does it not? I do not think that there can be any delegates here who will accept this formula. Comrade Krupskaya must excuse me for saying that she was talking nonsense about Nep. It is needless to take up the cudgels in defence of Lenin, whether against what Buharin said or against any similar absurdity.

7. State Capitalism

A mistake of Comrade Buharin is bound up with this question. What is his mistake? What were the questions concerning which Lenin disputed with Buharin? Lenin contended that State capitalism was compatible with the system of the dictatorship of the proletariat. Buharin disputed this assertion. He, and with him the left-wing communists (Comrade Safaroff among them) were of opinion that State capitalism is incompatible with the system of the proletarian dictatorship. Of course, Lenin was right, and Buharin was wrong. Buharin has admitted his error, so that matter belongs to the past. If now, in May 1925, he repeats that there were differences between him and Lenin in this matter of State capitalism, I think there must be a misunderstanding. Either he must repudiate his earlier statement, or else there is a misunderstanding, for the line he is now taking in regard to the character of State industry represents Lenin's own standpoint. It was not that Lenin came to accept Buharin's view, but, on the contrary, that Buharin came to accept Lenin's view. For that very reason, we are prepared to back up Buharin. (Applause.)

Comrade Kameneff's and Comrade Zinovieff's mistake consists in that they treat the question of State capitalism scholastically, undialectically, severed from its connexions with the historical situation. Such a treatment of the problem conflicts with the whole spirit of Leninism. How did Lenin contemplate the question? In the year 1921, when our manufacturing industry was very little developed and the peasants were in want of commodities, when our industry could not all at once be advanced to a higher stage, when there was a terrible scarcity of fuel—in this state of affairs, Lenin was of opinion that, among the various possibilities that offered, the best one was to attract foreign capital into the country, so that with its aid our industry might be set in order. He wanted to introduce State capitalism, and by this means to link up the Soviet authority with the rural areas, by this means to establish the smychka.[1] At that time, the plan was a perfectly sound one, for there was then no other way of satisfying the peasants, seeing that our industry was paralysed, our transport system was hardly working at all, and there was a widespread lack of fuel. Is it true that at that time Lenin favoured making State capitalism the dominant economic form in Russia? Yes, it is true. But that was in the year 1921. What about the present time? Can we say to-day that we have

[1] See note to p. 26.

no manufacturing industry, that our transport system will not work, that we have no fuel, and so on? No, that cannot be said. Can any one deny that our industry and our trade are competent, by their own forces, to establish direct ties between industry (our own industry) and the peasant economy? No, that cannot be denied. Can any one deny that, in industry, " State capitalism " and " socialism " have already exchanged roles, seeing that socialist industry has become predominant, seeing that the importance of the concessions and of the leased undertakings has remained minimal (the former employing a total of 50,000 workers, and the latter a total of 35,000)? No, this cannot be denied. As early as 1922, Lenin said that we had not got very far with concessions and with the leasing of enterprises.

What follows? It follows that, since 1921, circumstances have changed very much; that our socialist industry and our Soviet and cooperative trade have already gained the upper hand; that our own industry and our own trade have been able, of themselves, to cement the ties between town and village; that the most glaring forms of State capitalism (concessions and the leasing of enterprises) have not made serious headway. Now, in the year 1925, any one who speaks of State capitalism as the dominant form of economic life in Soviet Russia, is completely misrepresenting the socialist character of our State industry, is utterly misunderstanding the difference between the past and the present situation, is—as far as this problem of State capitalism is concerned—not thinking dialectically, but scholastically and metaphysically.

Hear what Comrade Sokolnikoff has to say. In his speech he declares:

> Our foreign commerce is carried on as a State capitalist undertaking. . . . Our trading societies within the borders are likewise State capitalist undertakings. I must insist, Comrades, that the State bank, likewise, is a State capitalist undertaking. What about our monetary system? Our monetary system is based upon this, that in the Soviet economy, where socialism is being upbuilt, we have a monetary system which is permeated with the principles of the capitalist economy.

That is the way Comrade Sokolnikoff talks.

Soon, I expect we shall hear him say that the People's Commissariat for Finance is a form of State capitalism. Hitherto I have thought, as we have all thought, that the State bank is a part of the State apparatus. Hitherto I have believed, as we all have, that our foreign commerce (apart from the State capitalist accessory undertakings) was likewise a part of our State apparatus, and that our State apparatus conformed to the type of a proletarian State. We all used to think this, seeing that the proletarian power is the sole possessor of these institutions. But now Sokolnikoff comes to tell us that these institutions which form parts of our State apparatus, are State capitalist. Perhaps, then, our Soviet apparatus is likewise a form of State capitalism, and does not, as Lenin declared, conform to the type of the proletarian State ? Why not ? Does not this State apparatus of ours make use of " a monetary system permeated with the principles of the capitalist economy " ? What nonsense people can talk !

Let me put before you Lenin's views concerning the character and the significance of the State bank. I want to quote a passage from a pamphlet written by Lenin in the year 1917, the pamphlet *Will the Bolsheviks retain Power?* At this time, he still had in view the control and not the nationalisation of industry. Nevertheless, he declared that the State bank in the hands of the proletarian State would be nine-tenths a socialist apparatus.

This is what Lenin wrote about the State bank :

> Great banks are the State apparatus which we need for the realisation of socialism, and which we take over ready-made from capitalism. When we do so, our main task is to cut away all the capitalist disfigurements of this excellent apparatus, and to remodel it on a larger scale, making it more democratic and more comprehensive. Quantity will give place to quality. A unified State bank of the most comprehensive kind, with branches in every district, in every factory—here we have an apparatus which is nine-tenths socialist. This means that there must be a bookkeeping system whose scope is State-wide, with a State-wide supervision and control of the production and distribution of products. This will constitute, as it were, the skeleton of a socialist society. (*Works*, Russian edition, vol. xiv., part II., p. 231.)

Compare what Lenin said with Comrade Sokolnikoff's speech, and you will understand whither Comrade Sokolnikoff is slipping down. I should not wonder if he were to call the People' Commissariat for Finance a form of State capitalism !

What is the meaning of all this? Why does Comrade Sokolnikoff make such mistakes?

They arise in this way, that Comrade Sokolnikoff fails to recognise the twofold character of Nep, the twofold character of commerce under the existing conditions of the struggle between the socialist and capitalist elements; from the fact that he fails to understand the dialectic of the development that is going on under the dictatorship of the proletariat, under the conditions that prevail in the transitional period, during which the socialist elements are employing the methods and the weapons of the bourgeoisie in order to overcome and to liquidate the capitalist elements. This does not mean that our commerce and our monetary system are methods of "capitalist economy". It means that the socialist elements of our economy, in their fight against the capitalist elements, utilise these methods and weapons of the bourgeoisie in order to overcome the capitalist elements— use them to good effect against the capitalist elements, use them to good effect for the upbuilding of the socialist foundations of our economy. It also means that the functions and the significance of these weapons of the bourgeoisie are changed, owing to the dialectic of our evolution, fundamentally and radically—in favour of socialism and to the detriment of capitalism. Comrade Sokolnikoff's mistake is that he fails to understand the complicated and contradictory character of the processes that are now going on in our economy.

In regard to this problem of the historical character of State capitalism, let me quote Lenin once more, to show when and why he recommended State capitalism as the dominant form, to show under what concrete conditions he made this proposal:

> We must always bear in mind what we often have occasion to observe, namely, the socialist behaviour of the workers in enterprises belonging to the State, enterprises in which the workers themselves furnish fuel, raw materials, and various products, or when the workers are concerned to distribute the products of industry satisfactorily among the peasants, conveying them by their own means of transport. *That is socialism.*[1] But side by side with this, there exist small-scale enterprises, which are *quite independent*[1] of the State enterprises. How can they exist independently? Because large-scale industry is not yet thoroughly re-established, because the socialist enterprises can secure, perhaps,

[1] Italicised by Stalin.

only a tenth of what they should secure ; and in so far as they do not secure it, the small-scale enterprises remain independent of the socialist factories. The devastation of the country, the lack of fuel, raw materials, and means of transport, render small-scale production independent of socialism. Under such conditions, what is State capitalism ? It is a unification of small-scale production. Capital groups together small-scale production, and grows out of small-scale production. We must not shut our eyes to the facts. *Of course freedom of the market signifies the development of capitalism.*[1] That is undeniable. Where small-scale production and a free market exist, there capitalism appears. But *have we any occasion to fear this capitalism, provided we keep the factories, the enterprises, the means of transport, and foreign commerce, in our own hands?*[1] That is why I say once more what I have said so often, that we have no occasion to fear such a capitalism. Concessions are a capitalism of this kind. (*Works*, Russian edition, vol. xviii., part I., p. 197.)

That is the way Lenin looked at the problem of State capitalism.

In the year 1921, when we had almost no manufacturing industry, when there was a lack of raw materials, and when transport was at a standstill, Lenin recommended State capitalism as a means whereby the peasant economy could be linked up with industry. The policy was sound. But is this tantamount to saying that Lenin thought it desirable in all circumstances? Of course not ! He was ready to establish the smychka, the alliance between the workers and the peasants, by means of State capitalism, because at that time we had no developed socialist industry. What about to-day ? Can any one say to-day that we have no developed industry ? Of course not. Evolution took another course ; the concessions did not strike deep roots ; our State industry, our State commerce, and our cooperatives, underwent a powerful development ; and the tie between town and country began to become established by means of socialist industry. Our situation has improved far more rapidly than we had expected. How, in view of these facts, can any one say that State capitalism is the main form of our economy ?

The mistake of the opposition is that it fails to understand these elementary things.

[1] Italicised by Stalin.

8. ZINOVIEFF AND THE PEASANTRY

I come back to the peasant question. In my report I said, and other speakers have confirmed my statement, that Comrade Zinovieff has succumbed to a deviation in the direction of underestimating the middle peasants, that quite recently he expressed himself once more as in favour of neutralising the middle peasants, and that only now, after the dispute within the Party, is he trying to move to a different standpoint, and is prepared to advocate a firm alliance with the middle peasants. Is that a correct statement of the facts? Let me refer to certain documents.

In his article, *Concerning Bolshevisation*, Comrade Zinovieff wrote during the present year:

> There are certain tasks which are *equally incumbent upon all the parties of the Comintern*.[1] One of these is the adoption of a correct attitude towards the peasants. Among the agricultural population all over the world, there are three strata which can and must be conquered by us and can and must be transformed into allies of the proletariat (agricultural proletariat, semi-proletariat—small holders and small peasants who do not employ wage labour). There is another stratum of the peasantry (the middle peasants), which must at least *be neutralised by us*.[1]

That is the way in which Comrade Zinovieff writes about the middle peasants four years after the Eighth Party Congress, at which Lenin rejected the slogan of neutralising the middle peasants and replaced it by the slogan of a firm alliance with the middle peasants. Comrade Bakaeff asks: "What is there so very dreadful in this?" I will ask you to compare Comrade Zinovieff's article with Lenin's thesis anent the policy of entering into an alliance with the middle peasants, and then to tell me whether Comrade Zinovieff has deviated from the Leninist thesis or not. (A voice: "He is referring to other countries than Russia". A clamour.) That explanation won't work, Comrades, for in Comrade Zinovieff's article he says that he is talking about "tasks which are equally incumbent upon all the parties of the Comintern". Does any one wish to deny

[1] Italicised by Stalin.

that our Party is one of the parties of the Comintern ? He says in plain terms : " all the parties ". (A voice, coming from the Leningrad delegation : " At certain moments ". Laughter.)

Compare this quotation with Comrade Zinovieff's article ; compare his remarks concerning the neutralisation of the middle peasants with the quotation from Lenin's speech at the Eighth Party Congress, wherein he says that we need to enter into a firm alliance with the middle peasants ; and you cannot fail to see that the two statements have nothing in common.

It is characteristic that Comrade Larin, the advocate of " a second revolution " in the rural areas, when he read Comrade Zinovieff's article, did not hesitate to join forces with him. Although of late Comrade Larin has made fairly successful onslaughts on Comrades Kameneff and Zinovieff, I fancy, none the less, that he is not quite of my way of thinking. This is what Comrade Larin writes about Comrade Zinovieff's before-mentioned article :

> The chairman, Comrade Zinovieff, is quite right in his formulation of the " correct attitude towards the peasants " from the outlook of the tasks incumbent upon *all*[1] parties of the Comintern.

Apparently Comrade Larin protests against my contention. He says that in his book he declared that he did not agree with Comrade Zinovieff, in so far as Zinovieff extended the slogan about the neutralisation of the middle peasants to Russia. It is true that in his book Comrade Larin said that for his scheme neutralisation was insufficient, that we must go " a step further " in the direction of " an understanding with the middle peasants against the kulaks ". But then Comrade Larin unfortunately lapses into his scheme of " a second revolution " against the power of the kulaks, a move which separates him from me and brings him close to Comrade Zinovieff, so that I am compelled to differentiate myself from him.

As you see, in the document I read to you, Comrade Zinovieff advocates in plain terms the slogan of the neutralisation of the middle peasants, in contradistinction to Lenin, who said that the neutralisation of the middle peasants was inadequate, that a firm alliance with the middle peasants was necessary.

[1] Italicised by Stalin.

Now I come to another document. In his book *Leninism*, Comrade Zinovieff quotes from Lenin the following passage, which relates to the year 1918 :

> With the whole of the peasantry, down to the end of the bourgeois democratic revolution ; with the poorest section of the peasantry, the proletarian and semi-proletarian section, forward to the socialist revolution.

From this Comrade Zinovieff draws the following conclusion :

> The fundamental problem which we are trying to solve to-day is fully and finally elucidated in the foregoing quotation from Lenin. *Not a word can be added, nor can a word be taken away.*[1] Everything is expressed in the concise and clear way characteristic of Lenin. (*Leninism*, p. 60.)

Zinovieff declares that this is an exhaustive characterisation of Leninist theory and practice as far as the peasant problem is concerned. With the peasantry against the bourgeoisie—that is the October revolution. So far, so good. Two of Lenin's slogans are given. But where is the third of Lenin's slogans : " With the middle peasants against the kulaks, on behalf of socialist construction " ? What has become of this third of Lenin's slogans ? We do not find it in Comrade Zinovieff's writings. It has vanished. True, Comrade Zinovieff tells us that nothing can be added. But we are in danger of distorting Lenin's views, and Comrade Zinovieff does in fact distort them, if we do not add Lenin's third slogan concerning a firm alliance between the proletariat and the poor peasants, on the one hand, and the middle peasants, on the other. Is it by chance that Lenin's third slogan, one which is now topical, has vanished, has been mislaid by Comrade Zinovieff ? No, this has not happened by chance, for Zinovieff's standpoint is that of neutralising the middle peasants. The only difference between the first document I quoted and the second is that in the former he expresses himself as opposed to the slogan of a firm alliance with the middle peasants, whereas in the latter he says nothing about this slogan.

Here is a third document, an article by Comrade Zinovieff

---

[1] Italicised by Stalin.

entitled *The Philosophy of the Epoch*. I am referring to the article as originally drafted, without the alterations and additions subsequently effected by the members of the Central Committee. It is characteristic of this article that, just like the second document I quoted, it has absolutely nothing to say about the problem of the middle peasants. It evades this topical question, and is content to speak of some vague " equality " like that which the narodniks were fond of talking about, an equality in which class distinctions are ignored ! In this article we can find everything : poor peasants, kulaks, capitalists, onslaughts on Buharin, such equality as the essers talk of, Ustryaloff. The only things missing are the middle peasants and Lenin's plans for cooperation. Yet the article is entitled *The Philosophy of the Epoch* ! When Comrade Molotoff sent me this article (I was travelling at the time), I answered it somewhat acrimoniously. Yes, Comrades, I am a plain-spoken and rather rough sort of fellow. I don't deny it. (Laughter.) I criticised it rather savagely, for really it is a little more than I can put up with when Comrade Zinovieff, for a whole year, systematically suppresses or misrepresents the most important features of Leninism as far as the peasant problem is concerned, and is dumb about the present slogan of our Party concerning the alliance with the great mass of the peasantry. This is what I wrote to Comrade Molotoff about the matter :

> Comrade Zinovieff's article, *The Philosophy of the Epoch*, is a distortion of the Party tactic, a distortion after the manner of Larin. The article discusses the Fourteenth Congress, but the main topics at this conference, the middle peasants and the cooperatives, are evaded. Zinovieff has nothing to say about the middle peasants or about Lenin's plans for cooperation. The evasion is no chance matter. After all this, to speak of a " dispute concerning the interpretation " of the resolutions of the Fourteenth Conference, is tantamount to an infringement of these resolutions. To confound Buharin with Stolypin, as Comrade Zinovieff does, is to calumniate Buharin. With equal justice he might compare Lenin to Stolypin, for Lenin said : " Trade, and learn how to trade ! " To raise the slogan of equality at this moment is esserite demagogy. There can be no equality as long as classes exist and as long as there are skilled and unskilled labour. (Cf. Lenin, *The State and Revolution*.) We must not talk about an undefined equality, but about the abolition of classes, about socialism. To speak of our revolution as a " non-class " revolution, is to draw near to menshevism.

> In my opinion, the article must be radically reconstructed, so that it may not bear the character of a platform for the Fourteenth Party Congress.
>
> J. STALIN.
>
> *September* 12, 1925.

I am prepared, to-day, to defend every word of this letter.

In an article intended to supply directives, no one is entitled to speak about "equality" without defining very strictly what he means by that term. Is the writer referring to equality between the peasants and the working class, or to equality within the peasantry, or to equality between skilled and unskilled workers within the working class, or to equality in the sense of an abolition of classes? In an article intended to convey directives, the writer is not entitled to ignore the actual slogans of the Party in the matter of work in the rural areas. He is not entitled to play with phrases about "equality", for this is playing with fire. Nor is the writer entitled to play with the phrases of Leninism while saying not a word about the chief Leninist slogan concerning the peasant problem.

There are my three exhibits: Comrade Zinovieff's article (January 1925) advocating the neutralisation of the middle peasants; Comrade Zinovieff's book entitled *Leninism* (September 1925), which is silent about Lenin's third slogan, the one concerning the middle peasants; and Comrade Zinovieff's latest article, *The Philosophy of the Epoch* (September 1925), which is silent about the middle peasants and Lenin's plans for cooperation.

Is Comrade Zinovieff's reiterated wobbling upon the peasant question a chance matter? You see that it is not.

Quite recently, Comrade Zinovieff has at length made up his mind to advocate the slogan of a firm alliance with the middle peasants, and he does so in his Leningrad report. This happened after the struggle, after the debates, after the conflict in the Central Committee. All very well, but I do not feel sure that he will not wobble once more. As the facts show, in the peasant question Comrade Zinovieff has never been able to follow a consistent line. (Applause.)

Let me give you a few facts concerning Comrade Zinovieff's vacillations in the peasant problem. In the year 1924, at the plenary session of the Central Committee, Comrade Zinovieff advocated a " peasant policy " which consisted in the organisation of non-Party peasant fractions at the centre and in the localities, coupled with the issue of a weekly paper. Owing to objections raised in the Central Committee, the proposal was rejected. A little while before, Comrade Zinovieff had actually boasted of exhibiting a " peasant deviation ". For instance, at the Twelfth Party Congress he said :

> When people say to me : " You have a deviation, you are deviating towards the peasantry ", I answer : " Yes, we must not only ' deviate ' towards the peasants and their economic needs, but we must incline very far to meet the economic needs of the peasants who follow our proletariat, and if needs must we must incline ourselves even to the earth ".

Do you hear : " we must deviate ", " we must incline very far ", " we must incline ourselves even to the earth ". (Laughter and applause.) Later, when our position in the rural areas began to improve, Comrade Zinovieff took a new line. The middle peasant had become suspect to him, and he uttered the slogan of neutralisation. Later still, he took a fresh turn, demanded (substantially) a revision of the resolutions of the Fourteenth Conference, accused almost the whole of the Central Committee of a peasant deviation, and began to draw decisively away from the middle peasants Finally, shortly before the Fourteenth Party Congress, he made yet another turn, this time in the direction of an alliance with the middle peasants ; and now perhaps we shall find him boasting once more of his readiness to prostrate himself before the peasantry.

What guarantee have we that Comrade Zinovieff will not, ere long, wobble in yet another direction ?

That sort of thing is see-saw, Comrades, and not a policy at all. (Laughter and applause.) That sort of thing is hysteria, and not a policy at all. (A voice : " Very true ! ") We are told that we need not take much trouble to fight the second deviation. That is a wrong view. While we have two deviations, that of Comrade Bogusheffsky and that of Comrade Zinovieff, you must understand that Comrade Bogusheffsky must on no account be compared with Comrade Zinovieff. Bogusheffsky is a spent force. (Laughter.) Bogusheffsky has no press organ. But the deviation in the direction of a neutralisation of the middle peasants, the deviation which takes the form of opposing a firm alliance with the middle peasants, Zinovieff's deviation, has its own press organ, and is still carrying on the campaign against the Central Committee to-day. This press organ is the "Leningrad Pravda". For this newspaper, the "Leningrad Pravda", has recently made much play with the phrase "middle-peasant bolshevism"; and what does this mean but that the newspaper has abandoned Leninism as far as the peasant question is concerned? Do we not see, then, that the struggle against the second deviation is a much more serious matter than the struggle against the first, against Bogusheffsky's deviation? That is why, when the second deviation is espoused by such a champion as the "Leningrad Pravda", we must see to it that we marshal the Party forces to combat the second deviation, and concentrate our fire upon it. ("Hear, hear" and applause.)

9. History of our Differences

I will now turn to the history of our internal struggle within the majority of the Central Committee. How did our differences begin? They began with the question: "What are we to do with Comrade Trotsky?" That was towards the end of 1924. To begin with, the Leningrad group wanted to expel Comrade Trotsky from the Party. I am talking of the discussions which took place in the year 1924. The Leningrad Provincial Committee passed a resolution demanding the expulsion of Comrade Trotsky. We, that is to say, the majority of the Central Committee, were not in favour of such a step. ("Quite right!") After a struggle, we were able to persuade the Leningrad comrades to delete the sentence about expulsion from their resolution. A little later, when the plenum of the Central Committee met, the Leningrad members, supported by Comrade Kameneff, proposed the immediate exclusion of Comrade Trotsky from the Political Bureau. We could not accept this proposal of the opposition either. We were in a majority on the Central Committee, and were content to remove Comrade Trotsky from his position as people's commissary for war. We did not agree with Comrades Zinovieff and Kameneff, for we knew that the policy of lopping-off might entail grave dangers for the Party. The method of lopping-off, the method of blood-letting (it was blood-letting they wanted) is dangerous, and infectious. To-day, you lop off one limb; to-morrow, another, the day after to-morrow, a third—and what is left of the Party? (Applause.)

In this first conflict, the fundamental difference between us in respect of matters of internal Party organisation became apparent.

The second question on which differences of opinion became apparent related to Comrade Sarkis' attack on Comrade Buharin. That was at the Thirteenth Conference, in January 1925. Comrade Sarkis accused Buharin of syndicalism. This is what Sarkis said:

> In the Moscow " Pravda ", we read Comrade Buharin's article concerning the worker correspondents and the peasant correspondents. Comrade Buharin's views find no supporters in our organisation. They are, in a sense, syndicalist and unbolshevik views, views adverse to the Party. Let me repeat, we do not hold such views in the Leningrad organisation, but certain comrades, even responsible comrades, do hold these views. Their advocates favour the independence and the extra-territoriality of the various proletarian and peasant social organisations, independence of the Communist Party.

This talk was, in the first place, an error in point of principle, for Comrade Buharin was absolutely right in the matter of the worker and peasant correspondents. In the second place, Comrade Sarkis' onslaught (to which the leader of the Leningrad organisation was accessory) was a gross infringement of the elementary rules of comradely discussion. I need hardly say, that this affair could not fail to make the relationships within the Central Committee worse than they were before. In the end, however, Comrade Sarkis frankly acknowledged his mistake in the columns of the public press.

This incident showed that open admission of a mistake is the best way of avoiding a public discussion.

The third question is that of the Leningrad Union of Young Communists. Some of the members of the Provincial Committee are present here, and they will probably remember that the Political Bureau passed resolutions concerning the Leningrad Provincial Committee of the Union of Young Communists, which had endeavoured, without the knowledge and approval of the Central Committee of the Union of Young Communists, to summon a sort of general conference of young communists. You know what the decision of the Central Committee of the Communist Party of Russia was. Of course we could not tolerate that, side by side with the Central Committee of the Union of Young Communists, there should come into existence another central body, competing with the former and setting itself up against the former. According to our bolshevist principles, no double leadership of this sort can be permitted. That is why the Central Committee considered it necessary to take disciplinary measures, and to dismiss Comrade Safaroff from his position as leader of the Leningrad Provincial Committee of the Union of Young Communists.

This incident shows that the Leningrad comrades have an inclination to transform their Leningrad organisation into a centre of opposition to the Central Committee.

The fourth question relates to Comrade Zinovieff's proposal to establish a special press organ in Leningrad, which was to discuss theoretical questions, was to be called the " Bolshevik ", and was to be edited by Comrades Zinovieff, Safaroff, Vardin, Sarkis, and Tarhanoff. We could not agree to this proposal, and declared that a newspaper of the sort, appearing side by side with the Moscow " Bolshevik ", would inevitably become the organ of a group, the organ of a fraction ; that such an opposition paper would endanger the unity of the Party. In plain terms, we prohibited the publication of this periodical. Now we are reproached because we issued a " prohibition ". This is absurd, Comrades. We are not liberals. We put the interests of the Party above the interests of formal democracy. Certainly we prohibited the publication of this organ of a fraction, and shall, if necessary, issue similar prohibitions in the future. (" Quite right ! " Loud applause.)

This incident showed that the upper circles in Leningrad wished to break away and to constitute themselves into a separate group.

Now we come to the question of Comrade Buharin.

I am thinking of the slogan : " Enrich yourselves ! " This phrase was uttered by Comrade Buharin in his April speech. Two days later, the April conference of our Party was opened. In the presidium of this conference, in the presence of Comrades

Sokolnikoff, Zinovieff, Kameneff, and Kalinin, I said that the slogan " Enrich yourselves ! " was not our slogan. I cannot recall that Comrade Zinovieff made any objection to this protest of mine. When, at the conference, Comrade Larin wished to speak, presumably against Buharin, Comrade Zinovieff demanded that Larin should not be allowed to speak against Buharin. Shortly afterwards, however, Comrade Krupskaya wrote an article against Buharin and demanded that it should be published. Comrade Buharin retaliated by writing an article against Comrade Krupskaya. The majority of the Central Committee decided that neither of the articles should appear, that no discussion of the kind should be opened, but that Comrade Buharin should be asked to admit publicly in the press that the slogan " Enrich yourselves ! " was an incorrect one. He agreed, and did what was required in an article directed against Ustryaloff, which he published after his return from a holiday. Now Comrades Kameneff and Zinovieff think they can frighten us by talking about " prohibitions ", and are as indignant as any liberal could be because we refused to allow the publication of Comrade Krupskaya's article. They won't frighten any one by this sort of talk. In the first place we did not only prohibit the appearance of Comrade Krupskaya's article but also the appearance of Comrade Buharin's article. In the second place, I should like to ask why we should not have the right of prohibiting the publication of an article by Comrade Krupskaya if we think that this prohibition is in the Party interest. What is the difference between Comrade Krupskaya's position and that of any other responsible comrade ? Do you think that the interests of any individual comrade are to take precedence of the interests and the unity of the Party ? Surely the comrades of the opposition know that for us bolsheviks formal democracy is a trifle, and that the real interests of the Party are all-important ! (Applause.)

Can the Comrades here present name a single article in " Pravda ", the central organ of the Party, which directly or indirectly justifies the slogan : " Enrich yourselves ! " ? They cannot name any such article, because there never was one. It is true that on one occasion Comrade Stetsky wrote in the central organ of the Union of Young Communists an article in which he tried to defend a mitigated form of this slogan. What happened ? Next day the secretariat of the Central

CONCLUDING WORDS AT THE CONGRESS

Committee reprimanded the editorial board of the newspaper in a letter sent by Comrades Molotoff, Andreeff, and Stalin. That was on June 2, 1925. A few days later, the organising bureau of the Central Committee, with Comrade Buharin's full agreement, decided to dismiss the editor-in-chief. Here are some extracts from this letter:

> Moscow, June 2, 1925. To all the members of the editorial board of the "Young Communists' Pravda", and to Comrade Vareikis, the chief of the press section of the Central Committee of the Communist Party of Russia. We are of opinion that certain passages in Comrade Stetsky's articles, *The New Stage of the New Economic Policy*, are calculated to arouse misgivings. In these articles, the slogan "Enrich yourselves!" finds expression, though in a mitigated form. This slogan is not ours; it is incorrect; it arouses misgivings and misunderstandings; and it ought not to appear in a leading article of the "Young Communists' Pravda". Our slogan is socialist accumulation. We remove the administrative restrictions in the way of the improvement of the wellbeing of agriculture. Beyond question, this facilitates every kind of accumulation, both socialist accumulation and private capitalist accumulation—but the Party has never said that private accumulation is its slogan.

Are these facts known to the opposition? Of course they are. Why, then, do not these comrades cease raising a clamour against Comrade Buharin? How much longer are they going on with their talk about Comrade Buharin's errors?

I know the mistakes that certain comrades made, for instance, in October (November) 1917, and they are so great that the mistakes of Comrade Buharin are hardly worth speaking of in comparison. These comrades did not merely go astray at that time, but they had the "impudence" to infringe on two occasions extremely important resolutions of the Central Committee, resolutions adopted under Lenin's leadership and in his presence. Nevertheless, the Party condoned these errors as soon as the comrades in question admitted their mistakes. In comparison with the comrades of whom I am speaking, Comrade Buharin's mistake was a trifle. He did not infringe any resolution of the Central Committee. Why, then, all this indignation against Buharin? What do they really want of Buharin? They are out for his blood! That is what Comrade Zinovieff demands when, in his concluding words, he returns to the Buharin question with so much acrimony. You want Buharin's blood? Well, you won't get it. (Applause.)

So much for Comrade Buharin's mistake.

Now I must return to the question of Comrade Zinovieff's article, *The Philosophy of the Epoch*, and must speak also of Comrade Kameneff's report to the Moscow plenum at the end of the summer, both of which contributed to complicate the internal situation of the Party. I need not go over all the ground again. At that time we were concerned with *The Philosophy of the Epoch*, with the errors contained in this article, with the way in which we corrected these errors, with the mistakes made by Comrade Kameneff in the matter of the grain supply, with his credulity in accepting the figures of the Central Statistical Board, according to which 61 per cent. of the marketable grain was in the hands of the rich peasants. Under pressure from the Comrades, Kameneff had to acknowledge his mistake in a special declaration made to the Council for Defence and Labour. In this declaration, which was published in the press, it is stated that more than half of the surplus is in the hands of the middle peasants. All this business, unquestionably, contributed to render our relationships more difficult.

.Subsequently, the questions that came up for discussion in the October plenum led to fresh complications. The opposition demanded an open discussion; the question of the so-called " Thermidor " propounded by Comrade Zalutsky came up for discussion; and finally there was a Leningrad conference, which from the first took the form of an attack upon the Central Committee. I think, in this connexion, of the speeches of such comrades as Safaroff, Sarkis, Shelavin, etc. I am thinking, also, of Comrade Zinovieff's speech, one of his last speeches before the close of the conference, in which he incited the conference to fight against Moscow, and proposed to elect a delegation of persons who were ready to carry on the struggle against the Central Committee. Such was the state of affairs. That was why such experienced bolshevist workers as Comrades Komaroff and Loboff were not appointed to the Leningrad delegation (for they would not accept the program of the fight against the Central Committee). In the delegation they were replaced by Comrades Gordon and Tarhanoff. If Gordon and Tarhanoff are weighed in the balance against Komaroff and Loboff every unprejudiced person will say that the scale holding the two former will kick the beam. (Applause.) What was wrong with Comrades Komaroff and Loboff in the eyes of the Leningraders ? Their whole offence was that they would not fight against the Central Committee. Why, it is only a month since the Leningraders proposed Comrade Komaroff for the post of first secretary of their organisation ! Was not that so ? ("Yes, yes !" from the Leningrad delegation.) Well, what had gone wrong with Komaroff within a month ? (Buharin : " He had ' degenerated ' within a month ! ")

What had happened within a month, that Komaroff, a member of the Central Committee, whom you yourselves recommended for the post of first secretary of your organisation, should be expelled from the secretariat of the Leningrad Committee and no longer be considered worthy to be elected as a delegate to the Congress ? (A voice from the Leningrad delegation : " He insulted the conference ! " Another voice : " That is a lie, Comrade Naumoff ! " Disturbance.)

10. Platform of the Opposition

Now I come to the platform of Comrades Zinovieff, Kameneff, Sokolnikoff, and Lashevich. It is time to speak about the platform of the opposition. This platform is rather an original one. The members of the opposition have made a number of conflicting speeches here. Kameneff said one thing and exhibited one trend. Zinovieff said another thing and exhibited another trend. Lashevich represented a third trend ; Sokolnikoff a fourth. Despite this diversity of opinion, they are all united upon one point. What is it upon which they are united ? What is their platform ? Their platform is that there is to be a reform of the secretariat of the Central Committee. That is the only point upon which they are fully united. The statement may seem strange, even ludicrous, but it is a fact.

There is a history behind all this. In the year 1923, after the Twelfth Party Congress, those who have now entered a " cave " (laughter), elaborated a platform in accordance with which the Political Bureau was to be abolished and the Secretariat was to become the leading political and organisational body. It was to consist of Zinovieff, Trotsky, and Stalin. What was the meaning of this platform ? It meant that the Party was to be led without Rykoff, without Kalinin, without Tomsky, without Molotoff, without Buharin. The platform came to nothing, not only because it did not represent any principles, but also because the Party cannot be led without the aid of the comrades I have just named. When a written question was addressed to me from the depths of Kislovodsk, I refused to have anything to do with the scheme, and said that, if the comrades should wish it, I was ready to give up my own position—quite quietly, without either open or hidden discussion, and without formulating demands for the protection of the rights of minorities. (Laughter.)

That may be called the first stage.

Now, it would seem a second stage has begun. Now, it would seem that what they want, is not that the Secretariat should undertake the political guidance of the Party, but that it should confine its attention to technical questions. What they want is, no longer the abolition of the Political Bureau, but the omnipotence of the Political Bureau.

Well, if the transformation of the Secretariat into a simple technical apparatus would really be to Comrade Kameneff's liking, perhaps we ought to see what can be done—but I am afraid the Party would never agree. (" Hear, hear ! ") I am very doubtful indeed whether a secretariat of this kind would be competent to elaborate the problems which come up for discussion at the Organising Bureau and at the Political Bureau.

But when they go on to talk about the omnipotence of the Political Bureau, is not a demand of this kind positively ludicrous ? Does not the Political Bureau already possess supreme authority ? Are not the Secretariat and the Organising Bureau already subject to the Political Bureau ? And what about the plenum of the Central Committee ? Why does not the opposition refer to this body ? Does the opposition wish to give the Political Bureau more extensive powers than those possessed by the plenum of the Central Committee ?

Certainly the opposition is in a bad way with its platform, or its platforms, in this matter of the Secretariat.

11. Their "Love of Peace"

You will ask, what are we to do now, in order to find a way out of the present situation. This question has occupied all our minds, not only during the Congress but before it as well. We want unity within the Party. That has now become the main question. The opposition likes to talk about difficulties. But there is one difficulty which is much more dangerous than all the others, one created by the opposition, the danger of dissensions within the Party, the danger of the disorganisation of the Party. (Applause.) This difficulty must, above all, be overcome. We made an attempt to overcome it when, two days before the Party Congress, we proposed to the opposition a compromise upon which it seemed to us that an understanding was possible. Here is, approximately, the text of our proposal:

> The undersigned members of the Central Committee are of opinion that various leading comrades of the Leningrad organisation have been preparing for the Party Congress in a spirit which is opposed to the general line of action of the Central Committee of the Party, and is opposed to the Leningrad supporters of this line of action. The undersigned members of the Central Committee consider that the resolutions of the Moscow Conference are thoroughly sound in respect alike of substance and of form; and they believe that it is the duty of the Central Committee to oppose all trends which are directed against the Party line of action and are likely to disorganise the Party.
>
> In the interests of the unity of the Party, in the interests of peace within the Party, in order to avoid the danger of a possible estrangement of the Leningrad organisation (one of the best organisations in the Communist Party of Russia) from the Central Committee of the Party, the undersigned nevertheless consider it possible to make a number of concessions (subject to the endorsement by the congress of the clear and distinct political line of the Central Committee). We therefore make the following proposals:
>
> (1) The resolution of the Moscow Conference, mitigated in certain respects, shall be the basis of the resolution on the report of the Central Committee.
> (2) Publication of the letter of the Leningrad Conference and the answer to the letter, both in the newspapers and in the bulletins, shall be regarded as undesirable in the interests of unity.
> (3) The members of the Political Bureau .. shall not attack one another in the congress.

(4) The speeches at the congress shall indicate disapproval of Sarkis (regulation of the composition of the Party) and Safaroff (State capitalism).

(5) The mistake concerning Comrades Komaroff, Loboff, and Moskvin shall be corrected by suitable organisational measures.

(6) The decision of the Central Committee concerning the inclusion of a Leningrad comrade in the secretariat of the Central Committee shall be carried into effect immediately after the congress.

(7) In the interests of a strengthening of the ties with the central organ, a comrade from Leningrad shall be incorporated into the editorial board of the central organ.

(8) In view of the inadequacy of the editor in chief of the " Leningrad Pravda " (Comrade Gladneff) he shall, in understanding with the Central Committee, be replaced by another comrade better fitted for the post.

Signed : Kalinin, Stalin, Buharin, Rykoff, Rudzutak, Tomsky, Molotoff, Dzherzhinsky.

December 15, 1925.

The opposition would not accept this compromise. It preferred open and savage war at the Party Congress. That shows you how genuine is their love of peace.

12. The Party will maintain its Unity

In essentials, we still remain at the standpoint of this document. In our draft resolution, as you know, we mitigated some of the formulas in the interests of peace within the Party.

We are opposed to the policy of lopping off. Of course this does not mean that the leaders will be entitled, with impunity, to do anything that takes their fancy. Certainly the Party will not prostrate itself before any individual leader. (" Hear, hear ! ")

We want unity. We are opposed to the policy of lopping off. The Party wants unity, and will establish unity, with Comrades Kameneff and Zinovieff, if they like, and without them, if they don't like. (" Hear, hear ! ")

Well, what does unity demand ? Unity demands that the minority should yield to the majority. Unless this rule be followed, there can be no unity, and there can be no Party.

We are opposed to the idea of a special press organ for discussion. There is a column for discussion in our newspaper, the "Bolshevik". That amply suffices. Discussion must not be driven too far. We must never forget that we are a *ruling* Party. We must not forget that any open expression of our differences may reduce our influence in the country—to say nothing of the effect it may have abroad.

The organs of the Central Committee, therefore, will retain their present form. I do not think that the Party will agree to their destruction. In any case, the Political Bureau has supreme authority, higher than that of all the other organs of the Central Committee, the plenum alone excepted. But the highest organ of all is the plenum of the Central Committee, though people are too ready to forget the fact. The plenum is the final arbiter and it calls its leaders to order when they are inclined to think too much of themselves. ("Hear, hear!" Laughter and applause.)

The unity of the Party must be and will be maintained—provided that the Party and the Party Congress do not allow themselves to be intimidated. (A voice: "We shall not allow ourselves to be intimidated. We have smelt powder before!") If any one of us should get a swelled head, he will be called to order. This is necessary, it is absolutely essential. The only possible way of leading the Party is by a collectivity of some sort. Now that Lenin is dead, it is absurd to think, or talk, or dream of anything else. (Applause.)

Collective work, collective leadership, unity in the Party, unity in the organs of the Central Committee, subordination of the minority to the majority—those are the essentials to-day.

As far as the worker-communists of Leningrad are concerned, I do not doubt that they will always be in the first ranks of our Party. In common with them, we built up the Party; in common with them, we have put it in its present high position; in common with them, we raised the banner of revolt in October (November) 1917; in common with them, we defeated the bourgeoisie; in common with them, we have fought to overcome the obstacles in the way of our constructive work; and in common with them, we shall continue the struggle. I am convinced that the worker-communists of Leningrad will not fall behind their comrades in other industrial centres in the struggle for the Leninist unity of the Party. (Loud applause. The Congress sings the *International*.)

INDEX

[N.B.—Readers in search of " Subject " entries should look under LENIN and MARX as well as in the general course of the Index.]

Abstentionism, 155
Abuse of Power in Rural Areas, 250, 318, 338
Address to the Moscow Soviet, 334
Against the Stream, 107
Agitprop Department, 405
Agricultural Cooperative, Central, 132, 133
 do. Credits, 385–386
Agricultural Tax, 296, 309, 312, 325, 432
Agriculture, gross Production in U.S.S.R., 390
 do., Reserves in, 385
Alliance between Proletariat and middle Peasants, 401, 403, 409
 do. do. do. do. Peasantry, see Smychka
All Power to the Soviets, 128, 153, 204, 205, 206, 281
Alsace-Lorraine, 362
American Spirit in practical Work, 176–177
ANDREEFF, 451
Antagonism, see also Conflict
Antagonisms between Russian Proletariat and Peasantry, 236–240, 308–311, 338
 do. within capitalist World classified, 354–355
Anti-Soviet Agitation in Villages, 324–325
April Demonstration (1917), 199, 200
 do. Party Conference, see Conference, Fourteenth
Archives of Central Committee, 434
Armaments, 367–368
Armed Peace, 368
Armenia, 275
Assembly, Constituent, see Constituent Assembly
Autonomy, cultural, 136
AXELROD, 167, 174

BAKAEFF, 441
Balance of Trade, 386, 394, 415, 431
Banking, see State Bank
Basle, 91, 92
BAUER, 14
Bauernfrage in Frankreich und Deutschland, 130, 131
" Bednota," 433, 434
Berlin Stipulations, 364
BISMARCK, 363
BOGUSHEFFSKY, 411, 413, 446, 477
" Bolshevik " (1925, No. 7), 240, 264, 407
 do. (1925, No. 11), 292
 do. (1925, No. 12), 292
Bolshevisation, 229, 441
Bolshevism or Trotskyism?, 13
Bolshevist Tactics during Preparation for October Revolution, 199–211
Bourgeoisie, new, 416
Boycott of Constituent Assembly, 209
 do. do. Duma, 149, 155
Brest-Litovsk, 153, 154
BRIAND, 363, 365
Brünn Platform, 322, 323
Budget, Russian, 252, 392–393
Budgets, local, 296
BUHARIN, 431, 435, 436, 444, 448, 449, 450, 451, 452, 453, 454, 456
Bureaucracy, 414, 416; see also Abuse of Power, also Officialdom
 do., Vestiges of, in Russian Industry, 388
Bureaucratic Elements must be cleared out of Party, 340; see also Officialdom
Buriats, 272

Capital, export of, 98, 358
 do. financial, see Financial Capital
 do. for large-scale Russian Industry. Is it procurable without foreign aid ?, 328–336

INDEX

Capital, supplementary, 328, 329, 331
Capitalism, partial Reinvigoration in Soviet Russia, 410, 429
  do., Stabilisation of, see Stabilisation, also Decay
  do., State, see State Capitalism
  do. no longer worldwide, 369
Capitalist Encirclement, see Encirclement
  do. Pressure on Soviet Union, 305
  do. World and Soviet Union, 369–374
Cave-Men, 434
  do. of Adullam at Kislovodsk, 426, 453
Central Committee C.P.R., 61, 62, 69
  do. do., Report to 14th Congress, 351–457
  do. Executive Committee of Soviets, 371
  do. do. do. of Trade Unions, 373
  do. Statistical Board, 406
CHAMBERLAIN, 250, 363, 365
CHANG TSO LIN, 379
Chechnya, 275
CHERNOFF, 18, 139, 201
CHICHERIN, 434
China, 139, 213, 226, 277, 278, 304, 337, 360, 367, 377, 378, 379
Choice between Debt Slavery and Vodka, 416
Choice Works of Lenin (Russian Edition, iii., 497), 49
CHURCHILL, 227
Civil War in France, 116
Class Struggle between poor Peasants and Kulaks, 313–314
  do. do. do. Proletariat and rural Bourgeoisie, 311–313
  do. do. in rural Areas, 308–314, 338
Classes (in Soviet Russia), their Activities and their mutual Relationships, 399–402
CLYNES, 139
Collected Works (Trotsky), 193, 195, 239
Collection of Materials relating to disputed Questions, 433, 434
Colonies and Dependencies in the East, 276–282
" Come out of the Unions !" a wrong-headed Slogan, 231

Comintern, see Communist International
Commercial Problems, 397–399
  do. Treaties, 375
Commercialism, Disease of, 176
Commissariat for Finance, 375, 393, 401, 437–438
  do. do. Foreign Affairs, 305
  do. do. Labour, 399
  do. do. Transport, 397
Commune of Paris, 41, 116, 121
Communism, War, see War Communism
Communist International, Right Wing of, 322–323
  do. do., 60, 172, 285, 377, 378; see also Enlarged Executive, also Congress
  do. *Manifesto*, 85
  do. Party of Checko-Slovakia, 322-323
  do. do. do. Great Britain, 9
  do. do. do. Russia, 9, 43, 46, 51, 54, 55, 58, 60, 61, 75, 76, 216–255, 418–425
  do. do. do. do., its Composition, 419–421
  do. do. do. not identical with State, 418
  do. do. do. Soviet Union, see Communist Party of Russia
  do. do. do. Yugoslavia, 288, 292
Community of Interests between Russian Proletariat and Peasantry, 237–240, 315–316
Compromisers, 202
Concerning Bolshevisation, 441
  do. *the Trade Unions*, 46
Concessions to Foreign Entrepreneurs, 387, 437
  do. do. Peasants, 428–431
Concluding Words at the Fourteenth Congress, 426–457
Conditions favouring October Revolution, 181–183
  do. *of Admission into the Communist International*, 171
Conference—
  Communist Party of Russia, Thirteenth, 448
    Fourteenth, 54, 55, 60, 61, 62, 216–255, 295, 318, 319, 401, 407, 408, 446, 449

Conference—*continued*
  Democratic, 152, 153
  Leningrad Provincial Party, 62
  of Powers,
    Genoa, 368
    Locarno, 361, 362, 363, 365, 381
Conflict, see also Antagonism
  do. between dominant and dependent Nations, 82
  do. do. Labour and Capital, 81
  do. do. victorious Countries, 366–369
  do. for Control of Sources of raw Material, 81–82
  do. of Ideas or Calumny, 433–434
Congress—
  All-Russian, of Sections for Political Education,
    Second, 175
  Communist International,
    Second, 33, 34, 49, 50, 402, 404, 405, 413, 414
    Fifth, 288, 292
  Communist Party of Russia,
    Second, 167
    Third, 104
    Eighth, 404, 441, 442
    Tenth, 43, 46, 173
    Eleventh, 51
    Twelfth, 446, 453
    Thirteenth, 9, 353, 394, 419, 421
    Fourteenth, 9, 54, 55, 58, 61, 62, 63, 69, 75, 76, 353, 421, 428, 429, 444, 445, 446
  Second International,
    Basle, 91, 92, 97
  Soviets,
    Third, 319
    Eighth, 240
  Union of Young Communists,
    Sixth, 348
Conquerors and Conquered, 361–365
Conquest of Power, 114
Constituent Assembly, 153, 207–209
Constitutional Method defined, 287
Contradictions of Imperialism (see also Contradictions of the Capitalist System), 82, 84, 87
  do. do. the Capitalist System, 81–82
Cooperation, 54, 59, 73, 74, 334
  do. and the Peasantry, 67–76, 249, 251

Core of Leninism, 15–16
Council for Defence and Labour, 452
  do. of People's Commissaries, 371
Counter-Claims by U.S.S.R., 375
Croats, 261, 264, 288
Cultural Autonomy, 136
Cutting Capers, 187

DAN, 139, 174, 201
Danger of losing sight of international revolutionary Goal, 303–305
  do. do. do. do. do. socialist Goal, 301–303
  do. that Party may become a Tailpiece of State Apparatus, 305–307
Dangers and Deviations in the Matter of Peasants, 410–414
Danzig, 363
DAWES, 225, 361, 362, 427, 428
Dawes Plan pregnant with German Revolution, 362
Dawesation of Russia, 426–428
Dead Souls, 164
Debts, tsarist, 83, 375
Decay of Capitalism, 223
Definition of Leninism, 13–14, 80 349
Delay in coming of World Revolution, 337–340, 384
Delegations, see Labour
Delusion that Working Class cannot get on without Bourgeoisie, 373
Democracy, bourgeois and proletarian, 115, 116
  do., Extension of its scope in rural Areas, 317–321
  do., Soviet, 249, 297, 408
Democratic Conference, 152, 153
DENIKIN, 142, 150, 153
Dictatorship does not consist exclusively of Force, 320
  do. *of one Party*, 49
  do. of Proletariat, 110–121, see also under Lenin
  do. do. do. as Instrument of proletarian Revolution, 110–121
  do. do. do. Rule of Proletariat over Bourgeoisie, 113–118
  do. do. do. defined, 115
  do. do. do. not End in itself, 297
Differentiation among Peasants, 308, 405–407, 412

INDEX

Drink Problem, 416
Duma, Boycott of, 149, 155
  do., Participation in, 154
DZHERZHINSKY, 253, 371, 456

East not a homogeneous Whole, 233
Ebb and Flow of Revolution, 247
Economic Forms in Soviet Russia, 386-389
  do. Policy, New, see New Economic Policy
  do. Position of Soviet Union, 382-394
Economists (a Group of Russian Doctrinaires), 96
Educating young Workers and young Peasants in Spirit of Leninism, 344-345
Egypt, 139, 226, 233, 277, 278, 360, 377, 378
"Ekonomicheskaya Zhizn," 383
Electrification of Russia, 240, 296, 391-392
Encirclement, capitalist, 328, 337, 418, 427
ENGELS, 85, 86, 90, 95, 116, 130, 131, 151
  Epoch of, 87
Enlarged Executive of Communist International, 60, 229, 232, 322
Enrich yourselves, 449, 450, 451
Enthüllungen über den Kommunistenprozess zu Köln, 113
ERENBURG, 175
Esthonia, 280
Exchange, Foreign, 386
Exploitation, Abolition of, 254
Extirpate Kulaks, 406, 408, 412, 413

February Revolution, 124, 127, 128, 146, 147, 149, 198, 230
Financial Capital, 98
  do. Exploitation, see DAWES
Flax Centre, 132
Food Tax, 240, 333
Forces of Production, Theory of, see Spontaneity
FORD, 389
Foreign Affairs, Commissariat for, 305
  do. Commerce of Soviet Russia, 393-394
  do. Situation of the Soviet Union, 374-379

Fostering Revolution, 109, 215, 227
Foundations of Leninism, 9, 13, 15, 31, 52, 64, 77-177
  do. of socialist Economy, 196
Fractions, non-Party, in Soviets, 326-327
Franco-German War, 363
Friends of the People, 91
Front, capitalist, Where can it be broken?, 101
  do., colonial, 99
  do., inter-capitalist, 99
  do., proletarian, 98
  do., united World, 99, 100
Fuel Problem in Soviet Russia, 396, 436
Fully-fledged Communist, 175
Future of Socialism in Soviet Union, 236-245

General Strike, 90, 287
Genoa, 368
GEORGE V, 143
Georgia, 275
GLADNEFF, 456
GOGOL, 164
GORDON, 452
Grabbing and pillaging Colonies, 328
Grain Supply, 398-399, 406

Hague, 364, 365
Half-Peasants, 308, 400
Hamlet Mentality, 212
Heavy Industry, 253; see also Metallurgical
"Help, help! the Kulak is coming!" 411
HENDERSON, 114, 139
HILFERING, 18, 209
Hilferdingery, 209
HILLQUIT, 18
HINDENBURG, 226
Hindustan, 101, 139, 213, 226, 233, 272, 276, 277, 278, 279, 360, 377, 378
Historical Roots of Leninism, 18-86
History of our Differences, 447-453
Home Rule, 136
HUGHES, 366
Hundred-per-cent. Leninism, 58, 63
Hvostism, see Tailism

Immediate Tasks of Communist Elements in Colonies and Dependencies, 233–235
do. do. do. do. Parties in capitalist Countries, 229–232
Imperialism, 14, 98, 99, 146, 173, 223
do., Colonies and Half-Colonies, 359–360
Impressions, 433, 434
Income Tax, 432
Independence comes by Revolution, not as a Gift, 277
India, British, see Hindustan
Industry and Agriculture in Soviet Russia, 395, 397
do. must be linked up with Agriculture, 134, 332, 333, 404
do., Russian, its Development without foreign Aid, 328–336, 410
do., Socialist, see Socialist Industry
do. do., Statistics of, 391–392
do., State, see State Industry
Inflation, 415
Insurance Fund, social, 400
Intelligentsia, 401, 416
Internal Situation of Soviet Union, 382–417
International, 457
do., Second, 80, 87, 88, 89, 91, 92, 97, 102, 122, 123, 135, 145, 146, 148, 156, 161, 162, 172, 173, 365, 368
do. Situation, 220–228, 354–381
do., Third, see Communist International
Internationalism, Spirit of, 345
Intervention, Danger of, 242–245, 337, 373
" Iskra," 96, 103
Isolation of Kulaks, 409, 413

Japan, Relations with Soviet Russia, 378–379
July Defeat of Bolsheviks (1917), 206, 221
do. Demonstration (1917), 199, 200, 221
June Demonstration (1917), 199, 200
do. Offensive, 128

Kabardia, 275
KALININ, 450, 454, 456.

KAMENEFF, 25, 26, 61, 62, 428, 429, 436, 442, 447, 450, 452, 453, 456
do. and Concessions to Peasants, 428–431
KAPP, 156
KAUTSKY, 14, 18, 87, 97, 115, 161, 272
KERENSKY, 22, 139
do. Regime, 128, 155, 203
Kindling Class War, 308–314
Kirghizistan, 275
Kislovodsk, 426, 454
KLYUSHCHNIKOFF, 416
KOLCHAK, 49, 142, 150, 153
KOMAROFF, 452, 453, 456
" Komsomolskaya Pravda," 341 ; see also " Young Communists' Pravda "
KORNILOFF, 156, 200, 206
do. Rising, 128, 203, 205, 221
KOSSIOR, 371
KRUPSKAYA, 435, 450
KUGELMANN, 116, 210
Kulaks, 70, 71, 72, 308–314, 401, 405, 406, 408, 409, 410–414, 428, 442, 444
Kuomintang, 278
" Kursk Pravda " (December 8, 1925), 58
do. Provincial Party Conference, 58
KUTUZOFF, 46

Labour Aristocracy, 173
do. Delegations, 370–371, 372, 381, 423, 424, 425
Language, universal, 272
LARIN, 375, 442, 444, 450
LASHEVICH, 426, 453
Leadership in Towns and in rural Areas contrasted, 307
do. of proletarian Class Struggle, 145–146
League of Nations, 365, 368, 381
do. do. Youth, 30, 31, 32
Left-Wing Communism, an Infantile Disorder, 14, 49, 50, 91, 92, 108, 146, 155, 170, 172, 323
Lena Gold Fields, 221
LENIN—
Accused of Bureaucratism, 167
Accuses Trotsky of denying Role of Peasantry, 187
Admission of Error, 92–93

INDEX

LENIN—*continued*
Agricultural Production must be increased, 407, 430
Alliance with middle Peasants, 404, 407, 441
Alternative Dictatorships, capitalist or proletarian, 49
Amicable Relationships with Peasantry, 240
Analysis of Preparations for October Revolution, 200–201
Aristocratic Anarchism, 166
Armed Intervention against Exploiters, 215
Blossoming of economic Life in Soviet Russia, 396
Bolshevism a model Tactic for all, 14, 186
Bourgeois Culture and proletarian Culture, 271
Bourgeois-minded Workers as Agents of Bourgeoisie, 173
Charge of Bureaucracy, 167
Cheapjack Phraseology, 92
Collaboration with capitalist world, 374
Communist Party as Vanguard, 40
do. Vanity, 175, 176
Communists are Drops in Ocean, and must give accurate Expression to Folk Consciousness, 51
do. form Party of Working Class, 164
do. must convince backward Members of Working Class, 45
Compromise, 157–158
Concessions to Foreign Entrepreneurs, 387, 437, 440
do. do. Peasantry, 429–431
Condemns bureaucratic Methods, 388
Conditions favouring October Revolution, 183
Contact with Masses, 91
Contrasts proletarian State with bourgeois State, 388–389
Convince first, keep Force in reserve, 46
Cooperative Enterprise and State capitalist Enterprise, 73
do. Organisation of Peasant Masses, 68, 70, 413
Course of agricultural Development in Russia, 133

LENIN—*continued*
Criticises Policy of waiting for Universal Revolution, 242
do. View that Russia is not ripe for Socialism, 241–242
Critics of, 13
Danger of Fractions, 172
do. do. Intervention, 243
Defensive Attitude fatal to armed Rising, 151
Definition of Dictatorship of Proletariat, 24, 25, 26, 35, 112, 170, 185
Democratic Movement, 138
Description of Soviets, 204–205
Development of Russian Industry without Foreign Aid, 330
Dictatorship of Leaders and Dictatorship of Masses not Alternatives, 41, 47
do. do. Proletariat and Peasantry not the Organisation of Order but the Organisation of War, 104
do. do. do. implies a higher Type of Organisation as well as the use of Force, 27
do. do. do. is Tap-Root of Revolution, 15
" Dictatorship of the Party," 48–51
Diffusing Spirit of Internationalism among Workers, 143
Disease of Commercialism, 176
Disinters Marx's and Engels' Ideas on Strategy and Tactics, 146
Distinction between Party and Class, 166
Does not identify guiding Role of Party with Dictatorship of Proletariat, 34
do. do. underrate Difficulties of upbuilding Socialism, 240
Dominion of financial Capital, 98
Economic Forms of Soviet Russia, 387
do. Reconstruction, 254
Electrification of Russia, 240, 330
Equitable Policy in regard to Peasantry, 241
Essentials for Revolution, 108
Extending Area of Revolution, 109, 215
Extension of Soviet Constitution to whole Population, 319

LENIN—continued
   Final Abolition of Class Divisions, 185
   Formulates Law of irregular and spasmodic Development of capitalist Countries, 189–191, 239
   Foundations of Socialist Economy, 196
   Free from "constitutional" Illusions, 259
   Greatest of Proletarian Thinkers, 16
   Growth of Cooperation identical with Growth of Socialism (in Russia), 66, 72–73
   Heavy Industry, 253
   His expert Knowledge of Peasant Question, 16
   do. Philosophy based on Marxism, 79
   Idea of continuous Revolution, 18
   Imminent Risk of foreign Intervention, 57
   Imperialism is Capitalism on its Deathbed, 81
      do. do. the immediate Forerunner of the Socialist Revolution, 99
   International Relationships, 213–214
   Law of Revolution, fundamental, 108
   Maintenance of Party Discipline, 39
   Marxism educates proletarian Vanguard, 43
   Marx's Use of "Popular" and "People", 210
   Means for establishment of fully socialised Society, 59, 241, 303, 334
   Mechanism of Dictatorship of Proletariat, 29, 32
   Metamorphosis of bourgeois Revolution into proletarian Revolution, 103–104
   Middle Peasants have become dominant in rural Districts, 430
   Mutual Testing as between party and non-party Workers, 327
      do. Trust between party Members and Sympathisers, 327

LENIN—continued
   Need for Alliance between Workers and Peasants, 26
   do. do. forcible Revolution and Destruction of old State Machine, 23, 117, 118, 210
   do. do. supporting Cooperation, 133
   Neutralisation of Peasants, 404
   Never play with Insurrection, 151
   New Economic Policy, 333, 334, 429–430
   do. kind of Democracy, 115
   Not hush up anything, 43
   Opposes Champions of permanent Revolution, 17
   Organisation means Transformation of Authority of Ideas into Authority of Power, 166
   do. of socialist Production, 58, 59
   Participation in Elections to Constituent Assembly, 208–209
   Party and Dictatorship of Proletariat, 33
      do. as highest Form of Class Organisation of Workers, 169
      do. do. Leader of Proletariat, 36
      do. do. organised Whole, 165
      do. Centralisation, 171
      do. Discipline, 170, 172
      do. must be purged of weak-kneed Elements, 174
   Peace of Brest-Litovsk, 153, 154
   Peculiar Features of Dictatorship of Proletariat in Russia, 14
   Persistence of bourgeois Strength, 111, 112
   Phases of Revolution, 106–107
   Possibility of peaceful Change in Britain and U.S.A., 117
   Power as fundamental Question of Revolution, 110
   Push democratic Revolution to an End, 147
   do. socialist Revolution to an End, 147
   Recruits, 77
   Relation of Reform to Revolution, 159–160
   Republic of Soviets, 121
   Requisites for Foundation of Soviet Economy, 129

INDEX

LENIN—*continued*
Revolution in several Countries at once rare and exceptional, 212
Revolutionary Conflagration will spread from Russia to the West of Europe, 104, 105
  do. Fantasy, 176
  do. Movement in East, 102
  do. Parties must go on learning, 153
  do. Possibilities, 44
  do. Theory indispensable to revolutionary Movement, 94, 95
  do. do. not a Dogma, 91
Right of Fusion, 144
  do. do. Secession, 143-144
Ripening revolutionary Movement in colonial Lands, 234-235
Russia of New Economic Policy will become socialist, 435
Russian Nihilism, 166
  do. Proletariat as Vanguard of international revolutionary Proletariat, 86, 95
Scope of the Russian Revolution, 105
Self-Determination, 290
Seizure of Power, 23, 24, 89, 90
Separation of Norway from Sweden, 263
Slogans on Peasant Problem, 402-410, 443, 445
Socialism in one Country, 52, 240, 243-245
  do. do. our Time, 196
Socialist Construction, 404
Soviet Power, 119-121
Soviets as Instruments of Dictatorship, 37
Speech at Eighth Party Congress, 404
State Apparatus, 298-299
  do. Bank, 438
  do. Capitalism compatible with Dictatorship of Proletariat, 436
  do. do. Socialism, Concessions, and small-scale Enterprise, 439-440
Struggle between socialist and non-socialist States, 215-216
Theory must serve Practice, 91

LENIN—*continued*
Theory of Dictatorship of Proletariat contrasted with Trotsky's Theory of permanent Revolution, 188-189
  do. do. proletarian Revolution, 190-192, 194
Theses concerning Smychka, 65
Those who confound Marxism with Liberalism, 105
To be a Revolutionist is not enough, 157
Trade and learn how to trade, 444
Trade-Union Support essential to Dictatorship of Proletariat, 230
Transition from Capitalism to Socialism occupies an entire historical Epoch, 111
  do. do. small-scale to large-scale Production, 74
Transitional Period between Capitalism and Socialism, 27, 113, 220-222
  do. do., when Proletariat must rule through military Organisation, 56
Trends in national Question, 141
Tsarism was feudal-militarist Imperialism, 83-84
Vanguard alone will not gain Victory, 155-156
Views on nationalist Problems, 259
  do. do. socialist Revolution, 21-22
When Time is ripe for Revolution, 152
Wholehearted Support by the Workers essential to Dictatorship, 38, 39, 42
Work of Party carried out through Soviets, 37
Workers' Participation in Government, 299
Leningrad Delegation, 442
  do. Organisation, C.P.R., 11, 405, 448, 455
" Leningrad Pravda," 447, 456
  do. provincial Committee, 447, 448, 449
  do. Union of Young Communists, 448
Leninism a Development of Marxism, 80, 93
  do., defined, 80, 349

Leninism, historical Roots of, 81–86
do., Method of, 87–93
do., Theory of, 94–109
Leninism (by Zinovieff), 47, 57, 60, 61, 62, 443, 445
Less but Better, 330
Lessons of October, 204
Letters to the Workers and Peasants about the Defeat of Kolchak, 49
LIBER, 201
Liberty of Nationalities, 259; see also Self-Determination, also Home Rule
Liquidationism, 302, 303, 333, 344, 423
Liquidators, 302, 423
LITVINOFF, 381
Livening up Soviets, 324, 401, 428
L'no-tsentr, 132
Loans, tsarist, see Debts
LOBOFF, 452, 453, 456
Locarno, 361, 362, 363, 365, 381
do. Conference pregnant with European War, 363
LONGUET, 18
LUXEMBURG, 197, 198
Lying Speeches about Freedom, 174

MACDONALD, 18, 114, 250, 376, 377
Manifesto of the Communist Party, see *Communist Manifesto*
Maniloffskyism, 164
MANUILSKY, 288, 292
March Revolution, see February Revolution
Market, free, 429–431, 440
MARTOFF, 18, 166, 167, 174
MARX—
A People which oppresses another People cannot itself be free, 140
Attitude towards nationalist Movements, 138
Communists pay special Attention to Germany, 85
Connexion of his Teachings with Leninism, 13
Destruction of bureaucratic and military State Machine as preliminary to popular Revolution, 210
Epoch of, 87
Formulates Idea of permanent Revolution, 17, 18, 106

MARX—*continued*
Founder of scientific Socialism, 86
Materialist Theory must not be content with explaining the World, but must change it, 97
Need for a second Edition of the Peasants' War, 89–90
On Insurrection, 151
On Phases of Revolution, 107
On Possibility of peaceful Change in Britain and U.S.A., 116, 117
On transitional Period between Capitalism and Socialism, 27, 113
Relation of Reform to Revolution, 159–160
Working Class must smash bourgeois State Machine, 116
Marxism and the Nationalist Question, 289
do. Betrayal by Leaders of Second International, 123
Marxists, Austrian and Russian contrasted, 259–260
Materialism and Empirio-Criticism, 98
Metallurgical Industry, 252–255, 392
Metals, Dearth of, 396–397
Metal Trust, 392; see also Metallurgical Industries
Middle-Peasant Bolshevism, 447
do. Peasants, 72, 308, 325, 401, 403, 407, 409, 410–414
do. do. turning to Kulaks for support, 324
MILYUKOFF, 302
MILYUTIN, 433
MOLOTOFF, 409, 422, 444, 451, 454, 456
Monopolism, 99
MORGAN, 116
Morocco, 226, 277, 337, 360, 367
Moscow Committee C.P.R., 61, 62
MOSKVIN, 456
Movement of oppressed Peoples and its Relation to proletarian Revolution, 140–144

National Question, 135–144
Nationalist Question in the Light of Marxist Theory, 288
Nationalist Question in Yugoslavia, 257–264, 283–292

INDEX 467

Naumoff, 453
Needy Year, 176
Nep, see New Economic Policy
Neutralisation of middle Peasants, 441, 442
New Economic Policy, 9, 43, 69, 70, 71, 75, 156, 157, 196, 230, 241, 244, 245, 248, 249, 301, 311, 333, 387, 405, 407, 411, 412, 416, 428, 429-431, 435, 439
  do. Life to the Soviets, 324, 401, 408
  do. Stage of New Economic Policy, 451
Nicholas II, 143
Nineteen-Five (by Trotsky), 187, 238, 334
Nineteen-Seventeen (by Trotsky), 192
Nosky, 114
November Revolution, see October Revolution

October and Trotsky's Theory of permanent Revolution, 184-198
  do. Revolution, 44, 58, 59, 60, 68, 127, 146-148, 150, 179-216, 221, 242, 259, 260, 272, 290, 298, 301, 302, 303, 305, 333, 403, 405, 443, 457
October Revolution and the Tactics of the Russian Communists, 9, 17, 25, 53, 54, 179-216
  do. do. as Prelude to World Revolution, 212-216
Offensive, see June Offensive
Officialdom, arrogant, 338; see also Abuse of Power
Ogpu, 409
Oil, 366, 369; see also Fuel
One Step Forward, Two Steps Backward, 93, 164, 166, 167
Opposition, 69, 72, 428, 432, 435, 440, 447-456
Opportunism, 87, 96, 166, 169, 174, 244; see also Tailism, also Reformism
Orders, the Day for them is over, 340
Organising Bureau, 454
Otzovism, 155
Our Revolution, 192, 238

Pacific, U.S.A. and Japan, 367
Participation in Duma, 154

Party and international Situation, 380-381
  do. do. the Working Class within the System of Dictatorship of Proletariat, 29-51
  do. as Expression of Unity of Will incompatible with Existence of Fractions, 171-173
  do. do. highest Form of class Organisation of Proletariat, 167-169
  do. do. Instrument for Dictatorship of Proletariat, 169-171
  do. do. organised Detachment of Working Class, 165-167
  do. do. Vanguard of Working Class, 162-164
  do. before and after Seizure of Power, 170
  do. erroneously identified with State, 298
  do. Policy in rural Districts, 246-251
  do. strengthened by purging itself of opportunist Elements, 173-174
  do., Tasks of, as concerns internal Policy, 414-417
  do., general Considerations, 161-174
  do. will maintain its Unity, 456-457
Parvus, 198, 323
Peaceful Cohabitation, 354, 373, 374, 375
Peasant Economy in Russia, its Course of Development, 66 et seq.
  do. Problem, 122-134
  do. Youth, Organisation of, 347-348
Peasantry after Consolidation of Soviet Power, 129-134
  do., Concessions to, 324-325
  do. during bourgeois-democratic Revolution, 124-127
  do. do. proletarian Revolution, 127-129
  do. of Soviet Union contrasted with that of Western Europe, 130-131
  do., revolutionary Possibilities, 123
  do., Zinovieff and, 441-447
Peasants, Categories of, 72, 308
  do., Middle, see Middle Peasants
  do., Poor, see Poor Peasants
  do., Rich, see Kulaks
  do. War, 90

Peculiarities of October Revolution, 184–198
do. do. Russian economic Life, 384–386
People's Commissariat, see Commissariat
Permanent Revolution, 17–19, 105, 106, 107, 184–198
Petrograd Municipal Council, 299
Petroleum, 366, 367; see also Fuel
Philosophy of the Epoch, 444, 445, 452
Pilgrimages, Labour, see Labour Delegations
PILNYAK, 176
Place in Sun, 99
Platform of the Opposition, 453–456
PLEHANOFF, 95, 210
Plenum of Central Committee, 55, 452, 454, 457
do. do. Communist International, see Enlarged Executive
POINCARÉ, 143
Politbureau, see Political Bureau
Political Bureau, 62, 353, 418, 432, 453, 454, 455, 457
Political Report of the Central Committee to the Fourteenth Congress of the Communist Party of the Soviet Union, 55, 351–457
do. Tasks of the Communist University of the Peoples of the East, 265–282
Policy, New Economic, see New Economic Policy
Poor Peasants, 72, 308, 313–314, 407, 408, 409
do. do. have Pensioners' Psychology, 409
do. do., Organisation of Groups among, 409
" Poslednie Novosti," 302
Possibilities of a Victory for Socialism in one Country alone, 333
POTRESOFF, 167, 174
Practical Work, American Spirit in, 176–177
" Pravda " (no Date mentioned), 198, 448, 450
do. (No. 83), 291
do. (February 13, 1924), 15
do. (February 21, 1924), 197
do. (November 30, 1924), 13
do. (December 14, 1924), 187
do. (January 14, 1925), 25

" Pravda " (November 29, 1925), 350
Press harder, 324–325
Problems of Leninism, 11–76
Program of Peace, 192, 194, 195, 334
Prohibition, Abandonment of, 416
Proletarian Culture, 271–273
do. Revolution and Dictatorship of Proletariat, 20–28
Proletarian Revolution and Kautsky the Renegade, 14, 50, 92, 105, 146
do. do., Theory of, 98–109
Propaganda, 377
Provisional Government, 104, 207
Purge of Communist Party of Russia, 327

Questions and Answers, 55, 293–304

RADEK, 186, 197, 198
" Radnik," 288
Railways, excessive Wear and Tear of Rolling Stock, 397
RAKOFFSKY, 367, 377
Realisation of Socialism, 64–76
Recognition of Soviet Russia, 374–375
Red Army, 320, 335
Reformism and Revolutionism, 157–160
Reformists endeavour to instil scepticism into Workers' Minds, 424
RENAUDEL, 139
Report of Central Committee, 351–457
do. to Party Officials in Moscow, 216–255, 333
Reserve Forces of Revolution, 149–151
Resolution concerning Colonies and Dependencies, 233–235
do. do. immediate Tasks of Communist Parties of West, 229–232
do. do. Peasant Problem, 402, 405, 409, 414
do. do. Tasks of Comintern and Communist Party of Russia, 54
do. do. do. do. do. International and Communist Party of Russia in conjunction with the enlarged Executive Committee of the Communist International, 60
do. on Unity of Party, 173
Restoration, see Safeguards

Results of the Discussion concerning Right to Self-Determination, 290
Revolution in one Country alone, 107, 108, 195
  do., permanent, see Permanent Revolution
Revolution, Russian—
  (1905), 122, 124, 146, 147, 149
  February (March) 1917, see February
  October (November) 1917, see October
Revolution, Russian, peculiar Course of, 125–127
  do. do., Phases of, 146–148
  do., Where will it begin?, 101
  do., World, see World Revolution
Revolutionary Possibilities of Nationalist Movement, 281
  do. Tempo, Slackening of, 247
Riga Telegraph Agency, 433, 434
Rising, see Korniloff
ROCKEFELLER, 116
ROTHSCHILD, 116
RUDZUTAK, 456
Ruhr, 361
Russia as Birthplace of Leninism, 85
  do. do. Focus of three Contradictions of Imperialism, 83–84
Russian Revolution, see Revolution
  do. rural Economy contrasted with that of Western Europe, 131–132
RYKOFF, 372, 454, 456

SAFAROFF, 436, 449, 452, 456
Safeguards against bourgeois Restoration, 53
SARKIS, 448, 449, 452, 456
SCHEIDEMANN, 114, 139
Scissors, 296, 310
Secretariat, 453–454
Self-Criticism, 246, 250
  do. Determination, Right of, 136, 290
Selskosoyus, 132, 133
SEMICH, 259, 260, 261, 262, 283–292
Semi-Proletarians, see Half-Peasants
SEREBROFFSKY, 371
Severance of Party and Trade Unions from Masses, 339, 340
SHANIN, 383, 426
Share of Spoils, 99
SHELAVIN, 452

Shell, 366
SHMERAL, 322–323
Significance of Gold, 157, 159
Skilled Workers, Dearth of, 397
Slovenes, 261, 288
Smenovehovstsy, 416, 417
Smychka, 26, 65, 120, 237, 248, 295, 297, 310, 311, 317, 338, 402–404, 436, 440
  do. as majoritarian Dictatorship, 120
  do. defined, 26
Social Democracy in Western Europe buttressed by Trade Unionism, 232
  do. Democrats, see Opportunists, also Reformists
Socialised Property gaining at Expense of non-socialised Property in U.S.S.R., 391–392
Socialism defined, 297
  do., final Victory of, 243
  do. in one Country alone, 52–63, 192, 304, 331–335
  do. not peculiar to Towns, 403
Socialist Industry, 387
Sofia Cathedral Outrage, 227, 280, 378
SOKOLNIKOFF, 426, 428, 431–433, 437, 438, 439, 450, 453
  do. and the Dawesation of Soviet Russia, 426–428
  do., how he defends poor Peasants, 432–433
SORIN, 33, 47, 50
Soviet Power as Form of State embodying Dictatorship of Proletariat, 118–121
  do. do., Characteristics of, 119–121
  do. Republics of the East, 269–275
  do. Russia predominantly agricultural, 395
  do. social System to-day neither capitalist nor socialist, but transitional, 391
Soviets, Characteristics of, 118–119
"Sozialdemokrat," 192
Spheres of Influence, 98, 99
Spontaneity, Theory of, 95–98
Stabilisation of Capitalism, 220, 222, 223, 224, 225–228, 236, 301–307, 311, 322–323, 337–340, 355–359

Stabilisation of Capitalism and Concessions to right-wing Deviations in Communist International, 322–323
  do. do. Soviet Regime, 222, 224, 228
Stalin's Letter to " Bednota," 434
  do. do. to Molotoff, 444–445
  do. do. to Young Communists' " Pravda ", 451
Standard Oil, 366
State and Revolution, 14, 43, 50, 115, 146, 444
  do. Apparatus, 298–300
  do. do. breaking loose from party Control, 338–339, 414
  do. do., soviet contrasted with bourgeois, 298
  do. Bank, 437, 438
  do., bourgeois and proletarian contrasted, 388–389
  do. Capitalism, 9, 387, 435–440
  do. do. contrasted with Soviet State Industry, 387–388
  do. Electrification Commission, 390
  do. Industry, 387
  do. Monopoly of foreign Trade, 309
  do. Planning Department, 400
  do. Political Administration Department, 409
  do. Purchase and Sale of agricultural Produce, 309
Stateless Society of Future, 121, 249, 297, 300
STETSKY, 450, 451
STINNES, 116
STOLYPIN, 444
Strategical Leadership, 149–154
Strategy and Tactics, 145–160
  do. and the Phases of the Revolution, 146–148
  do., basic Rule of, 202
STRESEMANN, 363, 365
Strike, General, see General Strike
Struggle for Power, 187
STRUVE, 210
Style in Work, 175–177
SUHANOFF, 58, 60
Supreme Economic Council, 371
Sverdloff University, 55, 77, 293–304
Sympathisers, dangerous Elements in Party, 165
Syria, 360, 367

Tactics and Ebb and Flow of the Movement, 148–149
Tailism, 96, 98, 162, 164 ; see also Opportunism
TANNER, 33, 49
TARHANOFF, 449, 452
Tax, see Agricultural, also Income
Taxation in Kind, 72, 74, 407
Their Love of Peace, 455–456
Theory, Importance of, 94–95
Theory and Practice of Leninism, 9
Thermidor, 452
To Lenin's Memory, 15
TOMSKY, 454, 456
To the Poor Peasants, 408
Towards October, 179, 333
Tractors, 296
Trade-Union Unity, 380
  do. Unionism in Soviet Russia and in Western Europe contrasted, 230–231
Transcaucasia, 269
Transport Workers' Union, 46
Treaties, commercial, 375
Trotsky, 60, 183, 184–198, 199, 209, 210, 238, 239, 333, 334, 447, 454
Trotskyists, 53
Tsarist Debts, see Debts
TSERETELLI, 139
TURATI, 18, 174
Turkestan, 269, 271
Turn your Face to the Villages, 339
Two Lines of Revolution, 107
Two Tactics, 103, 104, 105, 146

Union of Young Communists, 341–350, 448, 449, 450
United States of America now averse from War, 374
  do. do. of Europe, 192
Unity of Party, 455–457
Universal Language, 272
University of the Peoples of the East, 265–282
Upbuilding Socialism, 332–336
  do. do. Directives for, 382–386
Uskomchel, 175
USTRYALOFF, 416, 417, 444, 450
Uzbekistan, 270, 271

Vanguard, its Part in the Movement, 95–98
VARDIN, 449
VAREIKIS, 451

INDEX 471

Versailles, 304, 361, 362, 365
Village Correspondents, 433
Vodka, 416
Volkhov, 391

War against War, 91, 92, 97
  do. Communism, 247, 295, 318, 401, 428
Weakness of party Organisation in rural Areas, 324-325
What is to be done?, 86, 96, 146
What Lenin teaches about the Party, 33
Who have miscalculated?, 431-432
WILLIAM II, 143
Will the Bolsheviks retain Power?, 298, 438
Work of the Fourteenth Congress of the Communist Party of the Soviet Union, 54, 216-255
Workers' and Peasants' Alliance, see Smychka
  do. do. do. Government, Slogan of, 315-316
  do. Feeling of Class Dignity, 340
Works, the Reference in all Cases is to the Russian Edition of Lenin's Works,
  do. (v, 135-136), 94, 95
  do. (v, 138), 86
  do. (v, 307), 93
  do. (v, 356), 166
  do. (v, 438), 167
  do. (v, 442), 166
  do. (v, 462), 167
  do. (vi, 129), 104
  do. (vi, 171), 104
  do. (vi, 371), 103 147
  do. (vi, 449-450), 18
  do. (xiii, 133), 59, 191, 215, 216, 239, 333
  do. (xiii, 213), 107
  do. (xiii, 214), 105, 187
  do. (xiii, 243), 99
  do. (xiv, ii, 139), 210
  do. (xiv, ii, 228-230), 205
  do. (xiv, ii, 231), 438
  do. (xiv, ii, 236), 299
  do. (xiv, ii, 255), 44
  do. (xiv, ii, 270), 151
  do. (xiv, ii, 275), 209
  do. (xiv, ii, 284,) 201
  do. (xiv, ii, 302), 23
  do. (xiv, ii, 317), 43

Works—continued
  do. (xiv, ii, 324), 115
  do. (xiv, ii, 327-328), 117, 210
  do. (xv, 50), 121
  do. (xv, 68-69), 153
  do. (xv, 124-127), 22
  do. (xv, 161), 319
  do. (xv, 287), 242, 243
  do. (xv, 447), 15
  do. (xv, 453), 118
  do. (xv, 466-467), 111, 112, 212
  do. (xv, 493), 92
  do. (xv, 502), 109, 215
  do. (xv, 503), 14, 186
  do. (xv, 508-509), 105
  do. (xvi, 44-46), 36, 119, 120
  do. (xvi, 102), 56, 243
  do. (xvi, 222), 27
  do. (xvi, 226-227), 27
  do. (xvi, 240-241), 24, 25, 35, 185
  do. (xvi, 248), 185
  do. (xvi, 247-248), 27, 176
  do. (xvi, 256), 176
  do. (xvi, 296), 49
  do. (xvi, 306), 49
  do. (xvi, 348), 14
  do. (xvi, 450), 23
  do. (xvi, 456-457), 23
  do. (xvii, 116), 14
  do. (xvii, 117), 39, 112, 170
  do. (xvii, 118-119), 40, 112
  do. (xvii, 121), 153
  do. (xvii, 124), 37
  do. (xvii, 133-134), 41
  do. (xvii, 135, 136), 39, 112, 171, 172
  do. (xvii, 138-140), 37
  do. (xvii, 139), 32
  do. (xvii, 141), 169
  do. (xvii, 144), 45
  do. (xvii, 147), 93
  do. (xvii, 148-149), 209
  do. (xvii, 153), 183
  do. (xvii, 158), 158
  do. (xvii, 172), 44, 108
  do. (xvii, 173), 156
  do. (xvii, 179), 44
  do. (xvii, 180-181), 152
  do. (xvii, 197-198), 113
  do. (xvii, 232), 40
  do. (xvii, 246), 190
  do. (xvii, 248-249), 173
  do. (xvii, 270), 33
  do. (xvii, 355, 361), 26

Works—continued
  do. (xvii, 372–373), 174
  do. (xvii, 408–409), 243
  do. (xvii, 428), 240
  do. (xviii, i, 8–9), 33, 37
  do. (xviii, i, 19), 46
  do. (xviii, i, 112), 36
  do. (xviii, i, 135), 38, 46
  do. (xviii, i, 138), 26, 43
  do. (xviii, i, 146), 430
  do. (xviii, i, 175), 24
  do. (xviii, i, 195–196), 430
  do. (xviii, i, 220), 74
  do. (xviii, i, 282), 254
  do. (xviii, i, 331), 26
  do. (xviii, i, 355), 154
  do. (xviii, i, 365–366), 18
  do. (xviii, i, 384–385), 176
  do. (xviii, i, 412), 157
  do. (xviii, i, 414–415), 160
  do. (xviii, i, 425), 57
  do. (xviii, ii, 29–30), 248
  do. (xviii, ii, 55), 51
  do. (xviii, ii, 71), 248
  do. (xviii, ii, 74), 235
  do. (xviii, ii, 95), 253
  do. (xviii, ii, 108), 196
  do. (xviii, ii, 118–119), 241
  do. (xviii, ii, 135–136), 102, 214
  do. (xviii, ii, 138), 330
  do. (xviii, ii, 140), 59, 133, 196, 241

Works—continued
  do. (xviii, ii, 141), 133
  do. (xviii, ii, 143–144), 66, 73
  do. (xix, 46), 141
  do. (xix, 199–200), 138
  do. (xix, 203–205), 144
World Economy, 99, 100
  do. Revolution, 148, 212–216

YAKOVLEFF, 58, 59, 60, 61
"Young Communists' Pravda," 451 ; see also " Komsomolskaya Pravda "
Youth Organisations, 299, 335, 341–350
  do., see League of Youth
Yugoslav Committee of E.C.C.I., 257–264, 285–286, 288, 290, 291
Yugoslavia, 257–264

ZALUTSKY, 452
ZAPOTOTSKY, 322, 323
Zeal, revolutionary, inspired by the Russian Spirit, 175–176
Zemo-Avchalsk, 391
ZINOVIEFF, 13, 14, 15, 47, 48, 55, 57, 58, 59, 60, 61, 62, 63, 70, 288, 291, 436, 441–447, 449, 450, 451, 452, 453, 454, 456
  do. and Peasantry, 441-447

For Product Safety Concerns and Information please contact our EU
representative GPSR@taylorandfrancis.com
Taylor & Francis Verlag GmbH, Kaufingerstraße 24, 80331 München, Germany

www.ingramcontent.com/pod-product-compliance
Lightning Source LLC
Chambersburg PA
CBHW071233300426
44116CB00008B/1019